T0246083

HIT
GIRLS

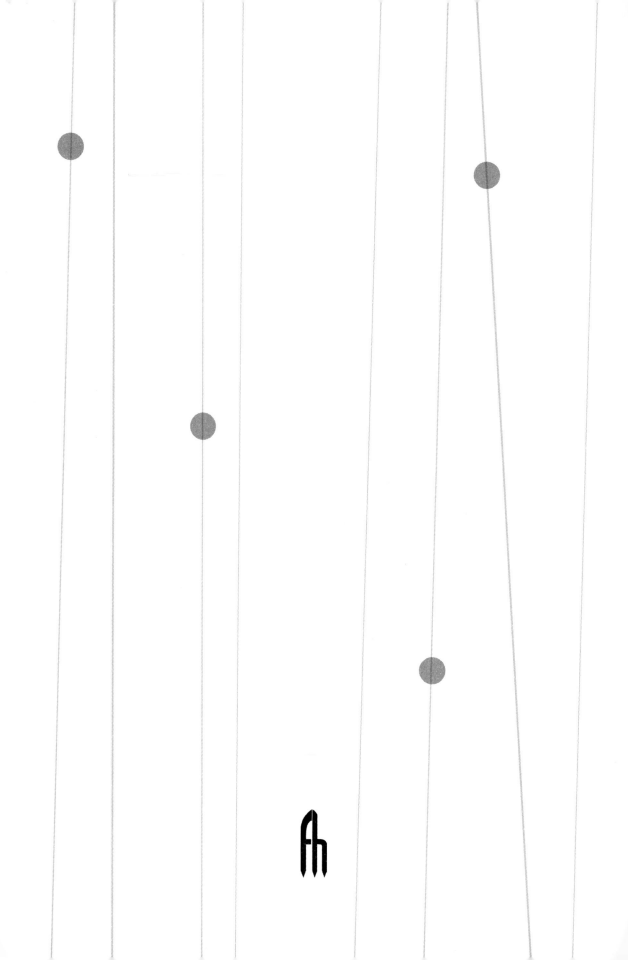

HIT GIRLS

WOMEN OF PUNK IN THE USA | 1975-1983

BY JEN B. LARSON

Hit Girls: Women of Punk in the USA, 1975-1983 © by Jen B. Larson
All Rights Reserved
ISBN: 978-1-62731-123-6

Feral House
1240 W Sims Way #124
Port Townsend WA 98368
www.feralhouse.com

10 9 8 7 6 5 4 3 2

Design: Bill Smith, designSimple
Cover photos: Ramona Jan by Catherine Riggs-Bergeson
Nikki & the Corvettes by Michael Carr
The Braphsmears by Janice Morlan

Foreword © Ann Magnuson. Used with permission.
"Feminista" © Alice Bag. Used with permission.
"Neo Boys Liner Notes" © Suzi Creamcheese. Used with permission.
"A Fable" © Nyna Crawford. Used with permission.

There are ten photographs included where the photographer is unknown.
These photos were provided by band members. Feral House would like to thank these
anonymous photographers by giving them, and all the fans that take pictures of their
favorite bands, thanks and credit for documenting their scene. If you recognize
YOUR photo, please contact us at: info@feralhouse.com.

*This book is for my brother, sister,
and father, who have all left this world.
They spun the first records I danced to and
taught me the art of the mixtape.*

CONTENTS

AUTHOR'S NOTE

8

FOREWORD BY ANN MAGNUSON

9

INTRODUCTION

12

ESSAYS
¡FEMINISTA!
BY ALICE BAG

20

NEO BOYS LINER NOTES BY SUZI CREAMCHEESE

21

1. MIDWEST
HIT GIRLS, HAUTE GIRLS

Destroy All Monsters, The Welders, Nikki & the Corvettes, Flirt, Chi-Pig, DA!, The Shivvers, The Waitresses, Bitch, The Dadistics, The Cubes, Unit 5, Ama-Dots, The Dents, Kate Fagan, Algebra Suicide, Dummy Club

INTERVIEWS: The Welders, Nikki Corvette, Jill Kossoris, Carolyn Striho

22

2. SOUTH
FEAST ON MY HEART

Pylon, Cichlids, The Klitz, The Delinquents, Mydolls, Screaming Sneakers, The Cold, F-Systems, Teddy and the Frat Girls, The Foams

INTERVIEWS: Vanessa Briscoe Hay, Marcia Clifton, Gail Elise Clifton

84

3. NORTHWEST
GUYS ARE NOT PROUD

The Dishrags, Chinas Comidas, The Accident, Neo Boys, The Anemic Boyfriends, Sado-Nation, Art Object, The Braphsmears, The Visible Targets, Bam Bam

INTERVIEWS: Karen Irving, Lisa Nansen Cram, The Braphsmears

MISCELLANEOUS: "Neo Boys" by Suzi Creamcheese Notes on *Peasant/Slave* cover by Cynthia Kraman

114

4. WEST COAST (SOUTH)
MANIC IN A PANIC

Backstage Pass, The Bags, The Controllers, Castration Squad, The Alley Cats, The Eyes, Suburban Lawns, The Dinettes, The Brat, 45 Grave, Tex & the Horseheads, Sin 34, The Pandoras, Screamin' Sirens

INTERVIEW: Alice Bag

154

5. WEST COAST (NORTH)
SHAKE THE HANDS OF TIME

Mary Monday, The Nuns, The Avengers, The Blowdryers, The Urge, VS, VKTMS, U.X.A., IXNA, Los Microwaves, Romeo Void, The Contractions, Inflatable Boy Clams, Wilma, Frightwig

INTERVIEWS: Deanna Mitchell, Mia d'Bruzzi, Penelope Houston, Jane Weems

MISCELLANEOUS: Fable by Nyna Crawford

190

6. EAST COAST
SUBVERSIVE PLEASURE

Jayne County, Mars, The Phantoms, Helen Wheels Band, 'B' Girls, Teenage Jesus & the Jerks, Cheap Perfume, DNA, Nasty Facts, UT, ESG, Plasmatics, Tiny Desk Unit, Disturbed Furniture, Bush Tetras, Y Pants, Egoslavia, Dizzy and the Romilars, Chalk Circle, The Excuses, Red C, The Bloods, Pulsallama

INTERVIEWS: Cynthia Sley, Cynthia Ross

240

IN MEMORIUM, AUTHOR'S ACKNOWL-EDGMENTS, CITATIONS, INDEX

296

Author's Note

≫ Lately, stories of women in early punk have been getting more attention in rock media. Mainstream audiences have viewed documentaries on Suzi Quatro, the Runaways, Poly Styrene, and the Go-Go's. Readers and audiobook listeners have had eyes and ears on autobiographies by Patti Smith, Debbie Harry, Kathy Valentine, and Viv Albertine.

While women who pioneered punk are becoming more visible, this book visits the obscure. As you'll notice, *Hit Girls* does not cover many artists with biographies, documentaries, inclusion in multiple compilations, or mainstream or worldwide acclaim, including the abovementioned artists, plus the likes of Poison Ivy from the Cramps, Tina from Talking Heads, and Exene from X. These women are of course admired by their peers and listed as influences by artists throughout the time period, but *Hit Girls* doesn't feature them by design. This book is written to peer beyond the prevailing consciousness, to illuminate the much-overlooked influential talents who kicked up dirt with loud guitars, vicious verse, and acerbic attitudes alongside (or imperiously over) boys way before riot grrrl emerged on North American soil. Some artists within the contents of this book are far more well-known than others.

I gathered information from as many sources I could get my hands on—from record sleeves to magazines, blog entries, and social media posts. I spoke with as many of the artists as I could. We emailed, chatted, texted, talked on the phone, Zoomed, and I even met with a few. Both my first- and secondhand research relies on human memory and its verbal or written transmissions as the stories and narratives of bands have been told anecdotally or through word of mouth. This means, of course, information may be subject to speculation and error. I am happy to correct errors if contacted. I do not claim to be an authority or omniscient historian in this work; hell, I wasn't even born until 1985. I am simply fanning the flames of the artists' lore.

I use the term "punk" loosely in the title and throughout. Within these pages, you will find artists who, upon hearing them, might make one question the genre descriptor. Some artists do or do not define themselves as "punk," and some adamantly refuse to (ahem, Lydia Lunch). Above all, "punk" represented energy and attitude; to some, punk was a community, to others, another fashion.

You'll also notice that though almost 90 below-the-radar bands are featured, plenty are not covered. Indeed, punk and genres adjacent to it involved so many women that hundreds of important artists were not included (an entire book on the bands left out from San Francisco or Portland could be written, for example). The point is, so many badass women played in bands in the mid-'70s to early '80s that this book could not contain them all. But, why on earth should badass women ever be contained? ●

Foreword by Ann Magnuson

❯❯ Danger is in the air.

In a spectacular display of Dionysian frenzy, girls are screaming, crying, jumping up and down, bodies gyrating wildly, hair flying, tears streaming down faces. Some faint, overcome with passions they have yet to understand let alone conquer. Chaos reigns.

Is this a scene from Euripides' *The Bacchae*? Having gone mad, are the Mae-nads now one with the god of wine and sexual abandon as they tear apart wild animals in the mountains with their bare hands?

Perhaps it's Bedlam, the notorious London asylum for the mentally ill where "problem" women with vague diagnoses of mania or hysteria were sequestered by husbands often because they viewed their wives as an inconvenience.

Or could this display of primitive savagery simply be an average night of wilding for the Manson girls flying high on LSD and biker speed down at the Spahn Ranch?

All of these scenarios sprang to mind while watching the first flush of Beat-lemania in Ron Howard's documentary *Eight Days a Week*. Featuring rare foot-age of female fans reacting to the Beatles during their first U.S. tour, the film reminded me, yet again, how the power of music—especially rock 'n' roll—can unleash the *daemon* like nothing else.

For the Greeks, the *daemon* was the spirit that acted as an intermediary between the gods and humans. Carl Jung saw it as our basic essence—an internal archetype that inspires and guides us, but whose guidance is too often ignored.

It is an energy the patriarchy has both desired and feared in women for millennia, renaming it 'demonic' and suppressing it by any means necessary. Yet the *daemon* is always there, desperately seeking to express itself.

The intensity of those teenage Bacchae worshipping at the temple of John, Paul, George, and Ringo reminded me of my own hormonal shift—and how music gave my confused excitement a form for the kind of expression that the misogynist culture sought to keep a lid on.

I was a tad too young for Beatlemania but years later my latent yearnings were aroused—at the lunchtime "sock hop" held daily at Thomas Jefferson Junior High School, located in the inner city of Charleston, West Virginia.

My seventh-grade self would sit with my bag lunch high up in the bleachers of the school gymnasium looking down at the older kids twisting, shouting, go-go dancing, and hippy-hippy-shaking on the basketball court below. The Black and white kids wildly dancing to the hits of Motown left little to the imagination. Frankly, it all scared the bejesus out of me. I was shocked by what those boys and girls were up to. But also intrigued.

By high school I had traded the exhilaration of riding horses to riding the sexy sonic waves of Mick Ronson's guitar and engaged in my own Dionysian frenzy, expressed through Isadora Duncan-style dance routines improvised down in the family basement. Bowie, Alice Cooper, and the New York Dolls were my gender-bending Beatles and I was finally one *gone girl!*

Girls weren't supposed to be *that* unhinged but my glam-rock hillbilly hippie friends and I could not help ourselves. (Quaaludes were only partially to blame.) The hormones surging out of our adolescent brains and into our loins were just too much to handle.

Music was the best—and often *only*—way to GET. THAT. SHIT. OUT!

Tragically, our mothers didn't have the same options. Feeling trapped by conventional rules imposed on them in the shame-based "olden days," they had nowhere to go to let loose except to Valium, vodka, infidelity, or endless crying jags. Subjugation was in their DNA. And they passed it down to us.

But the revolutions of the 1960s and 1970s gave us other ideas and, like Athena sprung fully grown from the head of Zeus, the concept of an *Alternative* was born.

A band made up entirely of women was absolutely unheard of back then. Yes, we had muses like folk goddesses Joni Mitchell and Joan Baez using their music to channel the poetry of the head and heart—as well as political outrage. Melanie added a ferocious "belt" that was as powerful as Merman's on Broadway (another strong female voice who inspired). Grace Slick was a divine banshee and Janis Joplin poured gasoline onto the twin flames of protest and desire.

Even the Laurel Canyon groupies whom Frank Zappa christened the GTO's (an acronym for Girls Together Outrageously) were pioneers—although it wasn't until much later that I discovered Zappa had put their outrageousness on vinyl. But the GTO's record was primarily spoken word and they certainly were not playing their own musical instruments.

But FANNY was.

FANNY was the first ALL-girl rock band I had ever heard of, discovered through ads for their debut album in *Rolling Stone* magazine. Sadly, I recall they were the butt of many juvenile jokes. Predictably, critics and audiences didn't take the band as seriously as they deserved. In the early 1970s, the idea of an all-girl group who wrote and played their own songs—without the help of men—was too revolutionary. David Bowie would later champion FANNY, saying "They're one of the finest fucking rock bands of their time…they're as important as anyone else who has ever been, ever!"

Then, as now, the Male Gaze was an insidious brain worm that wove sticky and tenacious cobwebs in our brains. Even the hippie chicks on so-called counterculture communes were relegated to the old 1950s housewife role, expected to be macrobiotic meal preparers and baby-makers.

Then Patti Smith arrived screaming SUCK ON THIS MOTHERFUCKERS!

Patti blew our minds. Her backup band was male but every girl my age who bought the debut album *Horses* was inspired to write poetry, show off her armpit hair and become a rock 'n' roll star! Not just by singing and writing and playing instruments but also calling the shots! We instinctively knew it was OUR time, time to ride our own untamed horses in this new Wild, Wild West!

The floodgates were opened and estrogen-fueled rock 'n' roll was everywhere, led by women like Patti as well as Debbie Harry, Chrissie Hynde, Poly Styrene, Siouxsie Sioux, Kate and Cindy from the B-52's…the list of names kept growing.

When I walked into CBGB one night in 1978 and saw the aggressively luminous Lydia Lunch banging atonally on an electric guitar while shrieking about "bloody orphans in the snow" I knew right then and there that the tables had turned—sending Grandma's good china and Mom's apple pie crashing to the floor.

Other female No Wave artists were doing the same. Badasses like Pat Place, Cynthia Sley, Anya Phillips, and Adele Bertei—all simultaneously intimidating and inspiring—were the new rock stars in my book.

All were dismembering the old concepts of womanhood—to a primal beat. The scene was right out of Euripides—but with a modern twist. While watching these performers do their thing, I envisioned a world where Playboy bunnies finally turn on SuperPimp Hef and rip him apart limb by limb (as the Maenads destroyed the macho king of Thebes) while the Manson girls cheer on like a demented Greek chorus (after picking their teeth clean with Charlie's freshly gnawed bones).

So many new role models were kicking ass on stage, either in groups or alone.

Diamanda Galás compressed all the mythological furies into one magnificent oracle as she ferried us, like Charon, across the River Styx, while deconstructing our collective emotional Hades. All she needed to do so was a piano and her own unleashed *daemonic* voice.

I was also in awe of the Erasers, a pioneering (almost all-) girl band who played CBGBs a lot. Formed in 1974 by unabashed feminist Susan Springfield (née Beschta) with drummer Jane Fire (later adding female bassist Jody Beach to the lineup), the Erasers always impressed me with their cool confidence and searing intelligence. The band was perfectly named because they helped wipe the toxic slate clean and inspire women to write fresh narratives for themselves.

And there were many others: The Scroggins sisters from the South Bronx redefined dance music with their groundbreaking avant-funk/post-punk band ESG. Kim Gordon may have been the only girl in Sonic Youth but she was the one you kept your eye on. The Bush Tetras had a male drummer but they were the first "girl band" I saw that inspired me to finally stop daydreaming and start my own band. Even the unique homemade sounds of the Shaggs (whom Frank Zappa famously called "better than the Beatles") was an influence.[1]

Move over Cock Rock, The Power of Pussy was taking center stage!

More and more girls were getting together outrageously and this massive tsunami was crashing its powerful New Wave all over the world. As more women released records and toured, they encouraged others to jump onto the DIY train!

That train was bound for glory for some, derailment for others, but those particular railroad tracks remained firmly in place to serve as a fast and furious route for the *Daemon* inside young women everywhere to break free and express desire, anger, passion, and pain.

It was as if all the female Beatles fans screaming in the stands at Shea Stadium fled the bleachers, trampled the cops and rushed the stage, pushing aside the Fab Four, grabbing their instruments and proclaiming "I don't wanna hold your hand, I wanna play your guitar."

Danger is still in the air. ●

---

1 EVERYone I knew had the Shaggs' album *Philosophy of the World*. Dany Johnson and I even created a tribute band playing their 'hits' with Yo La Tengo drummer Georgia Hubley.

Introduction

I was grounded for half of high school. Mouthing off, sneaking out to parties, getting my tongue pierced illegally at an underground tattoo parlor called "House of Pain" come to mind as reasons why. As a child of divorced parents, they didn't always agree on rules to raise me, so I never swore on oath to any of them. I rebelled and caused them many headaches. My family moved around, enduring unfathomable tragedies and emotional hardships; certainly, this all factored into my fashion. I wore wide-leg jeans, pencil-thin eyebrows, and layers of thrift-store T-shirts while most of my peers ironed tees from Abercrombie & Fitch, and the "freaks" who denounced conformity and designer culture unironically culled their wardrobes from Hot Topic.

Even if I wanted to, I couldn't fit in. I balanced this aesthetic and my misbehavior with honorable acts: playing sports, working several jobs (some under the table), getting along with most of my peers (and some teachers), and achieving decent grades while learning nothing academically. I thought it was enough to ensure freedom—but it wasn't. When not "working" or "at practice," I was regularly "grounded for two weeks." As an adult, I realize it probably was not entirely a bad thing. During this time alone, I was able to spend time getting to know myself. I climbed onto my roof and ate snacks. I plagiarized poetry from my English textbook, coated my furniture with acrylic paint, played guitar in my closet, and listened to CDs on my five-disc changer (it was 2001 and all the songs I had downloaded on Napster were on the off-limits desktop downstairs).

In my sophomore year, I signed up for a poetry class, and in junior year, I took creative writing. Ms. McClain and Mr. Cislo (well, Melissa and Joe—they are my friends now), the teachers of these classes, noticed my angst and took an interest in helping me cultivate an identity as a songwriter, and encouraged me to begin penning stories about my life. Ms. McClain gave me a copy of Annie Dillard's *An American Childhood*, and Mr. Cislo burned mixes for me. One I played a lot was titled "women," which included crooning by sonically-pretty-but-sad folk-oriented singer-songwriters like Lucinda Williams, PJ Harvey, and Juliana Hatfield.

But then, the 14th song on the CD was a woman with a dry, quivering voice slipping in and out of key, imperfect guitarwork, and wistful, sullen pleas, bad manners, and a salty disposition. Her name was Liz Phair. I found recordings of *Exile in Guyville* and *Whip Smart* in some music forum and burned them. I listened through my CD player via the auxiliary cord adapter in my car every day. I couldn't get enough of "Glory" or "Dance of the Seven Veils" or "Supernova" or any song on the albums, really. Liz Phair's lyrics became my creed. No one in my world had heard them, and they were all mine. Liz Phair isn't punk in the pure sense (what is punk in the pure sense?), but her first few albums were pissy and imperfect and created space for me to exist.

At the time, I only saw "punk" through MTV's lens. I knew of bands with punk or punkish women that I did like: No Doubt, Bif Naked, Garbage, and Hole. As a kid growing up in the '90s, however, my understanding of punk crossed wires with emo, grunge, ska, goth, and skating culture; visually, it was limited to mall styles. The punk boys at school defined punk music as a particular style of play: downstrokes and palm muting on guitar. You had to sing in a whiny voice something about "anti-authority." Fashion ranged but often included black band T-shirts, facial piercings, studded belts, and Vans or Converse kicks. There was always a member with an overly gelled mohawk or a tattoo sleeve. Punks were still the weird kids at school, and some of them played hacky sack in the courtyard, took visual art classes, and listened to shit like Rancid and NOFX. Aside from a few songs, I didn't love *that* type of punk. (Honestly, I'd rather have listened to the Monkees or the Kinks.)

My older sister Amy Beth Larson wearing a denim coat in high school. She was super fucking cool. Photographer unknown. Circa 1989.

At rehearsal for my first band, Random Delivery. I got kicked out after two practices, and the boys made an ad in search of my replacement. Photo by Jim Margle. Circa 1999.

"Punk," I thought, was overproduced pop songs that sold a style. It was another type of uniform. Excessively EQ'd distorted guitar, music videos that polished blemished skin, and curated locks of messy hair. It was just as dorky as being a jock. I went to overnight punk shows at a church with my Catholic school friends, where we ran around in our socks (WTF?) and slept in the pews. I got kicked out of an all-boy punk band in ninth grade and overall felt like I wouldn't "fit" into the subculture. Other than as sex symbols or in the shadow of their boyfriends, girls weren't allowed in the clubhouse where the music was being made. Girls were the subjects of songs, and present at shows to admire and swoon. Girls who played were the anomalies, boys were afraid of them, and lots of other girls were envious or secretly crushed on them.

To me, since I didn't know anything else, Liz Phair was feminist DIY. She was raw and rude, and totally relatable. Liz Phair is like if Cher from *Clueless* had a bad older sister. She crudely posed nude and sang things like "I'm a real cunt in spring." She wrote *Exile in Guyville* in response to *Exile on Main Street*. She said on MTV: "I treated Mick's lyrics as my love object. He was what the man was saying, and this is what I was coming back with." She did and sang whatever she wanted.

* * *

In my life, music has been my most consistent companion. My relationship with it is sacred. It's understood me and spoken to me in ways the people I am surrounded by cannot. When bonds with people have foundered, when loved ones have passed away, when friends have moved away or moved on, and anytime I've been emotionally shattered, music has held me securely in the world.

Music accounts for my earliest memories: Shimmying with my dad across the living room carpet as

"Straighten Up and Fly Right" spun from the record player. Butchering the lyrics of nursery rhymes as I cupped my mouth around the microphone of a Playskool cassette player. My brother lip-syncing to "Wake Me Up Before You Go-Go" and "Get Outta My Dreams, Get Into My Car" at his middle-school talent shows. Becoming fanatical about '60s pop with my sister Lisa. My mom taking me to see a Monkees reunion tour in seventh grade.

My oldest sister Amy made me a mixtape when I was three, six years before she died (the cassette was black with a yellow label covered in song-title scrawl, but I remember next to nothing about the tracklist, except that it included "Stand" by R.E.M. I looked for it in the garage for decades but never found it. I would give my right arm to have that tape). Throughout my life, I've laid awake at night, cursing God for taking her too soon. In my mind, we were going to start a band called the Larson 2 (terrible band name). Selfishly, I wish she'd introduced me earlier to all the music I learned about in my twenties. If she had lived past 1995, I know she would have made me a mixtape with Sleater-Kinney or played "Rebel Girl" for me.

Subcultures weren't part of my world until I was 19 or 20 when I was introduced to riot grrrl. I liked the idea of it and got into a few bands, a lot of them indie-leaning and some of the more well-known: Bikini Kill and Bratmobile. I really liked the short-lived Dischord indie band Autoclave and loved everything about Sleater-Kinney.

In 2010, my friends and I formed a band called Swimsuit Addition. We were influenced by the Wipers, Blur, and the Zombies.

Nevertheless, we spent the next six years hearing ourselves compared to or called 'riot grrrl,' even when we weren't much like it and, more importantly, not 20 years in the past. We were "just like the Donnas" or—the one I genuinely love—"the evil Go-Go's." We were, of course, Sleater-Kinney. These descriptors are all complimentary, don't get me wrong, and I wish they were true.

Until the 2010s, I knew women played rock 'n' roll, yet the only narrative I knew about "women in punk" were mainstream successes, and that riot grrrls reclaimed space in a misogynistic, aggressive, male-dominated genre, that they were the first women to push their way through mosh pits, fists in the air.

What I didn't grasp was precisely how fundamental and integrated women were to the foundation of punk in the first place. In the '70s, during the advent of punk, women worked alongside their male counterparts to create the movement a decade sooner than riot grrrl. The space girls made in the '90s was a restoration of a scene women had fashioned in the first place.

* * *

Collective pop-cultural consciousness may want to keep it a secret, but the truth endures. Women of '70s and '80s punk were the vanguards of the genre. They lit the path, blazed a trail, revved the engine, and wrote the map. They opened doors and flicked on the light. While most punk history focuses on bands with men in them, a few groups with well-known women (Patti Smith, Talking Heads, the Cramps) are acknowledged as anomalies. Women in punk scene after punk scene were treated as novelties. In the '80s and beyond, mixed-gender bands prevailed and women were considered a necessary ingredient to indie sounds.

What's left out of the story of punk are the many bands from the mid-'70s and early '80s in every scene that had or was run by women. How women booked shows and started fanzines. How women's style influenced. From Seattle to Miami (and worldwide), it was the first time women played in bands and worked in parity with men, so the phenomenon's significance should not be overlooked. Women were indeed present in rock music before punk; there was an abundance of all-women '60s garage bands where they played guitar, bass, and drums (the Pleasure Seekers, Goldie & the Gingerbreads, and Ace of Cups—to scratch the surface), and Black women in R&B inspired rock's very origins. However, punk was the first space in which women could defy mainstream gender roles and express themselves freely.

In the early 2000s, enlisting the help of other artists, Chalk Circle singer and guitarist Sharon Cheslow compiled a list of bands with women from '75–'80, when the first punk explosion hit, and wrote an essay on the significance of the roster. In her manifesto, she declares: "Respect is due. Women have been playing in punk bands since the beginning, yet only a handful have gotten recognition."

She writes,

> "It's amazing during this time period how many girls picked up instruments and formed bands, how many women were in all-female bands, how many women were in experimental or non-traditional bands…I want to break down the barriers that say that all-female bands sound alike or that women can't

My second or third band, Swimsuit Addition. One time, the *Chicago Sun-Times* mixed us up with another local all-girl band called Summer Girlfriends and referred to us as "Summer Addition" in print. From L–R: Sam Westerling, Becca Nisbet, Sarah Chmielewski, Jen B. Larson. Photo by Dave Rentauskas 2013.

play their instruments or that girls can only be in pretty-sounding pop bands. Once we realize the variety of bands out there that have existed and can see these women as our role models, maybe more girls will have a sense as to the long cycle of women expressing themselves musically…We must reclaim our rightful place in history. If women are to be truly recognized for the innovations we bring to music based on our creative expression and not on our gender, then the whole structure and mythology of rock 'n' roll criticism/history has to change."

Finally, she pleads: "What can we do?"

Musician and author Vivien Goldman expands on this notion when examining how writing about women in punk circled back into her life. She explains her thought process when asked to pen a blurb for a Pitchfork list: "I've got to write something that will rally the troops, younger and even older women than myself, everybody, to keep going, to keep producing culture, having self-expression as something that has weight and encouragement for others. I wanted to write something encouraging." It turned into a book project, *Revenge of the She-Punks*. In the book's introduction, she provides a reason for taking on the task:

> "This book is an attempt at healing…and yes, even a noncorrosive revenge…In the case of punky females, revenge means getting the same access as your male peers, to make your own music, look and sound how you want, and be able to draw enough people to ensure the continuation of the process. Sounds simple enough, talent permitting, but as this book shows, it's different for girls. Our path is beset with particular pitfalls, which makes our glories all the sweeter."

To go forward, we must identify and define the truth about punk history. We must preserve it. We must exalt our punk mothers. We must tell their stories, make documentaries, spread the word of their deeds in podcasts, share playlists, and showcase our record collections. We must cherish and hold on to our artifacts: flyers, records, videos, and photographs. We must have role models for young girls to express themselves freely, to excite their independence. We must keep the energy alive. And press against the gates the keepers want shut.

*   *   *

Politics and political culture had changed for the women coming of age during the late '70s and early '80s. It was a generation too young for second-wave feminism but before the third wave. It was in this societal no-man's-land that art, at least art worth serious discussion, was political. The contrast between the images of a '70s rock 'n' roller and a '70s suburban homemaker archetype is striking. On one hand, you have a woman in a soft-colored A-line skirt serving perfectly formed Jell-O molds to her family. On the other, a woman is singing, maybe screaming, dancing, shouting, and shredding on electric guitar on stage late into the night. In clubs and bars, wearing black leather, fishnet stockings, and high-heeled boots.

In mainstream America, the breaking of traditional gender roles was controversial. In the '60s and '70s, rock 'n' roll was a political statement that altered the consciousness of the status quo. For men, expressions of androgyny (long hair, tight pants) attracted dour, homophobic judgment. At the same time, women who were not getting married and beginning families in their early twenties were seen as the ultimate rule-breakers. But even in this subculture, where men were concerned, before punk, women were still not permitted to be loud, weird, crass, or angry.

It was only a matter of time. Hushed by their submissive roles in the presiding cultural gender binary, women embarked on various paths in bypassing cultural gatekeepers. Women executing their independence didn't all do so in the same way, either. Not all women were angry, but some were. Not all of them explored the avant-garde, but some did. Some created art alongside men and women on genderless terms. Some (women's music) excluded men entirely. Some dominated the men they worked with. Some played into the concept of binary gender roles as a means to expose them. All were powerful approaches that led to cultural freedoms that had not been achieved before this era. The women of this era opened doors for themselves as well as future artists and musicians of all genders—and, more importantly, had doors opened for them during punk's truest beginnings.

As a result of gospel/rhythm-&-blues player Sister Rosetta Tharpe striking a distorted chord on her electric guitar in the 1930s, because of Willie Mae Thornton's thundering wail on the original cut of "Hound Dog" in the 1950s, the women of punk were able to express themselves on their own terms.

All of whom influenced decades of music without decades of recognition.

However, these still-hidden stories aren't the tales we often hear in the popular punk narrative. And despite its significance, instead of being celebrated, the works of women in punk (and for that matter, every genre and movement) have often been ignored or the subject of critique—even by other women. Popular media and music history books haven't quite figured out how to remember and dignify the women at the core of punk and its sister genres.

But it must be done.

*   *   *

Luckily, many in my generation are nostalgic for an era we didn't experience. Garage rockers, DIY scenesters, and record and tape label launchers revel in and recreate a past predating our existence. Writers document—I write because it's how I gather, process, and organize information.

It's out of respect that I take this project on. I feel it is my and my generation's job to index and honor the work of artists who opened doors for us in the present. It's also life-affirming. Writing this book is the ultimate expression of gratitude for the artists whose work makes our current creative landscape possible.

I was drawn to women of early punk because first and foremost I like the music and I like the energy. The project has also been about making connections, forging real-life and internet friendships, and finding my past, current, and future self in the process.

During a lonely two years of my life (after a shitty breakup, a frustrating band ending, and a realization that a large number of my closest friends were living in different parts of the world), I found myself writing a lot. One project was *Punkette Respect*, a blog featuring videos of women in early punk from all over the world. I shared and wrote about videos from the Nuns, the Au Pairs, and the Welders. I found recordings of the Mo-dettes, Plastix, Wall Sockets, and Penetration. Recordings of women making punk in Japan, Australia, North America, and all over Europe. Radio hosts featuring some of these bands, blogs with lists and links, and people piecing together histories in YouTube comments inspired me to join them.

I started compiling bountiful lists of the artists and bands I found. I had always been told bands with women were rare. So, what was this? I talked with friends who also liked some of these bands, which was encouraging.

Knowledgeable collectors and label owners—CJ Del Mar from Girlsville, Jen Lemasters, Brian Carrizosa, Nick Mayor from Bric-a-Brac, and Todd Novak of HoZac—helped me gather information and understand my personal taste. Brian recommended the *Reference of Female-Fronted Punk Rock: 1977–89*. Lemasters, whose extensive record collection is featured throughout the book, suggested so many artists and geeked out with me about the ones we mutually enjoy. Del Mar of Girlsville shared personal obsessions and hooked me up with some writing gigs that were instrumental in getting my writing seen by others. Todd Novak started giving me records almost every time I saw him. He also enlisted me to contribute interviews on Victim of Time. I made friends on the internet, and we started sharing playlists with others. I started writing to women from these bands and asking to interview them. Then I emailed Christina Ward of Feral House a book proposal.

When the end of my band Swimsuit Addition came in the middle of recording our second album, just as we were starting to get larger, well-paying gigs, it sucked—I felt betrayed by the situation and by myself, like I've heard many of the women in these stories say about the demise of bands that were important to them. But there were also positives for my personal growth: It gave me a lot of time to sort myself out personally and understand myself as an artist. And it gave me more time to write. It gave me time to heal my once-toxic relationships with myself and with my bandmates and even figure out who my local friends actually were. But the space in my schedule also left me bored. And needing to connect. I had felt so disconnected. I wondered about bands of the past. About groups who were overlooked. Bands who ended too soon. What about the ones who never recorded? I thought about the women in punk music whose work has remained under the radar for longer than I've been on this planet. What was that like? I wondered. I researched, I contacted people, I asked. It kept me curious and alive.

I couldn't believe how much I found, how many people wanted to talk. I took notes. I dug and dug. Now, look where we are. All this material. All these stories. A whole book. Whole histories, deserving of three hundred more books. I probably wrote too much. I probably didn't write enough. There's enough material to fill an entire wing of an art museum, build curricula, a whole discipline. Information all music lovers, historians, and the general public should have at their fingertips.

(But actually, please don't ruin any of these artists by overplaying them.) ●

¡Feminista! by Alice Bag

>> It seems like the whole time I was growing up, the world was trying to teach me the role of women. From the first time I saw my mother cowering at my father's feet to the current state of insidious inequality, I've been confronted with the message that females are somehow weaker, less capable than men. I began questioning the validity of these messages early on, inspired by the women around me. My mother, my sisters, my friends, aunts, and cousins—each one constantly refined the definitions of femininity, androgyny, and the true nature of equality in small ways through their daily routines. Sometimes these women discarded antiquated clichés of ladylike behavior in favor of an assertive, can-do attitude. At other times, they tried to squeeze themselves into someone else's idea of womanhood. Either way, they helped me figure out that the tidy stereotype labeled "femininity" had some stretching to do to catch up with my evolving female consciousness.

In the 1970s, my mother found herself by stepping up to help my father in the male-dominated construction business; my girlfriends were pushing the boundaries, too. The L.A. punk scene was densely populated by female musicians, artists, writers, photographers, roadies, and more. These were the modern suffragettes in my life who, without banners or demonstrations, quietly led by example. Not that I oppose banners and demonstrations; I've participated in my share of marches, but it was the tiny changes that the women around me made in their personal lives that spoke the loudest.

Patricia and I learned early on from auditioning male musicians that every one of them thought they were the next Jimi Hendrix or another Keith Moon. While most of the women we auditioned apologized in advance for not being very good, all the males wielded their axes with a bravado that seemed like second nature to them. Even the lamest male guitarist would talk up his skills, acting cocky and confident, while the women underplayed their experience. After a bit of this, Patricia and I learned to adapt. We figured that when people wrote reviews about the band, they mentioned the two of us more often than they mentioned the guys. This gave us confidence, and after a while, we learned to do away with the modesty. It felt great to be able to say "I'm a musician" without feeling the need to tack on an apology.

Changing the way we spoke about ourselves as musicians and artists was like tossing tiny pebbles into a sea of conformity, making ripples, making waves, bringing about change that starts from within and spills out into the lives of those around us. The words were so powerful that the more often we said them, the truer they became. Now, when we stepped on the stage, we weren't asking for approval; we were flaunting our talent. ●

Liner Notes
by and courtesy of
Lesley Reece a.k.a. Suzi Creamcheese
(Included in Neo Boys *Sooner or Later* LP)

» Fall, 1979. There they were again: the two girls, disappearing into the fog by the park blocks in downtown Portland. One blonde, one redhead, bright berets floating over long wool coats.

The bus came once an hour and I'd missed it. Sometimes I missed it on purpose. But it was too cold to hang around much longer. I dug a book out of my backpack and sat down to wait.

Who were those girls? They weren't like anyone I knew in the suburbs, or at the big-box high school I was stuck at for two more years. They looked like they might be interesting. Maybe I could talk to them. But what if they were bitches? It didn't matter. The times I saw them, they were always at least a block away. Ghosts I could never catch.

I went back to my book. Then my bus came. Forty-five minutes later, it dropped me off in the middle of nowhere: the place I spent most of my time.

At home I had more books—mostly poetry—and records from Park Avenue and Renaissance. On Sundays I taped Joe Carducci's show from KBOO. I wanted to be in a band, but I wasn't old enough or cool enough. Worst of all, I wanted to play an instrument. Nobody wanted a girl in their band unless she was the singer. I knew that was stupid, but how could I argue? Obviously, there were rules not even punk could stop.

The eighties started. That summer, I went to an all-ages show at the Long Goodbye. The band came on. Four girls. Wow, two of them were THE girls. The redhead went to the microphone, the blonde picked up a bass. They even had a girl drummer.

How did they do that, start a band with other women, three of them not the singer? Maybe they thought the rules were stupid too. No, that hope was too big. I pushed it down. I watched them tune up, waited for them to be terrible or act campy.

But they weren't, and they didn't. The Neo-Boys had a strong pop energy, but Kim's hard-edged voice was never too sweet. KT wove her basslines around Pat's solid beat, while Jennifer played a twangy, clean guitar.

The lyrics were real poetry. None of their songs were about boys. THEY weren't about boys. They were a band. Four equals, up there on stage in their regular clothes, being their regular selves. And kicking ass.

Their regular selves kicked ass.

By the end of that year, I was in my own band with four other women. I got to know KT, Kim, and Pat. They were real. They were nice. I should have talked to them sooner. I should have thanked them sooner. Thirty-two years is a long time to wait. But here goes.

Over the decades here in the Northwest I've seen countless other all-female bands, good ones, up there on stage being their regular selves and kicking ass. KT, Kim, Pat, Jennifer, Meg, you knew the rules were stupid. Your music made them irrelevant. This work has aged well, but I'm not surprised. It's just proof.

Thank you, Neo-Boys. From the bottom of my teenage heart. ●

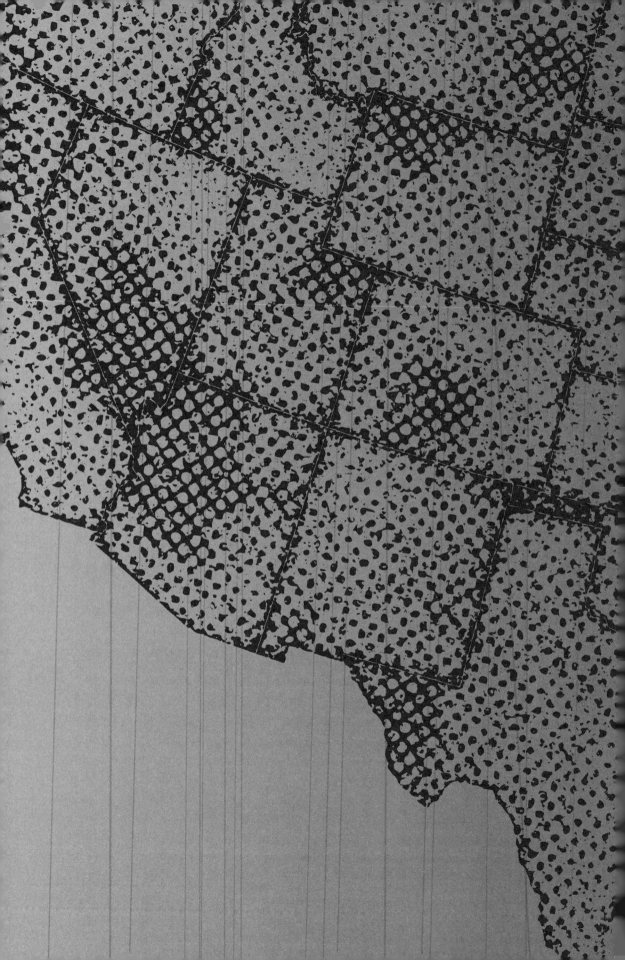

MIDWEST

Hit Girls, Haute Girls

DESTROY ALL MONSTERS

Ann Arbor, Michigan　»　Formed in 1974

M E M B E R S

Original Lineup
Niagara, Cary Loren, Jim Shaw, Mike Kelley

Second Generation Lineup
Niagara | VOCALS
Ron Asheton, Larry Miller | GUITAR
Ben Miller | SAXOPHONE
Michael Davis | BASS
Rob King, Larry Steel | DRUMS

»» Dangerously cocking an eyebrow, the artist poses at a worn vintage vanity cluttered with glass decanters. Her two-toned waist-length hair eclipses her right arm. Aiming a revolver at the ground, she leans on the furniture with her left arm, sucking a half-smoked cigarette. Long black gloves, gashed fishnet tights, and a short lacy strapless black dress imply she's just committed a murder and covered up the evidence. Confirming the allegations on the flip side of the page, she stands in the woods tugging at the seams of a bloodstained white slip.

Named after the 1953 Marilyn Monroe film and the world's wonder, Destroy All Monsters' frontwoman Niagara embodies a timeless aesthetic. Fellow art school students Cary Loren, Mike Kelley, and Jim Shaw were attracted to her look. Mike Kelley said, "Niagara was one of the first people I met in Ann Arbor: I sat next to her on a bus; she was the only freak in a denim sea of laid-back hippiedom. In contrast, Niagara had an alluring in-your-face drag queen kind of beauty. She was a 'superstar.' Her aesthetic was already formed. She ignored classes to spend time on her strange morbid drawings."

The Monsters entered the world in 1974 as a thought-provoking, chaotic performance art piece.

The misfit art kids from the University of Michigan united in subverting the sounds and aesthetics of popular culture, making experimental noise panoramas with toy keyboards, broken electronics, blenders, and trash cans. Their original sound evoked an anarchic, dystopian future with a dose of absurdity. Fittingly, their name comes from the title of a campy Japanese sci-fi horror movie in which a group of mind-controlled monsters (including Godzilla, Rodan, and Mothra), led by a group of she-aliens, attack the world's capitals. The artists also assembled *Destroy All Monsters* Magazine, curating the group's visual work and absurd writing. In the six issues of the magazine made between 1976 and 1979, perverse cartoons, Xeroxed collages, and photos of the band evoke film noir, monster movies, and psychedelic anarchy.

One would be misinformed to call the first version of this group "a band." The initial four-piece deemed themselves "anti-rock," and according to Loren, the group's "menagerie of words, images, and sounds were an attempt to thumb [their] noses at the pretentious circus of rock-star bullshit and musical emptiness that filled the airwaves during the early to mid-1970s."

Niagara's work is often recognized as the defining aesthetic of the band; much of her visual art was used for posters, record covers, band logos, the *Destroy All Monsters* magazine covers, as well as the cover of *Geisha This*, a collection of the six mags. Visually and musically, Destroy All Monsters' experimentation synthesized the mind-altering elements of psychedelia and the status-quo-rejecting elements of punk.

The band's bizarre sense of humor was apparent in their first public appearance, which very much upset its audience. Their first gig took place at a comic book convention in Ann Arbor, Michigan on New Year's Eve. They played a maniacal rendition of "Iron Man" by Black Sabbath, which featured violin, saxophone, a vacuum cleaner, and a coffee can. Ten minutes into the set, they were cut off and asked to leave.

Destroy All Monsters at Max's Kansas City New York. Oil on canvas by Niagara.

Committed to their visual explorations and avant-garde musical meanderings, Destroy All Monsters only played two formal gigs in their first years and rarely practiced. They were known for strange antics when they played live, and getting booed off the stage was commonplace. In *Niagara: Beyond the Pale*, Jerry Vile wrote, "We called them 'Destroy All Eardrums.'"

Shaw and Kelley left for art school in Los Angeles, so Niagara and Cary Loren brought in various backing members, including twin brothers Larry and Ben Miller (younger brothers of Roger Miller, a founding member of Mission of Burma), as well as MC5 bassist Mike Davis, and Stooges guitarist Ron Asheton. The late-'70s lineup changes inspired the "rockification" of their sound and helped them gain popularity. They began gigging more regularly and toured overseas in 1978 to critical acclaim. When Cary Loren left, Niagara led a new generation of Destroy All Monsters members through a new era, ultimately calling it quits and forming a new band called Dark Carnival in the mid-'80s with Asheton.

Despite their experimental noise and anti-rock beginnings, the new Destroy All Monsters lineup ironically transitioned to an identifiable rock sound with crunchy guitar, cutting solos, and heavy bass lines. Niagara acquired the space to focus on being a frontwoman with the standard garage-rock setup. Ron Asheton wrote, "After Iggy as front person, I could never settle for less." And, in 2004, she was one of four women named to *Classic Rock* magazine's list of the 100 best frontmen.

In "A Manifesto of Ignorance: Destroy All Monsters" (1996/1997), bandmate Cary Loren wrote, "Niagara also had a gift for grande black comedy, her voice a blend of Betty Boop and off-key Nico…her scratchy violin playing was equally anti-musical and lent a strong visual statement…indeed her costuming and ghostly complexion helped lend the group a gloomy gothic quality."

In "You're Gonna Die," she invokes macabre imagery. She sings,

> **I was looking out the window and a**
> **   witch flew by**
> **whipping her broomstick, she said**
> **   you're gonna die**

In "Bored," Niagara's creepy lyrics are juxtaposed with her coolness, singing:

> **When I woke up this morning**
> **There were ants crawlin' on**
> **   the floor**
> **When I woke up this morning**
> **There were moths crawlin'**
> **   around my door**
> **When I woke up in the**
> **   afternoon**
> **I was really bored**
> **When I woke up in the**
> **   afternoon**
> **I was really bored**
> **Really bored**
> **I was bored**

Like many poetic punk women, the timbre of her voice and beat-poetry-like delivery were likened to those of Patti Smith. However, the two have very little in common besides being chic, cultured, musical women adjacent to the MC5 who wore torn T-shirts. Niagara is risqué, sardonic, and aloof; Patti is androgynous, odic, and ecstatic. Nevertheless, their unique personas and styles exist in parallel evolution.

In the '70s, Niagara was given many labels ("Punk Rock Pin-Up Girl," "Queen of Detroit," and "Thrift Store Nico") by the likes of *Creem* Magazine, *PUNK*, as well as other publications. She carved out a niche identity, almost a prototype for what was reproduced faithfully in later punk. Niagara had a provocative stage presence with a runway model's body, black-and-white streaked hair, leather pants, and thigh-high boots. Mainstream rock stars, including Courtney Love and even Madonna, assumed similar bewitching looks and brassy attitudes.

Niagara's verbal terseness is a thread through her multiple disciplines and part of her charm. The band interviews itself in *Destroy All Monsters* fanzine #1. When a question is directed at Niagara, "What are your musical influences?" she responds, "I don't give interviews." Jim asks, "Why do you sing, Niagara?" and she says, "So people won't bother me."

Niagara is also an accomplished painter whose work has appeared in galleries worldwide. Her work comes from the Lowbrow movement, a humorous underground populist movement with roots in underground comix and punk. The pop-art she-devils in her paintings emulate her persona: ball-busting vixens

Destroy All Monsters live at The Roundhouse London. Oil on canvas by Niagara.

scantily clad in evening wear and sometimes topless. The subjects arch evil eyebrows, pucker their lips for cigarettes, point weapons, and grip makeup compacts while text bubbles flash sassy phrases like, "They Won't Let Me Be Good," "Kill Him," and "This Band Sucks."

Todd McGovern of Please Kill Me wrote of her work in 2016: "Every article about Niagara's art points out the obvious Pop Art influence of Warhol and Lichtenstein, but over the years she has created a world of tough-talking, wisecracking women, curvaceous gun molls, leggy broads with snub-nosed revolvers in their clutch purses, cheekbones, and hormones, a highball glass with a smudge of lipstick. Like the artist herself, the subjects of Niagara's paintings do not suffer fools gladly."

Niagara reflecting on her artistic path, said, "[While in the band], I wasn't painting a lot. I did the single covers, the album covers. I figured I'd be in a band for a couple years and go back to my art career. That was really where I was at, but I surely didn't mind doing the music thing with Ron. Then it was like, my God, it's 20 years later! I was like, I'm dropping everything and just doing art full-time."

Niagara's commitment to producing art in different media nonstop from a young age makes her an influential and prolific artist. In addition, her work as a painter and singer reflects and promotes strong roles for women, demonstrating what it means to evolve and advance artistically while chartering a defiant, formidable front. ●

THE WELDERS

St. Louis, Missouri   »   Formed in 1975

M E M B E R S

Stephanie von Drasek, Colleen O'Sullivan | VOCALS
Kelly "Rusty Welder" Draper | GUITAR
Caroline Fujimoto | BASS
Jane Fujimoto | DRUMS, KEYBOARDS
Lyla Turner | DRUMS

》 When you think "young punks," you might not imagine goofy junior high school Beatlemaniacs with straight A's and glasses who idolize the Marx Brothers, the Monkees, and Monty Python. But in 1975, St. Louis, four adolescent pop-culture geeks called the Welders were the first and certainly youngest punk rock band around. Besides being young girls with instruments, their initial formation as an all-girl punk band was unlike the media-famous teen punk stars, the Runaways. With decidedly prudish lyrics, the Welders moved in an entirely different direction from the provocative Los Angeles group.

Once a meeting of the minds occurred, the four girls were torn between making a magazine, forming a band, or creating a comedy troupe. They landed on calling themselves a band, but their work lingered in the visionary stage as they didn't yet have instruments. Four of the members worked as bus girls at a local Chinese restaurant to save money for gear. By 1976, they had drums and guitars. Ditching their glasses for contact lenses, the teenagers began applying makeup and dabbled in glitter and glam.

Drummer (and older sister of bassist Caroline Fujimoto) Jane Fujimoto said, "It had been a dream of mine to play drums in a rock 'n' roll band ever since I was nine years old and completely in love with the Beatles. I had been collecting rock magazines since about 1971. The other Welders used to come over and read them. It was like a rock 'n' roll library."

In their five years as a band, punk shows weren't exactly winning over bookers in St. Louis, so the Welders played only a handful of shows. Their first official show happened at a teen club in November of 1976, and they only played three songs, all of which were covers: "I Don't Wanna Walk Around with You" by the Ramones, "Wild Thing" by the Troggs, and "I Can't Explain" by the Who. (The best part is: Apparently, one member was playing an entirely different Who song.) Their second show was guitarist Julie's last and occurred at the first St. Louis Punk Rock Festival in January of 1977.

The girls integrated physical comedy into their shows, following loose scripts and using stage props. Some props included a white Styrofoam reindeer from a grocery store liquor display, a giant red plastic mallet, baby dolls, a life-size poster of the Osmonds, kazoos, and Silly String. At times, their off-kilter humor was compared to the Monkees, and they covered "I Trusted You" by Andy Kaufman.

Guitarist Kelly "Rusty Welder" Draper remembers, "We played in exotic locales like Breese, Illinois, where you could hear a pin drop. I believe we taunted the audience with questions like, 'Is this an audience or an oil painting?'"

In their own songs, they made light of serious subjects. Stephanie and Rusty wrote "P-E-R-V-E-R-T" when they were 15. The song is about being sexually harassed everywhere they went. They sing:

> You've got a Ph.D. in perversion
> you're a doctor of depravity
> you went through six years of school
> and graduated with a moral cavity

"Debutantes in Bondage" also satirizes unwanted sexual attention from men in the street. "We were kind of the anti-Runaways," Kelly said, inviting analysis of their song "S-O-S Now," which

The Welders

Cover of the Welders' self-titled 12-inch. From the collection of Jen B. Larson.

stands for "Stamp Out Sex," a song about being chaste. The lyrics include:

> It's so boring to be lewd,
> it's not shocking to be crude.
> Be a prude, prude, prude

In 1979, Colleen replaced Stephanie as their singer. Then, with a stockpile of original tunes, the Welders went into the recording studio. Their manager attempted to trade recording time for advertising in his newspaper and went out of business before paying his debt to the studio. The girls couldn't afford to pay for the recordings, so the music sat on dusty shelves for 30 years until finally being released on BDR Records. Passionate about pounding skins, Jane went on to play drums for the Strikers, once sat in with Beck, and played with Courtney Love; naturally, she named her son Ringo and plans to get back to her roots once he's an adult.

Email interview with the Welders, January 2021

Q: Where did the band name come from?

Stephanie: Brainstorming. As I recall, it got down to the Welders or the Atrial-Ventricular Nodes (AV Nodes for short, of course). The irony of Welders applying to petite girls appealed to us; also, we adopted Welder as our family name. I'm not sure if that was to obscure our identities or create a unified front. Either way, it was a marketing opportunity ahead of its time. I honestly can't remember if we landed on that before the Ramones came out or not.

Jane: Rusty came up with that name in one of our marathon hours-long telephone conversations. I believe she might have been hanging upside down off a chair and was reading a label on the underside. I liked the name for the sound of it and because it didn't sound like a girls' group. We did think of using it as our last names before we ever heard of the Ramones.

Rusty: We were constantly making lists of names, and during one session, I believe I was lying on the floor, looking at the underside of a chair; my mother said she needed a leg welded on a piece of furniture. We liked that it was free of any connotations and didn't scream "girl band."

Caroline: We did come up with lists of funny band names but ultimately, I think we went with the Welders since it seemed neutral and didn't have any association with anything in our realm.

Q: The Welders formed before the Runaways. As teenagers, what was your exposure to women playing rock music?

Stephanie: Back then, there would always be one token issue of any given rock magazine (*Creem, Circus,* even *Circus Raves*) featuring "women in rock." And it would always be Grace Slick, Pat Benatar, and Stevie Nicks. This was before Blondie. We didn't really connect with that; they were much older and just playing music other bands were playing. I don't recall us having any sense of being "women playing rock music." We just happened to be girls. We

certainly drew on that; that was not a persona we created; it's who we were.

I still don't have a take on women playing rock music, per se. Whoever makes music is fine with me if they're enjoying it. God gave rock 'n' roll to you, after all.

Jane: All of us were real rock 'n' roll fans. We thought about doing a fanzine or forming a comedy group but being a rock band sounded the coolest. It was the thing that bound our friendship together, being into unusual bands like Sparks or the New York Dolls. We would have done it if we were guys; we just happened to be girls. We didn't have any role models in that department.

Rusty: I'd say we were fascinated by some female musicians, that they were out there making a go of it, but stylistically, we weren't influenced by their music. Our tastes ran to glam bands, British Invasion, and New York punk music. We also had a keen interest in bands that used humor in their lyrics or presentation. What we discovered, in our experience, was that was something male bands had as a luxury but not something afforded to us as female teenagers.

Caroline: I saw photos of the band Fanny and thought they looked great but didn't get to hear their music until much later. I thought Nancy Wilson of Heart and Suzi Quatro also looked cool, but the music we were listening to was glitter, punk, and in my case, bubblegum, so the few women playing rock music then didn't provide any direction for us.

Due to the rarity of female musicians, I knew we would get attention, but it certainly was not the kind of attention any of us wanted. There were no deterrents to harassment back then, so I can only imagine what the women who actually made it in the music world must have gone through.

Throughout the decades, I always took note if a band included women, but now I think it's almost gotten to the point where female musicians are common enough so that gender is not a point of interest.

Summer of 1977 at Jamestown Mall in Florissant, Missouri. (L–R) Stephanie, Jane, Kelly ("Rusty"), and Caroline. Photo by Art Presson.

Q: You all poke fun at the idea of being "cool"—did you consider yourselves "punk"?

Stephanie: I don't think so. We considered ourselves "new wave." Funny, dressed cute, and reasonably well mannered.

Jane: We formed before punk rock was a movement. We were at the tail end of glitter. We realized we were, by definition, a punk rock band. We certainly subscribed to that punk attitude, but we did identify more with the colorful new wave movement—that seemed more fun. We really didn't have any business being punk—we weren't tough or particularly rebellious. We were scholarly types and National Honor students.

Rusty: I think we identified with the New York punk scene more than the British one. The stripped-down, anti-arena-rock stance suited us, and we identified with being outsiders because we didn't know anyone that was into the same thing at the time. We were outcasts in school, so it was a natural identification.

Caroline: I think we poked fun at being cool because we weren't! We weren't punk in the sense of being tough or political. We were punk because we didn't follow what the rest of the kids in high school were doing—we didn't dress like them, we didn't listen to the same music, and we refrained from drugs, booze, swearing, and boys.

Q: Did you make your stage props?

Stephanie: Sure, except the ones we found. I think I'm hugging a big Styrofoam reindeer in one pic from our first gig; that came from a grocery store liquor display. We used a Day-Glo Jim Morrison poster from our rehearsal space (a.k.a. Jane and Caroline's basement) at another gig.

Jane: In the beginning, we were really into our props. We got that from watching Flo and Eddie on the *Midnight Special*. I think because we were insecure in our playing, that a lot of props like signage and toys were a good, entertaining distraction.

Rusty: We made some and other times they were found objects, anything to illustrate a song and make for a good show.

Caroline: We used things we had around the house, like a huge poster of the Osmond Brothers that was in my *16 Magazine*, Silly String, a baby doll, kazoo, a sign saying "Wear Face Shield and Rubber Gloves When Handling," a squeaking red plastic mallet, Lawrence Welk musical spoons… anything that struck us as funny.

Q: What are some of your favorite memories or some funny stories about being in the Welders or from performing at shows?

Stephanie: We were friends first and foremost, and I really loved hanging out together and being a Welder. We overstayed our welcome at many a record store, generally being annoying. We went around telling anyone that would listen that we were a band long before we were a band. I believe we asked bands if we could play during their break and use their instruments—unsuccessfully, of course. But all these things were borne of enthusiasm, not brashness. We were not at all brash.

The best thing about shows was all of us deciding what to wear and working out the set list and little bits to say. I don't recall ever having any stage fright, but I do wish I'd been a little less self-conscious.

One funny part of Welder legend is that we never ever got a sound check. It's funny now, but I don't think it was then.

Rusty or Jane can tell the story about friends that came back from New York to see us, "only to be punched in a cornfield." It wasn't my favorite gig, but it's one of my favorite stories.

Jane: The friendships and just hanging out together was fun. We all were funny people. We started out as friends before we were a band, we had to pick instruments, buy them, and learn how to play! I think the first time we ever played several bars of a song together in our basement was so exciting. The song was "Kimberly" by Patti Smith, and we recorded it on a cassette. We were so impressed with ourselves we called the local rock station KSHE and played it for the DJ. He was not so impressed.

Rusty: We had fun hanging out, and the opportunity to have a creative outlet at that young age is something I'm glad we had. As an adult, I realize now how unusual it is to have such self-directed determination and focus at that age.

Caroline: The Jam were playing at a local club in 1978, and while plans to open for them fell through, we did meet Paul Weller. He told Stephanie that she smelled good, to which she responded that it was probably the beer someone spilled on her shirt.

When we played a reunion show in December of 2009, I hadn't picked up a bass in decades, so it was simultaneously exhilarating and nerve-wracking to be performing in front of an audience again. The best part was hooking up with the other Welder gals for our practices after all those years.

After the release of our EP in 2010, Henry Rollins played one of our songs on his radio show and was complimentary about the music and said something to the effect that it didn't make him want to swing a bag of kittens around.

Q: What were you thinking for all those years when your recordings sat on a shelf collecting dust? What was the impetus to put them out?

Jane: I never thought about it. I was always proud of what we did, and it gave me personal confidence in my life that I had done this cool thing as a youngster. It set the course for my life. I played in rock bands for 25 years. We didn't think of putting it out until Jason and Matt from BDR Records tracked us down.

Rusty: I didn't really think much about it after it was over because the reception we got at the time wasn't very positive. It seemed like we had failed after years of trying, so it was really gratifying when Jason and Matt from BDR Records convinced us to let them release it. We didn't think anyone would care.

Caroline: When Jason Ross and Matt Harnish approached us about releasing an EP of the songs, I had pretty much forgotten about it. I remember Rusty and me meeting up with them at a coffee house, and I kept questioning them on their motivation as to why they would even want to do that and why would anyone care. ●

NIKKI & THE CORVETTES

Detroit, Michigan   »   Formed in 1977

MEMBERS

Nikki Corvette { VOCALS, LYRICS, SONGWRITING
Lori Jeri, Krysti Kaye, Sally Dee { VOCALS
Pete James { GUITAR, SONGWRITING
Robert Mulrooney 'Bootsey X' { DRUMS
(a handful of additional members)

» Nikki Corvette played with a band for the first time on stage in front of a sold-out crowd. To her genuine surprise, a friend of hers who ran a club booked a show and told her, "I thought you could get a band together." He helped her find musicians. The players learned songs on their own and performed their very first show without ever rehearsing together. They played every weekend for the first six to eight months without practicing, as Nikki Corvette & the Convertibles. Members of the group came and went, and they added two backup singers (the ones you see with Nikki in photos brandishing salty stares and tough attitudes).

With this dynamic, they could execute the intended aesthetic: Shangri-Las meet the Ronettes meet the Ramones. On record, their sound is energetic, sugar-sweet, bubblegum punk, but live, they were far rawer—as you can imagine a group who practices less than they play. Shows were their rehearsals, and the crowd was their friends.

(L-R) Krysti Kaye, Nikki Corvette, and Lori Jeri. Photo by Michael Carr. Courtesy of Nikki Corvette.

HIT GIRLS, HAUTE GIRLS

Nikki danced wildly on stage as the front person, jumping into the crowd, grabbing guys by the shirt and kissing them. The young Nikki Corvette's rock 'n' roll lyrics swivel from boy-crazy lyrics:

I see you runnin' in the city
Sweet little boy, lookin' so
        young and pretty
And I know that you can
        understand
And I'm gonna do
        everything I can
To be with you tonight,
        'cuz…
Baby you're just what
        I need
Satisfaction guaranteed

to Wanda Jackson-style party-esque:

Mama killed a chicken, she
        thought it was a duck
She put it on the table with
        his legs sticking up
She had to shake it up
        and go
You good-looking people
        sure got to shake it
        up and go

The singer and lyricist grew up in Detroit, consumed by the live music evidenced in the band's signature sound: rock 'n' roll, pop, and Motown. "I went to every rock show that came to town even if I wasn't that into it," she remembers. "I had to see it all and absorb it, but bands like the MC5 and the Stooges were different; I felt like them, angsty, radical, glammy."

In high school in the early '70s, she bleached her hair and dyed it with food coloring. She rocked glitter, elevated platforms, and scarves. "I didn't fit in anywhere but at these shows," she said. "[Finding] garage, punk, glam was like finding my people."

34

(L-R) Lori Jeri, Nikki Corvette, and Sally Dee. Photo by David Zalkus. Courtesy of Nikki Corvette.

She famously ran away from home to see her first shows.

"I know it sounds totally made up, but it actually happened!" Nikki recalls being a wild child and giving her professor mom a lot to put up with. At 16, Nikki's mom thought she was too young to be running the streets. "She was probably right," Nikki admits. But that didn't stop her from hanging with the MC5 and White Panthers. "I snuck out of the house to go see the MC5 at the Lincoln Park Theater, then couldn't go home for a few days. I did let her know I was all right.

"My mom always taught me that I could do whatever I wanted, and I have always looked at life that way. If I want to do something, I will find a way to do it."

Nikki says she's always ignored people who tell her she can't do something. She wanted to be a singer in a band, so she did it. As Nikki Corvette & the Convertibles, they recorded their first singles, and then as Nikki & the Corvettes, recorded their only studio album in the late '70s in Detroit. Released in 1980 by Bomp! it includes 12 upbeat bangers that interlace power pop, garage, and vocal nods to early-'60s girl groups.

In the '70s and '80s, Nikki's infectious love of music was inspiring and opened doors for big names in music. The Donnas wrote "Gimme My Radio" about Nikki & the Corvettes breaking down gender barriers in the male-centric music scenes of the era. Prince is rumored to have written about her in "Little Red Corvette" and "Darling Nikki."

While the music business consists of many fun parties, gender roles have always been an omnipresent force. Nikki recalls the '70s being particularly difficult. "We got thrown off some shows when people found out there were girls in the band, some guys refused to play with us, guys would stand in front yelling nasty, rude, obscene things at us, and girls pretty much hated us."

Even girls behaved in misogynistic ways: "I got beat up by a bunch of punk girls because I wore super short skirts, makeup, and heels, and they got mad that their boyfriends were looking at me." With all the obstacles, Nikki remembers the positive outcomes as well. "Guys didn't want to listen to my ideas or what I had to say so many different battles. It didn't matter though; we forged ahead, had fun, made fans, got better shows than the ones we were thrown off of."

Nikki formed and played in several bands over the years—including a rockabilly version of Nikki & the Corvettes in the '80s—and sang backing vocals for other musicians' songs. Even when she took a 15-year hiatus from playing, she was involved in music. In 1977, she authored a book—a sort of encyclopedia of dead rock stars, how they died and where they are buried—called *Rock n Roll Heaven*.

She explains, "This was before you could get all the information in the world at your fingertips. I had millions of rock magazines, and I would go through them and write down information, and I talked about it all the time. I was talking about it for a year and a half, and this friend of mine said, 'You know, I talked to this literary agent, and he wants you to send him a chapter of the book,' and I hadn't written anything yet, so he said, 'You have a week.' It wasn't quite what I envisioned, they had editors that changed things, and they got facts wrong. I would like to publish the original book."

Later, she worked with Amy Gore of the Gore Gore Girls. "Working with Amy was really cool," she remembers. "I was a little hesitant because when I left Detroit—the girls there intensely disliked me, and I didn't think anything had changed. I was pleasantly surprised that she knew who I was, and we got along great right from the start."

The two started a side project (Gorevette) that yielded impressive results: playing with the Donnas, touring Japan, and opening for Blondie. Nikki Corvette has continued to play over the years, especially in Japan, where she has a strong fan base. Music and the relationships she formed around it bring her joy—and that's why she has kept making it.

Phone interview with Nikki Corvette, December 2020

Q: When was the moment you knew you wanted to be on stage?

Nikki: I always wanted to be on stage. I would watch bands and think, *That's what I want to do.* I knew from 15. I didn't think I could sing, and I don't have a lot of other musical talents. I mean, I can play guitar, but it doesn't work on stage, I've found. And so, I used to talk about it constantly. There weren't a ton of girls in bands then, but I knew all the guys in town. This friend of mine who ran a club was like, "Hey, I booked you a show," and I was like, "What do you mean??" and he's like, "I thought you could put a band together and play a show." I was like, "What!?" And it was already booked, so he helped me put a band together, and we learned the songs separately…Never had rehearsal. So, the first time I played with a band was when I walked on stage.

Q: Sounds terrifying…

Nikki: It was terrifying, but it was packed. It was a sold-out show. I knew everybody there. After the first song, I knew it couldn't get any worse than that! No place to go but up. And after that, we just kept getting booked. So, we just kept playing shows. I think I was in a band for three months before I ever had a rehearsal. We just kept doing shows. People would just keep asking, "Do you wanna play this?" and we were like, "Sure."

Q: What songs were you playing? Were you doing covers?

Nikki: Yeah, a lot of covers. The songs off the very first singles we did, I wrote those with the guitar player. But yeah, we did all kinds of stuff. We did like "Mony Mony" (Tommy James and the Shondells), some Kinks songs, the Who, the MC5, you know, early on we used to do the Stooges. This was like '78, and it wasn't cool to do Stooges songs or MC5 songs then, especially as a female, but I never cared. I was just like, "This is fun; I'm gonna do this."

Q: Why wasn't it cool to cover Stooges and MC5 then?

Nikki: Just timing, they weren't around anymore. You know, no one cared about them at that time. It was like '78. They cared earlier, and they cared later.

Q: Okay, so you were doing covers and originals. You were able to do originals without practicing?

Nikki: Yeah, we did. I know…I got to say I don't know how we did anything. Like we toured up and down the East Coast and down South, and there weren't computers; I would just meet people and write letters and make phone calls. You know, I'd meet a band and we'd call them up and be like, you know, "we want to play, could you book us a show," and they would, and then when they would come around, I'd book them a show and find them a place to stay. I called it the Nikki Network.

They were all good players, and we would just learn songs off tapes.

Q: Who was in the band?

Nikki: We went through people pretty fast. I started the band with Pete James—he was an ex-boyfriend and guitar player, and we wrote songs together. The first drummer we had was a guy named Bob Mulrooney; he later became Bootsey X. We were Nikki Corvette & the Convertibles for six to eight months, and that's when we put out our first single. Then we became Nikki & the Corvettes. That's when we got the girls. Lori was one of the original girls, and she was in every version. But there were a bunch of other girls. We went through a lot of girls because there were a lot of girls who thought that I wasn't that great of a singer and that they could take over, and I was like, "You know I started this band? And I write the songs? And it's called Nikki & the Corvettes, and I'm Nikki?"

We were just singing when we originally started. But when we went to L.A., and we were finally having rehearsals, after rehearsals the other girls and I would pick up drum and bass and guitar and whatever, and we would just play. But for me, I played guitar on stage once; I'd be dancing, and I'd think *I'm supposed to be playing this guitar right now*, but I couldn't sing and dance and play at the same time.

Q: Well, no, you're the front person. You have to be able to work the crowd, too!

Nikki: Right, it makes it harder when you have the guitar, you have to pay attention to that, and you can't move as much; you can't do as much on stage. When I'm on stage, I dance around crazy, and I don't think about it.

Q: Were you jumping into the crowd?

Nikki: Yeah, I've always danced in the crowd. But it depends on the height of the stage. I like the lower stage because I like to jump down and dance with people. Like, I used to grab a guy by the shirt and kiss him. Just whatever I felt like doing, I would do. Like in the studio, there was always someone to tell me, "You have to do this," but they couldn't tell me anything on stage. So, I just did whatever. I do like to interact with the crowd a lot.

Our live shows, like early on, were way more punk than our record was. Because you know, the guitar player was way more pop-oriented, and I wanted to be in a punk band. So, it was kind of a compromise. But like I said, on stage, I could do whatever I wanted. I was just going crazy, flailing around doing whatever. You don't think in 40 years people will think this is a cute little power-pop band who never saw us. Like our live shows were very different from how we sounded.

I know it's out there. I am just hoping someday someone comes up to me and says, "Hey, I recorded one of your shows!" I have cassette tapes, but the sound quality is just…unlistenable. It was like in a club, so the sound recording quality is just…It's not great.

Q: I am still wondering how you wrote songs when you were apart from your bandmates?

Nikki: I don't write a lot of music. It's more like something will inspire me. I write what ends up being lyrics, and I'll give it to someone and say, "can you put it to music?" I still write that way.

Back then, that's one of my problems with doing some of those songs still. I was like 20 years old when I wrote many of those songs. I have a different outlook on life than I did as 20-year-old me.

Q: In what way?

Nikki: Well, 'boys boys boys.' I mean, not that there's anything wrong with it, but it's just not what I really want to sing now. Not that I don't still feel that way, but people want to hear it. They don't care that it was 42 years ago. So, I end up singing a lot of those songs now. I've come to terms with it. Some of them, like "I Wanna Be Your Girlfriend," I don't think I would do that now. Some of them I can get past, like "He's a Mover" or "Let's Go." But I don't know if people didn't know the songs that I would still play them.

I have found that even over the years, I will write a song about what I'm thinking and what I'm feeling, and the people I am writing with will ask, "Why don't we write a song that sounds like Nikki & the Corvettes?" I wanna try to grow up a little bit! You know, when I did "Back to Detroit," I liked that because it was reminiscent of Nikki & the Corvettes, but it was a little more grown-up, like Nikki & the Corvettes but 30 years later.

Q: Yeah, you want to grow and evolve and change…

Nikki: Yeah, but people don't want me to.

Q: Do you think you got to with different versions of the band, like when you were doing rockabilly?

Nikki: We had so many different versions of the band. We had the versions where we were doing straight-up rockabilly for a while, although we were still doing a lot of punk songs, so I don't know what it was. Then, there came a time—I don't even remember, this was more towards the end—like the early '80s when we were a little harder band. And the girls weren't with us; so, we definitely went through some changes…

Q: What about when you were working with Amy (Gore)?

Nikki: Yeah. Stuff with Amy kind of just happened. We were hanging out when I moved back from L.A. I had met her out there. I moved back here, and I didn't really know anyone anymore. I had been gone for 23 years or something. And I had just told her I wanted to be in a punk cover band, and she was like "me too!" and that's what we were planning to do: a one-off side project where we picked a bunch of covers. Then one day I called her, and I was like, "Hey, I wrote these lyrics," and she wrote some music, and all of a sudden, we were writing songs, and we weren't just a punk cover band.

I've compromised. It's not that they don't want me to grow up; it's that people want to listen to music that takes them to a fun place. I need that too. It's just that personally I don't feel that. I'm not 20 anymore, so I feel stupid singing some of the songs, but nobody cares but me. That's what people want to hear, so that's why I am doing it. ●

FLIRT

Detroit, Michigan » Formed in 1977

MEMBERS

Rockee Berlin a.k.a. Rockee Re Marx | VOCALS
Skid Marx | BASS
Gaetano, Thomas St. Thomas | GUITAR
Mickey Church, Tom Cicola,
David Scott Bradley | GUITAR
Steve Sortor, Tommy 'Spud' Fremont | DRUMS

Cover of "Don't Push Me" / "Degenerator," Flirt's 1978
7-inch. From the collection of Jen B. Larson.

Celebrated style icons, Flirt embodied thrift-store fashion. On the cover of Flirt's 7-inch "Don't Push Me"/"Degenerator," pregnant punk Rockee Berlin embraces her round belly with a metallic glove while her shirtless ex Skid Marx poses in lace-up knee-high leather platform boots and a biker jacket. "That's my son," she said, referring to her gingerly placed hand. "He became a musician."

Before creating Flirt, the once husband-and-wife team were individually involved in Detroit music, playing with various groups and making money playing covers in local bars. Rockee's first experience in the studio was singing backup vocals on Bob Seger's hit "Katmandu."

"Nobody knew that officially until 2018. I did it in 1973; it was the first time I was ever in a studio. I was 17 years old, and I just thought, well, my dad told me, 'Whenever you want to get a job, just sort of fake it,' so I went in there and eh, you can hear my mistake, I was nervous. I did OK."

Presented with the idea that no one else would notice (it's a lo-fi backing track buried under dueling piano and guitar solos), she retorted: "Oh no, he noticed."

"I didn't really tell anyone that was me," she muses. "They found me in 2018, and now it's verified. I can officially claim it now. I was surprised it's been played 62 million times. He is a very noble, very

honorable person—I was not aware I was entitled to royalties. It could have just gone back in the closet. They only had my first name, Rockee."

Rockee started making musical connections when she answered an ad in the paper while in her mid-teens. She played in a group called the Kurbstone Beauteaze, which she describes as a "theatrical rock band, an Alice Cooper type of thing and advertised as an 'X-rated rock band' but by today's standards—no, but by those standards then—yeah." She reminisces, "We had props, we were doing silly things" and "we got kicked out of Canada for the inflatable doll."

She met her now ex-husband and Flirt co-creator, Skid Marx, and together they played in a cover band called Medusa, who got rowdy. They broke a tricycle on stage at bike clubs, and they managed other exploits, like Rockee would "shoot" Skid. Skid wanted a full record contract, and they formed an original punk band.

©℗ 1978 Real Records

Real Records
P.O. Box 19149
Detroit, MI 48219

FLIRT IS: Rockee Re Marx (Voc:
GUEST MUSICIANS: Gaetano (Guitar), T
Steve Sortor (Drur

SPECIAL THANX: Jim Cassily (Engineer),
Recorded at: A₂ Studios, Ann A
SLEEVE DESIGN: Dennis Loren for Solid Graphi

MIDWEST

40

"It's A Real Record"

Marx (Bass)
Thomas (Guitar)

ano (Assistance)
an
GRAPHY: Eric Smith.

"I believe we were [punk], although my aspirations were more for a thing that was a little bit more commercial, more on the pop edge." Skid played guitar in a way that goes beyond the limitations of punk, but he wanted to start a punk band. He convinced Rockee, whose vocals pushed the boundaries of punk and leaned toward more commercial sounds, that they should write original songs—a gutsy move in the mid-'70s when cover bands made money.

In Flirt, Rockee wrote most of the lyrics, centering on a woman's perspective. For example, "De-Generator" takes aim at the "boys will be boys" attitude. She sings:

> Pulled on my pigtails in school
> Stepped on my books to be cruel
> Told all your friends I was loose
> Called me a dog, such abuse

The underrated anthem "Don't Push Me Around" features proto-metal guitars and Rockee's tough front:

> You can laugh at me if you want
> You can't push me around.
> Baby baby watch what you say
> You can't push me around
> I'm just gonna set you straight
> You can't push me around
> I'm gonna follow you
> I'm gonna flag you down
> I'm gonna follow you

The phrase "smash your head in the ground" repeats so many times it's clearly a threat. Call-and-response backing vocals, handclaps, ripping guitar, and bass fill out the track.

Flirt self-released two records, a 7-inch single in 1978 and a 10-inch EP in 1980. They played in the Detroit area often, sharing bills with local bands such as Destroy All Monsters and opening for touring acts, including the Slits and Devo. But Flirt played in New York City perhaps more than in Detroit, becoming regulars at Max's Kansas City in New York. Notable music powerhouses noticed them, including Jimmy Ienner, manager for the Raspberries and Three Dog Night, and influential English disc jockey John Peel, who played them on his show in 1980. Pat Benatar also attended their shows and may have even learned a thing or two. On fame, Rockee says: "It's whoever gets there first… It's who is at the right place at the right time." ●

Back cover of "Don't Push Me" / "Degenerator." From the collection of Jen B. Larson.

CHI-PIG

Akron, Ohio   »   Formed in 1977

M E M B E R S

Susan Schmidt Horning { GUITAR, SYNTH, VOCALS
Deborah Smith { BASS, VOCALS
Rich Roberts { DRUMS

>> In 1968, a photograph of Sue Schmidt and Debbie Smith's first band, the Poor Girls, appeared in their high school yearbook. The photo was taken from behind the stage and captures the audience: a group of boys standing back about 20 feet with their arms crossed, directing imposing glares at the band. Off to the side, a lone girl cheers them on.

Outside of their high school, the girls drew both support and critical apprehension from outsiders. "We were still considered novelties at that point in the '60s," Susan remembers. "But we were serious about playing. We worked hard. We practiced regularly, we learned songs, and we weren't shabby."

Susan and Debbie started the Poor Girls with childhood friends Pam and Esta when they were in junior high. They played the Hullabaloo circuit, opened for Cream and Steppenwolf, and then broke up at the end of high school.

After high school, Susan went to Berklee College of Music for a year, and the girls continued jamming with guys around town. They played in Cinderella's Revenge and Friction with Peter Laughner, who was a major catalyst in the birth of Cleveland's proto-punk movement. Then, their friend, Devo's Mark Mothersbaugh, introduced them to drummer Richard Roberts, and Chi-Pig was born.

Susan says they held Devo in high esteem: "There was no sort of posing or being cool; it was just the opposite. Which was what was so attractive about them at the time. Here we are in the late '70s, and it's like 'how cool can you be' or, you know, the whole glam thing, but they really made fun of themselves," she says. "Their message was the paramount thing—the whole idea of de-evolution and all that."

Poaching their name from a local chicken and rib barbecue restaurant whose outdoor sign advertised dinners with a cartoon winged pig, Chi-Pig formed as an avant-garde new wave power-pop trio from Akron, Ohio.

When asked about the name, Susan shrugs. "We just thought it was a cool name. It was like 'why not?'"

Cover of "Bountiful Living" / "Ring Around the Collar," Chi-Pig's 1978 7-inch. From the collection of Jen B. Larson.

Chi-Pig performing live. Photo by Bill Samaras.

she says, remarking on the band's sense of humor and spontaneity. "It's not like we were advocating for eating chicken and ribs."

Quirky and experimental, their offbeat brand of post-punk featuring interwoven countermelodies and stop-and-go rhythms aligned them with a local community of supportive bands and fans.

Deb and Susan designed the sleeve for their 1979 45, which included "Bountiful Living" and "Ring Around the Collar." The record itself featured a flying pig cartoon, a nod to the style of a Magic Mirror record—a 1950s children's toy that looked like a carousel and gave images on vinyl labels the illusion of movement through an angled spinning mirror.

Chi-Pig only played together for five years but

significantly impacted the Akron sound—a post-punk movement that included well-known bands such as Devo, the Pretenders, and the Waitresses. Their 1978 song "Ring Around the Collar" features lyrics by Devo's Mark Mothersbaugh, and the girls of Chi-Pig wrote and were credited for the riff in Devo's "Gates of Steel." (The original version had the less pleasant title "Pimple in my Plans.")

Growing up, Motown and R&B were formative for them. When writing songs, the songwriting team of Susan and Deb played how they felt. They had been playing together so long that they genuinely collaborated by bouncing ideas off one another. They didn't intentionally switch time signatures or often obsess over lyrics.

Considered part of the second wave of punk in Akron, Ohio, Chi-Pig existed among a movement of interconnected bands and a community of supportive fans. After launching the careers of bands such as Devo and the Waitresses, the Akron scene became referred to as "The New Liverpool," a place where themes of prosperity with a hint of doom united the energy of like-minded artists.

"It was unique that there was that much collegiality and not a lot of infighting when everybody is going for the same donut. But I guess we were still coming from the mentality that there were dozens of donuts. Little did we know, you know, Krispy Kreme was going out of business," Deborah Smith said of the experience in the PBS documentary *If You're Not Dead, Play.*

Surrounded by a dynamic universe of creators and fans, Chi-Pig always put on a fantastic show. One of the popular venues at the time was called The Bank. There, crowds were energetic and eccentric without being violent. The band would sometimes pull people on stage, and the events were described by those attending as "just a big, fun party."

Stylistically, whether dressing in flashy flamenco style, floral patterns, or karate *gi*, Chi-Pig always intentionally matched (even in a documentary made decades later, the three musicians maintained their mission and dressed in all black). They picked up most of their outfits at thrift stores and from sidewalk sales, but their famous flamenco-style shirts were custom-made.

Musically, Chi-Pig made thoughtful pop songs with intelligent lyrics and a playful sense of humor critiquing a consumerist, patriarchal society through a feminist lens. In "You're Just Along for the Ride," they sing:

This pain in my heart
These tears in my eyes
These waves of disgust
Filling up inside
I've got chills and fevers
I've fears I can't hide
I've got a sneaking suspicion
You're just along for the ride

In "Waves of Disgust" they sing:

It might be something I said
Or maybe it's something I thought

I spend too much time believing
    in promises
and listening to small talk
I'm a hungry dog
and you're tossing me a bone
I'm a thirsty man
You've got me drinkin' alone

At the height of their career, Chi-Pig regularly played showcases in New York City and recorded at Criteria Studios in Florida, a reputable studio where 250 gold or platinum singles were engineered. Susan even laid down tracks on a piano Aretha Franklin played. Their recording session landed in the middle of a tour of the South. During that time, they lived on the beach and recorded. "It didn't matter; we hadn't arrived yet. It felt like it. You know, we were playing, we were just living our music," Susan said of the experience.

Though the group summoned large crowds and profoundly impacted the Akron scene, they couldn't land a record deal. They broke up in 1982. In 2004, they released a CD of 1979 recordings on an album titled *Miami*. It was hailed by the *Village Voice* as "25 years ahead of its time, even now." Susan even engineered the song "Apu Api," which appeared on *The Akron Album*, a scratch 'n' sniff record cover with the scent of burnt rubber, on her TEAC 3340 (a four-channel tape recorder).

Their demise occurred just as successful female-fronted bands such as the Go-Go's broke out of punk and into the mainstream. Like many women in '70s and '80s punk, Deborah and Susan moved on from underground music and turned to careers outside the music industry. Deborah became a lawyer, and Susan, a history professor, published a book in 2015 on recording studios' cultural and technological evolution in the United States. Susan says there were not too many women engineers besides Wilma Fine, a producer married to Bob Fine.

When asked why she believes music is male-dominated, she responded that recording is an old boys' network. In 2015, she says, she presented on all-girl bands of the 1960s at a social science history conference. One of the comments she received came from a guy in his thirties, who said something to the effect of "I don't know what it is, there is just something about a girl with an electric guitar that just doesn't seem right." ●

DA!

Chicago, Illinois » Formed in 1977

MEMBERS

Lorna Donley { BASS, VOCALS
Gaylene Goudreau { GUITAR
David Thomas { GUITAR
Dawn Fisher, Bob Furem { DRUMS

>> In the late '70s, the Chicago rock scene was saturated by heavy rock. The misunderstood downtempo punk outfit DA!, possibly the first post-punk band in the city, went relatively unnoticed. Being overlooked is a symptom of originality and often the case for complex creatives. Despite later being hailed as innovators or visionaries and opening doors for local scenes, artists in tune with a creative consciousness elsewhere don't quite fit into their hometown milieu.

With changing lineups, DA! played together until 1983. Despite leaving an impressive legacy, they never really packed a room until decades after breaking up. Then, in 2010, the band reunited to play a couple of shows, and in an interview with Gapers Block, singer Lorna Donley remarked, "The Empty Bottle was amazing; we never played for that many people when we were around. Maybe once, there was an art show we did, but we managed by the end of the set to drive the audience away."

Guitarist David Thomas told Victim of Time, "We were a struggling art-punk band in the Midwest. We often played to near-empty rooms." And in the documentary *You Weren't There*, fellow rockers from their scene remember DA! as being so unique that they didn't really fit in anywhere and in a "netherworld."

Writer Lene Cortina of the *Punk Girl Diaries* blog/zine suggests that DA!'s identity may not have fully aligned with their time and place. "Listening to them and watching the videos, their inner band seemed to be very much from the UK," she writes.

"Back in the day, there were still pronounced differences between English and American bands. The English were far more inclined to be pale, fey, with a taste for black and white films (not movies), and dressed up in hand-me-downs. Americans were not."

When DA! formed, Lorna was 17 years old. Lorna admired the guitar work of her older uncles since she was a toddler and began playing at age 11 and writing songs. However, as soon as she learned chords, she had dropped out of high school and was living on her own at 16.

Artistically, she was inspired by alternative pop—Magazine, Siouxsie, and Joy Division. The Jam, Kinks, Stranglers, and Captain Beefheart. "Lyrically, I was intent on not writing love songs," she asserts. In *Secret History of Chicago Music*, comic strip artist Steve Krakow likened the band to "Patti Smith fronting Joy Division."

Meeting people in the local music scene, friends would sneak her into La Mere Vipere, the notorious Chicago punk club that burned down in 1978. She quickly put a band together among artists and musicians, and their first lineup featured Dawn Fisher on drums and Evelyn Marquis on guitar and keyboard. They only played one show together, and guitarists Gaylene Goudreau (who had previously played with the all-girl punk band Lois Layne) and David Thomas (from the Singapores and Cool Jerk) stepped in.

Though not well-understood by their peers, DA! was appreciated and became an important fixture in Chicago's early punk music scene. Performing regularly at clubs like Exit, Oz, O'Banion's, and Tuts, they also opened for UK and East Coast groups like the Fall, DNA, Bauhaus, and Mission of Burma.

DA! also made artsy music videos for their songs. The video for "Dark Rooms" frequently appeared on pre-MTV cable station "Rock America," and Dave produced "Next to Nothing" on the CTA while he was in film school.

Left: Back cover of *Time Will Be Kind*, DA!'s 1982 12-inch. Above: Cover of *Time Stands Still*, Lorna Donley & the Veil's retrospective 12-inch (recordings from 1986–1989). Both from the collection of Jen B. Larson.

In the video, Lorna's lyrical delivery was both deadpan and powerful. She sings:

I've been eating next to nothing
On the run from place to place
My eyes won't close when I'm sleeping
And it's showing in my face
My face sometimes looks different
And though I like my face
Sometimes it works just like a mask on me.
I've been scrambled like a puzzle
Someone has shaken me around
I've tried to put some things together
Some of the pieces can't be found

Though many women played in the early punk scene in Chicago, according to Lorna, that fact didn't really make much of a difference in how audiences received women on stage or how other bands treated them. In *You Weren't There*, DA! was the only band with women featured, and an interviewer even referred to them as "the girl band DA." So, perhaps the hardcore bands DA! played alongside contributed to this feeling. "I never saw a recognizable shift in the way women musicians were perceived while I was in DA. I am not sure punk bands or audiences were more accepting of women," she indicates her impassivity. "I always felt a little out of place no matter what I did, so it didn't matter."

When the band broke up, guitarist Gaylene Goudreau went on to play hardcore music and formed Bag People in New York City, while Lorna and Dave continued to play together in various projects in Chicago. Lorna also played with a group called Silent Language. After that, she went back to school, and then, tragically and suddenly, she passed away in 2013 at 53. ●

THE SHIVVERS

Milwaukee, Wisconsin   »   Formed in 1978

MEMBERS

Jill Kossoris { SONGWRITING, PIANO, VOCALS
Scott Krueger { BASS, VOCALS
Jim Eannelli { LEAD GUITAR, VOCALS
Mike Pyle { RHYTHM GUITAR, VOCALS
Jim Richardson { DRUMS

》 Back in the day, live bands entertained bar crowds by keeping the music going for a good two to three hours. In Milwaukee in the '70s, the Shivvers were no stranger to this practice. Playing well-known covers and well-crafted original pop tunes, the seasoned musicians built their stamina for years in other projects before the Shivvers came into existence. They often played back-to-back shows—Friday, Saturday, and Sunday. With more than 150 songs in the band's repertoire, they could play for hours and always keep it interesting.

Jill Kossoris, the band's lead singer, keyboardist, and co-songwriter, demonstrates the depth of the Shivvers' appreciation for music by citing catchy, soulful, well-written songs as an influence—from Badfinger to Motown. "I love to mix it up and play an ABBA song and an Iggy Pop song after," she told the *Milwaukee Record* in 2017.

Dedicated to the craft, and a classically trained pianist, Kossoris wanted to be a musician from a very young age after seeing the Beatles' *Ed Sullivan Show* appearance. She began playing soul and rock music in junior high school, and by age 16, she had put out an ad to start her own original group. Jill played with many musicians who would join the band over the years and formed the Shivvers out of the ashes of many other Milwaukee groups, including In a Hot Coma, where Jill played keyboards.

Jill wrote songs but initially hesitated to bring them to the band. As a classical musician appreciative of impeccable pop tunes, she arranged songs to perfection, including every minor detail of a song's structure: the intro, the outro, and even the guitar solos. She would try to bring new material to practice each week to keep the momentum going. Open-minded and responsive to the ideas Jill brought to the table, her bandmates breathed life into the catchy, pop-perfect songs with gnarly guitars and complex harmonies. Lyrically, their message was sweet. In "Teen Line," Jill sings,

Last night I didn't know, I was wondering
I sit by the phone waiting for your ring
And the sound makes my heart beat fast
'Cause you had so much to say
And I know this love will last
'Cause my heart's on the teen line

And in "Please Stand By for Love," she sings,

I got two arms and want to hold you tight
I got a heart that's true, I can't get over you

In Milwaukee, the Shivvers were a big deal. They pulled in crowds and opened for nationally touring acts like the Shoes, the Romantics, and Iggy Pop. In 1980, "Teen Line" was released on the Fliptop independent label and underwent two distinct pressings—very few of them still exist today. Everything was going well, and the band was very popular locally. Crowds loved their punch-in-the-gut brand of power pop, with saccharine-sweet melodies and Jill's pouty delivery.

After Kossoris mailed tapes of the band's work to one of her heroes, Eric Carmen, who played in the Raspberries, Carmen suggested he produce the band's first major-label record—but it never happened. Their communication fizzled out, likely due to the physical distance between Milwaukee and California and the difficulty it took to stay in contact in those days. The Shivvers were also declared the "Best Band in Milwaukee" in 1982, but sadly, the talented group never actually caught a break during their active years.

One reason the band never landed a record deal may have been that they never signed with a manager who understood them. Many of the managers' criticisms of the band reflected misogynistic attitudes in the music industry: not only did management representatives criticize the single, suggesting that Jill was out of key, but several reps also suggested Jill change her style. They wanted her to dress more provocatively or change her makeup to mirror the look of a typical rocker-chick singer, which she didn't want to do. Despite being popular with crowds and praised by well-respected artists, managers didn't know how to describe the band. As a result, the Shivvers were rejected by major labels, including Arista and Elektra.

Music can be a cutthroat industry in many regards. Jill contends that her bandmates were supportive and crowds loved the band, but she never hides behind the idea that playing music is all sunshine and smiles or that everyone was kind and supportive. In an interview in the *Milwaukee Record*, Jill said, "There's a lot of posing. People say, '[Music] wasn't competitive.' Yes, it was. It's very competitive. I had quite a few circumstances where people would verbally attack me after a couple of drinks because we were popular."

The band tried their hand at moving out of Milwaukee in 1982 but didn't make the right connections. Luckily, they did make quality recordings of their tunes, and a retrospective album, *'Til the Word Gets Out*, was released in 2006 by Hyped to Death Records, welcoming a new demographic to their cult following. After the Shivvers broke up, Jill relocated to Nashville to work as a songwriter, releasing an album of solo material (*Invisible*) in 2001.

Email interview with Jill Kossoris, May 2019

Q: I've read a bit about how you transitioned from being a classically trained musician to writing pop songs, and I wonder what that evolution was like for you?

Jill: It wasn't really a transition or evolution. It was a means to an end. I had to take classical piano to learn how to play and please my parents. After I practiced my classical lessons, I could move on to Badfinger. This satisfied all involved! The plan was to learn an instrument so that maybe I could eventually learn how to write great pop songs. Don't get me wrong, I love Chopin, but it was always about rock 'n' roll. You can hear the classical influence at the end of "Teen Line."

It was the Beatles for me—just like everybody else—only I was only three years old when they changed my life. My only sister was 15 when the Beatles made their first appearance on *The Ed Sullivan Show*, and she didn't want her little sister ruining her experience, so I was sent to bed early. So, I'm lying in bed, dying of curiosity, and the TV is blasting in the living room with this otherworldly sound. It sounded too enthusiastic and exciting to be made by humans, so I pictured them in my mind like cartoon characters. I couldn't stand the suspense any longer, so I crawled down the hall on my hands and knees to avoid anyone detecting me and peeked around the corner of the living room wall, and BANG! The visual was as exciting as the sound. What is THAT??? Whatever it is, it's the most alive thing I've ever experienced, and I want to be a part of that. Little did the family know the forbidden aspect of not letting me watch them probably made it that much more exciting.

Q: What was the recording process with the Shivvers like?

Jill: We started recording very early in the band's development. We'd only played out a few times before we recorded "Teen Line," "When I Was Younger," "Don't Tell Me." We always recorded live, very quickly and with very few overdubs.

Q: In what ways has your approach to songwriting changed over the years?

Jill: I no longer believe in the romantic notion that the first draft is the best. There's almost always room for improvement, especially lyrically. You can find

Jill Kossoris of the Shivvers. Photo by Robert Uecke.

a more precise way to say something, bring something new to the second verse, find a more unique rhyme, choose a word that sings better or a better arrangement. I definitely take lyrics more seriously now. A great melody can't save a bad lyric. They don't necessarily have to be deep, or heavy, or even great, but they can't be lame!! Lame lyrics have ruined many a good song. By lame, I mean empty, meaningless, just taking up space. They say nothing, they don't make you think or feel anything, you don't care if you ever hear them again. A good lyric doesn't have to be literally true, but they must be emotionally true. You want the listener to feel that the writer/singer believes what they're saying. If the singer or writer doesn't believe, why should the listener?

I've also found that writing without an instrument is helpful in finding new melodies. Richard

Thompson said something about becoming so familiar with your instrument that you fall into the same old patterns, and that's very true. So, I write more in my mind now and work it out on an instrument later.

Q: Where do your song lyrics come from?

Jill: I usually start with a title, but not always. As David Lynch says, "you fall in love with an idea"… I think that's very true. The title will spark something, and then I'll explore different ways to approach it. I think a lot of the early writing takes place in the subconscious, and then you do the cleanup or critical work after you get that first rush of thoughts down on paper. If it's one thing I've learned, it's to write down or record as much as you can at the time you get the initial idea. Try not to think critically at that stage. The critical part comes later.

Most of the time, I don't know what I'm writing about until it's written.

Q: I can definitely hear a country sound on Invisible *that isn't necessarily present in the Shivvers' work. Where did that come from? How did your work as a songwriter in Nashville impact your songwriting?*

Jill: It happened very naturally before I ever set foot in Nashville or even thought about going there.

There was no deliberation, no feeling of "and now I will write country-influenced music." It just happened. I'd had a lot of heartbreak, disappointment, family issues, serious health problems, and depression in the years previous to writing anything country, just a deluge of bad stuff. I hadn't written in quite a while, and suddenly, a country-influenced song came into my brain. My first thought was, where is this coming from? But I stopped questioning after that and just followed my instincts and kept writing. I do come by it naturally; my mom loved country music and played Johnny Cash, Roy Orbison, and Hank Williams all the time. Real country music is very close to early rock 'n' roll. Chuck Berry, Buddy Holly, the Beatles, the Everly Brothers…were all very influenced by country music, and of course, Rockpile who were a huge influence on the Shivvers, so it makes sense. In the early 1990s, there was this little creative window on country radio. The O'Kanes, Dwight Yoakam, the Mavericks. Great stuff. It sounded real. Melodic, rootsy, inspired. It spoke to me more than the rock 'n' roll I was hearing at the time. So after a few months, I had written quite a few songs, and I went into a little studio with Mike Hoffmann[1] and made a few demos. I gave a cassette tape to the Mavericks when they were playing in Milwaukee, and they loved it! They eventually called and said they were constantly playing it on the tour bus! They even considered doing two of my songs. I took my first couple trips to Nashville laying on an air mattress in the back seat of a car because my back pain was so intense; thinking *I'm in too much pain to be a performer, but maybe I can write.* Robert Reynolds (bass player in the Mavericks) was my point man. Funny, clever, charismatic, generous, and a fan! I worked with publishers, I wrote with other writers, I tried to write more commercially, but the consensus was that I was "too left of center"… they said, "well, you might get a Mavericks cut, or a Yoakam cut"… but that's only $100,000.

Q: How did Nashville impact your songwriting?

Jill: In positive and negative ways. It made me more lyric-conscious, which is good, but it made me think in a more formulaic way. Verse Chorus Verse Chorus Bridge Chorus. I've been trying to unlearn that aspect for the last couple of years, and my natural writing style seems to be coming back.

Q: I personally (and a lot of people) think the Shivvers are one of the most underrated bands of the late '70s, early '80s. I've read a bit about how the band came close but didn't see commercial success. Yet, at the same time, you were successful locally in Milwaukee. What does "success" mean to you? Has that definition changed for you over the years?

Jill: Years ago, I would have said success is getting a recording contract and having hit songs. I LOVED the radio when I was a kid. 1960s AM radio was fantastic and very different from modern radio with its strict formatting. It was so diverse. You would hear a Byrds song, and then a Roy Orbison song, and then a Frank Sinatra song … all great, but all different.

Currently, I'd say maybe success is writing and performing songs that last. Songs that people want to hear over and over again without growing tired of them. I'm beyond thrilled that the band is currently being rediscovered, especially since we were always told we were great live, but we didn't have the songs.

Now all people have are the songs and some YouTube performances, and people are responding to them. We were a tight little unit. We were all road-tested, ready to go, and geared up for the next step. A band needs to keep moving forward; you need a new creative challenge. You'll stagnate if you're stuck in the bars playing three 50-minute sets a night. There are days when I'm a little bitter, especially when I hear a really lousy hit song from the era, and I think our songs could have competed well with it. And then I hear about how the songwriter is living in France in a chalet or something; it's a little hard to take! I'm a very ambitious person, but I was always willing to work hard. I don't think I'm owed anything; I don't think I have a huge ego, but of course, I wanted to be successful. People think you have to have a huge ego to be a performer or writer, not necessarily true. Many times, it's just the opposite. Most of the time, it's because you're not good at anything else, or it's the only thing you have confidence in doing! And everyone wants to be successful. People don't go to college and go into huge debt because they don't believe in themselves. I think it takes a lot of confidence to be a car mechanic. People's lives are in your hands! And here's the other thing. There wouldn't have necessarily been a wonderful outcome. Maybe we would have been a "success," but then we could have been in a terrible accident, or someone would have overdosed! There's no guarantee of a happily ever after and a chateau in France. The main thing we lost was the potential of hearing what we would have sounded like in a world-class studio with a creative producer that really believed in us. That is a shame, no matter how you look at it.

Q: At the time, what other women were you aware of playing rock 'n' roll or new wave music?

1 Mike Hoffmann (1954–October 21, 2021) was a musician and producer who had enormous influence on the Midwestern music scene. Among his many credits, Hoffmann produced, performed and recorded with melaniejane, EIEIO, Semi-Twang, Carnival Strippers, the Holy Ranger, Victor DeLorenzo, Nineteen Thirteen, the Spanic Boys, Arms, Legs and Feet, the Carolinas, Mike Fredrickson, Blue in the Face, Ward and His Troubles, and the Yell Leaders. Most recently he was collaborating with the Delta Routine, mood vertigo and Sam Llanas (of BoDeans).

Jill Kossoris of the Shivvers. Photo by Robert Uecke.

Jill: When I was growing up, the two most popular women in rock 'n' roll were Janis Joplin and Grace Slick. They were not role models to me. In fact, I wanted to be the opposite of both women! I have more respect for them now but growing up, I saw them as overly masculine and kind of desperate. I wanted to be a rocker, but I didn't want to give up my femininity. At the time, I didn't see anyone doing what I wanted to do: to show that girls could truly embody the spirit of rock 'n' roll without having to pretend they were men. It was very rare for women to be in bands in those days, especially as the main writer. There was no "rock band" in school like there is now. It wasn't cute to be in a band at that time; there was still a stigma about it. I was considered an absolute outcast and weirdo, and I took a lot of flak for it.

Q: Do you think being a woman has impacted your experience as a musician? If so, in what ways?

Jill: There was a positive and negative aspect to it. As I said before, there weren't many women in bands, so we were a bit of a novelty, and that probably attracted more immediate attention, which was great, but to sustain interest, you had to be good. There were the people who said, "you're only popular because there's a girl in the band,"… or "why didn't you just have an all-girl band? That probably would have garnered more attention." But that's ridiculous. It's silly to put a band together based on gender; you put a band together based on a mutual love of the same music and ability to sound and play well together. Men didn't necessarily get an easy pass either. I remember speaking to a booking agent who said he really liked a particular band, but they were too ugly!

Q: When Iggy Pop asked you out for coffee, but your drummer Jim [Richardson] said, "She's not going anywhere," you said [the guys in your band] were like your older brothers. Had you considered going to coffee with Iggy, or were you in your head like, "Hell no, someone help!"?

Jill: I wanted to have coffee with Iggy! But I thought it was just coffee, and Jim thought it was more than coffee. (Jim was always looking out for me, and he rescued me from some scary situations over the years, so I need to give him a big thank you.) Iggy was a very charming, extremely intelligent, personable guy. He was very cool about the whole thing. His response was, "Well, okay…. Anyway, you guys are great," and he hung out with us while we packed up. I don't flatter myself here; it's well documented that Iggy has had "coffee" with a lot of women.

Q: You've mentioned that you were so shy that your doctor told your parents to buy you a piano, so you'd have a way to communicate. What about playing piano helped you communicate?

Jill: My family had a lot of issues, and like most problematic families, you're taught to keep quiet and not question anything. When I was about five, my dad brought in a huge, ancient upright piano, and it just felt like maybe I could speak through it. My parents were major music lovers, and records were constantly on the turntable, but I thought, *what if I could create that sound myself someday?* Music just seemed so limitless, like you could never learn everything, and there were no rules.

Now I've mentioned that my parents were not exactly Ward and June Cleaver, but they supported the fact that I wanted to do something creative, and they helped me in any way they could. How many parents would let their 16-year-old daughter bring a bunch of punky guys into their suburban house to play loud rock 'n' roll four nights a week? Not many. So, there are advantages to families with problems. You can get away with more!

Q: Do you have recollections or stories on how you got over your shyness to perform?

Jill: It's like everything else. Little by little, you gain confidence. I was in my first band at 14; I joined In A Hot Coma when I was 16, so I had been in two bands by the time I was in the Shivvers at 18, but the Shivvers were the first band that felt like my band. The first band I was the creative leader of—not me solely, but I was a guiding force. If you really love something, you will overcome your fear to be part of it. ●

THE WAITRESSES

Kent, Ohio » Formed in 1978

MEMBERS

Patty Donahue { VOCALS
Tracy Wormworth { BASS
Chris Butler { GUITAR
Dan Klayman { ORGAN
Mars Williams { SAX
Billy Ficca { DRUMS

》》One day, Chris Butler nervously shared an original demo of "I Know What Boys Like" to his discerning and sophisticated all-male experimental rock band, Tin Huey. He hoped his bandmates would want to try something unconventional—pop songs elaborated with a quirky, off-kilter sense of humor, articulated from a female perspective. The cultural shift was inevitable, after all.

Met with silent stares followed by a polite decline, he realized he'd need to connect with like-minded folks, and perhaps women, to execute this plan. So, he walked into a bar one afternoon, and in a bizarre call to arms, stood on a chair and pitched his proposal to an entire room of unsuspecting employees and patrons. Then, magically, he summoned a new collaborator. An interested person, a 22-year-old waitress named Patty Donahue, was at the time working to fund her college tuition.

After their fateful meeting, the two began working collaboratively. Spinning together catchy hooks from varying genres, they attacked a pop sound from all the right angles and fleshed out a collection of songs into an entire set they were proud of.

In a male-dominated musical landscape, Chris wrote lyrics from a female perspective. He offered them to Patty to interpret and dramatize, and she delivered the writing to audiences with a unique, sardonic sense of humor. As Chris led the group and

wrote the songs, fans and music journalists often agreed that Patty's work attracted audiences. Patty's independence, sarcastic attitude, and overall approach to singing countered the idea that she was merely a performer reciting someone else's words; she was a strong woman who used her comedic sensibility to relate her own experiences.

At the very beginning of their working relationship, the Waitresses created the song "No Guilt," which depicted a woman asserting her independence and lack of regret after a breakup. Patty's deadpan delivery and Midwestern non-apologies are spot on in the recording. She sings,

> I know someone who really met Belushi.
> I fixed the toilet so it doesn't always run.
> I moved a chair over by the window.
> I feel better if my laundry's done.
> Getting by on less sleep than I used to.
> I had no trouble in setting up a desk.
> I learned the reason for a three-
>   pronged outlet.
> I got 100 on my driver's test.
> I got a trick to get them to deliver.
> I called the landlord when the
>   water turned brown.
> Did you know I own some
>   valuable records?
> I've learned a lot since you've been gone.
> I've done a lot since you've been gone.
> Not mad—beat a vicious cycle.
> Typecast as the model couple.
> I'm sorry but I never got suicidal.
> It wasn't the end of the world.
> I'm sorry I seem to be succeeding.
> It wasn't the end of the world

The song became a template for their later material: complex arrangements punctuated with

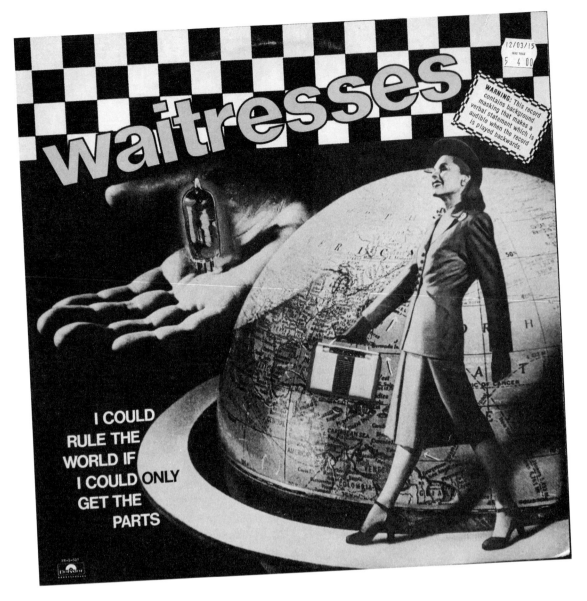

I COULD
RULE THE
WORLD IF
I COULD ONLY
GET THE
PARTS

WARNING: This record contains background masking that makes a verbal statement which is audible when the record is played backwards.

unexpected rhythms, doo-wop backing vocals, and a humorous bent. Decades later, in 2013, Chris told Perfect Sound Forever that "the early '80s were very much a time of strong feminist currents, and I didn't have to look very far to be influenced by that." While many men at the time stayed clueless or critical of women's liberation, he heard what second-wave feminists had been pointing out. One critique that struck him was the limiting stereotypes of women in music—the hard-rock babe, the sensitive folk artist, and the Black diva. Chris told *NME* in 2015 that he questioned the narrow representation of women in rock. "Where's the normal working woman? Where's the female Bruce Springsteen? It seemed pretty natural to build an honest personality that reflected what was going on around me," he queried. Butler understood the importance of the cultural shift as "a long overdue women's revolution." Before her untimely death, Patty also went on to work with Alice Cooper and in A&R for MCA Records as a recruiter of new talent. She was widely considered part of this shift—setting new standards and opening more doors for women in rock.

Patty may have been the ace up the band's sleeve, but the rest of the lineup was a stacked hand, composed of a swarm of superb musicians—including funk-jazz bassist Tracy Wormworth (The B-52's), drummer Billy Ficca (Television), saxophonist Mars Williams (Psychedelic Furs), and keyboard

Above: Cover of *I Could Rule the World If I Could Only Get the Parts*, the Waitresses' 1982 12-inch. From the collection of Jen Lemasters. Opposite page: Back cover of *Bruiseology*, the Waitresses' 1983 12-inch. From the collection of Jen B. Larson.

classicist Dan Klayman. Contemporaries of popular Akron-based artists Devo, the Dead Boys, and the Pretenders, the Waitresses (who were technically from Kent, Ohio) may not have gotten as much exposure as these other bands, but their songs hold up just as well. The collaboration between singer Patty Donahue and songwriter Chris Butler yielded handfuls of offbeat and timeless tunes that sit affably on a playlist among other art-rock outfits of the time—Sparks, the Tubes, Devo, Talking Heads, the B-52's, Captain Beefheart, and XTC, to name a few.

Of all the Waitresses' songs, "I Know What Boys Like" and "Christmas Wrapping" have gotten the most exposure, with the latter covered by the Spice Girls. They also have the distinct credit of creating the theme song for the short-lived prime time series *Square Pegs*.

Not only did the Waitresses convey uncharted aspects of female identity and showcase the talents of Patty Donahue, but the band also helped launch the career of the inimitable bassist Tracy Wormworth. Wormworth's musical talent brought her to later work with Sting, Cyndi Lauper, and more. She still plays with the B-52's. As a house band member for *The Rosie O'Donnell Show*, she performed with many artists, including Frank Sinatra and Liza Minnelli. She's also done studio work with artists from Paula Abdul to Moby. ●

BITCH

Chicago, Illinois » Formed in 1978

M E M B E R S

Original Lineup
Lorrie Kountz { GUITARS, VOCALS
Debbie Cielen { GUITARS, VOCALS
Donna Kirkendall { BASS, VOCALS
Donna Fraser { DRUMS, VOCALS

Second Generation Lineup
Lorrie Kountz { GUITAR, VOCALS
Gere Eddinger { GUITAR, VOCALS
Nancy Davis { VOCALS
Patti Prendergast { BASS, VOCALS
Leslie Kaye { DRUMS

» During the late '70s and early '80s, a coven of all-girl bands whipped through the Windy City like a pack of wild wraiths. Bitch, Tough Love, The Girls, Surrender Dorothy, Illicit, and Rash, to name a few. The tempest's catalyst was none other than songwriter and super-shredder guitarist Lorrie Kountz.

Lorrie began playing guitar at eight when her parents, unable to bear the everyday clamor of a yet-to-be-proficient percussionist, returned the drums they originally bought her and replaced them with a guitar and a promise of lessons. Lorrie studied classical guitar for several years, and at 14, began giving lessons. Once she heard Aerosmith and the Runaways, Lorrie abandoned nylon strings for a Strat and Marshall amp.

At 15, she saved up money from teaching guitar and bought a motocross motorcycle. On the bike, she cruised to school and went off-roading with friends. By 17, she traded in the motorcycle for a car to lug gear around for her first band, Bitch. Lorrie passed up a four-year college opportunity and

put ads in the *Illinois Entertainer.* Through that and word of mouth, she summoned the first lineup of Bitch. "My parents weren't pleased," she said.

She started writing songs and remembers, "It was good emotionally. It was a way to speak. Socially I felt better writing it down, writing music, and getting my point across, whatever my point was at that age. I felt I was better at writing music to describe my feelings."

Lorrie approached songwriting by beginning with guitar riffs or bass riffs and building from there. Her first songs reflected teen angst. Titles like "Committed," "Drag Her Under," "You Come Too Fast," and "I'm 18" (not the Alice Cooper song!) became Bitch originals. They also threw in covers like "These Boots Were Made for Walking" and "Heartbreaker."

"I was highly inspired by the Runaways," Lorrie recounts. The all-girl group put the idea in her head that an all-chick band would be cool.

In their three years together, Bitch underwent a lineup overhaul (adding a lead singer), put out two albums, *Love is Just a Crime* (on Orfeón Records) and *America's Sweethearts.* Bitch were often listed on marquees or billed in newspapers as "B" or "BIT**" by venues and media outlets; sometimes their entire name was blacked out. Despite this, they packed houses at local venues, performed at city events like Loopfest and Chicagofest, and zealously toured North America. They followed a six-weeks-on, two-weeks-off tour schedule during their prime and made it to 30 states. On tours of the States, they played alongside many legendary acts who were not yet household names.

"We toured with U2, the Cramps, and the Ramones," Lorrie recalls casually. Bitch opened for U2's first tour (5,000-seat venues) throughout the Midwest, played with the Cramps in the north (Wisconsin, Michigan, into the Dakotas), and the

Bitch

BOOKING INFO
266-9616

3	GREAT ILLINOIS PURCHASE	Rockfo
4-5	WAVERLY BEACH	Beloit, Wisc
11	DANVILLE JR. COLLEGE	
11-12	CHAMPAGNE JOHN'S	
17	ROCK GARDEN	
18-19	EDGEWATER	Twin Lakes, Wisc
22	HEADLINERS	Madison Wisc
24	B'GINNINGS	
26	WAVERLY BEACH	Beloit, Wisc
27	POISON APPLE	Peoria
6/1-2	B'GINNINGS	

Bitch in a locker room. An advertisement for booking, published in the *Illinois Entertainer* in May 1979.
Courtesy of Illinois Music Archives.

Ramones on the East Coast (New York City, Massachusetts, and the Carolinas). "That was a hoot, [the Ramones] were so nice." They also played with Ronnie Spector, the Kinks, and even the Scorpions.

Lorrie recalls touring endlessly, playing regularly in Texas, having a solid fan base in Guam and Mexico (where their label Orfeón was located), and once touring 28 straight days on the way to Los Angeles.

"It was much easier than now. There were actual booking agencies, and you actually made money," Lorrie says. "You had a lot of support from the crowds, too. The clubs would be packed five or six days a week, no matter who would be playing, so they had their own draw. They were very supportive of the original music back then."

In the city, women supported one another's bands fiercely as well. "There was a lot of camaraderie back then. All the females in music were supporting each other. When we were in town and not playing, we would go check out other female musicians and support them!" she says. "There was this band Barbie Army we used to go see."

"It's much different than now," she adds. "It wasn't competitive back then. When I play with a band now, and there are females in the band, there

Kwasniewski

Bitcly

4/6-7   Great Illinois Purchase
         (Rockford, Ill.)
4/13-15 The Ranch
         (Port Byron, Ill.)
4/19-21 Main Street
         (Cary, Ill.)
4/23   Rock Garden
         (Elmhurst, Ill.)
4/27-28 Squire Pub

BOOKING INFO
266-9616

Bitch on the cover of the *Illinois Entertainer* in May 1979. Courtesy of Illinois Music Archives.

is not as much camaraderie, not a lot of love going around. Is it generational? I don't know why it changed," she says.

Bitch sometimes egged on their male audiences, dedicating songs to "the boys in the room" and naming them "the ones who haven't become men yet," before launching into a riff-heavy song like "Come Too Fast."

The girls didn't let men push them around, especially the musicians they played with. "I think they were actually a little intimidated by us because we were a little bit edgier. Back then, long hair was in, like big poofy hair was in style, and we wore less makeup than they did. They'd be kind of hogging the mirrors and stuff, putting on their hairspray. So, we would come in there and be like, 'OK, clear the room' because it was our turn. They weren't really used to that. They were used to just kind of hanging out in the dressing room the whole time."

In 1980, Bitch headlined the Troubadour in West Hollywood to play for potential labels. Kim Fowley happened to be there and approached Bitch founder and lead guitarist Lorrie Kountz, interested in working with her and the band.

"He was a very crude man," Lorrie says unapologetically. "And I basically said, 'you know, I don't

think so,' and he got a big attitude. He would even call me when I was back in Chicago, and finally, I had to tell him to knock it off."

Even though the Runaways were one of Lorrie's biggest influences, both on her guitar playing and her vision for Bitch, she didn't budge. "I just didn't like him. I didn't care that he made the Runaways or some of those other bands. It was his attitude that I couldn't stand. He was too chauvinistic. We wouldn't go for that. I didn't want to go there."

Lorrie's patent integrity has always guided her decisions, even when it came to moving on from bands and beginning new ones. In 1981, Bitch changed their name to Tough Love to avoid censorship issues and make it easier to advertise. Tough Love added synths and tried to soften up their sound. With three second-generation Bitch members at the helm, Tough Love put out a few singles and got radio airplay. When Lorrie felt the band wasn't going in a direction she enjoyed, she left and tried out new outfits. She played in bands The Girls, Surrender Dorothy, Illicit, and Rash before doing solo work and starting her current band Whatismo.

Lorrie says she remembers the time in Bitch fondly. "We had a good time; we were good friends." ●

THE DADISTICS

Chicago, Illinois   »   Formed in 1978

MEMBERS

Audrey Stanzler { VOCALS
Fred Endsley { GUITAR, VOCALS
David Schutt, Eva Morgan { KEYBOARDS
Michael Hernandez, Ed Dietrich { BASS
Frank Eck { DRUMS

Cover of "Modern Girl," the Dadistics' 1980 7-inch. From the collection of Jen B. Larson.

» Before it burned down, La Mere Vipere was Chicago's premier punk club. DJs at La Mere dazzled clubgoers with offbeat records from new wave and punk paradises on the coasts while the dance floor lit up with freakish fashions.

One night, a friend invited Audrey Stanzler to La Mere, and the experience changed her life. Audrey felt like she found her people among the other misfits at La Mere. She began making the trek every night, traveling between the north Halsted location and Wilmette every night on the El, taking two different trains and nearly falling asleep every commute. Inspired by the eccentric folks she met or saw at the club, Audrey began to develop an original look, shopping at secondhand stores, where she discovered her own distinct style that would make a statement in the crowd.

Far before Madonna ever did it on TV, Audrey donned these trends not only at the club but in daylight, wearing slips, corsets, and colored hair out in the regular world, where squares would stare and sometimes make snide remarks. She remembers mean girls at her part-time job at the Board of Trade making comments such as "Your wig is falling off" and questions like "Is your skirt short enough?"

"I always had a reply," she remembers, laughing. "Like: 'I've got shorter ones at home.'"

Audrey studied photography at the School of the Art Institute Chicago (SAIC). Her ex-professor Fred

Endsley saw her out at La Mere and about and asked her to audition for his new wave punk band, the Dadistics. Audrey hesitated; having never sung or auditioned for a band before, she was unsure how to respond. On one hand, she adored the Beatles, Judy Garland, CSNY, and Emerson, Lake and Palmer—artists who explored intricate melodies and harmonies—and, when she was a kid, couldn't wait for her family to leave the house so she could practice belting out their songs uninhibited and uninterrupted. She also went to see Led Zeppelin and Jethro Tull live. But, on the other hand, she had been in art school studying photography, had a strong interest in fashion, and wasn't sure how to front a band.

She confessed these nervous feelings to a stranger on the train. The woman, whose sage advice influenced Audrey's decision, said, "If it's something you've dreamed of, just go for it! You don't want to find out you can sing five years from now and have regrets. Why wait?"

Audrey remembers: "Some lady on the bus, she really inspired me to get over the fear and audition." When she got to the audition, she met with the band, they gave her lyrics to practice, and she sat in the corner learning them. After nailing the audition, the band recruited her to be their singer, and she accepted the offer.

The Dadistics played for three years starting in 1978 and were mainstays at punk clubs like O'Banion's, Tuts, Gaspar's, Baby Hueys, and Exit (which took over after La Mere's demise)—and even Park West. Their clean and psychedelic guitar sounds, playful synth and danceable rhythms underscore Audrey Stanzler's luscious vocals. Audrey's doleful lyrics often contrast upbeat moments in her own hopeful melodies. For example, in "Paranoia Perceptions," she sings:

The Dadistics. Photo by Ed West.

> Lost my sense of reason
> It's beyond repair
> I need an explanation
> Gotta know you care

With the diverging layers, Dadistics songs expertly navigate mood shifts. Despite her plaintive lyrics and downbeat choruses, Audrey's presence in the scene as the singer of the Dadistics was feminine, fun, and energetic. In the chorus of the same song, she sings:

> You're a threat to me by your aggression
> I wish you wouldn't leave such
>   an impression

Audrey remembers spending a lot of time in the late '70s experimenting with fashion and surrounding herself with others who did as well. For one year, she studied at the Kansas City Art Institute. Over the summer of 1976 in Cape Cod, she befriended multi-disciplinary artist Cookie Mueller.

Her photographs of the underground star ended up in and on the cover of the book *Edgewise: A Picture of Cookie Mueller*. When she returned to Chicago, Audrey wore a lot of black eyeliner and came back to school with a completely different look.

While many of the women in bands at the time dressed androgynously, Audrey didn't, embracing a flirty and playful femininity. Audrey's outrageous fashion sense turned heads. She wore corset tops with tutus and donned ever-changing hairstyles: asymmetrical, blonde on top, brown on the bottom, red, pink, and tiger stripes. She had a friend attending beauty school at Vidal Sassoon Academy who recruited her as a hair model. For Audrey and the band, fashion was something fun to play with.

In the middle of recording an unreleased album, the Dadistics broke up, and Audrey spent a short time in what became the original lineup of the industrial metal band Ministry in their early synth-pop days. ●

THE CUBES

Detroit, Michigan » 1978

MEMBERS

Carolyn Striho { VOCALS, ORGAN
Gary Adams { GUITARS, SYNTHESIZER, VOCALS
Alan Sanchez { BASS, VOCALS
Tony Bojanic { DRUMS, VOCALS

Carolyn Striho performing with the Cubes.
Photo by Sue Rynski.

>> On the cover of the Cubes' 7-inch, "Spaceheart," the four members are edited onto a blank background. Their cropped bodies, placed in four cardinal directions, form a square. Gary, Alan, and Tony wear black suits, hands crossed over their groins, while Carolyn stands casually in a black dress and black beret with one bossy hand on her hip. "Cubes" is written in a four-dimensional font, parallel to each member. The vinyl label is designed with a similar logo and equal thoughtfulness.

The short-lived band took their songwriting and artistry seriously, while not taking themselves too seriously, and having a blast. The Detroit band played big shows around town with local favorites Flirt, Destroy All Monsters, and Nikki & the Corvettes. They also ventured to Toronto often.

Carolyn was immersed in music from an early age. Her parents loved all types of music and collected records: "Motown, big band, ethnic polka, Hungarian czardas, jazz, all the hip stuff," she recalls. "All the stuff people want to listen to now." She was in choir and glee club and took piano lessons. She has memories of going to her aunt's house and making up songs on her keyboard.

In high school, she felt shy growing up but being on stage and playing music was her way of communicating with others. Carolyn had been hanging around with musicians and forming bands since her early teens. One of the first was a band named Prong, which morphed into the Cubes. In Carolyn Striho's life, one thing has always led to another. That hasn't changed, from her joining the Cubes to playing in Rough Cut, Detroit Energy Asylum, to touring with Patti Smith, to her current work as a special education teacher and side work recording audiobooks.

"Things just happen. Next thing I know, I'm doing this, next thing that," she says, struggling to articulate her career trajectory.

Prong and the Cubes intermingled but were totally different bands with different lineups. Tony and Carolyn were dating when the Cubes formed,

Cover of "Spaceheart," the Cubes' 1979 7-inch. From the collection of Jen B. Larson.

and the whole band had chemistry. Carolyn played a Farfisa organ, wrote lyrics and many songs. "I wrote a lot in the verse-chorus structure." After that, the band came together naturally. "Gary wrote a lot, and Alan did a couple, too.

"I'd write stuff about women trying to look too pretty—like I think ugly is kind of pretty. It's in the eye of the beholder." In "Pickup," she sings:

He was over at the bar
sounds kept him waiting
blondes and floozies
everybody's dating
when she walked in now
glamourous and manly
a tight sweet dress
she looked at him banly[1]

And in the chorus:

She's so swishy and she's so cute
A woman with lots of loot
But he saw the hair under her chin
and she wanted to do him in

Once she graduated, she worked at WDET radio, where she hosted *Radios in Motion*, dedicated to new wave/punk music.

Gender never hindered her. "I never thought that much about being a girl. I wanted to be in a band. I didn't care who was playing with me," she affirms. "As long as they were cool and we had a vibe, which was the biggest thing for me—if everybody connected and the chemistry was there. It was all about chemistry. That was the most important thing. The Cubes had chemistry.

"There were other women playing, but I was always wondering why there weren't more," she muses. "I never thought about it consciously." As many other interviewees have noted, "Some were jealous, which was kind of weird because it's like, why bother being jealous?"

Some men gave Carolyn got flak for how she dressed. Sometimes she played in a slip and leather jacket. "I dressed any way I wanted, depending on the show…but I didn't feel like it was sexual—I mean, I didn't feel like a stripper, it was just what I liked to do."

At the same time, Carolyn wasn't afraid to use provocative metaphors for love. In the power-pop garage bop "I'm on a Leash," she sings:

For everything you've given me
I misunderstand and cannot see
why there's still this possibility
I'm hiding from you up a tree
I'm on a leash
I'm on a leash
stuck onto you

At the time, flyers were the general form of communication to get the word out about shows. "It was DIY—people were making fanzines, putting up flyers. It was all in the street. It was a little harder, I guess. But you know what, it's easier now, but then it's not."

In 1979, the Cubes put out the "Spaceheart" 7-inch and, after Carolyn left, a split album with the Americatz in 1981. The band was also featured on compilations by their label Tremor Records. After that, the Cubes stayed together, and Striho went on to form Rough Cut, later renamed Detroit Energy Asylum (following a lawsuit with an L.A.-area group of the same name but with a different spelling). Rough Cut toured Japan and played with the Slits.

After playing with Rough Cut, in the '90s, she went on tour with Patti Smith, whom she met in Ann Arbor at the Second Chance bar in 1979. Nowadays, Striho is a teacher and continues to make music, performing locally and internationally. In addition, she published a book of poetry last year. Detroit (Maiden Energy) is making a new record and continues being nominated for Detroit music awards.

Email from Carolyn Striho on the Cubes experiences, 2021:

The Cubes were getting ready for a heady weekend. Not only were the Clash playing at Masonic Temple, but the opener was David Johansen of the New York Dolls. And the Cubes were playing later at the New Miami nearby. So yes, of course, we were

---

1 According to songwriter Carolyn Striho, "banly" was a made up derivative of "banal."

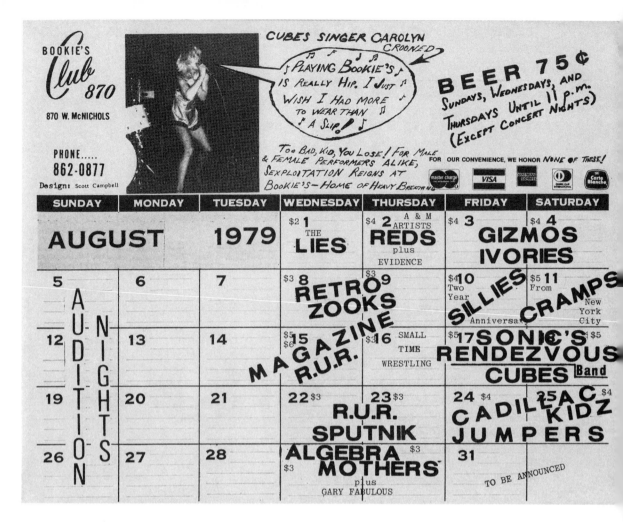

Bookie's calendar, August 1979. Someone drew a text bubble from a photo of Carolyn that read, "Playing Bookie's is Really Hip. I just wish I had more to wear than a slip!" Courtesy of Carolyn Striho.

at the concert, passing out flyers for our show later that night. Freddie and me, my sister, and friends, and some of the Cubes. The Clash! This was to be a pretty wild night. And it was, with people packed in at this beautiful palace in Detroit right down the street from where I was living. So, David Johansen as Buster Poindexter was amazing, just like he was in the New York Dolls. And afterward, he met us backstage, eating a pizza. He was so friendly and a regular guy! I gave him my record, and we gushed about the Clash who were coming on next. And the Clash was serious and fantastic. It was an intense night, but we had to get down the street to the New Miami to do the Cubes show later—much later—12:30 a.m., when the place was so crowded people that they were spilling beers and more on each other, everyone using whatever bathroom they could find and screaming as loud as ever, and here

comes the Clash bus! And David Johansen's band's tour bus driving right up outside! So, needless to say, some of the members of each group were inside. I was on stage and so busy performing, and this was a night to remember.

So, what did I wear? For M50, he was this person who came out of nowhere. He did a poster about the Cubes being sexist because of a flyer he saw, which I've attached—quote on it: "Playing Bookie's is really hip, I just wish I had something more to wear than a slip"—which was not my quote. I never said that. The booking type at Detroit's Bookie's put that in a cartoon blurb. Well, M50 went crazy, saying I (me) was promoting sexism because of how I dressed and this flyer and my attitude. This was when Blondie was doing shows, and Iggy, and the punk rock/art-rock era—so there were all kinds of ways to dress on stage. I dressed any way I wanted, depending on the show. So, after confronting him about it, he became a fan! And he started coming to all our shows! If I can find that flyer he put out, I'll send it, too.

EMI Records was interested in the Cubes, and someone from EMI England contacted the Cubes' manager to see if we could "pack our bags and move to NYC" at a moment's notice. Because of the attention we were getting and so many people showing up at our shows, people like Johnny Thunders from the New York Dolls and Glen Matlock from the Sex Pistols were at our show. I just didn't know what was next. Johnny jumped up on stage several times, and we opened for his band Gang War as well. Opening for the English band Ultravox was a huge night. And for the Dead Boys, who were the headliner at Bookie's. That was a crazy after-party with the Dead Boys and the lead singer, the late Stiv Bators.

The Cubes opened many times for Sonic's Rendezvous Band, which featured Fred "Sonic" Smith from the MC5 on guitar, who married Patti Smith in 1980, and Scott "Rock" Asheton on drums (from Iggy and Iggy and the Stooges band). These were major shows, with everyone attending from Patti (Smith) to Lenny Kaye. The Cubes always had an enthusiastic response. I was singing on stage with the Cubes and playing my Farfisa organ, and we would finish our set and get ready to watch Sonic's Rendezvous. Fred was a gentleman to me and the most intense and great guitar player on stage. His guitar melted ears with amazing songs. I met Patti at Bookie's, and that was special. We met on the dance floor when Sonic's Rendezvous was performing. Patti would stand on the dance floor and watch Fred and the band.

One early evening, when the Cubes weren't rehearsing, and I was down in Detroit, I locked myself in my bedroom at my apartment in the Cass Corridor of Detroit and had to jump down from a window into the alley. This is an infamous alley where Dally in the Alley is held every summer in the City. There was Fred Smith with Freddie Brooks (my ex, who became my manager), and they were in an old Cadillac-looking car with fins having a meeting in the car. Freddie was Fred's manager. They were laughing as I jumped out. I mean, what could they do?

It was just "normal" doing things like that then. There were no cell phones back then, nobody to call from my bedroom, but I had to get out. Jumping out the window was the only answer! I had to rescue myself. That was tame after hitting my head right on the stage while performing with the Cubes (and going to the hospital later) or dancing so hard I threw up (sorry) on a well-known Detroit band, the Mutants', amps!

The Ramones' shows were super high-energy, off-the-chart packed events with everybody dancing, standing throughout, and yelling in front—the toughest band with these amazing, yet melodic, fast, furious songs. Then we opened for the Ramones in Rough Cut, and everybody visited together another night. Pizza with Dee Dee Ramone and wife Vera and her super personality and gorgeous white leather jacket. You couldn't stop watching Johnny, Joey, and Dee Dee. This was so much how I felt. And how kind the Ramones were to everybody in the after-parties.

And in Rough Cut, a year later, we opened for Iggy in Ann Arbor at the Second Chance. This was also around the time we opened for the iconic all-female band the Slits, from England. At the Iggy show, everyone was throwing eggs, light bulbs, cups at the stage when Iggy was on, after our set. It was an Iggy ritual back then. It was a mess. They calmed down, but from the balcony, when I looked up from the stage, I swear people were going to jump down to the stage, landing on everybody in front. And people were landing on each other on the dance floor, starting the moshing pit trend maybe.

But what stands out to me is the sheer intensity and spirit of the times. I wrote and practiced a lot, and the entire band had regular rehearsals. The Cubes constantly played—often four nights a week, sometimes five or six days A WEEK. All ORIGINAL music. Clubs, Toronto adventures, and how did we get out of Canada when we played Windsor on one of our shows? We were still teenagers, trying to get to the show to perform, missing sound check, and possibly detained in Canada!

Anyway, I'm grateful for my songwriting and rehearsing and for so many creative people around me. I wrote lyrics, poems, and my diary and journals while attending a Detroit university and working at NPR radio WDET-FM. The Cubes' days began a long journey of so much music and more. ●

UNIT 5

Akron, Ohio » Formed in 1979

M E M B E R S

Tracey Thomas | VOCALS
Mike Johnson | GUITAR
Mark Jendrisak | BASS
Bob Ethington, Jr. | DRUMS
Paul "Augy" Teagle | KEYBOARDS

》》 On their LP *Scared of the Dark*, Unit 5 comes across so professionally polished, and Tracey's vocals are so pure it might be a crime to call them punk. With a tight rhythm section, keys high in the mix, minimalist rhythm guitar, and a vocalist performing elaborate runs, the group's pop sensibilities outweigh their transgressions.

The group started when Bob and Tracey worked at a record store together and jammed despite their musical differences. The whole band jelled immediately. Tracey had been singing her entire life— she would even hum tunes in perfect pitch back to her grandmother as a baby—and idolized singers like Loretta Lynn and Tanya Tucker. "I was always drawn to the country ladies; my family is Appalachian as far back as the eye can see," Tracey jokes.

Another artist important to Tracey was Linda Ronstadt, whom she describes as being in the center of the women-in-music universe. In the documentary *It's Everything, And Then It's Gone*, Bob teases Tracey for her "basic" music taste. But it's her affinity for vocalists that inspired her love of music in the first place—and the only role models visible to women aspiring to play music. So when Carole King put out *Tapestry*, it changed her life, making her aware that women could be more than just singers.

"I always thought it would be so cool to play lead guitar, but until the Runaways, women weren't playing their instruments," she recalls. "I always thought, *Why are only the guys allowed to get up there?*"

As a high schooler, Tracey started singing in a cover band. She played in barns and at parties; the band practiced at her cousin's horse farm. When punk and new wave hit, she wanted to emulate Debbie Harry. "At first, it was just mimicry. I wanted to be everyone from Carole King to Joan Jett."

Originally named the Vapors, they received a cease-and-desist from the "Turning Japanese" composers before changing their name to Unit 5. The band usually wrote songs democratically. Compositions were based on a core riff or lyric that a member presented at practice, and then the rest of the band added their own ingredients, and the vocals were last to layer on top.

Lyrically, Tracey sings about and from the perspective of independent women. On "Gracefully and Ladylike," Tracey sings:

Gracefully and ladylike
That's what they always told me
Gracefully and ladylike
They say that's how I should be

In "No One's Girl," she sings:

Things started out so nice
But then she called it off twice
Straighten up you better be smart
Don't fall in love, she'll break your heart

And in "Ready":

Treat me like a queen
buy me anything
only if you're ready
Take me to a show
anywhere I wanna go
only if you're ready

Tracey Thomas of Unit 5. Photo by Eddie Halamay.

"People didn't know what to call us. People called us 'new wave,'" Tracey says. "Punk and new wave were kind of the same, but we were by no means punk. I think we had some moments, and we flirted with it, but we called ourselves 'dark pop.'"

Dark pop is an apt descriptor; in songs like "Big Kids" she sings:

Big kids are really cruel
big kids can really hurt you
there's big kids on the playground

Complemented with a dueling chorus:

They spoil all our games
They punch our noses, and they
        spit on our clothes
They trip us when we're running
They make me so mad

And:

I wish big kids would die
I don't wanna be big

Tracey's striking looks, blonde hair, and distinguished vocals garnered a lot of attention for Unit 5. Unfortunately, it also summoned the demons of sexism. "[Misogyny] wasn't even noticeable because that's how the world was then," she says. "It was constant."

In one incident she remembers, a drunk guy came up to her before a show and abrasively declared, "You must be in the band because you're pretty," suggesting that she couldn't even sing. The event had her in tears in the bathroom. "It was always the guys [saying things like that]. And the girls hated you," she adds. "Women were jealous; guys were jealous because they thought it should be their job."

Her first husband, who was also a musician, used to feel threatened by her success. "When Unit 5 opened for the Dead Boys, which happened a lot, he would get mad. He thought it should be a harder-edged guy band."

"Everything was just divided into male and female. I do not miss that about the world at all. It's just how it was back then." Since then, she's gained confidence. "I had to talk myself into being a super badass."

In 1982, Unit 5 played at Danceteria in New York and was offered a potential major-label record deal that never came to fruition; the label didn't come

Tracey Thomas of Unit 5. Photo by Eddie Halamay.

through. The band put their album out on a local label and broke up, each member wanting to focus on other aspects of their lives.

Tracey stepped away from music for the next decade. Her then-husband's jealousy over her success was overwhelming. She chose to shrink herself and downplay her talents to avoid conflict over playing music in her marriage. But when he died, she was

free to create. A few years after his death, when Tracey was 34, she learned to play guitar and put out her first solo album, *Standing Alone*. She considers the work a purging of the relationship. "I picked up guitar because I was so fed up with living in the men's universe of music where I was at the mercy of them musically. I could throw lyrics and melody over what they did, but no one would let me compose! I didn't want to be directed anymore. I wanted free rein to do it how I wanted to do it."

After learning guitar, Tracey began writing her own music and has been writing freely in the last 25 years. Later in her career, she got to open for Judy Collins. At the time, Tracey felt the pressures of the industry's ageism. In the dressing room, Judy Collins said something along the lines of "don't let the fuckers get you down." •

AMA-DOTS

Milwaukee, Wisconsin » Formed in 1979

MEMBERS

Mary 'Boolah' Hayes { VOCALS, PERCUSSION
Connie Bam Bam Ruiz, Bill Stace { DRUMS
Gary Strasburg { GUITAR
Lisa Wicklund { BASS

» The covers of both Ama-Dots records illuminate shadowy figures. A half-skeleton bat spreads its wings menacingly on the Ama-Dots' LP, while the back cover features a negative image of the band playing their instruments. On their 7-inch, an obscure gothic figure traipses through the snow; inside on their mailing page, a fortune-teller peers ominously from under a pointed hat.

The images are an apt description of the band visually and sonically. But the categorization of Ama-Dots' arrestive and experimental sound can only be named through their individual talents: Lisa Wicklund's throbbing, robust bass lines, pulsating over Connie Ruiz and Bill Stace's drum work. Gary Strasburg's knife-like guitar and Mary "Boolah"'s maniacal vocals, which *Sub Pop* once quotably described as sounding "like a witch in need of a throat lozenge." The scary sound bites integrated into the music as if a foley artist added sound effects to a horror movie score.

Milwaukee has cultivated a phenomenal punk scene for decades. Yet another vital band overlooked by the coast-focused canon, Ama-Dots could easily be identified as subconscious seed material for industrial, goth, and anarcho-punk bands of the future.

Ama-Dots recorded a full-length album that was not released right away because of the spontaneous collapse of their label. They did, however, tour extensively around the Midwest and the South, bringing their wicked Wisconsin sounds to New York and Canada, opening for big names, including Captain Beefheart, Sun Ra, Gang of Four, and Talking Heads, along the way. In addition, they played with St. Paul's Hüsker Dü and Chicago's DA! in Milwaukee.

Opposite page: Boolah from the Ama-Dots. Photo by Kevin Hutchison. Above: Ama-Dots. Photo by Dan Hansen.

Regular performers at Zak's and the Starship scene on the east side in the early '80s, the band left fans hungry for decades, having only self-released one 7-inch on their own label, Hunky Recs, until 2014 when they released an LP. In the liner notes, Boolah writes about an expedition to Windsor, Canada, in which the band encountered an exceptionally aggressive and toothless crowd who threw glass and spit at them. She recalls the discomfort: "We had front teeth. We were pussies. Lily-white pussies from Milwaukee." An aloof granny with a motorcycle chain and shotgun who hosted the shows mesmerized her with her closing-time ritual: "When the gun came out, the punks and bikers scattered. It was surreal."

Their best-known songs on that album, "Hit Girls" and "The Cease Is Increase," were recorded Friday the 13th, 1980, at Shadetree Studios in Lake Geneva with their original lineup, which included Connie Ruiz on drums. The lyrics of "Hit Girls" empower women with togetherness:

> We move together
> We're together

and take jabs at men for seeing women as "covetous specimens on display." In the song, Boolah sings:

> Hit Girls, Haute Girls
> We're not timid coquettes
> We work with handsome struggles
> You're just an aperitif
> Filler with indifference
> The pleasure is ours ●

THE DENTS

Cincinnati, Ohio   »   Formed in 1979

MEMBERS

Vivien Pinger a.k.a. Vivien "Vinyl" Rusche { VOCALS
Doug Hallet { KEYBOARDS
John Murray, Pete Riffle { GUITAR
Chuck Swanson { BASS
Dale Adams, Mark Chanault { DRUMS

» "Punk was a political statement; it was an economic statement, a cry for change. It was across the world. So many people were so poor they couldn't pay their rent. So much change needed to be made, and it seemed like our voices were really heard," Vivien Vinyl, singer of the Dents, explains. "Punks were like 'fuck love!'"

When she was in her early twenties, Vivien Rusche's roommate overheard her singing in the shower and noted her vocal talent. She had no idea anyone was listening (the joys of communal spaces), and although she was a well-versed record collector, she had no plans to join a band. The roommate asked her to join his mostly-covers band called Malcontent as a backup singer, and she agreed. At a rehearsal session, she was overheard by musician Doug Hallet and, mesmerized by her abilities, he asked her to be the lead singer for the Dents.

Regulars on the Cincinnati scene, which they referred to as a "little big town," the Dents attracted more than local attention, embarking on small tours to Columbus, Ohio, Louisville, and Lexington, Kentucky. At the time, neural networks of underground musicians were just beginning to signal one another, so touring required a different type of planning. Without the internet, band members kept each other's phone numbers in physical address books and picked up the phone to dial one another and book gigs. On touring, she recalls: "It was so cool to make a network to know other small towns were doing exactly the same thing."

At a Gang of Four after-party at Vivien's house, the band's manager left their address book, and the next day she phoned to let him know. Because the little black book contained so much important information that was essential to the band's tour, she convinced him to buy her a plane ticket to deliver it directly to them in New York City: "I was so mean. I said, 'Well, that's too important. You're gonna have to fly me up there to hand it to you in person, make sure it doesn't get lost.' And they did! And so, I went up there with them, and it was so fun!"

Despite playing out locally and around Ohio, the Dents didn't release music during their active years. They finally saw their first song on vinyl in 2019 when songs by many Queen City bands were put out on a compilation titled *We Were Living in Cincinnati*, featuring never-before-released punk and underground sounds from between 1975 to 1982. It was a decades-long curatorial project masterminded by Peter Aaron (Chrome Cranks). As a teenager from New Jersey, he moved to Cincinnati and began collecting records and tapes from the local scene. In 2021, HoZac Records put out a proper Dents LP, where you can finally hear 17 Vivien Vinyl-sung tunes.

"I thought it was just for us, just for fun. It never occurred to me to record or to have higher goals," she says about her band's music release. On the record, listeners can hear several humorous, bouncy synth-driven tunes like "Do the Boob." They sing:

Don't say there's nothing to do
You can do the boob

The Dents also delve into fervent, sometimes political, post-punk propulsion. "Sleeping Around" is an alternate take of the same song from the *We Were Living in Cincinnati* comp. Vinyl sings urgently:

He was a fixture of the Cincinnati scene
I was a victim of the sex machine
He said, "Hey honey, come on home"
And I said, "no, I'm sleeping alone"

And in "Radioactive," she begins with:

Turn on your radio and flip through the dial
That condescending shit is sure to
     make you smile

And then tag-team vocals clock in to drag crappy corporate radio. Again, she emphasizes: "I wanna see aggression at a rock 'n' roll show!"

"[Punk] was a reaction to what was on the radio and what was happening to rock 'n' roll, which was really fun and exciting in the '60s when I was a kid. And then the rock 'n' roll on the radio merged into the prog-rock, the long drum solos, and the guitar solos; punk was a reaction to that long-winded stuff. People were just looking for something less complicated than the multi-track, heavy-duty concept album…"

Unraveling her memories, she continues: "In the '70s, I had turned to jazz because I was so bored with [where rock was headed]. The first couple things I heard were the Ramones, Elvis Costello, Patti Smith…pretty much all in the same month. I can remember where I was sitting. It was transformative for me. Patti Smith of all people. She was so different from the women rock singers before her, and I never went back to jazz."

After the Dents broke up, Vivien continued playing music in other bands, including Alterior Motives. In Alterior Motives, Vivien truly explored her vocal delivery and wrote profound and painful lyrics. However, after experiencing a brutal sexual assault, she says it changed how she expressed herself creatively. "After that, my songs started being anthems," she said.

When she wasn't playing punk shows, throwing parties at her place, or snarling in band photos, Vivien led a double life as a photojournalist for Channel 12. "Channel 12 was not happy about the things I was doing to my hair," she laughs. "They slapped me on the night shift so fast." Later, Vivien became a special education teacher in Cincinnati public schools. ●

Opposite page: Vivien "Vinyl" Rusche performing live with the Dents. Photo by Jean Brown.

Left: The Dents. Vivien "Vinyl" Rusche is on the far left. Courtesy of the Dents.

KATE FAGAN

Chicago, Illinois   »   1980

❯❯ After Rupert Murdoch bought *New York* Magazine and fired 80 staffers in the late '70s, Kate Fagan was out of a job. "He sat on my desk, and he fired all these people," she said. But a friend of hers living in Chicago sang the city's praises. So Kate visited the Windy City, where she picked up shifts as a waitress at the Little Corporal restaurant and stayed to make her mark. She loved Chicago for its creative energy and began bartending at the Jazz Bulls and Kingston Mines, where she saw all the blues greats perform. She also enjoyed folk music and lived with writers and actors, who inspired her. She lived above the liquor store across from the Biograph Theater and says, "Lincoln Avenue was vibrant!"

Kate had relocated a lot during childhood, moving from the outskirts of D.C. and going to college in Wisconsin, then lived in London and New York City. She never wanted to fit in, but to find herself. She said, "Moving around so much, you recognized how people created and identified with different kinds of groups. Everyone was searching for who they were and a way to express their feelings."

After living in London and New York, the art scene in Chicago seemed a little more down-to-earth at first. "In Chicago, there isn't as much phony-baloney—people are more straightforward."

Musically, she said, "Chicago fostered a lot of good punk music because of that. It's just that the framework isn't there for people to become nationally and internationally successful."

"[In Chicago], everyone wasn't standing around peering at each other from behind their shades," she says. Then, she started to see a particular type of conformity snake in. She approached BB Spin at La Mere Vipere. She writes,

"I took over the lead singing role in BB Spin. The original vocalist was a male, and I sang in the original keys. When we opened for the Ramones, Joey asked our manager, 'Where'd you find a girl that sings like a guy?' I took that as encouragement to be a 'front man,' like I was successful in a traditional man's role."

Then, she picked up a bass and wrote a bouncy five-note riff, adorned with her anti-cool culture critique "I Don't Wanna Be Too Cool." She calls out divisive hipster exclusivity in it—the idea of velvet ropes and the "who can get in and who couldn't get in" atmosphere invading creative spaces. She howls and sings:

I won't wait at Neo
Can't afford Park West
I don't really care
I'm just not impressed.
I don't know no rock stars
I don't snort the good stuff
I don't really care
I'm just not impressed

In the chorus, she sings:

I know your cool is chemical

The local scene loved being chastised. The anti-hipster anthem became a favorite of club DJs, radio stations, and Wax Trax. She had recorded the song at Chicago's Acme Studios and met the fellow artists with whom she'd formed the Disturbing Records label. This group staged warehouse parties and became a platform for many punk, new wave, and garage bands. Disturbing released the "I Don't Wanna Be Too Cool" single, as well as early singles by her later, legendary ska band Heavy Manners, for which she is most well-known.

Opposite: Kate Fagan. Photo by Amy Rothblatt.

Kate Fagan singing live.
Courtesy of Illinois
Music Archives.

After the original singles sold out in 1980, Kate Fagan did a second run of 1,000 copies out of her own pocket, but the records perished in a house fire where she lost everything she owned.

Another song she wrote and recorded, "Waiting for the Crisis," critiques U.S. international relations and the Reagan-era military-industrial complex. Over its singular plunky, eerie piano note, in the verses she sings:

> We sell guns to all our third world friends
> We sell guns if they will sell us oil
> We'll sell nukes
> if you will be our friend

With paranoia-inducing chanting choruses, she sings:

> Oh oh
> We're waiting for your crisis
> We sell hate to offset our deficit

Kate says she found herself writing protest music at a young age. She grew up outside of D.C. in a highly politicized environment during the Vietnam era when her father was a civil rights lawyer. "I'd run to get the newspaper in the morning to read the editorials on women's rights, Black power, and the sins of Richard Nixon," she told *Flaunt* in 2016. In high school, she wrote for her school paper; later, she earned a journalism degree from Indiana University's Ernie Pyle School. She states that she "found comrades among the editorial staff."

In Chicago, she became involved with Rock Against Racism as a political movement and taught art education at Chicago Academy for the Arts. She also fronted the ska band Heavy Manners, who shared bills with the likes of the Ramones, Grace Jones, the Clash, and Black Uhuru.

Kate hasn't stopped performing, as making music and entertaining is integral to who she is. Describing her experiences performing live, she says, "You're finding a little burning coal inside you—an essence, you're finding and expressing it. That's what punk was. You didn't just sit in the stands and watch people; you jumped down on the dance floor. That feeling is so contagious and punk really hit it right for a lot of people. They could open themselves up." ●

ALGEBRA SUICIDE

Chicago, Illinois » Formed in 1982

MEMBERS

Lydia Tomkiw { VOCALS, LYRICS
Don Hedeker { GUITAR, BASS, SYNTH,
AND DRUMBEATS

>> Lydia Tomkiw's verse charms and haunts audiences with its humorous, death-obsessed, and dreamlike wisdom. She arranges existential dread into gorgeous word bouquets of pithy quips, personal anecdotes, and pointed condescension as if she is an oracle peering through a spyhole from an unknown location in our galaxy. Her once-husband and Algebra Suicide guitarist Don Hedeker's hypnotic arpeggios echo ceremoniously, building a sanctuary where Lydia's lyrics grow.

The band performed behind handmade projections (made by slipping acetate and various materials into slides with tweezers), over drum machines, and on stages across the Midwest, Northeast, and Europe. The minimalist music operates as a vector for Lydia's poetic visions. While the impact is heightened by the swirling atmosphere and musical meter, Lydia's wit stands alone in its composition, homing in on universal human experiences.

In the poem "This is to Notify You," she laments:

I cannot bear the stars anymore;
They just hang there, silly, useless
    as neckties.

And in "Speed of Light," she philosophizes:

In previous lives we were
Born in cities we really didn't admire.
We ate atomic breakfasts,
Hid in map factories,

Cover of *Algebra Suicide 666* Show DVD, recorded August 30th, 1984. From the collection of Jen B. Larson.

Sang foreign hymns until
Our brain water ached.

Born to Soviet refugees and raised in Chicago's Humboldt Park and Ukrainian Village neighborhoods, she studied at Lane Tech, University of Illinois Chicago, and Columbia College. Initially pursuing visual art, she switched to poetry when a teacher helped her recognize her unique talent for it. Within a year, she had compiled enough poems to self-publish two collections in chapbooks, *Ballpoint Erections* (a reference to the click of a pen) and *Obsessions* (which she dedicated to her "friends who never read my stuff but tell me it's great").

Lydia's work is inspired. In her first chapbook, Lydia pays tribute to fellow punk poet Patti Smith in "I Wanna Be Like Patti Smith." With one foot in the poetry world and the other in Chicago's flourishing punk scene, Lydia and her fellow poet friends would perform with costumes and theatrics in bars, with a

ALGEBRA SU

band performing at the end. Lydia also wrote an ode in verse to the burning of La Mere Vipère and named local bands in a few of her other poems. (In "Benefit," she mentions Silver Abuse and Tutu and the Pirates; she has another poem called "My Favorite Dadistic.")

Less of a scene-girl and more of an enthusiastic art appreciator, Lydia attended live events at night and haunted bookstores and record stores by day. Tomkiw's enjoyment of nightlife sustained her obsession with art.

Lydia and Don met when Lydia saw Don's band Trouble Boys play. She struck up a conversation with him. "I noticed I was the only female in the audience. My old groupie tendencies came out. I approached him after the show and asked if he did private parties," Lydia said. With an instant spark, they fell in love and started a band, which took its name from Lydia's poem (and later Algebra Suicide song), "Recalling the Last Encounter." In it, she writes:

> There is no anemic embrace
>   on the street;
> A kiss is thrown, meets
>   another,
> Drops to the sidewalk and
>   goes for a tumble.
> You warn of tight clouds that
> Wriggle like army worms;
> A form of algebra suicide,
>   I guess.
> I want to telephone the sailors,
> Curse their songs of gasoline,
> As the light in the booth turns
>   me hideous.
> I want to become hydraulic,
> Hit the newsstands—
>   national exposure,
> Feel the world crawl into me
>   through the fingertips,

> As the traffic locks, stops,
>   goes soft.
> I want to talk about milk,
> About the invisible bones
>   of the face,
> About the brain that sits too
>   close to the skin
> While I hear you say that we
>   can be chainsaws
> Under the stars
>
> Under what stars?

As Algebra Suicide, the two put out their initial EP in 1982 on their independent record label Buzzerama Records but didn't play their first official show until 1983. The band played local Chicago clubs like O'Banion's, Tuts, and Lucky Number, whose patrons enjoyed both punk music and poetry, as readings were showcased between music sets.

Lydia's epic wit is only emboldened by her deadpan delivery. In "Little Dead Bodies," she famously articulates:

> I've heard that somebody is born
> Every eight seconds, so I
>   presume that someone
>   dies every eight seconds,
> Just to keep things even;
> It makes me feel shortchanged
> When I read the obituary page—
> Someone's holding back
> Information.

Algebra Suicide toured nationally and internationally before calling it quits in the mid-'90s. Lydia moved to New York City and worked on her solo career while Don continued to work and play music as a hobby. Lydia tragically died at the age of 48, but her clever verse remains alive on wax, in print, and with literary friends and fans who exalt her work. ●

Cover of *Feminine Squared*, Algebra Suicide's retrospective 12-inch (recordings from 1982–1986). From the collection of Jen B. Larson.

DUMMY CLUB

Milwaukee, Wisconsin　»　Formed in 1982

M E M B E R S

Stonie Rivera ⎰ VOCALS
Janna "Banana" Blackwell, Steve Del Rio ⎰ BASS
Paul "The Fly" Lawson ⎰ GUITAR
Andy Pagel, Eve Le Duc, Wild Bill Tanner ⎰ DRUMS

》 The cover art of Dummy Club's 7-inch "Ballad of a Lady Gun Slinger" invokes outlaws of the Wild West. A broad dressed in leather raises pistols in both hands on the cover and on the back; the band is clad in hybrid '80s and western wear. Sonically, the record features two psychobilly bops with walking bass and two-beat drums.

The woman in the photo is Mary Jean Dombeck, a good friend of the band, who also designed the cover using Xeroxed fabric for the border. "The cover is like a memorial to her," singer Stonie Rivera shares. "I've always been lucky to have been surrounded by creative and talented people. No matter what you're doing, being surrounded by creative people—it kind of bounces, it makes this circle, that everyone is influencing everybody else."

The Milwaukee-based band recorded in Chicago and put music out on a German record label. "I met Monika Döring[1], the most fabulous woman in Berlin back in the day. She ran a cluster of clubs and made it her point to showcase women in music. She was maybe

in her seventies, she wore these fabulous opera-length soft leather gloves, and she had this punk diamond bracelet. When she walked into a space, you could feel the respect she commanded, especially as a woman of her age. Because there is ageism that goes with our sexism. Just watching her, she had her own art of entertaining people, of knowing how to set things up."

According to Stonie, Monika Döring was wealthy and humble and invested in women artists. "A lot of times, there are women who are behind the opportunities," Stonie says.

In terms of misogyny in music, Stonie explains: "[Men have] this feeling of being threatened and a need for control over women. There's a perception of women in music that it's like, 'oh, you must be a whore.' There's no winning. Either you're a whore, or you're uptight. And you know how guys are; when they hit on you, if you won't talk to them, it's—'bitch,' 'whore,' 'lesbian,' or 'dyke.' They won't even take any onus that their behavior is why women won't talk to them. There are even a lot of women who are misogynists."

On race, she says, "There's this idea that there were no women of color in the punk movement, and that's total bullshit. Women of color have been in the forefront of music in every genre since day one."

Stonie was raised by a socially conscious mother in a racially diverse neighborhood in Milwaukee. Stonie's mom was a forklift operator in the 1960s, at a time when women were just beginning to work in factories.[2] However, she says it wasn't until

---

1 Monika Döring is a German concert organizer. With her club Loft she was one of the most important promoters of the avant-garde music scene in West Berlin in the 1980s. In 1982 Döring moved into the former rooms of the "Jesus People" above the Metropol on Nollendorfplatz, where she founded the 600-person club and the concert agency Loft for punk, avant-garde music, and alternative rock. Döring held there over 500 concerts with 800 bands in six years. It provided a stage for numerous, until then mostly unknown, musicians who were later seen as relevant and groundbreaking. Among other things, she organized concerts with Tuxedomoon, the Birthday Party, Cabaret Voltaire, Sonic Youth, the Doctors, Wire, Cocteau Twins, Diamanda Galás, Nick Cave, Stiff Little Fingers, the Bangles, Einstürzende Neubauten, Björk, Bad Brains, Swans, Johnny Thunders, Die Toten Hosen, Public Enemy and Run-DMC.

2 Women did work in factories and other traditional "men's jobs" during World War II, but were driven back to the "home" and "traditional" women's work when the war ended.

Dummy Club. Photo by Fred Fischer.

she was a teenager that she realized how segregated the rest of the city was (and still is), or how sexism impacted all facets of society: "It wasn't until I got older that I saw how men and women were treated so much differently.

"What radicalized me as a feminist was seeing a woman in my neighborhood whose abusive husband had seriously injured her, and I remember cops saying, 'He pay the bills?' and she says 'Yes,' and they were like 'well, there's nothing we can do about it,' and I knew it was wrong and my mother sat me down and told me why that was wrong, and that just freaked me out. It was the '60s; there were no women's shelters."

Stonie was taught to believe neither age nor gender creates actual barriers to self-expression. In her sixties, she still dances ballet, hip-hop, and contemporary dance. She rides a snow saucer down sledding hills, plays dodgeball, and shoots hoops with her grandkids. "In my family, age was never brought up in the negative; it was never a bad thing. This happens, especially for women— you're told if you're this age, you can't do this, or you can't dress this way. I think that's bullshit. Don't brace for impact."

A singer, writer, visual artist, and appreciator of fashion, Stonie also contends that creating art is personal. "[Art] feeds the soul," she shares. "And it takes you to the next place you need to be." She continues, "Especially for women of color, it's a way to deal with racial trauma; it enriches the soul. It's a way to holla—like I am just gonna put this out here, with my poetry, or dance or music—it's a way to release, to engage, to teach, and teach people who want to listen. You know, more and more women of color are emerging. But I have to say thank you to Bessie Smith and Big Mama Thornton and the women that came before, that really, really had to deal with insane adversity, so my hat is always off to them, big respect."

Stonie grew up listening to Motown, soul, and artists like Tina Turner, Nina Simone, Aretha Franklin, and her mom's favorite, Little Richard. "Music was the landscape for the Civil Rights movement; music has always been intertwined in any movement," she says.

But music was also always fun to her. She fondly remembers the first song she wrote as a young child:

Little shakin' shorts
shakin' shorts, shakin' shorts
Shakin' on the porch, on the porch

She admits the childhood song is "lost without the dance movements." She and her friends decked out basements with blue and red lights in her pre-teen years.

Dummy Club was formed in the early '80s. Country music, acid rock, and jazz are all influences that contribute to the essence of Dummy Club. In the '80s, they were called "rockabilly" when people needed a label, but truthfully, Dummy Club couldn't be confined to one genre. As an artist, one language Stonie speaks is cultural critique. She sings:

The American way, it stinks
the American way, it smells
If we could abolish the American way...
Damn well betcha we would!
'Cuz we don't like it
We don't like it

"Punk was the times," she says. "We came out of the '70s when there were a lot of rock ballads, and that morphed into people who wanted to come back to rock 'n' roll; the very succinct and danceable kind of rock 'n' roll. That's where we happened to land." The band fit under the punk umbrella but was also influenced by soul, rock 'n' roll, jazz, and Patsy Cline.

In Europe and the States, the band played to big, fun crowds. "I loved the audiences; people just cut loose. People just wanted to have fun and be their authentic selves," she says. "People didn't wanna follow societal norms. We were not our parents—not in a bad way—it was a new music movement, a natural flow."

In her view, sexism and racism in music haven't changed significantly. "It changed a little bit, but I don't see a big change. It's everywhere. It's not just the music industry; it's just everywhere. It just is. You have to navigate it. When we were on the road, traveling through the South with the band—this is where you have to educate people. [Janna and I] were bright yellow mixed chicks. Not wanting to go really into this off-road or gas station with guys hanging around because we weren't white women. So we had to take that into consideration and educate [our bandmates] as to why not.

"I think men, especially white men, take sexual assault for granted. They don't have to worry about it, whereas we women do. I mean, when was the last time you walked without your keys or your bulldog keyrings in your hand when you're out at night? Men don't really have to think about this, but we were raised to think about it. I can hear my mother in my head, my grandmother, my aunts: 'stay on well-lit streets, carry your keys between your fingers, don't park in parking structures that are really dark, always have cab fare'—we grew up pre-cell phone, so if your car broke down, you had to find a payphone."

However, opportunities for getting the music heard weren't an issue, and she supposes it could have been because of the transatlantic record labels. "They seem to be a little more enlightened in Europe, but I've run into misogyny everywhere, here and in Europe. There's always going to be a cluster of assholes."

Stonie and Janna began writing new material, and it felt like a different project, so they rebranded as the Psycho Bunnies, a band that played into the '90s. Then, in 2013, she fulfilled an important item on her bucket list by opening Dominion Gallery, an artist space that featured artists of all walks of life. For Milwaukeeans, the space was a gathering place for the community. Housed in the old Shepherd Express building (a local underground newspaper), she curated art shows featuring the works of women and people of all ages. ●

Dummy Club. Photo by Fred Fischer.

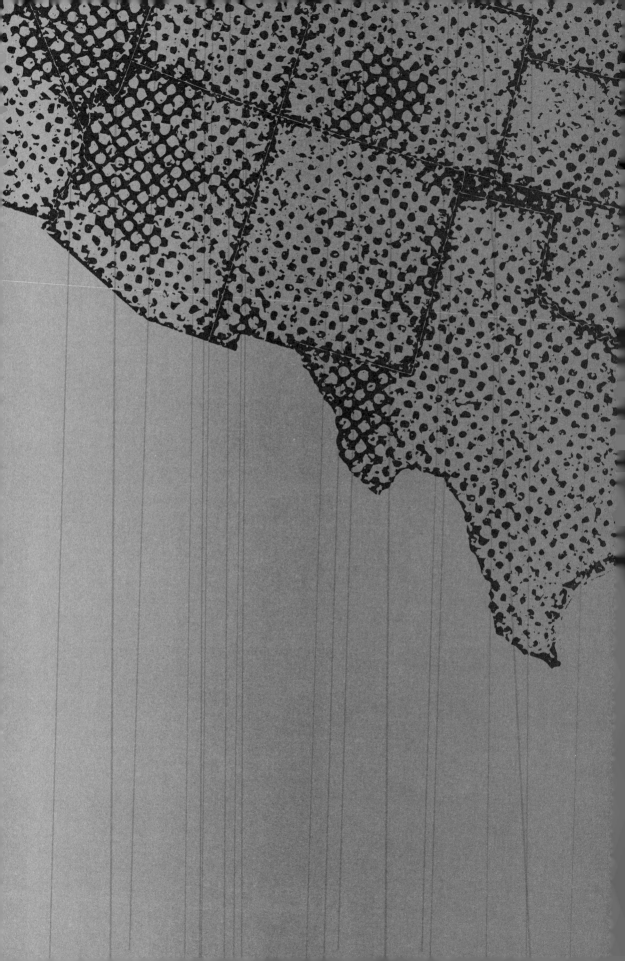

SOUTH

Feast on My Heart

PYLON

Athens, Georgia   »   Formed in 1978

MEMBERS

Vanessa Briscoe Hay { VOCALS
Randall Bewley { GUITAR
Curtis Crowe { DRUMS
Michael Lachowski { BASS

» Southern no wave pioneers Pylon prophesied the indie rock explosion of the '80s and '90s. Visual art students at the University of Georgia in Athens, the band members honored music as a new medium. Guitar, bass, and drums were established instinctively and sparsely while singer Vanessa treated their grooves as a canvas for her lyrics. She told WBUR, "I just tried to find myself, like, within the framework of the song, I would try to make something that fit."

Pylon honed repetition and an economy of language in their coolness lyrically and musically. They were geometric yet loose. They expressed disconnection through connection. The music featured Randall Bewley's original zigzag guitar playing, Michael Lachowski's steady, driving bass work, Curtis Crowe's minimal, dependable drumming, and Vanessa Briscoe's spastic, untamed poetry. They set themselves apart from popular music in Athens, and their secret weapon was in Vanessa's clever verse and uninhibited voice.

In "Stop It," Vanessa relies on brevity:

Don't rock 'n' roll, no

In "Gyrate," Vanessa sings:

Sometimes I feel like I speak a
    foreign tongue
At times I feel like I've got no destination

In "Danger," she sings:

Be careful, be cautious

I'll get you unaware
Look out, I'll get you

And in "Driving School":

The driving school, parking place
Seatbelt, windshield
Dashboard, floormat
Spare tire, lug wrench
AM - FM

In "Human Body," it's:

I can walk, I can run
I can talk, I can drive
I can steer, I can even hear

In "K":

Dissatisfaction, what?
Let's take a look at that ink
B-L-O-T

In "Crazy," she sings:

Listen.
Nothing can hurt you unless you want it to
There are no answers, only reasons
    to be strong

In "Feast on My Heart," she screeches in a tongue that registers as part wolf, part human:

Feast on my heart
Drill a hole in it
I want you to drown me in it
Pick up the scalpel and do it
I want you to do it
Feast on my heart
I missed the turnoff
This map has too many symbols
Punch a hole in it
I want you to do it
Drown me through my heart

Pylon in the desert. Photo by Michael Lachowski.

Pull down your eyebrows
Uncross your arms
I didn't choose your sorrow
No need to worry

While Athens, Georgia boasted world-famous acts like the B-52's and R.E.M., an underground scene sailed ahead with Pylon at the helm. Highly praised by the B-52's, Pylon's popularity expanded outside of Athens. They opened up for Gang of Four in New York City. They appealed to other bands and concert-goers for their musical creativity and danceability—angular guitar parts, a dynamic rhythm section, and commanding vocals—that impacted people physically and spiritually.

Their band name came from the orange road cones, inspired by band members' part-time factory gigs. They began their collaboration thinking they would play a small number of standout shows, get written up in *New York Rocker*, then disband soon after. Turns out, Pylon stayed together for nearly five years.

But by the time of the release of their second album, *Chomp*, in 1983, the band members were beginning to feel the burnout that so often comes with turning one's art into a business. So they did something unfathomable: Pylon turned down an offer to open for a nationwide U2 tour and decided to disband. They played their final show at Athens' Mad Hatter club on December 1. Vanessa, who later went on to play on the Elephant 6 roster in the band Supercluster, remembers, "For whatever reason, it was our decision. We were like, 'Let's just quit while we're having fun.' That was kind of the idea in the first place. We were just going to perform as long as it was fun. So, we broke up, and it was a decision we all made together."

Email interview with Vanessa Briscoe Hay, March 2020

Q: How have politics influenced or not influenced you creatively? Has that changed over the years?

Vanessa: Speaking as an artist, free speech, which includes artistic expression, influences me tremendously. As a human being, I have great empathy for those who do not have access—or think they don't have it—to this basic human right. That said, there are opportunists who have poisoned this pure idea and used it to control and manipulate others. As a child, I was encouraged by one grandmother who said, "you can do anything you want to do." As an adult, I have learned to be respectful of others' opinions but have become less afraid to express my own as time has gone on. Yes, I was a shy teen.

Q: Considering the strange pandemic we are living through, how has your relationship to art impacted your experience? How does making art help you personally and us collectively?

Vanessa: This horrible pandemic has forced us all to go back to focus on our small worlds of home and personal relationships. I feel fortunate that I am not completely alone as I live with my husband, younger adult daughter, cat, and dog. Number one—I have a home. If I want interaction, there is social media, telephone, and Skype.

I am listening to a lot of music and writing a little. I am also painting and spending time contemplating what is important. I am writing answers to this interview, it's spring here, and I have been watching two Carolina wrens build a nest and take care of their young. It's quiet here. Only an occasional plane in the sky. Much less traffic. The earth keeps turning. The wind blows, and the sun shines in a blue sky for the most part. The TV is mostly off.

What is next for humankind? No one knows. Has anyone ever really known? Historians and scientists can guess and give us their knowledge and advice. Artists are connected to everything all at once in an invisible web. It's a gift, and I think most human beings recognize that and know that man-made things would have no power or flavor without some type of beauty or creativity attached. We hunger for stories and connection; it keeps artists attached to the world. So, at some points in history, everything stops for most, and we are able to look and really see if we take the time. Collectively, we are all together on this beautiful planet, whether we wish it or not. Survival depends upon our actions and our feeling of responsibility to others. My personal mental survival depends on having a creative outlet of some type. I also feel responsible to share positive things as much as possible with the public. Negativity will defeat us if we aren't careful.

Q: If you had the power to change anything in the world, what would you change?

Vanessa: That is a challenging question. As a retired nurse, I would say free medical care for all.

As a mother, I would like to see hate and mistrust disappear, and kindness and tolerance take their place. That would solve many problems.

Q: You seemed so nonchalant about playing music in interviews when you were younger, but here you are, an iconic post-punk singer. What do you make of that?

Vanessa: That cracks me up. Iconic belongs in a museum—right? I'm not dead, and I'm still busy. But I am truly touched that so many get it now. Especially the younger people I've interacted with on tour with Pylon Reenactment Society. A lot of women love us. We have stalwart fans. An audience might be half in their 40–60s, and the other half will be underage.

Q: You've said you didn't have any plans to be in a band, but now you've been doing it for decades! What drew you to start singing in a band? What kept you singing?

Vanessa: To be honest, the guitarist for Pylon (Randy Bewley) must have seen something in me that I didn't know was there. He asked me to audition. I don't think the guys in Pylon even heard what I was doing until we went into the studio to record our first single. Why did I keep singing? …. Well, it was a lot of fun. I didn't have anything better to do at the time. I wasn't making plans. Now I have to and be responsible. I love to perform live. It is one of my favorite things in life.

Q: How did you begin working with Pylon? What was it like for you creatively? What had you been studying in art school?

Vanessa: Unknown to me, my former art school classmates, roommates Randy Bewley and Michael Lachowski, decided to start a band as an art project in the fall of 1978. They learned to play together by endlessly rehearsing the same riffs over and over. Upstairs, Curtis Crowe heard them and decided they needed a drummer and knocked on the door. They wrote some stuff and auditioned two other guys who were also classmates. They didn't work out for whatever reason. Then they were going to use found sounds like weather radio recordings or a record called "Teach Your Parakeet to Talk." They said that got old quickly. Randy had been teasing me for a while about asking me to audition and play an air organ. I didn't take it very seriously—but then he showed up at my job and asked me. So, I went and tried out on Valentine's Day 1979. The next day, they called and said I was in. It was explained that the premise was to play in New York and get written up in *New York Rocker* and break up. It didn't sound like it would take up too much of my life, so I said yes. My first husband could not seem to graduate from college. I was stuck in what was, at the time, a very quiet college town. This seemed like it would at least be a fun project, and it was! They had lyrics all neatly typed up during the first rehearsals but didn't give me any direction on what to do. So, I was given complete freedom. The whole object was to make a song and then present it live. We performed the first time just a few weeks later above Chapter Three Records.

I was a painting major. I have a BFA in drawing and painting.

Q: Was Pylon named after traffic cones?

Vanessa: Yes. Three of us—Curtis, Michael, and I—worked at DuPont making carpet fibers on the weekends. We loved the industrial look there. The traffic cones were interspersed through the building, warning of possible dangers. We found out what they were called, and that became the name of the band.

Q: Aside from your instruments, what were all your roles in the band? Like, who was the serious one? Who was always cracking jokes?

Vanessa: We worked as a collective, so to the outside world, it was all made by Pylon. Everyone contributed art, and we all wrote the music together. Michael has a degree and background in photographic design. He chose our typeface, Microgramma Bold Extended. Besides being naturally talented at guitar, Randy shared his love of Eames, Japanese robots, truck stop stickers, skateboards and was like having a pro driver onboard. He drove our van in big cities like NYC. Curtis could fix the van's brakes, tires (and did in parking lots and by the side of the road all over the U.S.), built his own road case and a cage in the back of the van. I don't know what I was good for, really. I could read a map or a Triptik by AAA and help keep the night driver awake. Everyone cracked jokes and pitched in. I remember laughing so much all time. We had so many adventures!

Q: What was playing music in Athens like in the late '70s/early '80s?

Vanessa: The B-52's had just left town. Pylon stepped into a ready-made house party scene. Athens parties were all about sweaty dancing to records, keg beer, thrift store clothes, and hanging out with your friends. No one had any money. It was cheap at the time to live here but tremendous fun. Our town had a real mixture of all different types of people—from art school, professors, cool townspeople like Jeremy Ayers, who had been a sidekick as crossdresser Silva Thin, of Warhol at the Factory—all colors and sexual identities and backgrounds. As time went on, more and more bands joined us, and each tried to have their own unique sound. A club or two allowed the new music in—first, it was a core group of maybe 50 people. Then, with the advent of R.E.M. and bands like the Side Effects, Love Tractor, Method Actors, the whole scene exploded.

Q: People have compared your stage presence to Ian Curtis. What do you think about that?

Vanessa: I have never heard that before. Wow! I wish I could have seen Joy Division—I love them. I found out about them a little before the time of his death. We were supposed to be playing some of the same clubs in the Northeast the same week they were going to do their first U.S. tour. He killed himself before that tour. What a tremendous loss. I guess there could be a level of intensity that we had in common in live performance. I can get into a zone where I feel like I am a channel, and the sounds are coming through me. I feel that sort of connection when I watch Joy Division's live video.

Q: So, it took me a while to notice the connections your more current bands have to the Elephant 6 collective. Bands in that collective were very influential on me in college! I love the stuff I've heard/seen of Supercluster. How did you get involved with Elephant 6? And can you tell me about Supercluster?

Vanessa: I was working as a registered nurse with two daughters from 1994 and had been in nursing schools from 1992–94. I didn't have much time for anything but family or work for a while there. When my oldest hit high school, she started bringing mix CDs home from her friend Naomi and buying her own stuff. Anyway, I wasn't going out at the time and became intrigued with some of the music that I was hearing—especially Olivia Tremor Control. A little later, I started going out again, and then Pylon reformed again. At Athens Popfest one year, I

Pylon's Vanessa Briscoe-Hay dancing. Photo by Randy Mayor.

saw two bands with women and was intrigued with what they were doing. They both had a lot of talent, power, and charisma. I started talking to drummer Hannah Jones right away about starting a band. I was having material come into my head that was not Pylon-type material. I wanted to mix acoustic and electric elements and get more in touch with my own Appalachian roots.

We assembled a dream team of Athens musicians who could and did rotate in and out as they were available. Multi-instrumentalist John Fernandes, Bill David on Mandolin. Bob Hay on acoustic guitar, Randy Bewley on electric, and others made up the core of the band along with Jones on drums. I tried to make it a democracy and let everyone sing—if they wanted. I would bring in some simple ideas on keys and sing, and they would do whatever they wanted to. Or we would jam at the Landfill. A few months later, the original bassist we had picked stopped showing up, so I asked a woman I had seen play with Casper & the Cookies at Athens Popfest—Kay Stanton—to come on board, and I have been working with her ever since.

With Jason NeSmith's help, Supercluster recorded a CD and three singles. He and Bryan Poole stepped in to play electric after Randy passed. Bradford Cox recorded three songs on the CD *Waves* that were unfinished at the time of Randy's death. Cellist Heather Macintosh graciously played on a few. My daughter Hana Hay both played cello on our song "Brave Tree," which is popular in China for some reason, and contributed a song that we recorded called "River." Supercluster also recorded an unrecorded Squalls song written by my husband Bob Hay called "Anyone."

We dissolved in early 2013 but never formally broke up. There was no big outcry about the lack of Supercluster in the world; it was a small recording project within what is now a very large and more worldly music town. It had served its purpose at the time for me, and I made some friends in the current music community through it. Who knows? It may surface again. I still have songs come into my head that aren't Pylon-type material. I also learned a lot about how other musicians worked and how to get self-released material produced. My bandmates helped me through a very hard time for me—my friend Randy's death in 2009. Pylon was no more at that point. Music is healing.

Q: What artists have impacted you or opened your eyes over the years? Were there any women in particular?

Vanessa: There are so many—I have pretty eclectic taste, and everything I listen to more than once has an impact—how could it not? That said, I had no dreams of becoming a musician. But I was a music fan. Here is a shortlist of artists I liked from childhood onward: Hank Williams, Patsy Cline, Mother Maybelle Carter, Johnny Cash, Janis Joplin, the Beatles, Yoko Ono, Cream, David Bowie, Frank Zappa, Captain Beefheart, Velvet Underground & Nico, Roxy Music, Elton John, Jackson Five, James Brown, Philip Glass, Heart, Ramones, B-52's, Gang of Four, Patti Smith, Talking Heads, Joy Division, Mission of Burma, Bongos, dBs, R.E.M., Love Tractor, Squalls, Side Effects, Oh-OK, Let's Active, Love of Diagrams, Olivia Tremor Control, Shellac, Sonic Youth, Sleater-Kinney, Dressy Bessy, New Sound of Numbers, Casper & the Cookies, The Glands, The Pauses, Priests, Fourth Mansions.

Women that I am a fan of include but are not limited to: Maybelle Carter, Yoko Ono, Kate Pierson, Cindy Wilson, Ann and Nancy Wilson, Nico, Christine McVie, Patti Smith, Tina Weymouth, Faye Hunter, Linda Hopper, Lynda Stipe, Antonia Sellbach, Carrie Brownstein, Corin Tucker, Tammy Ealom, Kay Stanton and the list keeps growing. I have been lucky to meet some of these women and become friends.

Q: What types of music were you into growing up? Did those bands influence the work you did with Pylon or other projects?

Vanessa: My parents were big country fans but listened to a lot of MOR in the a.m. on WSB before work and school. In the first grade, I wouldn't get out of bed until "Moon River" came on. My mom would pull the covers off and say, "Moon River's on—get up!" On the weekends, my Dad controlled the TV and country music shows like Porter Wagoner in the afternoon were followed by *The Grand Ole Opry*, *Hee Haw*, and the Johnny Cash show at night. He had seen Hank Williams perform twice at the Grand Ole Opry. My Dad could do no wrong when I was a kid; when I was able to listen to what I wanted to, I would buy 45 RPM records at the next town over for our portable record player with my allowance. I bought things like the Beatles and various songs I liked. For a short time around 1970, Atlanta had a station that played Top 40 hits of the day and regional hits to their own videos all weekend on a show called *Now Explosion*. You can see some of this online if you do a search. The ones made in Atlanta are the best. Weird video effects as opposed to later footage of women and men playing on the beach in Miami. I sometimes picked up an FM Chicago station on my tiny transistor radio late at night. That is where I first heard Hendrix.

When I got a job my junior year, I bought a cassette player and joined the Columbia House record club. I was also in the high school marching band.

Anything that is a part of your life has an influence. But I can't think of a direct influence other than I saw it was possible to do anything.

Q: When you started writing lyrics, what inspired you? Do you focus more on melody or the lyrics? Or how did you do it?

Vanessa: Each song evolved in a different way. Mostly I tried to find my place in the machinery of the song, I tried to not preconceive what it would be about or like, I would try to pare my words down to universal elements, but ultimately the sound was more important than the words.

Q: How did you feel when the band called it quits?

Vanessa: Pretty happy at the time because we had wildly exceeded our initial goals. We had performed across a good bit of the U.S., Canada, and England. I was 28 when we broke up the first time and felt like I still had my whole life in front of me. Bob and I decided to have a baby, so we did in 1987.

Q: You've mentioned that you didn't feel like you were treated differently because of your gender while in Pylon. Have you seen misogyny play out in the music industry outside your personal experiences? How do you think the presence of strong women like yourself helps other women?

Vanessa: Pylon made a point the few times I was given a sexist comment by a sound person or club person of turning their backs to them and asking me, 'what would you like to do' or 'what do you need?' Times were changing in the late 1970s, and more and more clubs were run, staffed, and/or booked by LGBTQ/women/people of color. My bandmates were like my brothers. We were a fun-loving bunch of nerds.

Yes, I have heard of some misogyny and pretty recently, though I only heard about it. The sound person gave an opening band for Pylon Reenactment Society, the Pauses, a hard time. He wasn't being very nice to her and said some mean things about her equipment and professionalism. I wasn't in the room at the time, but she handled it really well. She didn't put up with it, she talked to the promoter/stage manager directly, and he spoke to the soundman.

I have no idea what type of impact I have personally. I just try to give 110% of whatever I've got available. I hope I do have a positive effect. I've always tried to pitch in with the work. More and more, women are running the front of the house. Last year, Primavera 19 in Barcelona had women artists for their focus.

Q: What are some of the differences—in your process or aesthetically—in working with Pylon Reenactment Society?

Vanessa: It is a different group of people than Pylon. How can it not be different?

We do use Pylon as our guiding star when writing. We try to write more in favor of minimalism and being creative.

Q: I'm sure you get it a lot. How does it feel when people ask you that "woman in rock" question?

Vanessa: I'll echo what I've seen a few others say. I hope that someday being a musician or an artist doesn't have to have a tag like "woman" or "female" in front of it. Why not just say—artist or musician?

Q: I've read/heard some of your responses about not encountering that much sexism from guys when you were in Pylon. Have there been other instances of sexism from men, or women, when you've been in other bands? Also, have you or do you encounter sexism in other ways outside of music?

Vanessa: Not that much as a musician. Grandma also told me, be careful who you lie down with; you might get fleas. Of course, having grown up in a small town in the South, I encountered sexist comments along with racism. But, when I got to college and met others of my own kind at art school, things greatly improved.

When I was a child, I thought things would be better—like the bridge of the Starship Enterprise. Unfortunately, things seem to be regressing. A large group of people, who might have kept their mouths shut a few years ago instead of saying what they are thinking, have been disinhibited by certain news organizations and the current administration.

I will say this to all the other young women—from small towns and elsewhere—you can do anything you want to do. Don't forget who you really are. ●

CICHLIDS

Miami, Florida   »   Formed in 1978

MEMBERS

Debbie DeNeese { VOCALS, GUITAR
Susan Robins { BASS
Bobby Tak { DRUMS, VOCALS
Allan Portman { GUITAR, VOCALS

On a stormy Halloween night in 1979, the Cichlids entered Peaches Records and Tapes in Ft. Lauderdale to play live on-air. Outside, thunder, rain, and lightning raged against the walls of the building, which in its former life as a supermarket had not been wired to handle the torrential assault of rock 'n' roll, especially during a tempestuous tropical squall. The broadcast resulted in an electrical mess that conjured a psychedelic dirge over the airwaves, into people's homes, and perhaps summoned a few demons.

Despite what most might have thought based on their debut on mainstream radio, the Cichlids were not an experimental noise rock band. Based on their record, you'll believe they were pure co-ed pop-punk fun—but that's another misnomer. The album, 1980's *Be True To Your School,* didn't quite capture their live sound either. Miami's TK Records, a disco label that put out stuff like KC & the Sunshine Band, signed the Cichlids (the first and only rock band on their roster) and pushed the punk band into a more mainstream, new wave sound for bankability. The hooky *Be True To Your School* found middle ground between punk and new wave, receiving good reviews. But because of bad management decisions and strange, contemptuous relationships within and around the band, the group broke up pretty quickly after their short-lived rise to Florida fame.

Before Cichlids, Debbie put together a handful of groups with women; one was called Sheba, and another called Pandora's Box, trying out Screaming Sneakers singer Lisa Nash on bass for a short spell. At one point, the Cichlids were even all women (and, in fact, went through a handful of lineups before landing on their crew). The original lineup, the Kitlids, was an all-girl band. This lineup included an accomplished jazz bass player, Diane Barron; a girl named Heidi; a thief who indiscreetly left blood trails as evidence of her stolen items, Kit Carson[1]; and a drummer named Lisa who was born without legs. After these members didn't work out, Debbie played with three guys, including Bobby and Alan, and then found the perfect match in Susan.

As bandleader, Debbie was indiscriminate about the gender of her collaborators, as long as there was chemistry between them. Debbie told *Trash Fever*: "[Being a woman in rock] was really hard. It was one thing to be a singer, but to be a guitar player or a bass player, and to be taken seriously." She says that her gender didn't inhibit her. And she gives credit to the

---

1 Kit Carson's real name was Catherine Brayley. She was involved in punk bands the Nike Chix and Sybil in Washington D.C., and apparently her 1989 heroin overdose inspired the Fugazi song "Shut the Door."

On the album cover:

MISSIONARY MAN
WITH MY GIRL
BUBBLE GUM
JEWISH GIRLS
LIFEGUARD DAN
UPS AND DOWNS
LET'S GO MENTAL
J 4 OR FIGHT
FOLLOW THE TREND
THESE BOOTS WERE MADE FOR WALKIN
DID YOU EVER
PLANNED OBSOLESCENCE
UBANGI STOMP

THE CICHLIDS ARE:
DEBBIE MASCARO GUITAR
SUSAN ROBINS BASS, ORGAN
ALLAN PORTMAN GUITAR
BOBBY TAK DRUMS

PRODUCED BY ANN HOLLOWAY

ENGINEERED BY THOMAS HOLLOWAY
& ANN HOLLOWAY

MANAGEMENT ROBERT MASCARO

WRITE THE CICHLIDS
P.O. BOX 397
DANIA, FL 33004

PHOTOGRAPHY LYNN GOLDSMITH

ART DIRECTION BOB HEIMALL

Runaways: "They did give girls the incentive to say, 'If they can do it, we can do it too!' For the Bangles, and everybody that came along after that."

Debbie had a boyfriend whose presence imposed upon the band so strongly that it's hard to know how anything would have shaken out without him. The boyfriend, Robert Mascaro, had an authoritarian, fascist-like command over the band. Intending to uphold their allure, Mascaro demanded the group stay away from the public at gigs and did not allow anyone in the band to go out socially unless they went together. In addition, he decided what they wore, how they presented themselves, and who would record them. In the same interview, Debbie said, "anytime Robert felt something was getting out of his grasp, or he might become obsolete, he found a way to shut it down."

The band experienced extravagant drama, they met many celebrities, and a 17-year-old Johnny Depp almost replaced their guitarist. On their one release, they covered Nancy Sinatra's "These Boots Were Made for Walkin'" and showed off their original songs like "Missionary Man" and "With My Girl." Unfortunately, once they set out on tour to support the record, the band came to a foreseeable demise. ●

Opposite: Cover of *Be True to Your School*, the Cichlids' 1980 12-inch. Above: Back cover. Both from the collection of Jen B. Larson.

THE KLITZ

Memphis, Tennessee » Formed in 1978

M E M B E R S

Lesa Aldridge { GUITAR, VOCALS
Gail Elise Clifton { VOCALS, KEYBOARDS
Marcia Clifton { DRUMS, VOCALS
Amy Gassner Starks, Sarah Fulcher { BASS

» Too depraved to say or see on a marquee, Memphis group the Klitz' moniker was often left off promotional material and could not be mentioned on the radio. As a result, their band name never made it to the newspaper blurb when they played at the premiere party for Lorne Michaels' *Mondo Video*. Let's just say the name was unthinkable to many at the time.

But to the group, it was hilarious and wry. The girls named the band one drunken night. "It was ridiculous we had the band name that we did," Marcia tells Ryan Leach in the band's oral history.

Often cited as the Bluff City's first "all-girl band" and one of the city's original punk bands, these ladies rallied against their region's status quo in more ways than having a vulgar name. Instead of playing polished Southern rock or following the formulas of '60s British Invasion-style garage, they took an unfettered and intuitive approach to their instruments, inevitably leaving an enduring mark on guitar-based music of the South. The once long-haired free spirits chopped their locks and laced up their combat boots to achieve their desired aesthetic.

When interviewed by *Oxford American* writer Holly George-Warren in 2017, Lesa said, "I actually meant to sound beautiful and sing well and play nicely—it just didn't work out that way. We were so loud and simplistic we got labeled as punk. So, what to do? We embraced it."

"I have to say, we sounded better than I thought we did. Even better than some of the punk bands I've heard in the decades since," bassist Amy Gassner told Ryan Leach in the oral history.

In a song Gail Elise wrote called "Two Chords," they sing and play "Two chords/going out of my mind," descending into madness by mid-song. In "Hard Up," Gail's bold vocals dominate the instrumentation. In addition to writing original songs, the girls recorded popular covers like ? and the Mysterians' "96 Tears," the Beatles' "I Should Have Known Better," and "Hanky Panky."

Playing in the band wasn't the long-standing members' first rock 'n' roll rodeo either. Gail and Marcia Clifton sang on a Christmas record when they were nine or ten years old, and both had played instruments throughout their youth. Later, Marcia took her experience with dance to experiment on the drums—as she said, "Yeah, I figure if you can count, you can be a drummer." Gail, vocalist, keyboardist, and later guitarist, had been in a short-lived punk band before the Klitz called the Malverns, in which she wrote the song "Two Chords" that was later recorded by the Klitz. Lesa Aldridge worked with her boyfriend, Alex Chilton, on Big Star recordings, co-writing the tune "Downs," an experimental song that used a basketball for the snare. Lesa wrote the lyrics, but in her on-and-off relationship with Alex, recalled that "he'd get mad at me and just remove me from the recordings."

According to Chilton's producer Jim Dickinson, "Lesa is a muse, unquestionably…Nearly every song on *3rd* (*Sister Lovers*) is about her. The world will never know the extent to which Lesa was responsible for that record."

During the band's original run between 1978 and 1980, the Klitz worked with big names and turned many heads. They opened for the Cramps

THE KLITZ - ROCKING THE MEMPHIS UNDERGROUND 1978-1980

Cover of *Rocking the Memphis Underground 1978–1980*, the Klitz' 12-inch cover. From the collection of Jen B. Larson.

multiple times in Memphis and New York. Marcia told *Terminal Boredom*, "Everyone was curious about us because of Alex and Lesa. They both got us a lot of attention. Everyone knew who Alex was. Lesa was [photographer William] Eggleston's cousin. They were part of the cool Midtown art scene." After Alex Chilton and Lesa broke up, Jim Blake of Barbarian Records and Jim Dickinson started working with the group, recording them at Barry Shankman's studio, BR Toad, and getting their name into *Rolling Stone*.

They also appeared on a local TV special—*Captain Memphis Meets the Klitz*. In the show, Dickinson mused, "If the Klitz stay together, we'll hear them progress on every record just like the Beatles." They didn't stay together long enough to reach such a status, but they did have the attention of major labels, including mainstream producer Miles Copeland, who sniffed them out. "He came to see us play. I think we weren't polished enough for him. Then, a short time later, the Go-Go's came out, and I went, 'Oh, so that's what they were looking for.'

"I guess we just thought, 'Okay, we've done the band for three years now. Let's just stop pretending and be grownups now,'" Marcia expresses.

After the band dissolved the first time in 1980, the Klitz recordings disappeared from consciousness into the dark abyss of recording history. As a result, many of their recordings didn't see the light of day. However, in the time since, the band has reunited and released old and new material, including an online-only album, *Glad We're Girls*.

Email interviews with Marcia Clifton and Gail Elise Clifton, August 2021

Q: You said it was ridiculous you had the band name you did. Lesa said it's German slang for "pistol." How did you decide on the name? What were the pros and cons?

Marcia: I would like to clarify the context of my comment a little bit… Yes, I did say it was ridiculous we named ourselves The Klitz. But in the sense that we actually thought we could get away with it and that it would not be censored or considered shocking. We found it to be funny and ironic. I love the name and am very proud that it was my idea! It was Alex Chilton who suggested we change the spelling. You might argue that it held us back at the time. The local newspaper didn't print the name, and our friends at Ardent Recording Studio (makers of Big Star records, among others) thought we should change the name. We got and still get a lot of attention based solely on the name. Currently, a documentary is in production about us. It is called *Say the Name: The Story of the KLITZ*.

As for the comment "Klitz is German for pistol," we made that up! There is some rumor that my German grandma said that, but I'm not sure she did. Gail and Lesa kept that comment out there when they got the Klitz back together in 2007. It's been attributed to Lesa in an article from that time.

Q: I've read interviews with members of the band, where, in some cases, you identify the Klitz as a punk band, and others you brush it off as a label that was put on you by others. How do you feel about the term punk? And how does it apply, or not apply, to the band?

Marcia: I definitely think we fit the description of punk, especially early punk. We were unabashedly unrefined and just learning to play. We also didn't care what people thought of us. We were being creative and putting it out there without any preconceived notions of what was good or bad. We were definitely rebelling against the commercial music of the day, and we had the Ramones, Patti Smith, and the Sex Pistols to look up to! Gail and Lesa both had piano lessons, and Lesa and Amy could play guitar, but none of us were polished in any way. I think Amy and Lesa might have some issue with the punk label, but not me!

Gail Elise: I liked being called punk. I had just spent a year in 1977 (pre-Klitz) going to Peaches Record Store every night to buy vinyl punk imports with my boyfriend, Dave Branyan from the Scruffs. I started a collection of punk vinyl: Sex Pistols, the Clash, Ramones, to name a few. Then I wrote "Two Chords" later that year around Dec. 1977

when I joined Ross Johnson's band the Malverns. I had no idea at the time that I would take that song with me to start the Klitz with Marcia and Lesa in early 1978! About that time, Ross joined Alex's band the Yard Dogs. They were punk as well.

Q: At the time, there weren't many women in Memphis playing rock. What other women making music similar to you all were you aware of at the time?

Marcia: Nope, just us, playing punk, that is. Memphis is such a music town, and we were surrounded by great blues singers like Jesse May Hemphill and Ma Rainey II, who played at local clubs, and more traditional white rock 'n' roll singers in the style of Heart had gigs but no one else playing punk styles. By 1983, more punkish all-female bands like the Marilyns and the Hellcats were on the scene. But no one else but us in the late '70s - early '80s.

Q: What did being in the band do for you personally?

Marcia: Being in the band was freedom! And for me, it gave purpose to my life as a college dropout! Plus, it was great fun! I love that we have a legacy that people are still curious about. We were well-timed to be able to hang out with Alex Chilton and Jim Dickinson and Teeny Hodges, and Roland Robinson. It was amazing to know them and record with them.

Q: What's your favorite Klitz song? Why?

Marcia: I have two… "Hard Up" and "Two Chords." Both are kind of like the soundtrack of our life then. I think "Hard Up" defines us and shows that we were not afraid to talk about our desperation and sexuality of being young women on our own in a

Klitz poster. Courtesy of Marcia Clifton.

man's world in the late '70s. I think that's the song that defines our feminist roots. And I just love "Two Chords"! It's so fun. Gail wrote that song for an earlier band she had called the Malverns. They were short-lived, and "Two Chords" became one of our first, best, and most memorable songs. It is still a lot of fun to play and takes on its own shape every time, making it a perfect punk song.

Gail Elise: My favorite Klitz song is "Two Chords." But I love "Hook or Crook," which Alex wrote and produced on *Sounds of Memphis* 7-inch vinyl. After that, I like the pop songs on *Glad We're Girls*. Greg Roberson from Reigning Sound produced it. (Engineered by Adam Hill who worked on Big Star's *In Space* at Ardent Studios.)

Q: What memories do you have of New York or CBGBs?

Marcia: It was only Gail and Lesa who played at CBGBs. Amy and I had already left town. The whole band played at Irving Plaza with the Cramps and a few months later at Tango Palace as part of the *Mr. Mike's Mondo Video* movie premiere. Those are great memories. In hindsight, we should have been more inspired to tour and stay together based on those experiences. A tape of us at the Irving Plaza gig recently surfaced, and we really sounded good. The Tango Palace show was not as good. Amy didn't come along, and Gail and Lesa got too drunk to play well. I was sober and out of place. That's the gig that made *Rolling Stone* magazine with a quote by Sylvia Miles, who said she "wasn't sure what was worse, the Klitz or the *Mondo Video* Party Punch." Ouch! That hurt. I see that as a missed opportunity for sure. Oh well, it's punk for ya…

Q: A lot of writing about the Klitz gives Alex Chilton credit for encouraging your work or guiding the band. In what ways did that relationship impact the band personally, professionally? Do you like that narrative?

Marcia: I'd say that's accurate, and we were often caught up in the ups and downs of Lesa and Alex's relationship. When the Cars toured Memphis, they came to our show hoping to see Alex, but he wasn't there that night because he and Lesa had had a fight. We got to hang out with them anyway, and that was fun. Miles Copeland came to see us too because he was managing the Cramps. The gig was good, and he said we were versatile, but we got too wild at the afterparty. We scared him away with our drugged antics. It was soon after that he launched the Go-Go's. ●

THE DELINQUENTS

Austin, Texas   »   Formed in 1978

MEMBERS

Layna Pogue { VOCALS
Becky Bickham { VOCALS, GUITAR
Mindy Curley { KEYBOARDS
Andy Fuertsch { GUITAR, VOCALS
Brian Curley { BASS
Halsey Taylor, Tim Loughran,
Willie Alleman { DRUMS

» Mindy Curley's minimalist, haunting Farfisa organ arpeggios, paired with the band's distinct vocal delivery, distinguishes the Delinquents' sound from other new wave punk gems of the late '70s. The band, put together by friends Andy Fuertsch and Brian Curley, played together for three years and featured two different singers, Layna Pogue and Becky Bickham, over their short run. At an informal audition in the parking lot of the popular rock club Raul's, Layna impressed the band in 1978 with her distinctive rendition of a Tammy Wynette song.

The two singers only recorded one song in common ("Alien Beach Party"). The first version of the song, with Layna singing, was recorded by then-drummer Tim Loughran in their garage with a TEAC four-track reel-to-reel and then released as a 7-inch on Live Wire label. (Over their three years as a band, the group saw drummers spin in and out of their orbit.) After the song was chosen as the Single of the Week in *New Musical Express*, the band planned a tour, but Layna didn't want to travel. She stepped down, and they enlisted another vocalist who quit shortly after. Then they found Becky Bickham, who joined for the remainder of the band's tenure.

Layna and Becky's vocal abilities are a good match, as evidenced on the alternate recordings of "Alien Beach Party." Album credits and slight distinctions in vocal patterns are the only evidence of different singers. However, the two brought complementary elements to the band: Layna co-wrote much of the Delinquents' material, including "Alien Beach Party" and at least three other tracks from their self-titled LP, and Becky played guitar.

Before moving to Austin, future Delinquents Andy Fuertsch and Brian Curley were friends in Albuquerque, New Mexico, where they learned how to play guitar together as teenagers. Both moved to Texas and reconnected. Attending shows in the city's underground music scene, the two started the Delinquents with Brian's wife Mindy on organ, whose wobbly, supernatural hooks became integral to the band's signature sound. The band's songs recalled upbeat bops of '60s surf rock with the addition of spooky keys, distorted chords, and bizarre lyrics written and delivered with a lively sense of humor.

In the song "Do You Have a Job For a Girl Like Me," Layna sings from the perspective of a young derelict struggling against the demands of an individualist, capitalist system. In the verse, she sings:

I've been in the same hospital for
    17 weeks
I've gotta get some money 'cuz I'm living
    on the streets
I need an easy job that don't need too
    much strength
I've gotta pay the doctor or he'll
    repossess my brain

And the chorus:

And I don't wanna go on welfare
I don't want to be a parasite
I'm not trying to be a millionaire

THE DELINQUENTS

I'm only trying to do what's right
I don't have no experience I've got
     no degree
You have a job for a girl like me?
I burned out my brain on PCP!
But you got a job for a girl like me?

As a final move, the group made a full-length album with rock critic Lester Bangs called *Jook Savages on the Brazos*, an early example of country-western punk, in which Becky's backing vocals received high praise. After that, the band broke up for the reasons bands do. Many of the members have gotten back together to play reunion shows over the years. ●

Top: Cover of the Delinquents' self-titled 1981 7-inch. Bottom: Back cover. Both from the collection of Jen B. Larson.

MYDOLLS

Houston, Texas   »   Formed in 1978

M E M B E R S

Trish Herrera { GUITAR, VOCALS
Dianna Ray { BASS, VOCALS
Linda Younger { GUITAR, VOCALS
Kathy Johnston { GUITAR
George Reyes { DRUMS

» Both good hair and authenticity go a long way in punk. Guitarist and salon owner Trish Herrera got to know two of her bandmates bonding over hairstyles, which led to conversations about music and other creative pursuits. Trish's first encounter with guitarist Linda Younger was when Linda came into Trish's salon to get her bangs cut. Around the same time, Trish met bassist Dianna Ray through friends at a show and offered to update Dianna's feathered Cherie Currie cut. The ladies dished on different types of music and decided they could come up with something more unique than what they had been hearing on mainstream radio and what they had been seeing around town.

Dianna told *Maximum Rocknroll* in 2013, "Music was central to both of us, and we went out to the Island, Houston's original punk rock club, most every night…A number of the bands were just this side of terrible, but it never stopped us from going. One night we decided we can't be any worse, so let's start our own band; it'll be fun." Trish has played guitar and piano since childhood, and she enlisted her cousin George to play drums. However, Dianna and Linda were novices, so they experimented with their instruments as they went, which made the band's creativity all that more genuine.

At the time, few clubs in Austin would book the Mydolls and other punk bands. Other venues only welcomed country-western groups and cover bands.

Much of what inspired the band artistically was railing against the corruption and hatred they witnessed and experienced in the world. Police brutality in Houston had become an anger-inducing issue. Once, Trish herself was strip-searched and arrested for not using blinkers to change lanes while driving. The band expressed their political fury artistically, speaking out against misogyny, racism, and homophobia in their lyrics. Aside from gender politics, members of the band have experienced other forms of marginalization: Trish and George as Hispanic, Dianna as gay, and Linda as Cajun.

Similar to other cities, for a short time, punk offered exclusive space for artists to express themselves in a way that challenged the mainstream, but by the early '80s, aggressive, macho energy began to take over. At punk shows, audiences were becoming violent and mosh pits were getting dangerous. For example, at a Butthole Surfers show in 1982, Dianna lost her two front teeth when a guy in the pit shoved her face-first into the ground.

Trish explains, "The inclusiveness of punk was sweet…until boys got all sweaty and spiky and started pushing us out of the slam thrash. Then it became a uniform just like Dockers, Nikes, and printed T-shirts are now."

At the same time, their punk identities overruled any others. Dianna says, "I am gay, but I wasn't 'raised' in the gay subculture; I was 'raised' in the punk rock subculture. Labels like 'butch' and 'femme' didn't exist there. People were punk first and queer, Mexican, Black, secondarily."

Having had these individual experiences, the Mydolls have invested time empowering and mentoring young women and minorities in punk (and have strong opinions about making mosh pits safe). Repurposing a nursery rhyme, lyrics for their song "A World of Her Own" speak to the independent nature of young people's creative experiences. They sing,

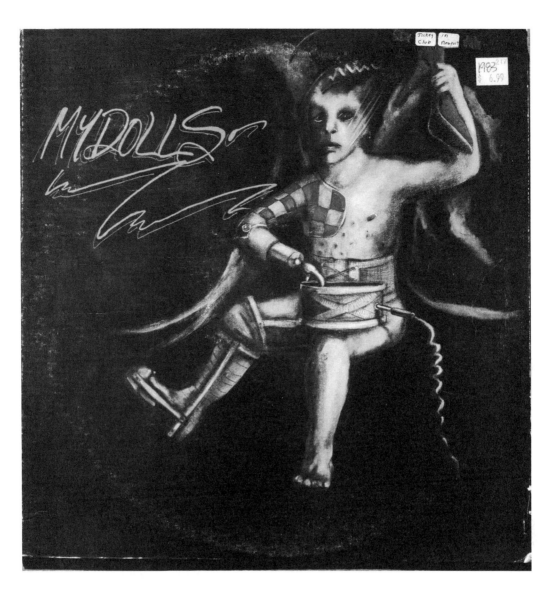

Cover of *Speak Softly and Carry a Big Stick*, the Mydolls' 1983 12-inch. From the collection of Jen Lemasters.

Once there was a girl
Who built a little world
Right and left in the middle of her brain
When she was good
She did what she was told
When she was bad
She built a world of her own
Once there was a boy
Who loved the little girl
He wanted in her world
Though he loved her
And she loved him
He couldn't get in

CIA Records put out the Mydolls' first three records, "Nova Grows Up"/"The/Rapist" (1980), "Exorcism"/"Imposter" (1982), and the full-length *Speak Softly and Carry a Big Stick* (1983). In the '80s, they toured the coasts, Europe, the Midwest, and one of their songs was used in Wim Wenders' movie *Paris, Texas*. The band played together until 1986, then reformed in 2008. The group has been recognized for their important work by the Contemporary Art Museum Houston, Lawndale Art Center, Houston Press Music Hall of Fame, and most recently, the University of Houston Special Collection. ●

SCREAMING SNEAKERS

Miami, Florida » Formed in 1979

MEMBERS

Lisa Nash { VOCALS
Mark Evans { DRUMS
Bud Gangemi { BASS
Gary Sunshine { GUITAR

» They had the tunes, they had the look, and they had the audience. So why did the Screaming Sneakers not "make it big" when they relocated to New York City? And what happened on their mysterious recording journey with Polydor Records in England?

Their only recorded EP, *Marching Orders*, combines punk, power pop, and '80s sensibilities with deep hooks, drum flourishes, layered guitar, and powerhouse vocals. Live versions of their unrecorded tracks have surfaced online, and every cymbal crash keeps the adrenaline elevated.

Their anthemic song "Violent Days" seems like hyperbole and sarcasm, but in reality, reveals an uncomfortable truth. In the song, Lisa Nash sings:

I see violence as a rising tide
Backed up to the wall, no room to hide
Perfect weather for a homicide
Feelings over now by many died
In the violent days, the violent
    ways of our lives
These are violent days within our lives
Crime committed against your dog,
    your wife
Crime committed every single day
Criminal people teaching violent ways
But I don't see tomorrow, I can
    barely see today
I can't predict tomorrow
But I know it will be violent anyway
I know it will be violent anyway

When the band began, Lisa wasn't old enough to patronize the bars they played at. Because of this, she usually couldn't watch the other bands on the bills play. Perhaps, to local musicians, this gave the impression that she was unsupportive, shy, or aloof; but for audiences, when she was nowhere to be found offstage at venues, it added to the mystique of her stage persona. Her underage status was a legitimate alibi, but she also enjoyed the benefits of performance glamour. As she told Greg McLaughlin in an interview for Invisible Bands, "I used to tell the band, you should never go out and hang out with people before the show."

As a band, the Screaming Sneakers have often elicited inapt comparisons to the Cichlids, who they were not similar to, likely only because they were both from south Florida and had women in their lineups. (It just happens that Lisa played bass for a short period in an early lineup of the Cichlids.) Screaming

SIDE 1

VIOLENT DAYS
GRIN AND BEAR

SIDE 2

I CAN'T HELP IT
REFLECTIONS

Left To Right:
Mark Evans: Drums
Bud Gangemi: Bass
Lisa Nash: Vocals
Gary Sunshine: Guitars

In memory of
Mark Evans and
Bud Gangemi

This extended play record with four cuts on it was produced and mixed by John Hanti and Screaming Sneakers. It was recorded at Songshop Studios in New York City. The engineer was Frankie Quinn. The cover was designed by Screaming Sneakers. Photos by Debbie Baylis. Nice one Debbie!

We would very much like to thank: Barbara, Allen Jacobi, Skip brown, Wayne Vlcan, Eddie Gregg, Randy Blitz, Joey Calari, Jay Cohen, Bob Roberts, Dave Parsons, The Rat Cage, Lenny Kaye, David Sunshine, Mike Manwel, The Reactions, Hillary, Brandee, Rich Desantos, Eric Haskal, Robert Lefsatz, David Goldstein. Special thanks to all our families (who've been a great help) and a very special thank you to our friends in South Florida, New York, and the East End of London...

Screaming
Sneakers
Records
© 1982 / ℗ 1982. Warning: All Rights Reserved
Unauthorized duplication is a violation of applicable laws

45 RPM

GENERATION
RECORDS NEW YORK CITY

Sneakers often cited the Reactions as an influence, recording their song "I Can't Help It" on *Marching Orders*. And they once did a cover of Tommy James and the Shondells' "Mony Mony," which Billy Idol saw, commented on, and suspiciously, shortly after debuted his cover of.

That isn't the only way the music industry showed its teeth to the Sneakers. The band was a big fish in a little pond in Florida, but when they moved to New York, the city swallowed them up. Audiences at CBGBs enjoyed their shows but didn't really know who they were. People at CBGBs were often just there for the party. Lisa mentions that, in hindsight, she would rather have been the "big fish" at home.

In 1982, Polydor Records courted the Sneakers and brought them to England. They stayed in the West End at a swanky castle and went into the recording studio during the day. With radio airplay in mind, the engineers sterilized the music by having Lisa punch in notes. When the label revealed they were only interested in keeping her as a singer and wanted to replace the band with studio musicians to create a new wave pop sound, Lisa was unable to betray her rock roots and put her foot down. ●

Opposite: Cover of *Marching Orders*, Screaming Sneakers' 1982 12-inch. Above: Back cover. Both from the collection of Jen B. Larson.

THE COLD

New Orleans, Louisiana » Formed in 1979

MEMBERS

Barbara Menendez { VOCALS, ORGAN
Vance DeGeneres { BASS
(Ellen's brother, by the way)
Kevin Radecker { GUITAR
Bert Smith { GUITAR
Chris Luckette { DRUMS

Cover of "Take All the Time" / "I Go to Pieces," the Cold's 1984 7-inch. From the collection of Jen B. Larson.

»On the second-to-last day of the decade, the Cold debuted its classic lineup, a technicality that cements its status as a late-'70s band. Though the guitarists had formed the band the summer before as Totally Cold (a parody of Olivia Newton-John's *Totally Hot*), the quintet wasn't realized until December, ironically, in a city where it doesn't snow.

The popular band covered upbeat '60s pop tunes and played originals. They packed venues with dancing crowds in New Orleans, putting on 90-minute-long gigs, and booking up to ten shows a month. As an unusually egalitarian feat, all five members of the band sang, trading off vocals between songs. Barbara's signature aerobic dance moves—vigorous headbangs, arm flaps, off-kilter leg kicks, and windmill hair whips—energized the room and the other members of the band. When she wasn't singing front and center, she played the organ.

The Cold put out gobs of singles between 1980 and 1982. Halfway through 1982, Barbara made a sudden decision to leave the rock 'n' roll lifestyle for domestic normalcy. She told the *Times-Picayune*, "I've just had enough. I want to lay low for a while, and I want to take art lessons because I've been meaning to do that for a long time. I've been drawing all my life, but I never took it seriously. It was always self-taught. Everybody always said I was pretty good. I didn't pursue it, but now I think I should. I think I could maybe make a living doing something with art. I love it, so it's going to be good for me. I'd love to be the next Norman Rockwell."

Menendez explained that she had lost the excitement she once had for music and that she no longer appreciated the lifestyle of a rock musician—late hours, smoky bars, drinking all night, and partying. When asked what she would say to fans upset by her departure, she responded with conviction, "I've got a message: It's my life, and I'll do what I want. What am I going to tell these people: 'Oh, I'm sorry, I know you're right. I'll do whatever you say. Why don't you come over for cocktails some night'?"

Barbara's departure was a foreboding of the band's fickle run. They broke up and got back together a handful of times, releasing albums of retrospective material. The Cold was inducted into the Louisiana Music Hall of Fame in 2018 thanks to dedicated lobbying by their fans. ●

F-SYSTEMS

Austin, Texas » Formed in 1979

M E M B E R S

Lorenda Ash { VOCALS
Neil Ruttenberg { BASS
Dick Ross, Mark Lander { PERCUSSION
Randy Franklin { GUITAR, KEYBOARDS
Jerry Barton, Kerry Crafton { GUITAR
Andres Andujar { KEYBOARDS

》 In Austin in the late '70s, singer Lorenda Ash used to visit Sanctum Records, where she met film student and KUT radio DJ Reverend Neil X. She would carry a notebook brimming with original poetry and wear a beret flopped on her head. Once they got to talking, they discovered their creative compatibility.

Hosting a local weekly radio show, future F-Systems bassist Neil Ruttenberg was responsible for revealing the secrets of punk rock to the Austin underground. Learning about bands through *NME*, *New York Rocker*, and *Melody Maker*, the punk music people heard in Austin—like most other cities—came from the UK, Los Angeles, and New York.

Neil formed the art-punk outfit F-Systems with Lorenda singing in 1979. Over the years, the band's changing lineup impacted their fluid sound. What remained static over the years was the collaboration between Lorenda and Neil. First, Neil laid down groove-oriented basslines and offered lyrical ideas, and then Lorenda built upon the foundations and delivered poetic melodies over the tunes.

In a surreal 1981 video series, the band performed in a studio in the University of Texas' radio/television and film department. Lorenda wears a metallic gold long-sleeve shirt and dances coolly among the band members. A TV of the band performing sits on stage, and a background holds various spacey visuals while glitches illuminate the band's transcendental aura.

As the band's focal point, Lorenda had a sizable following of men and women. Fans idolized her for her great stage presence and charisma. Offstage, however, she was more private. Quieter than Neil, she didn't go out a lot and stayed home reading while he bounced from bar to bar socially.

Though danceable and upbeat, the band also had existential, avant-garde qualities. Lorena typically wore black, and many songs were referential to horror

Back cover of "People" / "Naked Kiss," F-Systems' 1980 7-inch. From the collection of Jen Lemasters.

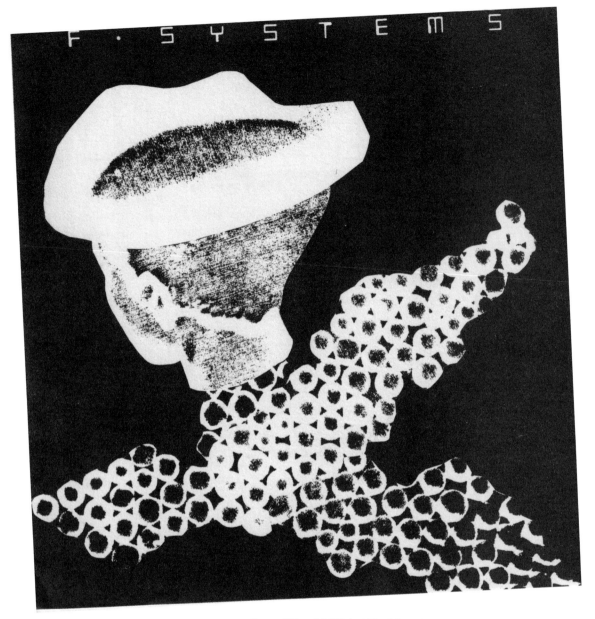

Cover of "People" / "Naked Kiss." From the collection of Jen Lemasters.

films, including "Dawn of the Dead," "Exorcism," and "Four Flies on Grey Velvet." Other songs, such as "People," show themes of social isolation:

I can't feel anything
I don't touch anything
I can't feel anything
I'm walking wounded romance
I never understood emotions
I never cried, I never danced

while repeating "People/People" in the chorus.

The band was popular in the Austin punk scene, and regular headliners at Raul's. They could pack a room, but outside of punk spaces, they were side-eyed like other punk bands that played at non-punk venues. The band's manager once booked a show at an Air Force base that promised the group $600. The show ended up being an hour and a half of dead silence from the audience, and only about five soldiers remained in the room by the time the show was over. Their songs were played on local radio, and they opened for Gang of Four, Grace Jones, Joan Jett, and U2. ●

TEDDY AND THE FRAT GIRLS

South Palm Beach, Florida   »   Formed in 1980

MEMBERS

Cookie Mold { VOCALS
Pam Axley a.k.a. Spam Ax { GUITAR
Sarah Parsons a.k.a. Fish { BASS
Joesaphine Dupont { DRUMS

>> In 1980, Sheer Smegma recorded the EP *Audio Suicide* and then changed their name to Ted Bundy and the Frat Girls. It is unclear which name is more vile. They later shortened the name to Teddy and the Frat Girls, a subtler reference to a gruesome killer.

The strangeness of this band cannot be understated. In their songs, audible chaos ensues. Drumsticks gallop and beat drumheads wickedly, accenting uncalculated measures with nasty cymbal crashes. Guitar fills the void of what could be a calming silence with broad strokes of distortion and indiscernible chord changes. Vocals gasp and screech in a bewitching terror, unapologetically reciting depraved and insulting language. It is music to piss off parents, neighbors, and anyone with taste.

Soon after recording *Audio Suicide*, Cookie Mold and Spam Ax also moved to Cincinnati and, with a new lineup, continued as Teddy and the Frat Girls. Of the four songs on the *I Wanna Be a Man* EP, two of the songs, "Clubnite" and "I Owe It to the Girls," were both written by Fish (who also wrote for the legendary *Mouth of Rat* fanzine). According to her son, when he was 13 years old, he co-wrote the other two, "Alophen Baby" and "I Wanna Be a Man," with Cookie Mold and his seven-year-old sister Lona. He states that despite his mother's contributions, Cookie and Spam sold the rights to the tapes to Jello Biafra, who reissued their recordings without Fish's consent.

Cover of Sheer Smegma, *Audio Suicide* EP, 1980.
From the collection of Jen Lemasters.

Cookie Mold was an infamously bellicose artist, throwing punches and bottles while the band freaked out audiences with their wretched musicianship and foul lyrics. In "I Owe It to the Girls," a song with a pretty cool chorus, they sing,

I've got the clap
I'm going crazy
I'm getting mad
I'm awful lazy

Their notoriously disgusting song "Alophen Baby" begins with:

Some people like ass
Some people like tit
But nothing gets me going
Like liquid shit

(And it only gets worse from there…)

The lyrics in "I Wanna Be a Man" maliciously critique society's low standards for men. Recited in a bad German accent, the lyrics, like most of the band's prose, are meant to shock and offend. They chant in a piercing tone:

TEDDY and the frat GIRLS

CLUBNITE

ALOPHEN BABY

I WANNA BE A MAN

I OWE IT TO THE GIRLS

THE EGG MAN DON'T COMETH

45rpm

Cover of *I Wanna Be a Man*, Teddy and the Frat Girls' 1984 12-inch. From the collection of Jen B. Larson.

I'm sorry I'm a girl
And not a man
Then I could come all the time
In the palm of my precious little hand

And:

And if I was a man
I could piss anywhere
Piss on your wrist, you sonofabitch
When you're a man, you don't care
I could fuck any time
And be hard as a rock
Spend my life worrying about

The size of my teeny, little cock

(Chorus)

And if I was a man
All you sluts would give me head
(I'd) Get my rocks off
Then I'd kick you out of bed
Be tactless and boring
With nauseating breath
I'd be a worthless piece of shit
From birth until death

So…yeah. ●

THE FOAMS

Austin, Texas » Formed in 1980

M E M B E R S

Irene Hardwicke { VOCALS
Cathy Crane, Alison Rogers { GUITAR
Sarah Cunningham { BASS
Jozann Kelly { DRUMS

》 The cover of the Foams' coveted only release, *Gay Boys*, is a xerox of the band with potato-stamp print skirts. It was made by the group's singer Irene Hardwicke, who also drew a picture of the band for the record.

The oddball all-girl four-piece from Austin was once named to a Top 10 list of Texas bands in the *Austin Chronicle*. In it, the writer unsparingly describes the band as "charmingly incompetent." Favorites at Raul's, Austin's premier punk club, the Foams started just for fun. They were described as a lighthearted yet socially critical performance art piece, and they put out a limited-run 7-inch of live recordings called *Gay Boys*. After the recording, the Foams disappeared into the night.

Singer Irene Hardwicke moved to Austin from southern Texas to study painting at the University of Texas. She loved dancing at night and discovered bands like the Skunks and Terminal Wave. Living in a solar-powered co-op that hosted parties and put on

The Foams performing live. Photographer unknown. Courtesy of Irene Hardwicke Olivieri.

bands, one day, on a whim, she and friends thought up the idea to get a set list together and play a set at one of their parties.

Bassist Sarah Cunningham channeled her cello abilities into jerky funk grooves, Jozann kept a steady but off-kilter rhythm on the drums, and Cathy fiddled with guitar. With Irene, an untrained singer (the most untrained singer of the four, according to her), on the mic, the group wrote three songs, concocted outlandish outfits, and made their stage debut at the co-op. The show was such a blast, it impressed the manager of the Huns—the hottest band in town—who called and asked if they would open for them at Raul's that following week. So, with three songs in their repertoire, the girls got down to brass tacks and slapped a 45-minute set together. They skipped a week of classes and set up a makeshift studio in Jozann's living room to write and rehearse.

"We went crazy trying to write and play enough songs and make outfits and posters to put up and down the drag (Guadalupe Street in Austin). At that time, we were the only all-girl band in Austin, and we got an awesome reaction," Irene remembers with glee. "Being on stage at Raul's was like nothing I'd ever experienced. We were addicted to the feeling and started getting gigs."

Their pal Larry Deemer, an artist who wore outfits made from bubble wrap, became somewhat of an auxiliary member of the group. As their manager, he booked them wherever he could in Austin and out of town. Larry also added to the band creatively, helping author songs and coming up with style ideas.

Guitarist Alison Rogers joined, Cathy left, and the band continued writing original tunes and doing covers. One cover they performed was the New York Dolls' "Girls" (but they changed the lyrics to "Boys"). "Jozann sang this one, and I played the drums. I LOVED playing drums, but the drum kit would travel all over the stage because I played so hard," Irene says.

Training as a painter, Irene found music to be a new, refreshing outlet for her creative expression. Sometimes she wore her heart plainly on her sleeve, singing about her love of art. In "Paint Me" she shrieks "I have loads of brush of color," and sings the chorus, "Paint me Paint me." Irene continues, "Clay is too messy, ice is too cold, let's cast some plaster; that may be the mold."

Focused as much on their stage show as their songsmithing and fun-having, Irene recalls carting carloads of clothes across the state in her VW Bug for the band to make costumes out of. As for looks, they went for the unexpected: Irene occasionally wore a

lampshade as a skirt or an airplane on her head. Once, the group rode giant ducks out on stage. Another time, they brought a small oven on stage and baked cake during their set. Disinterested in drinking and drugs, their intentions were pure: they would drink high-energy vitamin shakes to prepare for shows.

The Foams performing live. Photographer unknown. Courtesy of Irene Hardwicke Olivieri.

"At the time, I was in art school, and being in the band was such a great opportunity to make street art. I painted a mural at 21st Street co-op of a girl turning into a mermaid. I was always making posters for our band and many other local bands. The excitement of the punk scene was so wild and creative, it just felt so free like every day anything could happen," Irene exclaims. "I remember when the Ramones came to town. They were signing records at Inner Sanctum, and I went to see them, and when I saw Joey Ramone, I ran up and kissed him." Aptly, the Foams had a song called "I Wanna Marry Joey Ramone." ●

NORTHWEST

Guys Are Not Proud

THE DISHRAGS

Vancouver, Canada » Formed in 1976

MEMBERS

Jill "Jade Blade" Bain { GUITAR, VOCALS
Carmen "Scout" Michaud { DRUMS
Chris "Dale Powers" Lalonde { BASS

» Three girls with dark windblown shags loiter in front of a brick wall wearing leather coats. "The Dishrags" hovers above them in a bold, blocky sans serif font, holding the iconic Ramones record they reference. The photograph of the girls was superimposed over a brick background for the cover of a 2010 CD compilation, *Past is Past*. It illustrates the Dishrags' adoration of the Ramones, whom they consider one of their biggest influences.

The band officially formed in 1977 and was first booked as Dee Dee & the Dishrags after a promoter lost patience with the girls for not giving them a name in time for the show's poster. "Dee Dee," of course, came from the name of their favorite Ramone, but where "the Dishrags" came from still puzzles them.

In Carmen Pollard's short *Madame Dishrags*, Scout jokes, shaking her head, "[The promoter who named us] was probably just standing in her kitchen."

"She was [probably] just looking at us," Jade jokingly piles on, presumably referring to their rumpled haircuts, patchy jeans, baggy shirts, and loosened ties.

Jade Blade, Scout, and Dale Powers. Three bored teenagers from British Columbia, turned on by the sounds of Suzi Quatro, T.Rex, Alice Cooper, and '60s girl groups, started a punk band in tenth grade. It was 1976 and they are considered one of the first all-girl punk bands in North America.

Dale says, "I don't think we set out to be an all-girl band; it's just that that's who we are."

Despite creating tight, three-chord earworms hookier than those of many notorious all-male bands and outperforming the short-lived locals, the trio of high schoolers were given ample attention but not anywhere near equal amounts of respect from their musical peers, mainstream audiences, or even in hindsight by historians. Once, for example, the all-girl band was invited to open for a Battle of the Bands. They were not taken seriously enough to participate as contenders, so they had to warm up for the event.

Before the Dishrags officially formed, the girls played at a family New Year's Eve party at Jade's parents' house when they were 14 and 15 years old. Growing up in Central Saanich, a conservative rural town outside of Victoria, B.C. that hadn't quite been exposed to punk, the Dishrags hauled their gear to Vancouver by ferry to play shows, and they ventured down to Seattle and San Francisco where punk scenes thrived. A punk scene emerged in Vancouver, so the girls quit high school and moved there.

Their no-nonsense tunes linger around the two-minute mark and are crafted with scratchy guitar riffs, knife's-edge rhythms, and pure punk meanness. Embedded with unapologetic honesty and cool austerity, the song "Bullshit" taunts the audience with

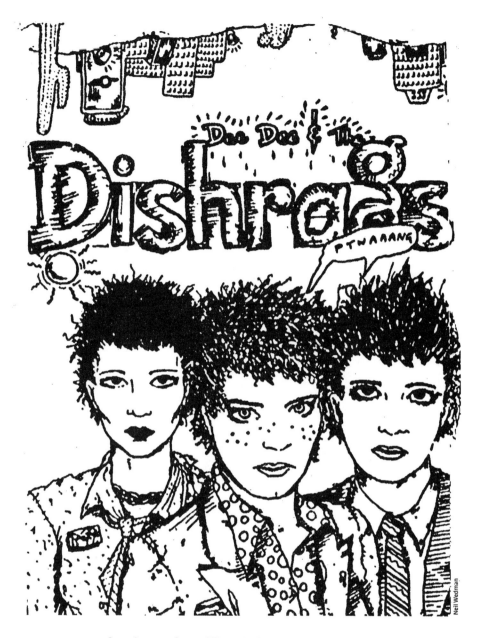

Opposite page: Cover of *Three*, the Dishrags' retrospective 12-inch (recordings from 1978–79).
Above: Cover of a Dishrags zine accompanying *Three*. Both from the collection of Jen B. Larson.

its repeating titular chorus, while "I Don't Love You" contains threats and declarations. They sing:

> I could make you cry
> Get you on your knees
> My heart is ice
> No pity inside

Though they were well-liked by punk audiences, mainstream audiences often reacted adversely to their performances. Bombarded by boos, pelted with objects, and forced to leave the stage, the negative reactions became so commonplace that the band's memories of them happening run together. "That was one way that we couldn't help but be political, because people objected to us just because we were three young women on stage," Jade Blade told the *Georgia Straight* in 2014. Even the punk bands who liked them often treated the Dishrags more like a novelty act than a

the DISHRAGS
JADE plays guitar
DALE plays bass
SCOUT plays drums
IT'S 1977... THREE 15-YEAR-OLD GIRLS ARE INSPIRED... TO START A BAND
FURIES
BELIEVE IT OR NOT
JULY 30
ROCK
SNOT RAG
FREE
SUB HUMANS
DISHRAGS
SATURDAY NOV. 11 8 PM
ENDLESS
SIDE 78
I Don't Love You
Bullshit
What Do You Want Me To Be?
High Society Snob
I Don't Wanna Walk Around With You
Rebel Kind
Tormented
Double Checkin' Woman
Quick Step
Friday Nite Date
SIDE 79
Past Is Past
Tormented
Love Is Shit (It's Goodbye)
Just Another Girl
Sold Out
Cravin' A...
Public Enemy
Bullshit
I Don't Love You
London's Burning
SIDE 78 1–2 Produced & engineered by Chris Cutress & Jay Leslie. Recorded at Sabre Sound, Burnaby, BC, November 1978.
3–9 Recorded by Nancy Smith and Grant McDonagh live at the Windmill, Vancouver, BC, October 23, 1978.
10 Recorded by Tom Harrison live at Gary Taylor's Rock Room, Vancouver, BC, October 1979.
SIDE 79 1–3 Produced by Harry Cool & Colin Griffiths. Engineered by Eric Betten & Mathew Sutton. Recorded at Triangle Studios, Seattle, WA, summer 1979.
4–10 Recorded by Nancy Smith and Grant McDonagh live at the Commodore Ballroom, Vancouver, BC, January 31, 1979.
Windmill & Commodore audio from the personal archives of Nancy Smith.
Compiled, Remastered & Produced by Jason Flower at Rockland Studio, 2012.
• Jade Blade – guitar / vocals
• Dale Powers – bass / vocals
SUPREME ECHO

Back cover of *Three*. From the collection of Jen B. Larson.

serious band. These reactions can be explained simply as anger at just the sight of young women on stage. And then there were the sexist comments about their clothes. "There were certain people who suggested that if we were to dress differently, we might be more popular," Scout says in the documentary *Madame Dishrags*. Jade finishes her sentence, adding: "Including an early manager who literally did want us to wear hot pants on stage. It's like, *ahh, I don't think so*."

"We wanted to be taken seriously, so that was really annoying. We would never get sound checks, and we got crappy equipment; people would never let us use their drums or amps," Jade says during a group interview in *Bloodied But Unbowed*. The band also laments their status as the opener, never the headliner, for gigs. While they opened for incredible touring acts like the Clash and the Avengers, they weren't given the opportunity to headline their own shows the way adjacent male bands in the city were. Also, unlike many male bands, three years into the project, the Dishrags still didn't have any songs released on vinyl.

Though the trio remained friends, Dale Powers left the group during the band's final year in 1979, and the Dishrags teamed up with two members of another all-girl group called the Devices. With Kim Henriksen on bass and Susan MacGillivray on guitar, the Dishrags played for a year before disbanding for good. While the girls only recorded five studio singles from their extensive repertoire, a collection of live tapes of soundboard recordings surfaced and were finally released more than 30 years later on the LP *Three*. ●

CHINAS COMIDAS

Seattle, Washington　»　Formed in 1977

MEMBERS

Cynthia Kraman (Genser)
a.k.a. Chinas Comidas { VOCALS, LYRICS
Richard Riggins { GUITAR
Lynn Paulson, Dag Midtskog { BASS
Shawna Holt, Mark Wheaton { KEYBOARDS
Brock Wheaton { DRUMS

》 Seated at a table inside a shadowy apartment, four mystics interpret your fortune. Three devoted protectors surround a serious woman—a poet—wearing an oversized black cloak. She casts her gaze squarely into the camera. The man opposite her fans a deck of cards. She's just ashed into a heart-shaped tray and rests a cigarette between two fingers. Below her hand, a bloomed rose, two unopened packets of sugar, a near-empty mug, and a cigarette carton are tools she possesses to manifest her intentions and aspirations. The poet, Cynthia Kraman (Genser), illuminates the scene, the cultural influence of the objects carefully arranged around the room, and the ghosts whose presence was known.

Studying, penning, and performing poetry in New York City in the mid-'70s, Cynthia Kraman grew inattentive to the demands of the big city, mentioning to a friend she dreamt of the West. The friend, a fellow poet, urged her not to fly but travel across the country to fully experience the trip. Agreeing, Cynthia decided to catch rides for her first trip across the states, describing the journey to Dennis White of Jive Time Records:

"I picked up a ride with a person I didn't know. His name was Miles which I thought was fictitious. He turned out to be a big bore. We parted ways in Pennsylvania, then I started to just get rides off of ride boards, and occasionally I'd hitch solo...

Even in the '70s, it was a little dicey going alone … It turned out wonderfully! I met a lot of really interesting people. When I got to the Mississippi River…for me, being from New York, that was *mythic!* I said, *'I have to get out of this car! I have to put my boots in the Mississippi mud!'* To me, this was like *'America for real.'*"

Cynthia's book of poems (*Taking on the Local Color*) was published in 1976. Other work of hers was included in *The Paris Review* (issue number 57, Spring 1974), and she had been performing spoken word live in New York City. In Issue #8, she told *Search & Destroy* that she was getting sick of

Cynthia Kraman performing live with Chinas Comidas. Photographer unknown. Courtesy of Chinas Comidas.

Chinas Comidas. Photo by Abbot Genser.

dull academic poets and wanted to do something more interesting. The writer ricocheted between coasts, landing in the Bay Area and biding her time as a journalist. In Berkeley, she worked as a culture critic for the underground journal *The Berkeley Barb* and began writing under the pen name 'Chinas Comidas.' She covered the trial of the San Quentin Six, which she attended with radical leftist cartoonist Spain Rodriguez.

Having experienced the explosion of punk rock in New York City, she sought out a similar scene in Seattle, where she began connecting with underground musicians. With Red Dress guitarist Rich Riggins, she formed her own band. Rich started writing melodies and Cynthia supplied lyrics inspired by and referencing Marxism and feminism.

In "For the Rich," she warbles:

You see them walking down the street you
see them driving in their cars you
see them sitting on their yachts you
see them sipping on their Scotch...
They dream of money and of cars they
Dream of shooting out the stars they
dream of sucking on your bones after
they have eaten up your homes

Other band members came and went, as they had an open-door policy. The original lineup included members of other local art-punk group the Tupperwares (who later became the Screamers in L.A.) and drummer Eldon "El Duce" Hoke (of shock-rock band Mentors and later a regular on *The Jerry Springer Show*).

By 1978, their most stable lineup went full steam ahead. Performances often included confrontations, which connected Chinas Comidas on lineups with aggressive punk bands like the Germs, the Bags, D.O.A., and Black Flag. Walking the tightrope of punk taxonomies, Chinas Comidas exists at the intersection of punk cultures: the intellectual New York poetry scene, the more relaxed beginnings of art-rock, and the antagonistic and assertive political music that would follow. More traditional punk rock crowds sometimes resisted the art nature of the group, and violence would often occur during shows.

Cynthia told *Search & Destroy*:

There's some impromptu responses brought about by the show or by me —'cause I look somebody in the eye—'cause sometimes I'm up there and I want to wipe the smile OFF EVERYBODY'S FACE, and sure enough I'm gonna catch somebody's eye, and they're going to be pissed off and feel attacked and throw stuff... but there's staged violence mostly by—people who are reading too much *Rolling Stone*—and that's what I can't stand!

After releasing and receiving praise for "Peasant/Slave," Chinas Comidas packed their bags for L.A. Rich said, "We probably would continue to be given the news of another band like the Go-Go's being signed. Chinas Comidas were newcomers to town, so they got shoved to the side because Slash Records were more interested in the Germs and X, so they put us on hold…."

Cynthia's brazen nature and aversion to conformity guided her decisions. For example, in conversation about Marxist thinker Henri Lefebvre in *Search & Destroy*, she said:

Some people are on the outs with everybody because you know if you're getting support, it means that somebody's buying your line, which means that it can't possibly be true ... because nobody buys the truth. Everybody throws it away! They buy the big lie!

When the band dispersed, Cynthia went back to New York to focus on her poetry, then continued to get her Ph.D. in medieval literature at the University of London. Rich moved back to Seattle. The remainder of the band went on to play with transgressive performance artist Johanna Went.

On a remastered compilation of their studio recordings, Chinas Comidas is remembered by Bill White:

[They] were never scenesters; they didn't hide behind somebody else's attitude. They were the first band to take punk out of the punk clubs and into the Lumberjack bars, where working people danced to country rock. I don't know how many times Cynthia had to listen to some assholes yell at her to 'shut the fuck up' now it's their turn to shut up.

Cynthia Kraman
on the cover of "Peasant/Slave"

According to my best recollection, the photo was taken in our apartment in Seattle above the Comet Tavern. The whole building was filled with ghosts since drunks live on the astral plane, but this apartment was haunted by a particular old woman we'd actually met when we were living in our first tiny apartment in the same building. After she died, her family came, slit the mattress and the soft furniture (no doubt looking for cash or jewelry), and left. She had only been found because her dog was crying…I believe she was buried in a pauper's grave by the city. Rich and I found a photo of a tough little sailor in her room. We decided he was an old beau, and we made an altar with it and a few dried flowers and one of her gloves so that her spirit could hang out there and leave us alone. That worked pretty well. Later we used his image for our label, Exquisite Corpse Records.

At the time of the photo, I was very much under the influence of my trip to Mexico, to Mexico City and the Pyramid of the Sun and the Moon, and Casa Azul, Frida Kahlo's house. The heart and the rose come from that lineage. The cigarettes, which were mine, probably come more from Papa Legba or even Baron Samedi, whom I knew from Maya Deren's great book: *Divine Horsemen; The Voodoo Gods Of Haiti*. The cup may have been a reminder from Lawrence's *The Virgin and the Gypsy* of the scene of the gypsy wife's method of telling fortunes from dregs, but also all the objects are simply mine and came readily to hand.

When I look at the photo, I'm tempted to give it a good dream analysis via Northrop Frye's system of alternative worlds. "Where are we? How did we get here?" The dream elements are very strong with the foreground use of four symbols, the four humans seated in a row, the blackened window, the stripes leading like roads to the viewer, and also back to the camera's subjects.

Each of us is also wearing standard dream clothing: uniforms for Brock and Rich (he's in his white mechanic overalls; Brock is the universal American biker outfit) and then there's Mark with his game of chance, the cards in his hand and on his lapel, with

Cover of "Peasant" / "Slave," Chinas Comidas' 1979 7-inch. From the collection of Jen B. Larson.

his flowing fingers underlining the 'crossed' negating wrist. I'm dead center in dead black, looking straight into the camera, demonstrating something with my hand—the Corazón. There's also the lit cigarette separating that little heart from the big artificial full-blown rose.

I think that's a globe hanging above us. And the hat is from the East, perhaps a nod to Vietnam, or the sun…I like our logo over it—I made that logo in under a minute with a thick brush and a can of paint lent by Carl Smool when we needed it for our poster, and we always used it. One try, and it was done.

I guess I'd say we're sort of guides to the underworld here, the boys all so handsome and uninflected, and me in my sorcerer's robe absorbing the light, beckoning ever so slightly as if to say, these are our wares: the heart, the rose, the burning fire, the liquid in a cup—the four elements of creation, but recreated, therefore an alternative universe, which was very much where we lived—we were living the "other" life, not the one given to us, but the one we're making with every song. ●

THE ACCIDENT

Bellingham/Olympia, Washington   »   Formed in 1977

MEMBERS

Lisa Nansen Cram, Megan Chance,
Jennifer Warp { VOCALS
Doug Cram, Bruce Poot { GUITAR
Trent Kelly { BASS, VOCALS
Mike Stein { DRUMS, VOCALS

Outside a loading dock in an alley, three boys holding instruments look around, and a voice offscreen whispers, "Is everybody around here REALLY a bunch of wimps?" There's a countdown, the bassist hangs on one note, and the drummer—railing only on a snare—punishes the skins with two sticks evenly before rolling into a chunky guitar riff. A girl in white go-go boots runs into the shot and leaps off the drummer's knee onto the platform before the song kicks off. She sings:

**Well you listen to the radio
you hear an awful thing**

Gang vocals underscore the chorus. They chant:

Kill the Bee Gees right now!

The song escalates; the bassist boasts a solo, the guitarist headbangs with his long blond hair cloaking his face, the drummer wrecks his snare while the singer's moves become bossier, more violent. She screeches "Kiiiillll," opening the floodgates for a hard rock guitar solo. The jam is punctuated by a mouthed fart noise.

Singer Lisa Nansen captures the feeling: "Nothing felt intentional in The Accident. Trial and error." Part Ramones, part Monkees (see their video for "True Detective"), the group began in 1977 with four

college kids playing raucous party music and having a good time. The guitars were loud, the drums were fast, the bass bounced, and the vocals hit "like a cheerleader from hell."

Over their four-year span, the band was led by three different frontwomen, all of whom were wild and captivating in distinct ways—Jennifer Warp and Lisa Nansen Cram, and for one memorable weekend of shows, the author Megan Chance. When Jennifer wasn't available to play their very first show, they enlisted longtime friend Megan to fill in at the Windmill, a former strip club in Vancouver.

Megan writes, "For nearly the entire winter break, I ended up in this heatless house they'd rented in Bellingham, learning the songs and practicing in the only room that had heat (a space heater)." The band traveled up to Vancouver for the weekend, got pulled over at the border, slept on the booker's floor, ate fast food once a day, and then she caught pneumonia. But she said that it helped muster a gruffness in her voice, and that this danger was all part of the experience.

"It was exciting, but really on the edge," Megan remembers. "Punk at that time was really male-dominated, and I think I subconsciously did things to fit in." She recalled that she wore a men's shirt, trousers, and tie she picked up at a thrift shop in Bellingham. "I went out of my way to have no sexuality. Otherwise, it would have felt too dangerous, I think." She evokes her past self: "I wasn't a woman on that stage; I was a badass—fuck you all you assholes, get back and let me work."

Simultaneously intense and lighthearted, the band pulled off a proportional fun-to-punk ratio. Their sought-after EP *Kill the Bee Gees* maligned the white disco trio (and was recorded by Art Object guitarist Myles Boisen). And during their song "Jonestown Hop," the band would pass out Kool-Aid to their audience where everyone would drink it or splash it on each other and then fall to the ground and flop around on cue.

The Accident playing live at Washington Hall, Seattle in 1979. Photo by Randy Hall.

"It was an awesome time to be creating music. So much creativity. Anything was possible," singer Lisa reminisces. "The energy came from all of us, especially once we got together. A spark to flame... It was always fun; it never felt like a job."

"[The Jonestown Hop bit] was Michael and Trent's macabre sense of humor. I was happy to oblige," Lisa adds. "The audience participation was that link that completed the circle, the energy, and vibe. We fed off each other."

They played their beer-filled, loud set regularly in Vancouver, and two years after forming, played perhaps the first punk show in Bellingham, Washington, opening for the Subhumans. The Accident played with other punk legends, the Avengers, Subhumans, Pointed Sticks, and D.O.A.

Recalling the intensity, Lisa says: "There were some shows when I thought I'd have a heart attack. My heart was pounding so hard. And I was only 18!"

Michael Stein remembers all three singers as driving the band's energy on stage and connecting with audiences. In 1997, he wrote, "Our first [singer] was Megan Chance, our friend from high school. She became a wild woman on stage, making our first few shows at the Windmill very memorable." He continues, "Jennifer Warp [was] a four-foot bundle of Hiss who ROCKED. She meant it, man! When she and Bruce left, we had big shoes to fill—and that's when we met Doug Cram and Lisa Nansen. They were more 'straight rockers' than we were but liked the Power of Punk Rock. Lisa had a very strong voice. Plus, Doug had a Marshall amp... we could be even LOUDER. It was a natural fit!"

About their demise, Lisa said, "The city wasn't quite ready for what we had to offer."

Email interview with Lisa Nansen Cram, September 2020

Q: Had you seen the Accident before you tried out for the group? If so, what did you think about them?

Lisa: No, I had not. I learned about The Accident from my husband, Doug. We had met a few months prior in September of 1978; I loved his long blond hair and the way he played the guitar. Our first couple of months together was wild and passionate, then we

The Accident. Photo by Jeff Kelly, drummer from Village Green.

broke up, hard. Like, not acknowledging each other or talking to each other. At the time, we lived within four flights of stairs and a short hallway from each other in the dorms at Western Washington University.

One night I barely made it to the nearby food hall before closing for dinner. The place was nearly empty, but there was Doug, and he asked me if I wanted to join him. I told him I'd heard he had joined a band. He told me they needed a lead singer. He suggested I try out. I replied, "Why not? Sounds like fun!"

That's how I heard about The Accident. Never had met Michael or Trent until I tried out.

Q: What made you want to be in a band like The Accident?

Lisa: To be truthful, I never thought about it. I just stumbled into it, with Doug leading the way. It felt like the right thing to do. I was drawn to the new boys in my life. It was serendipitous. To this day, we are all still friends. Doug and I have been married for over 35 years (although we were only friends during our time together in The Accident). This shared experience has left a profound mark on my life. Both of ours, actually. And most positively.

Q: I've heard your vocals described as "cheerleader from hell." So many later bands have tapped into this exact vibe/sound (even a band I was in a few years back!) Where did that energy come from? Was it intentional?

Lisa: I laugh because nothing felt intentional in The Accident. Trial and error.

It was an awesome time to be creating music. So much creativity. Anything was possible. I actually was a cheerleader in high school for my freshman and junior years. My senior year, I discovered the parking lot and the crowd that hung there. Picked up a few bad habits. So maybe that's where the hell part comes from.

I was comfortable playing a role (Halloween is my favorite holiday). So, when the boys encouraged me to put that short skirt back on, I did, and it felt right.

The energy came from all of us, especially once we got together. A spark to flame. There were some shows when I thought I'd have a heart attack; my heart was pounding so hard. And I was only 18!

Q: On his website, Mike remembers you and Doug as "straight rockers"—Doug had a Marshall amp, but other than that, what do you think made him say that? What kind of stuff were you into?

Lisa: When I was 13, the first album I bought was Deep Purple *Machine Head*. Doug is a closet metal head. We like the same kind of music. It's one of the things that drew us to each other and keeps us together today.

My brother is six years older than me, and when he left the house when I was in middle school, he left his album collection. I had a record player in my room and spent hours listening to them all. From Iron Butterfly to the Beatles... soon I added to the collection, Grand Funk Railroad, Aerosmith, Foghat, Elton John (still love *Yellow Brick Road*), Led Zeppelin, Van Halen... I was open to whatever I could get my hands on.

I love the music and energy that came out of the punk and new wave scene. I credit Michael and Trent for introducing me to it and moving my musical tastes beyond a "straight rocker."

Q: Can you tell me about how the idea to pass out Kool-Aid for the Jonestown Hop came about? What did it look like on stage from your end?

Lisa: That was Michael and Trent's macabre sense of humor. I was happy to oblige. The audience participation was that link that completed the circle, the energy, and vibe. We fed off each other. Without that connection, it makes it hard to stay engaged. I learned that in later gigs, usually in bars in Seattle before the music scene and Nirvana had exploded there. We really tried to make it work, but the city wasn't quite ready for what we had to offer.

Q: Do you have any other silly memories like that from shows?

Lisa: Smilin' Buddha in Vancouver, BC. That was my first punk awakening. Lots to unpack from that weekend.

I grew up middle class, though not your typical middle class as we moved around a lot. But I had never been to a punk rock show. My first concert was seeing Chicago. I had no idea what was about to happen.

It was a two-night gig. The first night we started to play, and I remember it took a couple of songs to warm up the crowd. Then they started spitting. One after another, punk boys took turns running up to spit on me. I had no idea what it meant.

The boys kept playing. I had loogies dangling from my bangs and stuck to my cheeks, but I kept going, singing then screaming. I can't remember which song it was, but it was a heart-pounder; the crowd was pogoing by this point, a silhouetted sea of spiky-haired heads bobbing to Michael's frantic beat. Doug stepped forward for his solo, stepping on the wrong button on his effects pedal, max volume. Mind-numbing loud. Electricity flowed through my body. The crowd went crazy. The connection was made. Spit, beer, and God only knows what else was flying through the air at us. Doug was soaked through, hair dripping beer onto the blur of his fingers across metallic strings. Rivers of beer running down the body of his prized red '62 Gibson SG. I remember thinking, "my God, he's going to be electrocuted!"

Q: Do you still play and sing music?

Lisa: I play it while I garden, work out, cook dinner, drive in the car, socialize with friends. Love the new technology where you can put wi-fi speakers all around the house, so it follows you everywhere!

I like almost all music except country, angry rap, and canned pop. So it's sad to see live shows with lip-syncing. If you can't sing for real live, then it's cheating, right? Somehow, we did it. Heart pounding up your throat, belting out the words. Maybe not studio-perfect, but the energy was there. It was real. That's what I love.

Over the years, I'd sing in the car when alone and dabbled in karaoke for fun. But it was last summer (2019) that we put together a two-night, weekend gig including Michael, Doug, me, and two musician friends. We did covers. I got to channel Joan Jett, Cherie Currie, Led Zeppelin, Lenny Kravitz, and more. We had two practices then the real deal. It was a bit chaotic, but that's what added to the success of it. We had hoped to do it again this summer, but... There is always next year!

Q: What kind of stuff do you play for your kids?

Lisa: Doug fed them metal and grunge at an age much younger than most people might feel is okay. I turned them on to '80s alternative.

In turn, our daughter who is 26 goes to music events and has turned us on to stuff like Queens of the Stone Age, Tame Impala, the Yeah Yeah Yeahs... Our son who is 24 is into EDM (electronic dance music). He is writing and producing. The computer is his instrument. We've learned it's all about THE DROP.

In essence, we shared with them and now they share with us, keeping us up-to-date on the music scene. We feel very lucky and fortunate. We didn't corrupt them after all. The circle is complete! ●

NEO BOYS

Portland, Oregon » Formed in 1978

> ## MEMBERS
>
> Kim Kincaid { VOCALS
> KT Kincaid { BASS
> Pat Baum { DRUMS
> Jennifer Lobiciano, Carol Steinel,
> Meg Hentges { GUITAR

>> When Neo Boys singer Kim Kincaid was 16, the Ramones played a tavern in Portland, Oregon. She wasn't old enough to get in, but she and the sound guy had a plan: Stuff her into an empty bass cabinet and take her backstage. She says, "The plan was I would just sit in that cabinet until the show started, and once the audience was there, I could just go see the show. The concert promoter and the club owner wouldn't see me; I would just blend into the crowd." Hours passed, and her bladder reached its threshold. "It was to the point that I was going to pee my pants if I didn't go," she said.

From inside the bass cabinet, she heard the Ramones chitchatting in the room. "So, I pop out of the cabinet, and I'm like 'Hi! Please don't tell anyone. I really want to see the show, but I have to go to the bathroom so bad!'" The Ramones laugh at her, and she runs to the bathroom. "As I am coming back, I'll never forget it: I saw the club owner. It was like a western. He's at one end of the hall. I'm at the other end of the hall. We lock eyes. And he knows I am underage." The club owner and concert promoter escort her out. She said, "I felt like the kid that was being pulled by the ear. And I didn't get to see the Ramones."

In Portland, "punk" (which didn't have a name at the time) was a youth movement. Because there were so many high schoolers involved, the Neo Boys always made a point to play underage shows. Bassist and Kim's older sister KT Kincaid explains, "If we played

an over-age show—a 21-and-older—we would also play an underage show at the same venue early that day." And also, "We put on a lot of shows ourselves… at colleges or renting halls."

The girls started playing when they were young teenagers. KT and Kim Kincaid allied with their friend and guitarist Jennifer Lobiciano to create their first band, Formica and the Bitches. The group, whose name wasn't exactly apropos for promotion in 1977, played a few shows and broke up. In *The Oregonian* in 2013, Jennifer said: "We had a rehearsal space in our friend's house where they had put mattresses on the floors and walls." She played a borrowed guitar, Kim had a cookie tin for drums, and they covered a Germs song. "It was like a rattletrap trying to get off the ground. It really was absolutely amazing."

Soon after disbanding, the three members reconvened, adding drummer Pat Baum, as a fleshed-out four-piece with Jennifer on guitar, Kim singing, and KT on bass. In a 2004 interview on KBOO, Pat said, "I always wanted to play drums, but they would never let me in school because they said girls can't play drums. My brother and I used to jam—he played the piano. I had some bongos with drumsticks, and I think a pie-plate cymbal or a pan-lid cymbal." She adds, "When I moved into a house that had a drum set, I started playing secretly when no one was home…"

At first, playing in the band was about letting loose, being expressive, and not perfecting a craft. Kim said, "I never really felt like it was that premeditated. It just kinda happened. We wanted to play music, and it was a good creative outlet, and we hooked up with the group, and we just went from there." Retaliating against popular music from the time, they approached their instruments scrappily, and as a guitarist, Jennifer played straightforward chunky three-chord rock. Recalling their first show in which they opened for Television, Pat and Kim both say, "We just weren't really very good… And we were really nervous…"

Neo Boys. Photographer unknown. Courtesy of Neo Boys.

After the event, the girls were determined to improve, so they practiced every day. At the time, 15-year-old Kim's brother had guardianship of her, and by his rules, she was not allowed to play in the band. So, she would sneak out to make gigs. "They didn't really [like what I was doing]… they didn't really realize how good the band was for me in so many ways. It was a tremendous amount of discipline and dedication. I think that they thought the people I was hanging with were a bad influence." The band helped Kim hide her participation from her older siblings, going so far as to not put her pictures on the promo posters.

For Kim, writing lyrics was instrumental to her growth. Candidly exploring political topics, like gender and economic inequality, Kim's lyrics carried the songs and were written without a melody in mind. When Jennifer left for Los Angeles, KT would craft melodies on the bass. Guitarist Meg Hentes joined, and their songwriting flourished. The evolution from simple, compact chords and two-beat drums to intertwining riffs with high-end guitar jangles can be heard distinctly on their double-LP release *Sooner or Later*, an archival treasure chronologically compiling all their songs over their five years.

Kim says, "It was really important that we were merited as musicians rather than just being girls, a novelty to go see girls playing music." And KT adds, "There was an awareness early on that we didn't want to sing about boys. We didn't want to just be thought of as girls and what that meant previously. It was so narrow what a girl could sing about. It was pretty conscious that we didn't want to be thought of as a girly band."

The lyrics take on a rhythm of their own. In "Poor Man's Jungle," they sing call-and-response:

> Looking through life with an angry eye
> This is what I get for fighting a
>   poor man's war
> Looking through life with an angry eye
> This is what I get and pray I'll get more
> Looking through life with an angry eye
> This is my class because my
>   pocketbook says so
> Looking through life with an angry eye
> This is a system that strips me
>   of my dignity

In "Running in the Shadows," the song bends around the repetition of the lines,

> Running in the shadows
> Rolling in the gutter

Neo Boys. Photo by Kristine Larsen.

In the rockabilly tune "Cheap Labor," Kim sings,

Do I dare resist the favor
Do I dare forget the offer
No, it's not for me
I won't forget my company

Kim addresses sex work and in "Image of Guilt," laments the impossible beauty standards of women.

Kim recounts, "At that time there wasn't even a name for it—I remember being in high school and punk rock was happening, but no one had a name for it, they just called you a freak," and Pat adds, "You really had to hunt it out at that time."

From the early days of punk to the heart of post-punk, women's roles changed drastically. Jennifer,

who went on to form Randy and the Randies, in Los Angeles, shared her feelings about women's roles in the Portland scene before the band got together: "A lot of women were helping their male partners be musicians. There really weren't that many women out there…If you wanted to get backstage, pretty much you were a groupie. Those were the challenges we were up against before we even started the band."

After a time, the "punk" scene became more aggressive. Kim says, "I personally felt that once more of the hardcore and thrash music became more popular, there was just more testosterone and this harder edge of masculinity."

KT adds, "It became more intolerant, more narrow. It felt like the jocks came in and took over." Pat says, "I didn't want to go to shows anymore because the

In a speech at the Oregon Historical Society, KT and Kim reflected on the roles of women in punk:

"Within this context, what was NOT lacking was the involvement of women. It's sometimes hard to imagine now—the landscape of rock has changed so much—but during the late '70s and early '80s, the number of girls who picked up a guitar, grabbed a mic, played found objects, or sat behind a drum set in order to express themselves musically was unprecedented. There had been so few female role models in rock before this time. And while we may not have known it—ALL of us contribute to what would become one of punk's most valuable legacies: the deterioration of gender roles within rock 'n' roll."

Following this declaration, they remember and acknowledge more than 20 women in the punk scene they were part of, in Portland alone: "Girls, we applaud you and are proud to have been among you! Please forgive us if we've forgotten anyone!"

More than other cities, the Portland DIY scene felt like a collective effort. The band partook of the underground circuit, shaking up basements, college stages, art galleries, even in their practice space. Generally, events were organized by the small punk community in Portland. Pat remembers, "There were no male/female roles…everyone doing it for the good of the scene…"

KT adds, "We generally played within the parameters of the punk rock community, and within the punk rock community, gender was not an issue, ever, ever. But once we went out of that community, it was very different. Either you were ignored, or they thought you were gonna be a tits-and-ass band."

Though preferring to be judged by their musical merits alone, perhaps on instinct, Neo Boys addressed feminist issues head-on. They have always openly discussed the frustrations of being an all-female band. They recently shared publicly on Facebook, "When we tried to find a place to play outside [the Portland] community, and the word got out that we were girls, like some kind of freak sideshow, we were inevitably billed as an 'all-girl band' and often disappointed our audience, not being the tits and ass act expected. This was particularly apparent at the men's prison in Salem and another venue in the same town where unbeknownst to us, and much to our outrage, we were followed by a wet T-shirt contest! Kinda underscored our reason for choosing the name." ●

moshpit would get bigger and bigger, and you could get hurt just by standing on the sidelines—something could get thrown." KT adds, "[Hardcore] was a narrowing of the definition of punk rock, and it all became that. That's not how punk rock started. There was no definition, and that was the whole fucking point."

Pat says, "It wasn't even called punk when it started. It didn't have a name." And Kim says, "There was more room to explore before that. There was room to discover your gender, of your belonging in the world. There was even more room for feminine men. Before any of that, you didn't even look at people in terms of gender in their music. I didn't think about it until hardcore started happening."

More than a decade before a battalion of riot grrrls ripped a hole through that testosterone-fueled Portland music bubble in the early '90s, the Neo Boys were far from the only women pioneering punk, but they were among the most influential.

THE ANEMIC BOYFRIENDS

Anchorage, Alaska » Formed in 1978

M E M B E R S

Louise Disease { VOCALS
Ellen Johnson { BACKING VOCALS
Maggie Johnson { LYRICS
John A. Firmin { SAXOPHONE
Chris Goddard { GUITAR
Dave Tremper { DRUMS

>> When Louise Disease was 18 years old, her older sister Maggie wrote lyrics to a song she didn't want to sing herself. Louise had previously been in a garage band, so it wasn't difficult for Maggie to persuade her to perform the misandry-tinged tune "Guys Are Not Proud." What else are sisters for?

The song taunts oversexed boys, snidely accusing them of engaging in bestiality. Now a punk anthem, the song became a favorite on college radio stations due to its jeering lyrics and the spirit in which they were sung. Louise Disease chants, like a schoolyard ruffian:

Guys are not proud
They'll do it anytime
Guys do not care,
They'll stick it anywhere
Guys are disgusting
They're always lusting
Guys are obscene
Vile and unclean
Guys are such creeps
They'll even do it with sheep

Until then, Maggie's husband, John Firmin, a saxophonist and member of David Bromberg's band, wanted to do something different. So he and Maggie composed the initial tune "Guys Are Not Proud," then gathered a group and called themselves the Anemic Boyfriends.

Louise Disease performing live. Photographer unknown. Courtesy of Louise Disease.

Louise and Maggie's other sister Ellen also crooned backing vocals along with Alaskan author Kim Rich.

Released by Red Sweater Records, an independent label with no other apparent titles, the girls took matters into their own hands to get "Guys Are Not Proud" heard. Ellen shopped the 45 around in the San Francisco Bay Area, while Maggie took it to radio stations while adventuring with the Bromberg band. As a result, the song rose to cult status on college radio stations.

In the late '70s, punk wasn't popular in Anchorage. There wasn't a scene for it; Alaskan bar bands typically played covers and country music. So, the band traveled 3,000 miles away to play at clubs like Mabuhay Gardens in San Francisco and sometimes made the even farther trek to Los Angeles. They were once offered a show at CBGBs, clear across the continent, but they couldn't make it.

As the youngest of six, Louise grew up with eclectic tastes, listening to whatever her sisters put on. She remembers hearing Frank Zappa at ten and spinning Tower of Power on repeat. At Odyssey Records, the chain record store where Louise worked, she mostly heard Top 40 tunes or whatever her coworkers were interested in. Once the Flying Lizards came into her orbit, she was tapped for punk greatness.

While "Guys Are Not Proud" was the most played Boyfriends' tune at the time, the band had other songs, including "Bad Girls in Love" and "Love Attack." In the tongue-in-cheek "Fake ID," Louise sings about underage rebellion:

You can't go party when you're only 15
So here's what I'm going to do
Going to find me some guy with a
　　real big car
And we'll go out cruising to a
　　rock and roll bar
A ton of mascara and my real tight pants
'Cuz I want to go out and get drunk
　　and dance!
I got a fake ID
It's got a picture of me
Says 1953
Does it look like me?

Louise contributed lyrics to a handful of songs that she describes as "a bit harder," but the recordings aren't available anywhere. Like many bands, the Anemic Boyfriends self-destructed, and the members moved on to other ventures. Since then, Louise has focused on visual art and writing. ●

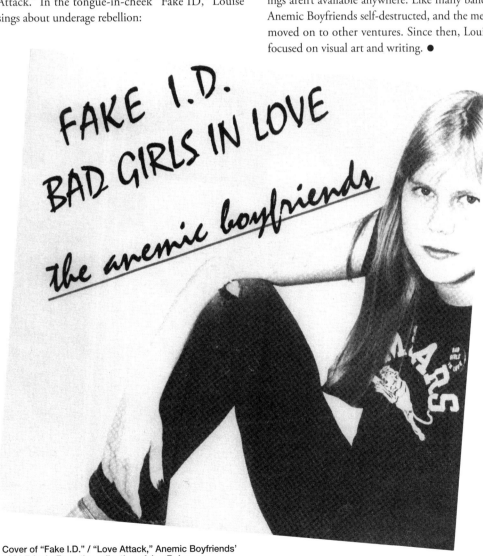

Cover of "Fake I.D." / "Love Attack," Anemic Boyfriends' 1981 7-inch. From the collection of Jen B. Larson.

SADO-NATION

Portland, Oregon » Formed in 1978

M E M B E R S

Mish Bondage, Leesa Nation,
John Shirley { VOCALS
David Corboy { GUITAR
Dave Propp, Steve Casmano,
Dan Pozniak, Ric Couch { BASS
Chuck Arjavac { DRUMS
(*a handful of additional members*)

》 When Michelle Miller was 15 years old, she ventured out to see punk bands in Portland. Her older brother played in bands and drew her into the scene. At shows, she met an early incarnation of Sado-Nation, a band she later joined as singer. She and her friends were inspired by the energy of the live performances and started an all-female band called the Braphsmears. Braphsmears' drummer Leesa was singing in Sado-Nation at the time. When Leesa moved out of Portland, Sado-Nation needed a new voice, and Michelle Bondage stepped up to be their singer.

"I told Corboy I was the voice for Sado, and I was who he was looking for," Michelle says. "He made me audition anyway and sit in while other (two, maybe) women auditioned. I had an authentic and more hardcore voice, and he gave me the job. Later he said I always had the job, but I think he wanted to give me a little bit of a hard time."

In the early days, David Corboy—a child guitar prodigy who played on *The Dick Clark Show* at a young age—arranged most tunes, and Leesa sang. The band had a pop appeal, seemingly inspired by '60s garage rock framed in a tight and abrasive punk sound. Dynamic arrangements allowed Leesa Nation's voice to boomerang between sweet and fierce. Songs like "Gimme You" even included handclaps and "oohs" and "ahhs" overlapping screaming lyrics. Michelle writes:

Leesa and I [had] very different stage presences and vocal styles. I knew this going into it, and knowing I could never fill Leesa's fun power-pop style vocal/presence, I could be me, which was darker; I prowled the stage like a panther and spat out lyrics like a bad taste, hurling them at the audience. Leesa was very energetic and was more power pop. That was her style, and she was very good with that style. Powerful, very pretty, and fun. I liked Black Flag and D.O.A., Pistols, Clash and Stranglers, amongst other bands, like Ramones, Dead Boys and Richard Hell, also English bands, Stiff Little Fingers, Sham 69, Adverts and X-Ray Spex… I was an early female hardcore/old school voice. I thought punk should be in

Opposite page: Mish Bondage singing live with Sado-Nation.
Above: Mish Bondage's aggressive stage antics while performing with Sado-Nation. Both photos by Janice Morlan.

your face, shocking and accusatory; I suppose I was never interested in being pretty or power pop. It just wasn't in me to carry that off.

In a 1983 *Maximum Rocknroll* interview, the band discusses the themes on *We're Not Equal*, the album they made with Mish on vocals. They all chime in that its themes include conflicts between races, ages, genders. They also discuss the significance of having a female singer. David states, "We [have a female singer] because…men writing for women really can't do it. It's gotta come from a female point of view…It's not like we're really heavy into that women's lib and all that junk."

Then Chuck says, "It's not like we went out and were like 'let's get a girl singer' either."

David adds, "Plus, she's got a good presence on stage… she's like a little animal there."

After singing "Cut Off the Cord" live, Michelle's intensity doubles. She yells,

**I'm bleeding! I want to see
someone else's blood!**

On "Stand Up, Fight Back," Michelle barks,

**Don't take their crap
Stand up, fight back**

On "Messed Up, Mixed Up," she takes the sins of society to task:

**They won't give you work
or recognize you're there
They look right through you
like you were thin air**

**They smile to your face
Then they stab you in the back
but they won't really push you
they're afraid that you'll attack
They envy you so much
They're filled with hate
They've got you so confused
that you can't think straight**

She says, "I already had a high bar to be held up to; Sado was one of Portland's best and tightest bands at the time. However, my look, style, approach, and voice were way different than Leesa's, and I had to sing the songs my own way."

When Mish joined Sado-Nation, the songs got faster and more contentious. Mish's presence was described as ferocious, frightening, and thrilling; skulking from one end of the stage to another, hissing momentous lyrics at the crowd. She made such an impression on audiences she was recognized as "female" vocalist of the year by *Flipside* magazine in 1984. Less than a year later, Michelle moved to L.A. to expand her horizons. About that experience, she reflects:

"At the time, we were playing a lot and touring up and down the coast. I worked very hard to be an equal to the guys in hardcore bands. It was very primal for me, and I could reach deep inside and let out this primal energy. I was surprised since we weren't as well-known as many bands and mainly stayed on the West Coast. I remember thinking that was pretty rad, and cool they would recognize female [vocals] as well as general all-around [vocals]." ●

Sado-Nation's first singer, Leesa Nation performing live. Photo by Janice Morlan.

ART OBJECT

Bellingham, Washington   »   Formed in 1979

M E M B E R S

Karen Irving "Anna Klisis" { VOCALS
Myles Boisen { GUITAR, VOCALS,
ENGINEERING
Jim Fricke "Ed Media" { GUITAR, VOCALS
Oren Sreebny { BASS
Kim Kleinschmidt { DRUMS

**I always thought he was so enlight-tened
about his sex-ual-ity I always thought he
told the truth I always thought he
knew the deep-er meaning
though I knew he danced the poot**

Art Object flyer for a show benefiting Blackwell Womyn's Health Resource Center. Courtesy of Art Object.

》 With a sigh and two attempts at a two-beat start-stop intro, "So Enlightened," the second song on the B-side of their only EP, *Ride the Metro*, begins. Vicious jazz chaos ensues. Back and forth, poetry and jazz hopscotch, and then the rhythm section loses its footing across the finish line, and the android-inflected singer flubs a line. "Oh shit. Stop the song," she says. "I blew it."

As fate would have it, Karen Irving met bassist Oren Sreebny at Fairhaven College in 1974. Oren spontaneously invited her to perform in an impromptu band for a Valentine's Day dance at the college—that night. She said yes, and so began the collaborative relationship that led to Art Object. The brand new band sensibly named themselves Wet Paint when they found some free and available posters on a freshly coated bench. A straightforward '70s rock outfit with rotating members, Wet Paint played as a working tavern band and toured regionally for the next several years. In the meantime, a few of the members created an offshoot band that toyed with different aesthetics.

One winter, the piano player of Wet Paint took a vacation. During the time off from the group, some of the members of the band bonded over punk music and formed a side project. They originally called this group Art Object and the Van Gogh-Gos (a variation of a nickname given to Oren), but later shortened it to Art Object. They put together a set for a benefit for a women's health cooperative, a repertoire which consisted of '60s garage rock covers and a few original tunes. The band went over well, and they were asked to play another show, for which they had more original tunes ready. Truly a collaborative effort, Karen and Myles wrote the initial stages of most songs; Karen came up with lyrics, Myles tweaked the music, and Oren, Jim, and their drummer Kim wrote parts for their own instruments. While they participated in many benefit shows and were very politically minded in conversation and lyrically, Art Object's playful nature showed through. Karen wrote, "We performed a song called 'Do the Dead Rock Star' where we all swapped instruments—then, within the song, we each took a turn singing a line from a dead rock star's song, and then 'died' on the stage… at the end of the song the whole tavern did the same—about 200 people lying on top of each other on the beer-soaked tavern floor."

Another time, they played a half-hour set before two showings of *Eraserhead*. Jim tells the story: "Truly surreal—a big stage in a big auditorium, playing far enough back that the movie screen could be lowered in front of us while we finished our set. Then getting off the darkened stage without knocking instruments over, with *Eraserhead* visible, huge, through the screen pinholes."

The band's peculiar sense of humor led them to craft songs that were simultaneously socially aware and weird. "Art Object pushed some of the audience past their limits of musical understanding. Their music is not like any that has come out of Bellingham before," a fan told the press in 1981.

The combination of Karen's spoken word poetry, their free-jazz meltdowns, and tongue-in-cheek post-industrial-warfare social commentary fuels their combative persona. The song "USANRK" (say it out loud) boasts lyrics like,

> I'm a mess, I'm a bomb
> I'm a tool, I'm a pawn
> I'm a threat, I'm a fright
> I'm bound and gagged
> and I'm ready to fight!

In *The Western Front*, the singing in "(I Want to Grow Up to Be a) Juvenile Delinquent" was described as "like Johnny Rotten after a breakfast of Brillo pads":

> I coulda been a lawyer but I just don't
>   have the wardrobe
> I could be a priest but I'm rotten
>   to the core
> Since I got no social conscience
>   I might as well be obnoxious…
> I was born the wrong sex
> I could be the right sex
> if I only had the money

In "Confused," a musical intro explodes into deranged opera-turned-poetry. Their "hit" "Ride the Metro" enters with a city soundscape and persists with a fuzzed out '60s guitar riff turned proto-indie pre-chorus, plus Karen's apt description of city life:

> Get in line, door slams
> Press my nose to the window
> Watch the people all dressed like me
> Go by
> They're standing still
> I go by
> I'm standing still
> Ride the Metro!

Almost immediately after forming, the band was offered a record deal and began recording their material. Myles, an instructor at Fairhaven (and engineer of the Accident, the Subhumans, Frightwig, the Donnas, and other notable bands), produced 15 songs at the school's recording studio. Only five songs were mastered and made it to the EP. The record was never distributed, and, sadly, the other songs didn't make it to vinyl.

Email interview with Karen Irving, 2020

Q: What was Fairhaven College like?

Karen: Fairhaven College is a cluster college of Western Washington University. It was a very fun, adventurous, and progressive place at that time. Without grades, our work was critiqued by our mentors, and we created our own majors… 'concentrations.' The classes delved into non-traditional studies—in non-traditional ways... and we learned better how to learn—I think... or to think, I think.

I took classes in meta-communications, radical feminism, global religions, Marxist economics, linguistics, and organic gardening... and did lots of different types and forms of music—which I loved. Operettas, a barber shop quartet, madrigals, choirs, and the bands.

We would also take traditional classes at the larger university—if our interests led us there. I took physics classes, and some other science classes—music theory and voice lessons, and a lot of dance there.

Q: I know Penelope Houston went there—did you ever meet her?

Karen: Penelope Houston lived in the same co-op dorm that I did. We had set up several co-op dorms there—Oren was in the one a couple of buildings over. We cooked and ate together—a big old household type of dormitory.

If I remember, Penelope was a real youngster—like in her mid-teens, I think—when she came to college. I used to call her Peeps. I adored her and would watch her watching all us older students very closely—sitting back and drinking it all in. I was in a barbershop quartet at Fairhaven, led by Professor David Mason, with Penelope's brother Mark. He was beautiful and gentle and had a lovely tenor voice.

Q: When did you start making music?

Karen: I took piano lessons when I was very young. As a kid, I would sing along with the radio all the time. I was in a glee choir and musicals in junior high—and a friend helped me learn to sing harmonies during our lunch hours.

When I was at Fairhaven, Oren invited me to sing in a spontaneously formed band for a Valentine's Day dance—that night. Wet Paint became a working tavern band that toured the Pacific Northwest (PNW) for many years. I was in the band for about three years.

I spent some time perusing my musical history and found the first album I ever sang on YouTube. Rebecca Valrejean's *Songs for Silent Lovers* in 1976. Rebecca was very bold and out during those challenging times. Check out her one-woman play, *The Lavender Troubadour.*

Q: What about the writing process—when did you get involved?

Karen: One of my thoughts is that I didn't ever think that I was in a leadership position in Art Object. I felt that we were all in it together. We were a group of musical friends creating together in a wonderfully playful and adventurous way. We all had enthusiasm and willingness. We all led or stepped back in moments.

Anyway, I seemed to have a whole lot to say at the time... a lot bubbling up... so I wrote and co-wrote a lot of the songs. We all had creative input. Several of my songs were written from a specifically female perspective, expressing things about the societal inequities within the U.S. and things that affected me from my personal history—some with anger, some with humor. This certainly influenced the band's direction. Though, there was a lot to the

Karen Irving performing live with Art Object. Photo by RDB.

band—improvisation—experimenting with instrumental and vocal sounds and rhythms, songs ranging from rebellion to Jim's puppy and more.

I am so thankful that I was so embraced and had the opportunity to make music and say whatever I wanted to say in that music; however, I wanted to say that within this band, I am honored I got to create with such incredibly talented and playfully creative musicians.

I am very lucky.

Q: What did you love about creating music with your comrades in Art Object?

Karen: I loved that we laughed a lot together, and I loved all the talent, playfulness, and creativity.

I think we as a band were pretty unique and spontaneous, and I think we all enjoyed the freedom of that. We all had a multitude of different things, music, experiences, which influenced and guided us. Some in common, some not.

Q: Where all have you lived?

Karen: I grew up in Los Angeles, mostly, and moved to Bellingham for college, after a year working in the Sierra Nevada and traveling in Mexico.

I left Bellingham many years ago... starting with a year living in London, England with Myles—working in bistros and movie theaters. I had a lot of musical experiences while there… busking with Myles in the tube stations, performing at the London Musician Collective, playing with the Axminster Orchestra, improvising with Phil Minton, creating music with Fred Frith in the RAI[1] in Rome, traveling around Europe with Obstacles—a women's multi-media improvising group with musicians, dancers, and shadow puppetry.

When we returned to the Pacific Northwest, Art Object did one more gig. I studied at WPI—and after several years of study, I was ordained. I moved to Vashon, Washington, then Seattle. I had to move again and couldn't find a place to rent. Some friends helped me out and gave me shelter with them. I ended up (mostly) living there for several years.

Jumping ahead, I had worked as a clairvoyant reader and healer, and I did several years of volunteer environmental work and bird surveying. After a difficult injury from a hit-and-run car crash, I slowly returned to life by turning to music again—playing at community centers with mostly street folks. Some of the people were wonderful musicians, and I found it an easier place to be broken while I was healing. Socializing with healthy, active people was way too much for me at the time. And the woman that ran the music sessions at the community center was very kind, patient, and understanding. I began to pick up the guitar, share my singing and harmonies, and embark on a different musical adventure.

After many years of enjoying myself and that community—playing music several times a week for the joy of it, meeting new people, having lots of opportunities to share with others, and performing occasionally—it came to a point where I had to face some hard truths, and I sadly left that life.

Q: Were you motivated politically to make art back then? Are you politically motivated now?

Karen: Sure... sometimes it was something specific. But one is at least affected by just being part of the larger picture of America—figuring out where you fit or don't fit in, and then expressing your sense of self in this world. Even if someone tries to remain politically uninvolved, that becomes a political stance because this country is not benign. It's inescapable.

We called it "Living in the Belly of the Beast" when I was growing up. When I was young, we watched so many people in pain and dying in Vietnam every day on our TVs. (This was before the U.S. stopped allowing free and honest journalism that shows the reality of war.) We saw the corruption of Nixon. We had the Cold War with Russia—with nuclear attack drills at school. We marched to end the war, and we marched to gain civil rights for everyone.

America has been too full of itself for as long as I know about, preaching righteousness while wreaking violence and destruction around the world—down the road—and setting the tone for violence inside the home—for its own callous selfish motivations.

In the time of Art Object, we had been acting to stop a nuclear power plant being built in our area for a few years. Three Mile Island had just melted down in Pennsylvania. We also continued to fight for civil rights and against American imperialism. The same fights for human rights and dignity continue today... some have come back as the *exact* same fights after all of these years.

This country remains slow to move—ignorant of its own truths—and it often, painfully, resists a better way.

Who knows what is on the horizon next.

Q: Yeah, it seems like people with different political philosophies live in entirely different realities…

Karen: I was listening to an interview with LL Cool J on *The Beat with Ari Melber* yesterday. They were talking, and LL repeated this quote from Rabindranath Tagore. I think it is beautiful in its harsh clarity, and since you like words, I would like to share it with you.

The quote: "Power takes as ingratitude the writhing of its victims."

Then LL said: "In other words, I put my foot on your throat—your neck—and you disrespect me when you bleed on my shoe."

Whew…huh? That word "ingratitude" rings some bell. ●

---

1 RAI or Rai is Radiotelevisione italiana, the national public broadcasting company of Italy. It has been commercially styled as Rai since 2000 and it was known until 1954 as Radio Audizioni Italiane.

THE BRAPHSMEARS

Portland, Oregon » Formed in 1980

MEMBERS

Shellee Harper Post
a.k.a. Ami L. Nitrate { VOCALS
Mish Bondage { BASS, VOCALS
Lesley Reece
a.k.a. Suzi Creamcheese { BASS, GUITAR
Angie Mima { VOCALS
Leesa Nation, Suzette, Crystal { DRUMS

"OK! This song… could be about someone YOU know," the singer announces. "It's called… 'She's a Cunt.'" A honky-tonk bass and lopsided guitar riff duel, and the lyrics jet in:

"She's just a cunt, cunt, country-western girl…"

The song descends into chaos as an untuned, distorted guitar gushes over the rhythm section and singer Shellee Harper Post (Ami L. Nitrate) shrieks, telling a story: "I went out on the street the other day… and this girl, see I live right outside of the west hills, ya know… and there are all these people running around in their stupid jogging suits, and it really makes me sick…" Bassist Michelle Miller (Mish Bondage) says the song is about "a snotty society girl who looked down her nose at us wild punk girls."

The Braphsmears, a band inspired by and friends with the Neo Boys, turned out two Sado-Nation singers (Leesa Nation and Michelle "Mish Bondage" Miller) and shared a song ("Messed Up Mixed Up"). They were loud, abrasive, and years ahead of riot grrrl. Church of Girl documents the history of the band: "People either worshipped them—or hated them— and they frequently experienced an ashtray or partially consumed pitcher of beer flying in their direction."

In the late '70s, the future Braphsmears met as teenagers in Portland. All having moved to the city for one idea or another, they connected through their affinity for music. They learned about the artists they loved in music mags, radio, and mutual friends, listening to everything from Karen Carpenter to AC/DC.

The girls lived together, dropped acid together, saw Devo together, and then decided to form a band together. True to their own selves and aligned with the raw energy of punk, they formed an all-girl band and named it after the stains on a girl's underwear. Whether it was German slang they learned from an older friend or they just made the word up, there is no consensus. They behaved wildly on and off stage, wore mix-n-match clothing, and didn't give a shit about rules. Vocalist Angie says, "We were quite disdainful of being lumped into anything, but it was still somehow easier at that age, in that time, to work with other girls."

While guys in the Portland music scene were supportive and may have seen the inclusion of women at all as evidence of a "gender balance" in the scene, the girls in Braphsmears felt that there were nuances and microaggressions men wouldn't have been aware of.

Mostly, they were around to be wild and have fun. The Braphs experienced a few members come and go, and after two years as a band, broke up. Members joined other bands, moved out of Portland, and moved on to other things.

Email interview with Angie, Shellee, Mish, and Lesley of the Braphsmears, June 2020

Angie Mima sadly passed away in October 2020 and this is likely her last interview.

Q: What brought everyone to Portland? What drew you there?

Shellee: I was in a band from Ashland, a great band called Felix. I was the singer, and Angie was a fan of the band. We met and became fast friends. I was 16, she 14. I quit school, wanting to go to a city. It was San Francisco or Portland. I decided on Portland. It's smaller so I could work on my chops. I stole some jewelry from my parents and hocked them in Portland. Got an apartment. That same day, Carlotta Court. Tammy saw us and introduced us to Mish. The rest is history.

Angie: Yeah, pretty much how Shellee puts it. I quit school the first day of my junior year with my mom's permission. All we wanted was a band. I was barely 16, Shellee was 18, and we were determined.

Mish: I grew up just outside of Portland. Originally, we were in Happy Valley, and I would have attended Clackamas High School but ended up moving out to Gresham. I was 15 and met Jerry A from Poison Idea; my brother was in bands with friends and family of the Ice 9 guys, so I was drawn into the punk scene. Jerry A's mom lived in the apartment complex near our duplex at the time, and he and I became friends. He would tell me about the scene and when shows were happening. I moved to Hollywood with my girl Johnny Cat in late 1984, and we spent a couple of years there before returning to Portland.

Lesley: I grew up in an area that was literally nowhere, in between Portland, Beaverton, and Tigard. The metaphor was not lost on me. The area I lived in is part of Beaverton now. Portland was close, but I did move to San Francisco in the '80s, and now I'm in Seattle.

Q: How did you all meet?

Angie: I was 16. And Mish moved in with us at our studio at Carlotta Courts for a while. I remember the loft bed in the big closet that Mish put up somehow. And yeah, Tammy lived downstairs from us. We got to Portland in September 1980.

Shellee: I was 17 Angie was 15. My God, we got in trouble! Everyone who came to town was there. I think Mish and Lesley had an apartment in the Northwest. I remember dying my hair pink and black. I thought I was Dave Vanian.

Mish: Lesley was one of my earliest friends in the scene, and we were besties! We had a couple of apartments together. The night that Devo played, we took acid. I lived in a small studio apartment near the Galleria up on the top level, and the lift there was rather

wonky. Someone gave my address out at Devo, saying the party was at my place. So many people showed up they ended up breaking the lift that night. I was run out of that apartment by the manager. After that, Lesley and I got our first apartment together. We had a couple of apartments, and at one time, the Braphs had an apartment in an old building owned by an old Russian anarchist. We wanted to start a band, and we met Ami (Shellee) and Angie, we already knew Leesa Nation from Sado, and we got together after that and formed the Braphsmears.

Lesley: I met Mish first at Urban Noize around 1980. I was 17. We were drinking quarts of beer outside. I don't remember the show. She said she wanted to start a band, and I was in for that, but we hung out a lot that summer; we took acid and went to see Devo. I might not be remembering this right, but I think Angie and Shellee had moved into the same apartment building with one of Mish's and my friends (Tammy Stotik), and that's how we all met.

Q: How did you get drawn to punk music? What were you listening to?

Angie: Ashland was a really small, backwoods kinda town in the '70s. I was always listening for something new. My little brother's girlfriend, who moved up from California, introduced me to the Clash and Siouxsie. I also hung out with a lot of older college guys who played Devo and the Sex Pistols for me. Then Shellee and I became friends. She had somehow got her hands on X's first album, *Los Angeles,* and came straight over to my house. We sat on the floor and listened to it closely, all the way through. At the end of the album, we went out on the porch to smoke cigarettes and ended up writing our first song together, "Institutional Hangout." We were inspired! "Los Angeles," the song itself, really got to me. When you listen to that song now, it's loaded with racism and homophobia, but what I got from it around the age of 15 was that I wanted to go where that other girl wanted to leave.

Shellee: Shit, I was listening to everything! X was a favorite. We haunted the little record shop "Singles Going Steady." We didn't have any money, so we would listen to what was hip. We met so many important people there. The reason I got into punk was my first ever boyfriend, Bob Noxious. We were dating in high school in California. I'm the only member of the band from California. Bob was the

The Braphsmears performing live. Photo by Janice Morlan.

lead singer from the Fuck Ups. We met in high school my freshman year. We were 14 then. Punk wasn't even a name yet. In terms of what I listened to: my favorite singer is Karen Carpenter, my favorite composer is Burt Bacharach, and my favorite lyricist is Bernie Taupin. Isn't that a twist!

Mish: My brother, Matt, is a guitar player; he now owns his own custom amplifier business called Miller Ampwerks in Portland. I grew up in a house where rock 'n' roll was always played in the basement. Matt was playing in a band (after we moved from Clackamas to Gresham) and he always had guitar and rock magazines around, so I would often peruse those. My brother was more of a prog-rock guy, and I just couldn't get into that. I listened to Iggy, Bowie, Black Sabbath, the Sweet, Thin Lizzy, the Saints, Elvis Costello, Rockpile (Nick Lowe and Dave Edmunds), Clash, Pistols, Stranglers, and the Ramones. That was all it took. Once Suzi and I became friends, a whole new musical world opened up; we had a lot of the same taste musically. Also, my close friend Leatherboy Chad who was really into the early English punk stuff would bring me records of all the early British punk

bands. He was a big influence on me. I've lost touch with him, but I've tried over the years to find him.

Lesley: Music magazines were the first place I heard of it. I liked *Creem*, *Crawdaddy*, all those, and punk was making things interesting. I loved Lester Bangs in particular, and I wanted to be a journalist, so I just read magazines all the time. I liked a lot of different kinds of music already; there was a lot of really good funk music back then, and there were more conventional rock bands that were disrupting that end of the spectrum, like AC/DC. I saw AC/DC open up for somebody, and they just owned everything.

I liked how short and good their songs were because a lot of the popular stuff back then was prog rock with like 800 keyboards and songs that were 20 minutes or longer. Boring! Who's got time for that? I already liked blues and stuff, and I liked glam pop music like Bowie and Sweet. The first place I got to hear a lot of new music was Joe Carducci's show on KBOO[1] on Sundays which I always taped, and then I'd listen to the tape over and over, and that was all the really crazy old stuff like the Mekons, Glaxo Babies, Electric Eels. But I also would just go to the used

---

1 A community radio station in Portland.

record store and buy records for a buck because why not. That's how I discovered the Saints (from Australia) and, believe it or not, the Ramones.

Q: What does 'Braphsmears' mean?

Shellee: I came up with the name! I thought it was insanely funny. It's the panty stain on a girl's underwear! Now I was kinda leading the band. I thought it was hilarious! I just love a good cry your eyes out laughter. Too bad we never made shirts. Shit, I'll make my own with a sharpie and sign it myself! I don't know what 'Braph' means. I just made it up.

Angie: Nope. That's not how it came about, Shellee. It was this guy, Rick Stanek. He was an older kid who lived next door to me from when I was 10. I didn't really know him, but then when I was 15, I went to a garage show in east Ashland and ran into him. He was like seven or eight years older than me, but we got to talking. He knew so much about Patti Smith and literature, and he had a killer record collection. HE told me (possibly Shellee was there too) that it was German slang for the stain on a girl's underwear. Never knew if it was true or not, but the idea was rad. We already had the name before we left Ashland.

Mish: Shellee threw that one out. We thought... oh... a raw band of all teenage girls who can barely play named after panty stains... yup that's us! We figured that was pretty shocking. At one point, a recording was made of a live set which we put on cassette and sold in a Ziploc baggie with a pair of used panties. "The Scratch n Sniff Panty Cassette." Fifty were made, I believe, and some are still in existence.

Lesley: I have no bloody idea. Seriously. I think Shellee thought of it, but I don't remember ever asking her. It was her thing, so I just went with it because I couldn't think of anything better!

Q: How did being women impact your experiences in Portland music at the time?

Angie: I think it made us more obnoxious, if anything. We were quite disdainful of being lumped into anything, but it was still somehow easier at that age, in that time, to work with other girls. Portland's scene was really diverse, though, and we didn't really get shut out of it.

Shellee: I guess it was cool, the dudes would rib us sometimes, but if you look at the photos, we are playing Poison Idea's equipment, and they are standing in front!

Mish: I grew up being the little sister of the boys in the band, tomboy and athletc. My brother was the 'musician,' so I was the tagalong. Having grown up in a house with rock bands, I knew from a young age that I wanted to rock and roll. I wanted to be as good as 'the boys.' I could never be a pin-up. I would take no prisoners. Punk gave us a platform where it was OK to not necessarily be the best, and a safe enough place to take a chance. The older musicians mentored us and supported us to take the next brave step to get out there and make music. Lesley played bass, and she was good. We made a strong team and once we met the other girls, we realized we could be a force of nature or at least make a ruckus. I think with the Braphs we were all already somewhat different and adamant to be 'who we were,' no apologies. I never wanted a male or female audience to like us because we were hot or cute. Hardcore was just coming up, and I could unleash all of my primal energy and angst with this music. I never saw women as my competition, I felt like we were all our own personalities which we were comfortable with. My role models early on were Johnny Rotten and Poly Styrene and I wanted to be a combination of the two. I wanted to be a strong female voice with a snarl. Like Lesley, I didn't want to be a good *girl* vocalist. I wanted to stand on my own two feet. I was purposefully ambiguous as far as presentation of my gender identity. I wanted to be accepted for my songwriting, stage presence, and vocal presentation skills alone. In Portland, there were several women in the early scene, so we didn't have an issue there. Later, when I was fronting Sado, we tried to play the On Broadway. I had been out partying with people at the Vats. My band went in early to sound check along with my drummer's girlfriend who was very striking. I came along a bit late and tried to get in for my soundcheck. I was in army boots, boxer shorts with a skate, dirty from sitting in a van for days. They refused to let me in, said the 'singer' was already there. I called for Corboy to come to the door. He weighed the situation up, laughed and said put her on the guest list. What a surprise to the crew of the club when I ran up on stage and proceeded to own it.

Lesley: I was a pretty good bass player, and I was better than pretty good by the time I stopped playing in bands, but I was always "the best girl bass player" which I hated. Not that I was the best overall; Glenn Estes was better than me (just for one example!). But even "the second best" or "a good bass player" would have been better than "the best girl bass player" for fuck's sake!

I wrote the liner notes for a re-release of the Neo Boys stuff a few years back, which was essentially a personal essay about how I wanted to be in a band, but I wasn't old enough or cool enough, and worst of all I was a girl which meant I would have to be the singer. I am an OK singer, but I didn't want to be the damn singer; I wanted to play bass which I already knew how to do. Or guitar, which I sorta knew how to play and eventually got better at.

But I didn't know any other women in bands, and it seemed like an impossibility until I saw the Neo Boys up there wearing their regular clothes (not some spandex costume) and playing instruments. And that is why representation matters. I had no model for how I could be myself and be in a band before that. And then suddenly I did. Then I met Mish and for the first time it seemed like a possible reality.

I agree with Mish—I didn't see other women as competition either. That was one really good thing about the whole scene is the women stuck together.

Q: A male author from Portland wrote "there were [a lot of women in bands in Portland in the late '70s, early '80s]. No one even thought about it, either. There was no consciousness of achieving a gender balance. It just worked out that way." Did you all feel there was a total balance of genders in the music scene? Why/why not?

Angie: I wouldn't say there was a total balance. I also think you have to remember the times, and how strange we looked in them. The other people in the scene were all really pretty good and accepting of us, it was to the outside world that we were shocking. I took a lot of flak on the streets when I shaved my head, but the punks all loved it and remember it.

Shellee: Yeah, we took shit, but I wouldn't back down. It was new crazy for guys to deal with. One time Angie got a strawberry milkshake thrown on her head at McDonald's. Mark Rabner, a photographer we knew, chased the guy down,

Lesley: So, the short answer is, it depends on how you define "gender balance." As I said, there were a lot of woman musicians, but I don't think "nobody had to think about it" because we had to think about being

women and doing what we wanted to do. I don't think the male author fully appreciates how easy it is for a male to get up on stage and just play instruments and be himself. (If we are talking about the same male author, I believe he genuinely supported our right to play, although I don't believe he fully understood our work but that's another question.)

So yes, there was a balance in terms of sheer numbers, but not really in terms of gender as a whole. For women, there was and probably still is a whole other dimension of what we were "supposed to be" doing vs. what we were doing. What we were doing did not fit easily into a male fantasy (slutty girl, tough girl, slutty tough girl, mysterious chanteuse, whatever) and with some men, which meant they didn't know how to compartmentalize the sight of us.

Mish has reminded me that compared to some of the other women around, we were kind of crazy-looking. We got all our clothes at Goodwill by the pound and all our makeup at Newberry's (dimestore lipsticks—Hazel Bishop[2] would stain absolutely anything, but they were a buck). We did our own hair with varying results. Mine started out naturally orange but I hated it; I bleached it first and then I dyed it black. I painted leopard spots on Mish's head once when she wore it really short! So that's probably part of why some men didn't know what to do with us except accuse us of being lesbians. For me that was just confusing—I'm not a lesbian, but is that supposed to be insulting?

Men don't have to fight that, not really, because there's an expectation that they're going to get on stage and do their thing, whatever their thing is. They do not have to fit into a female fantasy to be valid. There is a longer history for male performers bucking stereotypes, like David Bowie of course but going all the way back to Little Richard, men were allowed to wear makeup and camp it up as long as they were on stage. It comes out in their recordings too, if you listen to the intro for Sweet's "Ballroom Blitz" it's very campy ("All right, fellas! Let's go!" and the very next

---

2 Hazel Bishop was an American chemist and the founder of the cosmetics company Hazel Bishop Inc. She invented the first non-drying, long-lasting, no-smear lipstick soon after World War II.

The Braphsmears performing live. Photo by Janice Morlan.

thing he says is "Well it's been getting so hard…"). But that song was a huge hit with everybody, including straight men.

I have no problems at all with gay or bisexual men or campiness, of course, but for me this just points out how much more accepting we all are of what men do versus what women do. The power dynamic was different; according to men we were not allowed to be our actual selves and rock out. They had to do something about it, like call us lesbians or throw milkshakes at us. Men didn't have that issue themselves, not as much and not because they were men.

Mish: I agree with Lesley, I wouldn't trust a male journalist to decide how easy it was for us as radical teenage girls to first of all figure out how to play our instruments, and then figure out song construction, and finally to get up there and perform and interpret it, especially in front of a group of men who were accomplished musicians already with years of expe-

rience already behind them in bands. The Neo Boys maybe had it easier. They were non-threatening. We just weren't. We were raw and wild, and we didn't play by the rules, we made them up as we went along. We also didn't take no for an answer. We did get labeled lesbians or dykes at the time. I was punched by guys more than once for my wild ways. People used to throw things at us on stage. Having said that… David Ensminger has written quite a bit on women in punk over the last few years, and he has a fair and objective and supportive take on our situation.

Q: In what ways was punk political to you?

Angie: All art is political. Punk just brings it right up in your face. If you make a statement of any sort, even an apathetic one, that is still political.

Shellee: I know that the music and performers have a message. I personally took the other route of avant-garde. I didn't want to fit the mold of what "punk" was. I didn't really care about it, still don't.

Mish: I was interested in current events and politics both nationally and internationally. I was curious about where we had our dirty little fingers and read everything I could find. I then would interpret it, and as a vocalist and lyricist, I had a platform to express my opinions. I used to write scene reports for *Maximum Rocknroll* and other smaller zines I often kept in touch with. I have mail from all over the world during that time period because young punks would write to me and tell me about their scene. There were quite a few young punk girls who would write to me and tell me about what they were facing, and I wrote back to every one of them and offered a supportive, strong female voice as much as I could. I think, for the most part, we were on the same page politically. We hated Reagan.

Lesley: I absolutely hated every atom in Ronald Reagan's shriveled brain and still do. For me, he was the face of everything bad that happens in this country—racism, sexism, fake moral panics, complacency in the face of AIDS, trickle-down economics, and suffering fueled by rampant capitalist greed. If I wanted to do something and I thought it might piss him off, those were bonus points. I could just see him wrinkling his nose at punk rock or Nancy going into a moral panic, so hell yes, I was in. If it would piss off his fascist robot followers, double bonus points.

Q: In what way did politics impact your attitude?

Angie: I am a child of politically minded, intellectual parents. Critical thinking has always been important to me. I also had a grandmother (RIP Celia) who always told me, "an empty can rattles the loudest, Angie," and from that I learned to actually have something to say.

Shellee: None really as I stated before. It's all a puppet show to me.

Mish: I later worked jobs at the local government level and eventually took a contract in Europe at the Parliament while I was completing law school in Britain. It opened my eyes as I had criticized enough as a punk on my own platforms. I found myself in a position of having to analyze legislation and the pros and cons of how it would affect not only the country, but a variety of constituents. I had to research my topics

and not merely voice my opinion. I learned tolerance and objectivity. I learned not to be a reactionary, but to weigh things heavily and try to find facts and background information to make an informed opinion or analysis. I currently work as a policy analyst with the state Department of Energy and while I have to analyze legislation and report on it objectively, I can take a stand with music. I tend to look at issues and not side with any party. The Braphsmears wrote songs about being radical teenage girls in a world that did not necessarily want girls rocking on stage. I don't think we wrote many political songs. I did later when I joined Sado-Nation.

Lesley: I wasn't "political" in the conventional sense other than being a feminist, but I didn't have a choice about being a feminist if I wanted any kind of life at all. There was a group of anarcho-syndicalists or something similar, but I never got into that. Clockwork Joe's was run as a cooperative, but it seemed like there were a lot of arguments about various petty bullshit and I'll be honest, that turned me the hell off. Especially when I could see that some animals were evidently more equal than others in that environment (mostly it was the older animals who were more equal and since I couldn't change my age I just kinda gave it the finger and walked away).

I always read the paper and watched the news because I originally wanted to be a journalist, and I wanted to see what all was going on in the country and the world. But I just wanted to live my life and make my own choices from the set of all available choices, not just approved choices for a white middle-class woman in that time and space. Doing that was itself a political act but that was as specific as I ever got.

Q: Can you tell me the story of "She's a Cunt"? What's it about?

Mish: The lyrics were a spin on words, they weren't about a country girl, more like a snotty society girl who looked down her nose at us wild punk girls.

Lesley: I loved that Johnny Cash riff. I was playing that at practice one day because I felt like it and Shellee and Angie, or maybe it was Mish, started singing "She's just a cunt, cunt, cunt, cunt, country-western gal!" Then we all laughed until we choked, and we worked it into a song we could play on stage. As I remember, it was mostly just the pun. I forget whether the lyrics are about an actual person, but I don't think so. ●

THE VISIBLE TARGETS

Seattle, Washington » Formed in 1982

M E M B E R S

Pamela Golden { GUITAR, VOCALS
Rebecca Hamilton { BASS, VOCALS
Laura Keane { VOCALS
Ron Simmons { DRUMS

>> A full-spectrum light show illuminates the musicians on stage. In a large room, silhouettes of audience members pogo in a packed crowd. The song is catchy and melodic; the scene could be a band cameo in an '80s teen flick. The music is an intersection of new wave and power pop, but the band's physical style—their attire and hair—feels slightly glam metal.

Sporting an elaborately coiffed mullet, the lead singer slings a low-hanging sunburst Strat, while a drummer in a muscle shirt, leather gloves, and spiked collar tightens his grip on his sticks. In an angular outfit, the bassist keeps a steady funk rhythm, and a third player, in the shadows opposite the stage, reels a cabasa.

The song, "Autistic Savant," is complex: a pop sense permeates, including a devotion to rhythm and melody, with a uniqueness only very studied or very creative musicians possess that pulls it toward avant-garde. Repetition of the chorus, "It's just a dream/it's not reality," requests listeners to imagine a parallel Earth where this band—Visible Targets—is as well-known as the Cars or Blondie (they should have been).

In another video for the song "Just for Money," the same musicians, three blue-eyed clairvoyants, who are real-life sisters, cast spells upon the rich. Their eyes sear through the screen, and their guitars are switchblades. Stand in a threatening, horizontal line at the front of the stage, it's clear they might jump you. They sing,

Back cover of the Visible Targets' self-titled 1982 12-inch. From the collection of Jen B. Larson.

> You! Just work for money
> We live on the edge of the poverty line
> How can u ever sleep at night
> When you know what rules the
>   middle class kind?

The song progresses at a rapid pace. Later the bassist sings a chorus nestled within eerie harmonies:

> You give them diamonds to depend on you
> I pay my bills, that's all I ev-er do!

On YouTube, mention of an unreleased video featuring men in penguin suits sparks discussion. The three mysterious sisters from Yakima, Washington—Rebecca Hamilton, Pamela Golden, and Laura Keane—are notoriously guarded about what they share with the world. Perhaps their collective perfectionist nature is why their songs are so worthy of mainstream praise.

The Visible Targets

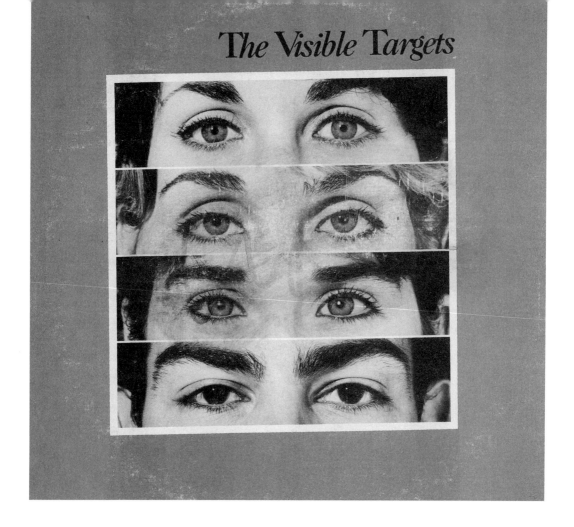

Cover of the Visible Targets self-titled 12-inch. From the collection of Jen B. Larson.

Before forming and naming the Visible Targets, the group spent years playing cover songs (and some time in England). Their original name, Wreckless, didn't stick, but describes a bellicose vibe woven throughout their aesthetic. And once they changed their name to the Visible Targets and began playing original songs, the group attracted a reliable fan base. Musically, producing unique rhythm-driven tunes with pop sense—strong melodies, attractive harmonies, and marked guitarwork—they didn't belong to one genre or scene, nor were they well understood, but they were eye-catching to their peers. Dennis White writes for Jive Time Records:

"It's no wonder that the band was often scoffed at by the supposedly hip, more cynical and 'serious' bands. The irony is those 'hipper' more cynical audiences always showed up at their shows… The Visible Targets were original, musically talented and…fun. They were secure in their musical talent and determination."

They recorded "Autistic Savant" with Mick Ronson and toured with Simple Minds in Canada. Considering their talent, drive, and well-connectedness, it's puzzling that the band didn't get much national attention. In 1980, the 'cassettezine' *Sub Pop 5* brought the Visible Targets to light for many, including Bob Jeniker, a successful record store owner in Portland and Seattle who founded Park Avenue Records (the label, with record store locations of the same name in Seattle and Portland). Jeniker had released the Wipers' "Alien Boy," "Youth of America," and "Is This Real." Taken by the Visible Targets' talent, he not only signed them, but became the band's manager.

The group disbanded in the early 1990s due to exhaustion, and while attempts to reunite have presented themselves, only bits and pieces have come to fruition. Their song "Life in the Twilight Zone" is a well-known and timeless local underground jam that still receives airplay. ●

BAM BAM

Seattle, Washington　»　Formed in 1983

M E M B E R S

Tina Bell ⟨ VOCALS
Tommy Martin ⟨ GUITAR
Scotty "Buttocks" Ledgerwood ⟨ BASS, VOCALS
Matt Cameron, Tom Hendrickson ⟨ DRUMS

» Searching for a location to shoot their sludge-metal single "Ground Zero," Bam Bam trespassed on a U.S. naval base before military police escorted them off and suggested a new location for them to film. Scotty recalls, "We didn't 'break'

in; we opened a gate and drove in for a bit. The military police showed up as we were straddling our bums over a short second fence. They weren't smiling. But they didn't have their guns pointing at us either."

In the video, the singer, Tina Bell, a stunning, short-haired vision clad in a white leather jacket, standing on rocks at the shore, grooves subtly while the band goofs around behind her. She mouths the line,

Don't want to be a dead hero

and looks up to heaven—or, perhaps, rolls her eyes—then pulls her gaze away from the camera and smirks. She gently sings,

Bam Bam photoshoot. Courtesy of Scotty "Buttocks" Ledgerwood.

Tina Bell singing live with Bam Bam. Photo by David Ledgerwood. Courtesy of Scotty "Buttocks" Ledgerwood.

Faced with opposition from mankind, that's not kind

In faster songs (such as "Goin' Down," "Villains Also Wear White"), Tina takes command of the stage, fires vocals fiercely, and throws her whole body into the performance.

Unlike most singers of hard rock groups in the '80s, Tina was both Black and a woman. And Bam Bam's down-tuned, overdriven, and riff-based guitar-work was recorded almost a decade before the mainstream heeded the sounds of "grunge." The influential sludge-metal post-punk Seattle band planted seeds for the genre but was omitted from compilations, ignored by labels, and breezed over in retrospective histories of the city's contribution to the rock canon.

To boot, essential artifacts of Bam Bam's legacy might have been destroyed for good if it weren't for valiant acts and divine intervention. In 2017, bassist Scott Ledgerwood was living at his in-laws' ranch. He had just moved his '56 Les Paul and precious Bam Bam master tapes out of storage into the house. When it caught fire, he knew there was no way he was going to stand there and watch as the band's work melted into the ground.

"It was like in those nature films when you see the waves crashing under the water…it looked like that except it was orange and black…rolling across the ceiling," he explains. The fire went up fast. The building was near old chemicals and tanks. Scotty recalls a refrigerator, full of soda water, exploding and pushing him out of the house. He broke an arm and got sliced with shrapnel. An oxygen tank shot perfect holes through the walls.

That's when the building where the tapes were started smoking. A firefighter standing in front told him he couldn't go in. "I was like, 'listen, man, I am going in there and you can either chase me or help me' and he chose the latter and that was way cool."

Less than a decade before, the tapes survived another natural disaster when a flood devastated guitarist Tommy's home while he was on the road. Stored on a shelf three feet off the ground, Bam Bam's master tapes avoided total waterlogging by mere inches.

Tina Bell died in 2012 after years of personal health struggles. Tommy, her ex-husband and the band's mastermind guitarist, followed her in death seven years later. The couple, who named the band after an acronym of their initials (Bell and Martin), also had a son, T.J. Martin, before even starting the band.

T.J. is a filmmaker and made a documentary about another Tina—Tina Turner. He told *The Stranger*, "My relationship with Tina Turner was unique in the sense that my early association with her is through people, like men on the street, hitting on my mom—not because they knew who she was but because she has a rock aesthetic," Martin said. "They would say, 'Hey Tina—Tina Turner!' That was the only other Black woman in rock they could associate her with."

Bam Bam was the first Seattle band to record at Reciprocal, with their EP *Villains (Also Wear White)*, but never made their roster. They headlined a 1984 show in which the Melvins—with Kurt Cobain as their tour roadie—opened for them. Bam Bam played scores of local fests, toured the U.S. and Europe, and played with huge acts like Alice in Chains and Guns n' Roses. They made music videos and were named Best NW Band on KCMU/KEXP by listeners.

The band formed at the tail end of punk and, alongside other acts like Green River, predated the rise of grunge by several years. They experimented with sludgy sounds, unconventional tunings, and key signatures. Tina's vocals vary between growls and vocal techniques, showcasing her depth of expression. Lyrically, she was irritated with the status quo and even realistic about death. Over thrashing guitar, in "It Stinks," she snarls,

> Everybody says this and that
> Their social commentaries on life.
> Where do I stand?
> Bitch and complain, it's not fair
> I think it stinks. But why should I care?
> Everybody says here or there
> they leave no room for simple
> compromise
> I don't believe in where you put your faith
> I just live for now. It's all make-believe
> But why should I care?!

Another song, "I'm Dead," launches with a vocal call and response, "So this is the end… or is it just another beginning?" but lands with Tina on a lead:

> I'm dead, I'm dead
> Well open the door
> I'll be for, and over, and of your life
> Don't worry, your work is done here

Forty years later, due in part to the stubborn determination of Scotty Buttocks (a name Tina gave him during the "Ground Zero" recording when the titles guy asked how his name was spelled—Tina piped up, "B-U-T-T-O-C-K-S!"), interest in Bam Bam has increased, with tributes to her coming from visual artists, writers, and music appreciators. Her son T.J. has toyed with the idea of making a documentary about his mother.

"She would be absolutely honored," Ledgerwood says. "She was a woman of awareness of herself… she knew she was good, but she wasn't arrogant about it.

She was very nonchalant. She didn't put herself above others… She was so different there was no one like her anyway, so it's not like there was a comparison of her and the others."

One-time drummer Matt Cameron (of Soundgarden and Pearl Jam) told KEXP, "I'd meet these people in Seattle that were just like…these kinda unicorn people like Chris (Cornell), and Kurt (Cobain) and Tina (Bell), (Mark) Lanegan, like all these like incredible singers, man."

Scotty describes meeting Tina the first time: he remembers Tina as talented and beautiful, with hypnotizing and confident energy that today radiates through the band's music, photos, and film. Tommy and Scotty describe her as "cynical, loving, loyal, tough, generous, brooding deep thinker, a bit of a clown, quick to anger—quicker to laugh, socially bored, and politically angry."

Tina was an original and a natural. Growing up, her influences included Johnny Cash, Jim Morrison, Janis Joplin, Chrissie Hynde, and Metallica. Tina's mom was also an artist and songwriter.

In the early '80s, both the anti-woman and anti-Blackness of rock scenes was very palpable, and the band recalls multiple times Tina was called the N-word at venues the band was playing. Scotty recalls an incident that still enrages him.

"In Seattle [Tina] grabbed the mic stand, and with all of her 90-odd pounds, she swirled it around her head two to three times for centrifugal assist and smashed both these skinhead wanks in the front row. She fuckin' NAILED 'em!…Tina stormed off humiliated and fucking furious. Tommy dove into the fray with his guitar still strapped on, but the crowd was already clearing them out…Took a while for Tina to calm down enough to come back and finish the show."

But, when asked why the band didn't see more success, Scotty later contends, "Tina didn't want to say it was racism. Bell had a harder time than I did believing that was part of the issue, but it was clearly a big part of the issue. Just a lot of questions. It's puzzling. I don't really know the answers…I know there was a little friction with the band and some of these entities…But overall, I have no idea."

Although Bam Bam didn't get the recognition they deserved during her lifetime, their legacy lives through their music and in Tina's image. In the last few years, the counterculture has picked up on her story and amplified it in the media. Bric-a-Brac Records released an LP of their work; fan art has been shared; and, potentially, a future documentary about her life is in the works. ●

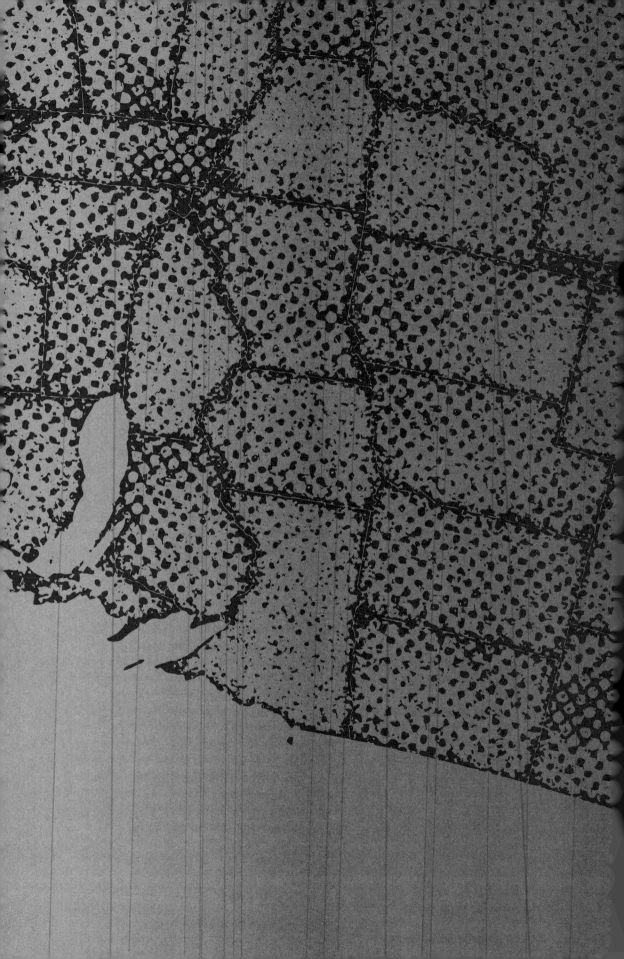

WEST COAST (SOUTH)

Manic in a Panic

BACKSTAGE PASS

Los Angeles, California » Formed in 1976

M E M B E R S

Original Lineup

Joanne Russo a.k.a. Marina Del Rey
a.k.a. Marina Muhlfriedel | KEYBOARDS
Joanna "Spock" Dean | BASS, VOCALS
Genny Body | LEAD GUITAR, VOCALS
Holly Beth Vincent,
Ché Zuro | RHYTHM GUITAR, VOCALS
Rod Mitchell, Michael Ruiz | DRUMS

》On the timeline between the Runaways and the Go-Go's sits a band crucial to the advent of L.A. punk: Backstage Pass. Groupies-turned-performers, the ladies of the band had their hands in everything, all while influencing and making space for the scene known and documented as early Los Angeles punk. Their story, however, has not gotten its deserved space in that scene's history.

In 1971, long before Joanne Russo discovered the alias 'Marina Del Rey,' and before her move to England for college, a friend introduced her to bassist Joanna Dean (Spock). Marina says, "She wasn't Spock yet… she was Joanna, and Joanna knew how to play it. She knew how to meet guys; she knew how to flirt… she was this remarkable force."

Joanna gave Joanne a long list of tour managers' phone numbers, then, cross-referencing them against show announcements in *Melody Maker*, Joanne would call band tour managers and ask to get put on the guest list. Doing this, she regularly got backstage for Led Zeppelin, the Kinks, and Thin Lizzy (to name a few).

Having made connections in Los Angeles, the two girls, along with other friends, would charm their way backstage. They met Genny Body, a teenage runaway from outside L.A., in 1976 at a Dr. Feelgood show. According to themselves and others on the scene, the

girls of Backstage Pass were "legendary groupies." Pleasant Gehman remembers hanging out with them at the Continental rooftop's "Riot House," the Starwood, the Masque, and many after-parties.

Spock confirms, "[We were] unapologetic groupies, and I think the fact that that was a big part of us, and that we were proud of it, added to the band."

It was between the crossroads of glitter and punk that they formed a band. "It was spontaneous," said Marina Del Rey, whose pseudonym separated her from her workaday persona as Joanne Russo, editor for *Teen* Magazine from 1975–1977.

A year after the Runaways were assembled (truthfully, Joan Jett and Sandy West started the band, and their notorious producer glommed on) and a good two years before the Go-Go's formed, the mostly all-girl band Backstage Pass began on a whim. Doing it more for fun than fame, Backstage Pass helped usher in early L.A. punk—for everybody. Marina recalls:

"Kim Fowley invited me to see the Runaways at the Whisky [a Go Go]. I got there and I was watching these porny girls prancing around in their bustiers and garters and doing this cherry bomb thing and it was appalling to me because it didn't come from anywhere. It was so manufactured—some fantasy. I was embarrassed. I mean, who am I to know they would find great success. But in the moment, I was appalled…"

After the show, down the block at the Rainbow Bar & Grill, drinking wine with girlfriends, she shared criticisms of the Runaways. (Marina remembers in conversation with Alice Bag that over time she grew to admire and very much respect the band members—Joan Jett, Lita Ford, Cherie Currie—all the girls—but that something about the performance irked her.)

"I said 'we can do better!' Of course, we never were better—it had nothing to do with it. The instinct in the moment was 'I'm gonna do this because women can have bands for themselves. We don't need Kim Fowley or any man molding what we do. No one is

Cover of *Backstage Pass 77*, Backstage Pass' retrospective tape (recordings from 1976–1979). From the collection of Jen B. Larson.

ever going to tell me what to wear. No one is ever going to put cherry bomb lyrics in my mouth.' I just wanted to turn the dial 180 degrees from that."

Begrudgingly, she decided she and a gang of gals were going to start a band, and when KROQ DJ Rodney Bingenheimer (known for breaking new bands like Blondie, the Ramones, and the Sex Pistols, as well as sparking interest in local bands) walked by their table, she shouted, "Hey Rodney, we started a new band!" He asked, "What's your band?" and she said, "Backstage Pass!" The name flew out of her mouth.

"We hung around with a lot of bands. Backstage Pass was part of our fluency, our life," she muses. "Between knowing so many bands and industry types and interviewing artists for magazines and Westwood One AND getting to know bands while hanging out at the Rainbow, Rodney's English Disco, the Roxy, and other clubs, I was almost always able to coast backstage."

Backstage Pass attracted press before they even played together. Talk of the band appeared in British music newspapers *Melody Maker* and *Sounds*, as well as Rodney Bingenheimer's column in *Phonograph Record Magazine*.

They rehearsed for a while and were finally goaded into playing their first show, opening for the Damned. In the scene, the girls of Backstage Pass were friends

with and fans of all the usual suspects. They were instrumental in the L.A. punk scene; Marina even co-signed the initial lease for the Masque as a favor to its Scottish owner Brendan Mullen. The venue, which hosted some of the first performances of the Bags, X, the Go-Go's, and the Alley Cats, was their home base, their clubhouse. They rehearsed there, hung out there, and sometimes slept there.

Spock said, "Women showed how creative and ballsy they were and inspired both men and women to be in bands."

Marina muses: "It wasn't really consciously about breaking down doors at the same time…but I knew somewhere in the back of my mind that by doing so we would encourage other people to do it, maybe inspire other people to do so. I just really wanted women not to feel controlled creatively."

Women within the L.A. scene generally got along, supported one another, and fangirled each other; but not all women, especially the women who weren't in bands, automatically supported one another. Spock recalls a time when she defended the band against an envious girl in the audience harassing the band, jumping off stage to fight her. And Marina recalls, "I saw people roll their eyes and shrug their shoulders, but that didn't really bother me…The irreverence, it

MANIC IN A PANIC

157

Spock, Marina, and Genny of Backstage Pass playing live. Photo by Donna Santisi.

was more about how you felt, how you put yourself out there than whether you went to Juilliard or Berkeley, had some fancy music degree. I think punk was liberating and it was so fucking fun."

Genny dressed as half feminine, half masculine. Splitting her clothing in half—one side a bra and garter belt, and the other, a vest and jeans—as well as half-face makeup. "It was a yin/yang kind of thing…" she says, "a psychic they/them kind of thing…My thought process was, I'm gonna play guitar, I don't care that I'm a girl playing guitar. I want to play electric guitar, too."

Growing up, Genny Body, the band's guitarist, had been playing guitar since age eight and picked up the electric guitar in high school, and as she recalls, the people at her school thought she was a freak.

"I don't remember getting a lot of love playing electric guitar as a girl…There were a lot of guys in bands, and they were kinda like, 'no.' But then I met these kids who lived in Hollywood, and they were way more into it."

To find her kind, she would travel to Hollywood, frequenting Rodney's English Disco and the Rainbow. She even auditioned for the Runaways while still in high school (Kim Fowley told her, "yeah, you need to lose weight") and years later was considered to play bass in the Go-Go's during one of their transition phases (she said, "They ended up with Kathy, which was the better choice").

She says, "The punk scene was the perfect scene for me to express myself—I really needed it—I had a lot of hurt and anger that I needed to release in some

kind of way… Anybody was accepted in that scene… so it was happening organically; we were coming from this glam and dinosaur rock…" After her mother's death, the guitar is what pulled her through.

Influenced by the Kinks and the Beatles, Genny and Spock co-wrote and co-sang most of the songs. They played extensively up and down the California coast (with Devo, the Mumps, Wall of Voodoo, the Nuns, and opening for Elvis Costello's first U.S. tour), were featured in seminal punk publications (*Back Door Man*, *Slash* Magazine, and *Flipside*), and captured by luminary rock photographers (Jenny Lens, Brad Elterman, and Donna Santisi).

Other Backstage Pass members included Ché Zuro (of the Orchids) and Holly Beth Vincent, who later went on to create Holly and the Italians (and also sang in the Waitresses for a short spell). With Holly and the Italians, Holly Beth Vincent is known for the song "Tell That Girl to Shut Up."

Outside of the band, Spock also played bass in MnMs and managed Redd Kross; in fact, the band's song "Legend (Come on Up to Me)" was covered by Redd Kross in the underground cult film *Desperate Teenage Lovedolls* (made by SIN 34 drummer David Markey) with Spock singing lead. Marina Del Rey played in the Vidiots and formed Vivabeat, which got signed and toured the world. Genny was in the first lineup of Screamin' Sirens and became a wardrobe stylist, co-founding Strait Jacket and working as a personal stylist for Linda Ronstadt and working with the Bangles. ●

THE BAGS

Los Angeles, California » Formed in 1977

M E M B E R S

Alice Bag { VOCALS
Patricia Morrison a.k.a. Pat Bag { BASS
Craig Lee { GUITAR
Rob Ritter { GUITAR
Terry Graham { DRUMS

>> The idea for the Bags began during hours-long three-way phone calls between a group of girl-friends. Initially, they were supposed to be an all-girl glam band. But once punk took over counterculture youth consciousness, the group became a new concept entirely, taking on many forms before settling into their classic lineup.

In her memoir *Violence Girl*, Alice Bag relives the details of the Bags' existence—starting with the excitement of inventing band names with Patricia and Marlene (Lipstick and Femme Fatale were strong contenders). She documents the trials and tribulations of getting a dedicated group together, personal relationships, and the wild parties with friends and through the band's final moments.

In the mid-'70s, teenage Alice and Patricia swooned over flamboyant rock stars like Elton John and Freddie Mercury, dreaming of playing glam rock themselves. However, they encountered a few obstacles. "We were unsuccessful [at creating a glam band] for a variety of reasons. One important reason was that we didn't have the technical ability required to perform the type of glam we most liked (Queen or Mott the Hoople)," Alice writes on her website. They also moved on from glam once they saw their first punk show. That show featured the Weirdos, the Zeros, and the Germs. Alice writes, "It was an unforgettable night. I think seeing the scope of diversity, creativity, and raw nerve that was presented on that stage really struck a chord with us."

Back cover of "Survive," the Bags' 1978 7-inch.
From the collection of Jen Lemasters.

Patricia contends that they faced dismissive misogyny as they worked to put a band together. She says, "Boys at the time thought we were so darn cute. Didn't take us seriously at all." When some did, however, they reluctantly let guys in the group on a trial basis. They landed on the name the Bags, a concept in which they would play with paper grocery bags on their heads, concealing their identities. The band played up and down the West Coast for about two years, piling into cars to travel to San Francisco, sharing stages with the Neo Boys in Portland, and getting into trouble in Hollywood.

Often dubbed 'hardcore before there was hardcore,' the Bags attracted wild audiences, where rambunctious youngsters let out their inner rage, and sometimes even incited violence. Alice commanded the stage. She was chaotic, raucous, and powerful as a singer. In a black-and-white video of their song "Violence Girl" from the Troubadour in 1978, Alice explodes onto the stage wearing a baggy white collared shirt over a T-shirt and thigh-high fishnet tights. She shakes so erratically the collared shirt almost slips down her arms. Halfway through the song, an audience member launches a chair on stage, and when it's apparent her microphone isn't working, she commandeers the one in front of the guitarist.

Alice's lyrics were poetic, political, and aggressive. In "Babylonian Gorgon," she sings,

> Don't need no false reasons for
>   why I'm out of place.
> I don't goose-step for the masquerade.
> I don't scream and twist just for the
>   fun of it.
> I'm poisoned blood when I'm pissed!

And,

> Don't want! Don't need!
> The seed that you sow!
> Get out of my way I'm ready to go!
> Tear down, rip up your idol's photograph.
> They do it all just for a laugh

And,

> Here I go Babylonian gorgon.
>   I'm gonna babble babble on

Alice has often described the early punk scene as being fluid and free. She said, "The early punk scene was one of diversity of class, gender, ethnicity, education, religion, sexual orientation." And, "Most of us had punk names so it was sometimes difficult to make a quick assessment of someone's ethnicity based on their last name. Also, a lot of us dyed our hair crazy colors, wore tons of extreme makeup, and wore customized thrift store clothes which made a person's ethnicity and economic background difficult to gauge."

Once the scene went from colorful outsiders finding their own styles to a black leather jacket uniform, the band checked out. Parties, drugs, and personal differences all contributed to their demise. Although the band never achieved their desired all-girl status, their influence and contributions toward women's empowerment in the L.A. scene cannot be understated.

After years of estrangement, Alice and Patricia reunited, and Alice interviewed Patricia in 2015. She asked Patricia how she saw the role of women in the Los Angeles music scene. Patricia responded,

"I wouldn't look at it as the role of women, it was a field of equality. Anyone could do it. It was shocking to a lot of people on the outside but within the scene it was fine, it was acceptable, it was as it should be."

Patricia later played in the Gun Club, the Sisters of Mercy, and the Damned. Alice played with Castration Squad and at least seven more bands (Fun House, the Fire Engines, She-Riffs, Afro Sisters, Cholita, Las Tres, Stay at Home Bomb, to name a few).

"Punk rock has evolved over time and there have been periods when it seemed to be dominated by aggressive, straight white male energy, but those periods didn't last. I think women, people of color, queers, and anyone who identified as 'other' were always involved. Even when bros in leather jackets were trying to push us off the dance floor, we've persisted. Punk has found its way back to its roots, which means inclusivity, diversity, a rejection of conservative patriarchal values, and challenging the things we want changed in our world." —**Alice Bag**

Email interview with Alice Bag, 2021

Q: Someone recently said to me that men dressing and behaving more effeminately in music in the late '60s and early '70s opened the doors for more women to be taken seriously holding guitars and playing rock. What is your take on that?

Alice: When guys in glam bands started wearing dresses and makeup, it wasn't always consciously done as an assertion of gender fluidity though it definitely had that effect. Some of those early rock musicians were just dressing the part while others were expressing who they genuinely were. Performers like Wayne County (who transitioned to become Jayne County) made a huge impact on our thinking about gender. Other rock dudes might have just enjoyed experimenting with their appearance and presentation without being fully aware of what their actions meant to others. I think that exposure to androgyny was helpful in opening up new possibilities of gender expression but I'm not sure that it opened doors for female musicians; perhaps it just left the door unlocked for women who wanted to push it open? I believe in the importance of intersectionality,

Cover of "Survive," the Bags' 1978 7-inch. From the collection of Jen Lemasters.

so when gender roles are questioned by trans musicians like Jayne County or Laura Jane Grace, those gains have a ripple effect. Even if advancing feminism may not have been the principal goal, having a more gender-expansive way of thinking inevitably creates more opportunities for people pushing against gender stereotypes.

Q: What is a particular power that women hold?

Alice: People who are oppressed have the power to use their experience as the fuel for change. There's a saying that what doesn't kill you makes you stronger and I think it's true. Life can be like boot camp. If you're constantly facing, jumping over, or smashing hurdles, you become better at getting past them than those who travel a smooth road.

Q: When did you notice that the music industry was male-dominated? Do you think it still is? Did you see it as being as male-dominated in the same way as, say, a construction business or the workforce of the '60s/'70s?

Alice: I noticed the male dominance pretty early on. I grew up reading comics and watching Saturday morning cartoons and I remember how exciting it was to see a band like Josie and the Pussycats. Even though they were a fictional band, imagining that an all-female band like that could exist was inspiring. I don't remember seeing any real all-girl bands when I was growing up, but that doesn't mean they didn't exist. In fact, I know now that several of them did exist, they just didn't receive the type of support that male bands got. I think the whole idea of domination is not so much about whether female bands or musicians exist, but about who makes the decisions about who gets financial support, who gets publicity, who is seen as and remembered as a "serious" musician.

In the 1940s, there were all these women joining jazz bands, playing as well as or better than male musicians. They were allowed opportunities because so many of the male jazz musicians were off fighting in WWII. Those women briefly enjoyed the freedom and appreciation that is usually reserved for men. Bands like the International Sweethearts of Rhythm were popular and successful until the war ended, then they were expected to "step back" into more traditional female roles. That domination manifested as a lack of access but there are many kinds of domination

and subjugation of female musicians. Some are obvious and overt; others are more insidious.

I don't know enough about the construction business to make an informed comparison.

Q: How and in what way did punk change the music industry? Culture?

Alice: Punk provided an alternative to the big corporate record labels. The existence of small indie labels and of DIY pressings meant that artists could be more creative and diverse without feeling like they had to try to appeal to record labels that were driven by the bottom line and were more likely to be moved by profits than by talent.

Q: In Violence Girl, *you mention that as a little girl you always imagined yourself in an all-girl band. Do you know where the desire originated?*

Alice: Probably from *Josie and the Pussycats*. I think that comic book writers and science fiction writers are visionaries who feed our imaginations and help us stay open to possibilities of what can and should be.

Q: What's the first image you remember of women holding guitars or playing drums?

Alice: As a child, I'd seen female musicians in other genres. For example, in mariachi music you might see a woman playing a guitar or a guitarrón or violin. On the occasions that I saw a woman in a predominantly male mariachi, I thought it was cool. Mariachi members typically sing together and take turns being in the spotlight and supporting each other, so to me it looked like an egalitarian situation. Of course, those instances were rare; when I was growing up, mariachis were typically male.

Q: What were the most challenging obstacles you met when trying to form that all-girl band?

Alice: It was hard finding female musicians who felt confident enough to want to join up. My earliest experience of women entering the male-dominated music world was strange because it seemed that every woman I met, regardless of her skill level, felt she wasn't good enough. It was like widespread imposter syndrome. The lack of visibility in the rock world had convinced many women they couldn't play rock. That's why punk was so important. Punk wasn't skill-centered, it was about creativity, uniqueness and nerve—in other words, the perfect place for outsiders. Punk was good for women and women were good for punk because punk is at its best when it's amplifying new and original voices and that's what we had in abundance.

Q: Women comprised much of the punk scene as writers, artists, musicians, and photographers. Why do you think women's roles in early punk were originally diminished in the "history" of the genre?

Alice: Who was telling the story? We need people to tell their own stories, otherwise the old patriarchal structures will surely erase those that don't mirror its goals and makeup. We need to look at the patriarchy as a structure that has to be attacked on many different fronts because it is constantly attacking us on many different fronts. To defeat patriarchy, we need to not only make culture, but we must also disseminate, archive and fight against erasure. It's a lot of work but we can do it!

Q: How did the women "quietly lead by example"? What is meant by "quietly"?

Alice: I think many women who were part of the early punk scene weren't always aware of the power they were wielding. It felt natural to us, because of course, it is natural for women to have power. In the early L.A. punk scene, most of us were surrounded by men who were not threatened by us, so we didn't outwardly come out as feminists. We just went about our business treating punk rock as if it was our baby and we were going to own it, which we did.

Q: You published Violence Girl *in 2011. What do you think about all the books and documentaries coming out now about women in early punk today? (More than ever!)*

Alice: I think it's wonderful! I want to see more books by women, queers, trans folk, Mexicans, Filipinas, African Americans, Asians. I want to read a book about the Deaf Club in late 1970s San Francisco and find out more about the Deaf experience of punk rock.

Q: Why do you think punk takes these turns from being diverse and inclusive to straight white male energy and then back?

Alice: Because people with power want to hang on to power and the structures that support the straight white rock star are already in place. The rest of us are fighting an uphill battle but damn, but that stuff can get boring. Creativity and originality are on our side!

Q: How would you characterize the similarities and differences between the women of early punk, riot grrrls, and the current punk scenes?

Alice: We've all experienced different punk scenes, so we all interact with our realities in different ways, but the feeling of empowerment only grows stronger with each generation. For example, the work of Chilean feminists Las Tesis—their performance of *Un Violador en Tu Camino*—was an international tidal wave that could not have happened in 1977 but today a feminist collective in Chile can write a song that gets translated into different languages and is performed by women across the globe—without a record company, without radio play, without management or tours. That shit is powerful! This generation is powerful. Of course, I see the work of so many women forming the foundation of what's happening today. From Violeta Parra to Pussy Riot, from the Sweethearts of Rhythm to the Linda Lindas: there's an international, intersectional, intergenerational connection.

Q: How does economics impact punk?

Alice: I think punk can function pretty well outside of traditional economic limitations. Punks have always been resourceful, and DIY recordings are very common, as are homemade tapes and self-produced records. Some of us work with small punk record labels for support with distribution and manufacturing but those labels are largely owned by members of the punk community who are invested in the scene and want to help it grow.

Q: What economic and/or political structure do you think we need to better meet people's social and cultural needs?

Alice: We need to support music, art, and dance in public schools and provide a more accurate narrative of American history. It's no wonder that some stupid white dudes think they're the center of the universe, because that's exactly what they're being taught. And I don't just mean history textbooks, I'm tired of seeing all those buildings and streets named after "important" white men, all those white men's faces on our currency. Let me earn some Tubman Twenties, let me drive on Dolores Huerta Street, let me take a class at Wilma Mankiller University! ●

THE CONTROLLERS

Los Angeles, California » Formed in 1977

MEMBERS

Kidd Spike, Johnny Stingray | GUITAR, VOCALS

D.O.A. Danny | BASS

Charlie Trash, Gaye Austin, Hillary Dillary,
Karla "Maddog" Duplantier | DRUMS

» In 1977, when Controllers drummer Karla "Maddog" Duplantier was 21 years old, she worked for the U.S. Postal Service. She recalls in her blog, "I had two priorities then: fix up my 1970 Mustang and buy every punk rock record I could get my hands on." After hearing "Sheena is a Punk Rocker" on *Rodney on the ROQ*[1], she went out and bought the record immediately. She wrote in her blog, "My brother looked at me

and said, 'These guys rule,' and I said, 'It's about time somebody started playing the real true rock 'n' roll.'" She continues, "I began practicing my drums more furiously now cuz I could smell the return of rock 'n' roll. So, I started learning every Ramones song, every Dead Boys song, Blondie songs that I liked."

Karla's brothers gave her the nickname "mad dog" because of all the trouble she would get into. She began playing drums her senior year of high school because she was forced to choose a fine arts class. She told *Search & Destroy* (#11), "I didn't want to go to college—there was nothing I wanted to take. Then I took drums, and I said, 'I want to be a musician.'"

Unconvinced she'd find a punk scene in L.A., she thought she might need to relocate to New York. In Los Angeles, she'd go see New York bands playing live. She writes, "I had a few days off in September, so

---

1 A radio program (hosted by Rodney Bingenheimer) that ran on the Los Angeles rock station KROQ from 1976 to 2017.

The baddest Mad Dog drummer on the West Coast is KARLA MICHELLE DU PLANTIER the only black girl in punk rock, and undoubtedly the best girl drummer. She drums for LA's THE CONTROLLERS, with KIDDSPIKE on guitar (he broke one the last time they played the Mabuhay) and multi-talented JOHNNY STINGRAY playing Fender Mustang Bass. They've got a recent 45 out: DO THE UGANDA/SUBURBAN SUICIDE/SLOW BOY, available from Siamese Records, 1214 Clark St. West Hollywood, CA 90069 ($2). And they're even better live -- they may move to San Francisco... (intv by Vale)

up!" And they used to b the time -- take his hoa B&D: Do you have a surf KARLA: No, I used to. in about 4 years, becaus real bad, and my doctor out of the water. I was my mom has it. I was re ing ALL THE TIME -- I was good at it. I was paddl Santa Monica Pier, it wa there were 6-foot waves. hard time breathing, and ed hurting. I thought, little tired, I'll go on

CONTROLLER : KARLA
MADDOG

I decided to go to Hollywood and terrorize the tourists by riding my skateboard up and down the boulevard and scaring the shit out of 'em, the Dogtown (Santa Monica) way." She had a custom skateboard and would skate with her brothers at Torrance Skate Park. She writes, "We were the only negros skating there but in the '80s our numbers grew." As she was skating home, she saw something that excited her. She writes, "A guy and a girl dressed like the punk rockers I'd seen on TV in magazines and on the records I had; punk rockers in LA!!!!!"

From them, she learned about a club where punk rockers were dancing. "I had found my place: I was gonna come back and join a band." Some of the bands she got to know were the Eyes, the Skulls, and the Controllers, who she saw play at the Whisky with the Dils, the Zeros, the Bags, and the Germs. She befriended Paul and Kira Roessler. The Avengers made a great impression on her. She called them "the best-looking band on the West Coast" and wrote, "They could play well. That mattered to me; it separated the real musicians from the bandwagon jumpers."

In 1978, she quit her job and joined the Controllers, who had formed less than a year before. The Controllers was founded by Kid Spike (Jeff Austin) and Johnny Stingray—two guys from Lansing, Michigan—in Santa Monica. They had a few female drummers before Maddog joined, including Charlie Trash, but Maddog's presence in the band is the most well-known. She called the year she joined the band "the happiest year of [her] life" because she was in a band that played rock 'n' roll "the way it's supposed to be played." They recorded and toured to San Francisco and Austin, Texas.

She wrote, "In June '79, the band broke up because of a stupid reason that I'll only explain if you

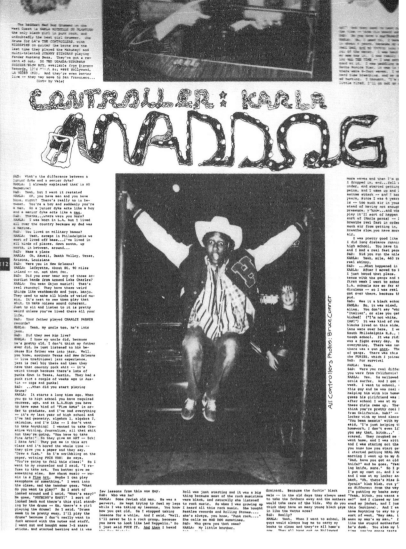

Opposite page: Karla Maddog shooting a carnival rifle with bandmate, featured in *Search & Destroy* #10. Photo by Bruce Conner.

Above: Karla Maddog goofing around as Penelope Houston looks on. Featured in *Search & Destroy* #10. Photo by Bruce Conner. From the collection of Jen B. Larson.

call me on the phone and I can talk about it, but it's too fuckin stupid to write down."

After the Controllers broke up, Maddog went on to be in many bands over the years, including Sexsick with Black Flag's Kira Roessler, Legal Weapon, and El Rey. She lived in San Francisco and London, where she attempted to play in Siouxsie and the Banshees, and attracted the likes of Malcolm McLaren, who helped promote her band Jimmy the Hoover.

Though they formed before she joined, Karla is credited with helping the Controllers get attention in L.A. Her personal magnetism combined with her promotional skills and talent on the drums attracted audiences, press, and show opportunities. ●

CASTRATION SQUAD

Los Angeles, California   »   Formed in 1980

M E M B E R S

Mary Bat-Thing a.k.a. Dinah Cancer { VOCALS
Shannon Wilhelm { VOCALS
Alice Bag { BASS
Tracy Lea { GUITAR
Elissa Bello { DRUMS
Tiffany Kennedy { KEYBOARDS
Phranc { GUITAR

❱❱ In a live performance of "A Date with the Late Jack Kennedy," the goth rock intro—a three-note bassline and steady drums—kicks in and two frightening figures, a stoic, pale black-haired beauty wearing dangling cross earrings, and a hooded platinum blonde, both wearing dark lipstick and thick black eyeliner, turn their heads in the same direction before delivering a deadpan ode to the deceased president.

Before the advent of death rock, there was Castration Squad. The group of militaristic goth women supported, and almost achieved, the impossible mission not to smile. Their work was so silly, however, that laughing was inevitable. An interview following the performance reveals the group's bizarre obsession with JFK and RFK. Other songs the group sings are "No Mercy for the Dead," covers of the Cruella DeVil theme, and "Wild Thing" with lyrics changed to "Bat Thing."

Shannon Wilhelm and the Bags' bassist Patricia Morrison unseriously started Castration Squad one day. Their longtime friend Alice believed it to be a joke. But, later, after the Bags broke up, Shannon phoned Alice and asked her to play bass in the band, stating that Patricia was too busy. Alice, who wrote in *Violence Girl* that she didn't really play bass at the time, also never fully committed to the band,

always agreeing to play one more show, but remaining part of the lineup longer than she anticipated.

Probably the most important part of the project was that the full lineup of Castration Squad was a powerhouse of women, several from other bands or art projects on the L.A. scene. Besides Alice Bag and Shannon Wilhelm, the group included Mary "Bat Thing" Sims (Dinah Cancer) of 45 Grave, Tracy Lea of Redd Kross, Phranc (who also played in Nervous Gender and Catholic Discipline), and Elissa Bello, original drummer of the Go-Go's. (Several of the members also formed an offshoot band, the Cambridge Apostles.)

Their platform, based on Valerie Solanas' *SCUM Manifesto*, read:

> Life in this society being, at best, an utter bore and no aspect of society being at all relevant to any woman, there remains to civic-minded, responsible, thrill-seeking girls only to undermine the government; to reasess [sic] and reorganize the senseless, archaic legal system (and initiate a more effective method of enforcement), to stop the blind acceptance of implausible media role models, to re-educate apathetic female puppets who distort the image and impair the evolution of women… and to repair men.

The band predated many goth rock bands in its sound and imagery. Other than the track "The X-Girlfriend" which appears on the vinyl-only Redrum Records *Killed By Death #13* LP (a collection of '78–'83-era demos from bands that never put out a record), and "A Date with Jack" on Alice Bag's *Violence Girl* compilation, no official recordings of Castration Squad have been released; however, demos and live recordings are in circulation. ●

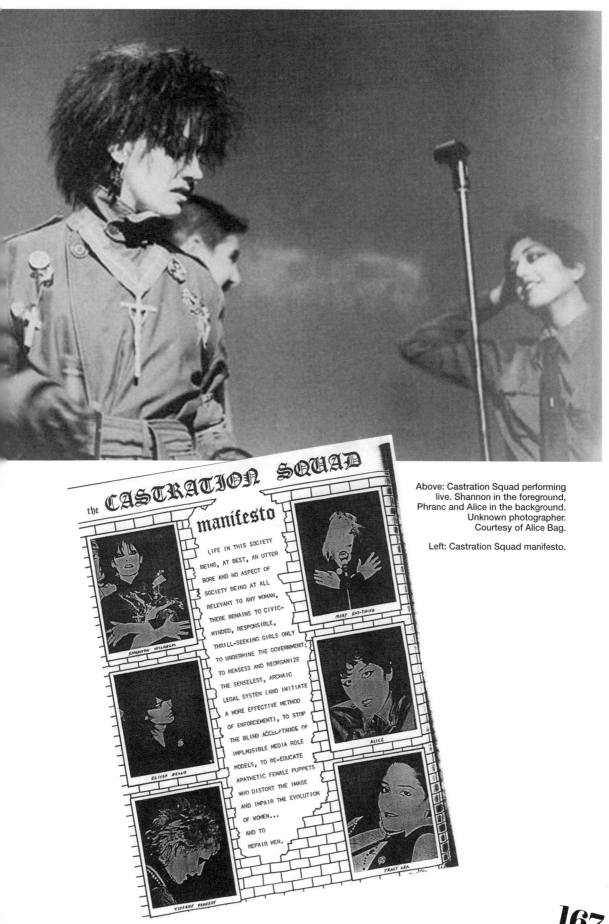

the CASTRATION SQUAD

manifesto

LIFE IN THIS SOCIETY BEING, AT BEST, AN UTTER BORE AND NO ASPECT OF SOCIETY BEING AT ALL RELEVANT TO ANY WOMAN, THERE REMAINS TO CIVIC-MINDED, RESPONSIBLE, THRILL-SEEKING GIRLS ONLY TO UNDERMINE THE GOVERNMENT; TO REASESS AND REORGANIZE THE SENSELESS, ARCHAIC LEGAL SYSTEM (AND INITIATE A MORE EFFECTIVE METHOD OF ENFORCEMENT), TO STOP THE BLIND ACCEPTANCE OF IMPLAUSIBLE MEDIA ROLE MODELS, TO RE-EDUCATE APATHETIC FEMALE PUPPETS WHO DISTORT THE IMAGE AND IMPAIR THE EVOLUTION OF WOMEN...
AND TO
REPAIR MEN.

SHANNON WILHELM

ELISSA BELLO

TIFFANY KENNEDY

MARY BAT-THING

ALICE

TRACY LEA

Above: Castration Squad performing live. Shannon in the foreground, Phranc and Alice in the background. Unknown photographer. Courtesy of Alice Bag.

Left: Castration Squad manifesto.

167

THE ALLEY CATS

Los Angeles, California » Formed in 1977

MEMBERS

Original Lineup
Dianne Chai { BASS, VOCALS
Randy Stodola { GUITAR, VOCALS
John McCarthy { DRUMS

As evidenced by their recordings and live performances, the Alley Cats are pure L.A. Chai plays lean basslines, alternating between punchy root notes and scales that tether the drums and guitar together. Her vocals soar soulfully with a sense of urgency. In "It Only Hurts the First Time," she wails:

**Life is just one small moment
We are born and then we die
It only hurts the first time**

» It's maddening that a band could be so well-loved by fans, so righteously recorded and photographed, so attractive and respected by their peers, but their story exists with barely a trace in the history books, minimal mentions in blogs, no memoirs, few to no interviews. For many reasons, their legacy is their music; but their story is somewhat of a mystery.

They were a husband-and-wife-fronted punk trio who frequently played Hong Kong Café, the Masque, the Whisky a Go Go in Los Angeles. And they regularly trekked up to San Francisco. In the late '70s and early '80s, they put out an incredible recording, broke up, and re-emerged as a different band with a new name (as the Zarkons, with the additions of Terry Cooley and Freda Rente') in the mid-'80s that didn't get as much attention and vanished.

Dianne Chai-Bass, vocals
John McCarthy-Drums
Randy Stodola-Guitar, vocals
Cover & photos by Fayette Hauser
Produced by Randy Stodola &
DANGERHOUSE
LOM-2

Back cover of "Nothing Means Nothing Anymore" / "Give Me a Little Pain," the Alley Cats' 1978 7-inch back cover of first pressing. From the collection of Jen Lemasters.

ALLEY CATS

nothing means nothing anymore

Cover of "Nothing Means Nothing Anymore," the Alley Cats' 1978 7-inch (second pressing).
From the collection of Jen Lemasters.

On their only LP, *Nightmare City*, her bass work underscores every song, and she takes lead on another song called "Too Much Junk" on the perils of the drug that wreaked havoc on many in the scene. Despite the little notoriety the Alley Cats have received, David Ensminger gives the band a lot of credit in his book *Punk Women*. He credits Chai with "[creating] a template for a pre/post-hardcore sound that remains ever distinct, wiry and powerfully cogent." ●

THE EYES

Los Angeles, California » Formed in 1977

MEMBERS

Charlotte Caffey, Jimmy Leach { BASS, VOCALS
Joe Ramirez { GUITAR, LEAD VOCALS
D.J. Bonebrake, Joe Nanini { DRUMS
David Brown { ORGAN

>> In *The Go-Go's* 2020 documentary, Kathleen Hanna calls the Eyes' "Don't Talk to Me" a feminist anthem. It certainly has a riot grrrl appeal. The song is the perfect punk concoction: simple and catchy, with what seems a predictable hook with one off-kilter note that sets it apart. The lyrics don't surprise but arm you against strangers and enemies alike. Playing bass, the future Go-Go Charlotte Caffey sings,

Don't talk to me
Don't look at me
Don't talk to me
Oh yeah!

Promotional photo of The Eyes circa 1978.

Before playing lead guitar and composing hits like "We Got the Beat," co-writing "Head Over Heels" and "Lust to Love," and adding a touch of magic to "Vacation" for the Go-Go's, Charlotte Caffey played in a three-piece outfit called the Eyes. The band had a handful of other song titles like "Little Girl From Hell," the hopefully tongue-in-cheek "Kill Your Parents," and the auspicious "Go-Go Bee," none of which she sang, but played bass frenetically.

Charlotte was a trained musician with a music degree and began writing songs at 15. In the Eyes, she frequently played at the Masque with them before joining the Go-Go's. When Belinda Carlisle asked her to join the Go-Go's, she couldn't pass up the opportunity. On Pleasant Gehman's podcast *The Devil's Music*, Belinda reveals that the group had their sights on Charlotte because of her musical competency. "She knew how to plug her guitar into her amp," she says, laughing.

The fate of the Go-Go's hinged on its members crossing paths in the early L.A. scene. In an excerpt from John Doe and Tom DeSavia's *More Fun in the New World: The Unmaking and Legacy of L.A. Punk*, Charlotte Caffey writes, "I was fortunate enough to be living in Hollywood, CA, when the underground punk rock music scene started. It was a small group of artists, misfits, and weirdos, where everyone was welcomed and encouraged to express themselves." ●

SUBURBAN LAWNS

Long Beach, California » Formed in 1978

M E M B E R S

Su Tissue a.k.a. Sue McLane { VOCALS,
KEYBOARD, BASS
Vex Billingsgate a.k.a.
William Ranson { BASS, VOCALS
Frankie Ennui a.k.a.
Richard Whitney { RHYTHM GUITAR, VOCALS
Chuck Roast a.k.a.
Charles Rodriguez { DRUMS
John Gleur a.k.a.
John McBurney { LEAD GUITAR

» On a large stage, a band kicks off an upbeat song. The camera pans around the stage. Wild boys in mismatched clothing groove with their instruments and a composed, expressionless girl with straight, long hair and a Victorian dress sings into the microphone, looking down at the floor.

It's not possible to know her impression of the band, because enigmatic Suburban Lawns multi-instrumentalist and singer Su Tissue has never been one to speak to the press. She once proclaimed to the *Los Angeles Times* that "interviews are obsolete." The reluctant star of the group rarely spoke in band interviews or appeared on film in live performances. Su left behind a trail of spellbinding performances and recordings, inspiring a near-cult-like obsession from fans across generational lines. Fans have learned through years of attempts that she doesn't want to be found. What we can do is appreciate what she left us.

The band's most famous work, the pre-MTV music video for Suburban Lawns' iconic jam "Janitor," is somehow less bizarre than the song itself. In the video, a periodic table prefaces images of the band. The screen flashes between color reversals and transition slides to reveal the band in shiny

alien outfits. Singer Su Tissue appears in a series of costume changes, mouthing lyrics in deadpan lip movements, dipping between monotone and high-pitched squeals. She sings:

> All action is reaction
> Expansion, contraction
> Man the manipulator
> Underwater, does it matter
> Antimatter, nuclear reactor
> Boom boom boom boom

According to band members, the song was about the dangers of technology, and the costumes were all Su's doing. From the first verse, the rise to the chorus unfolds with Yoko Ono-esque vocalizations in the second. Then begins the chorus everyone remembers, laughed about, and loved. Su wrote it herself. She sings:

> I'm a janitor
> Oh my genitals
> I'm a janitor
> Oh my genitals

The video was put together by filmmaker Denise Gallant, who also did the effects on "Baby"—a video Su Tissue imagined into existence.

The backstory is that the band were friends and began making music in Long Beach, California, in 1978. Cal Arts students Sue "Su Tissue" McLane and William "Vex Billingsgate" Ranson joined with the latter's hometown friends Richard "Frankie Ennui" Whitney, Charles "Chuck Roast" Rodriguez, and John McBurney (a.k.a. "John Gleur"), as well as another friend who left the band early on. They played around Los Angeles as Art Attack and the Fabulons before dubbing themselves Suburban Lawns.

Influenced by the convulsive art-rock of bands like Devo, Talking Heads, and Richard Hell and the Voidoids, while rebelling against pop outfits like the Beach Boys, the group achieved an authentic sound. Humor

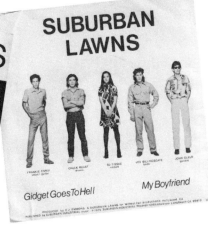

Left to right: Back cover of Suburban Lawns' self-titled 1981 12-inch. Back cover of "Gidget Goes to Hell" / "My Boyfriend," Suburban Lawns' 1979 7-inch. From the collection of Jen Lemasters.

SUBURBAN LAWNS continued

was undoubtedly integral to their writing process. In an interview in *Vice* in 2015, Frankie remembers, "We wrote a bunch of pretty funny songs and started playing around L.A."

Chuck chimes in: "We always strived to be original. We were a terrible cover band. We were always lampooning something. We could get pretty silly and laugh a lot at rehearsals. We didn't take ourselves too seriously."

And the band was popular. By 1979, their debut single "Gidget Goes to Hell," a song written as a satirical take on the Gidget franchise[1], had a music video directed by Jonathan Demme, later famous for directing *Silence of the Lambs* and *Philadelphia*, featured on *Saturday Night Live*. Suburban Lawns received regular airplay on KROQ, and the first single sold out its first pressing. They played with locals the Dickies, X, the Germs, Black Flag, and Geza X. They opened for huge touring acts like Bow Wow Wow, U2, the Clash, Siouxsie and the Banshees, Oingo Boingo, and Ultravox, growing their audience each time.

Su's performances intrigued and impressed audiences. In a 1979 live review in *Slash* magazine, the author penned:

"When Su Tissue sings, nothing else matters. I don't even know if she's got a great voice (their really good single doesn't quite convey what's it's about) or if she's sexy or anything, all I know is that you can't keep your fuckin' eyes off her, so strange is her presence, so surprising is her way AROUND the songs."

Noting her authenticity, Chuck said: "What you saw and heard from Su was unvarnished and uncalculated. It was an extension of who she was; very organic. She had a wicked sense of humor; a reluctant star."

Su espoused a unique, unconventional fashion sense, never smiling, and wearing blow-up pants, three-piece suits, pumps with nails driven into the soles, aggressively clashing patterns, Victorian blouses, and prairie dresses. She played with makeup sometimes but didn't apply it for sex appeal. She mostly objected to performances being recorded live. A few were, but Su's performance was best understood live. It has been said she expressed a range of conflicting emotions, interacted aggressively and sarcastically.

Due to internal band conflicts, the band broke up in 1983. Su attended Berklee College of Music, where she studied piano and recorded a captivating if not hypnotic solo album with three movements, *Salon de Musique*. She also played a side role in the "Gidget Goes to Hell" director Jonathan Demme's 1986 comedy movie *Something Wild*. In it, she played the role of Peggy Dillman, an uncomfortably and charmingly awkward pregnant wife of a Manhattan suit.

But these days, Su Tissue's whereabouts are shrouded in mystery, and it seems as though she'd like to keep it that way. Rumors from message boards and online social channels include bizarre claims like *she's been a lawyer for 20 years*, that *she had her Ph.D. from Stanford in astrophysics by the time she turned 14*, that *she has a 194 IQ*, and also, *she memorized Ovid in Latin and recites in seven different languages effortlessly*, that *she is a suburban housewife*, and the most likely answer: she disappeared from public life and is living a quiet life doing whatever the fuck she wants. ●

1 Based on Frederick Kohner's 1957 novel *Gidget, The Little Girl With Big Ideas*.

THE DINETTES

San Diego, California » Formed in 1979

MEMBERS

Doriot Negrette Lair { VOCALS, SONGWRITING
Joyce Rooks { GUITAR, VOCALS
Lisa Aston-Emerson { LEAD GUITAR
Sue Ferguson Delguidice { KEYBOARDS
Cindy Brisco { BASS
Irene Liberatore-Dolan { DRUMS

>> An all-women five-piece powerhouse fleshes out a set of quirky new wave songs at the Deaf Club in San Francisco.[1] Phase-delayed guitar and herky-jerk drums underlay the melodic chanting of Doriot Lair, who wears a waitress' apron and gesticulates wildly, blinking her eyes at the audience with a purpose. A lyric from the first song ("social norms") punctuates the standard structure. By the finale, it descends from the bridge into a half-time drone.

The Dinettes are defined by spirited performances, potent songs with pop and blues precision, and a robust sound. In an earlier iteration of the band, they called themselves the Cockpits. They decided "Cockpits" was a funny name for an all-female band and recruited a group.

Guitarist Joyce Rooks studied classical music and was a trained cellist. She had been reading about the Sex Pistols and other punk bands when she recognized punk as an opportunity to play music that "wasn't Boston," or whatever cock-rock was playing on FM radio at the time. In 2010, she said, "I had a guitar, and I had an amp, and I was looking for a band to play with. I joined the Cockpits in 1978 by answering a *Reader* ad," elaborating,

"I had a cello which I kept hidden, as it didn't seem punk rock enough at the time."

The Cockpits lineup was slightly different from what would become the Dinettes, and included punk pioneer cartoonist Shawn Kerri, who played drums. Kerri made posters for the Germs and most notably created the Circle Jerks' iconic 'Skank Man' (for which she received no compensation).

Their first gig was at a pub on the campus of the University of California San Diego, and they opened for the Alley Cats. They played with the Alley Cats a few times after that. Joyce said, "We were so blown away by Dianne Chai. She was such a great bass player."

The Cockpits played gigs and then after membership shifts, the group transformed into the Dinettes. In San Diego they were an anomaly at that time as an all-girl band. "It was both an advantage and a disadvantage," Doriot Lair told the *Chicago Tribune*. "People's insistence at calling us an 'all-girl' band really drove me crazy. I'd been brought up to be a feminist and it was really difficult to get away from people labeling us a novelty act. It was never about our musicianship, even though all of us were classically trained. It was: 'Oh, an all-female band.'"

She contends that the group met many obstacles in their brief existence. "We didn't have a chance; we weren't being taken seriously and I think that really affected what happened to us next..."

Rooks said, "It's still a sexist business, but it was pretty bad back then. All the stuff with the Runaways, and we had encounters with Kim Fowley. He came sniffing around."

---

1 The show was part of the Western Front festival in 1979, organized by Jello Biafra. It took place at the Deaf Club—the famous San Francisco social club for the Deaf.

The Dinettes in their original form as the Cockpits. Photo by their occasional backup singer and manager, Edie Paul. Front row (L-R): Joyce Rooks, Jolie Gardener, Doriot Negrette. Back row (L-R): Barbara Brouhl, Shawn Kerri.

THE DINETTES continued

The group traveled a handful of times to Los Angeles and San Francisco to play shows, and opened for a lot of familiar outfits who came to San Diego. They played with the Bags, Lydia Lunch, and the Go-Go's at the beginning of their career.

Rooks said, "The whole scene was happening in L.A. and San Diego was considered a joke. San Diego was always looked at as a sleepy Navy town, not to be taken seriously. It always seemed like even Orange County got more love than San Diego."

The Dinettes didn't put out an album, but they did release a single ("Poison" b/w "T.V.") and did two national tours. The Dinettes, like so many punk bands of the era, collapsed under the stress of touring, interpersonal conflict, and the constant struggle to get their music heard. It might have been the lost opportunity of their career when the band fell apart just as they had confirmed an opening spot for Joan Jett in 1981. ●

THE BRAT

Los Angeles, California » Formed in 1979

M E M B E R S

Teresa Covarrubias { VOCALS
Rudy Medina { GUITAR
Sidney Medina { GUITAR
Robert Soto, Michael Rummens,
Mark Stewart { DRUMS
Luis Soto, George Garcia { BASS

Front cover of generic black-and-white outer sleeve of "The Wolf," a single-sided 7-inch by the Brat with an unknown release date. From the collection of Jen B. Larson.

>> Unable to be neatly packaged, bought, or sold, the spirit of the Brat is the spirit of punk itself. Vocalist Teresa Covarrubias told *Razorcake* in their Eastside Punks series in 2020:

> "I always felt like an outsider, I didn't really feel like I fit in. And I think that whole punk thing when it came around, it sorta catered to the outsider in a way. It was sorta like a movement for people that didn't fit into the mainstream."

An introvert growing up with seven siblings in a Catholic family, who had been singing since her youth, Teresa wasn't totally comfortable going out or meeting people and felt socially shy. One night, attending the Jam's record release show in Hollywood with a friend, she ran into future Brat collaborator Rudy Medina, the brother of one of her schoolmates, and the two got to talking about music and their respective bands. At the time, Teresa was writing about her observations and personal experiences growing up in East L.A.—sitting on the corner at Yum Yum watching the world go by. Rudy, whose older brother had turned him onto glam rock, found punk and loved the simple approach to songwriting, despite being a classically trained musician. Rudy's nephew Sidney, who was close in age, joined them.

While experiences varied and a similar ethos united the punk bands of Hollywood and East L.A., there was still a relative divide forged by location, race, and class. Many Chicano punk bands from East L.A. were excluded from performing in many of the elite West Los Angeles clubs, where many—not all—of the punks were self-isolated from the status quo based on personal choice.

Because it was hard to get booked at Hollywood clubs, and another East L.A. band, Los Illegals, practiced down the block, they booked the Brat at a show at the Vex with the Plugz. The Vex became the East L.A. bands' DIY epicenter—a community of artists, painters, and poets who inspired new ways of thinking, performing in backyards and gymnasiums.

The Brat's sound was simple three-chord pop drowned in distortion and layered with powerful vocals with a political point and attitude. They started getting radio airplay, signed to Fatima Records, and put out the extremely rare and coveted *Attitudes* E.P.

While many Hollywood kids were reluctant to come to East L.A., John Doe and Exene Cervenka of

THE BRAT — STRAIGHT OUTTA EAST L.A.

FEATURES BRAND NEW MIXES OF SONGS FROM THE BRAT'S LONG-OUT-OF-PRINT EP "ATTITUDES," PRODUCED BY SINGER/ GUITARIST TITO LARRIVA OF L.A. PUNK LUMINARIES THE PLUGZ

INCLUDES THE COMPLETE "ROTHCHILD SESSIONS," THE BRAT'S NEVER-RELEASED TEN-SONG ALBUM RECORDED UNDER THE AUSPICES OF LEGENDARY RECORD PRODUCER PAUL A. ROTHCHILD

1. SLAUGHTER OF AN ANCIENT TRIBE†
2. VICIOUS LOVE
3. SWIFT MOVES*
4. LEAVE ME ALONE*
5. STARRY NIGHT*
6. TOMBSTONE BLUES†
7. THE WOLF
8. THE PROMISE†
9. HIGH SCHOOL*
10. MISOGYNY
11. BRAIN SPARKS
12. ATTITUDES*
13. CORNER OF THE WORLD
14. THE CRY†
15. INDIAN INK TEARS†
16. HARD SOMETIMES†
17. BELIEVE†
18. JUST ANOTHER DAY†
19. SOLDIER†
20. IT'S A CLIMB†
21. WE ARE THE ONE

Executive Producer: Rudy S. Medina • Compilation & Direction: Michael Olsen
Drums: Mark Stewart and Robert Solo • Additional Bass: Lou Soto and Larry Arrieta

Additional Recording, Production and Mix: Anthony Valli, Helik Hadar, Mark Wolfson, Neil Citron and Carmine J. D'Amico, Jr.
Recording Engineer: Russ Castillo
Art Direction/Design: Mark Kalmus at Blue Fondue • Photos: Ann Summa
*Produced by Tito Larriva   †Produced by Paul A. Rothchild

To see our entire catalog of LP, CD and DVD titles, visit RockBeatRecords.com
© 2017 Mao Sounds. Packaging © 2016 S'more Entertainment/Rockbeat Records, 2934 1/2 Beverly Glen Circle, Suite 113, Bel Air, CA 90077.

THE BRAT continued

X came to one of their parties and asked the Brat to open for them at the Whisky in Hollywood. Because popular members of the West L.A. clique approved, they got an "in" with the Hollywood kids, and from there, more opportunities appeared.

But some of the opportunities didn't lead them to a road they wanted to be on. They got management and were being scouted by a major label and invited into the studio. Teresa was never impressed and grew increasingly skeptical. The band recalls the managers trying to play up their Chicano culture.

"We wanted to expand what a Chicano is but here were these guys playing up that image again," Rudy recalls.

Teresa tells a story of management renting a fleet of lowriders and driving them over to Capitol Records, then driving them around Hollywood blasting the Brat demo. "It was more people outside the group that started to label. They had these really strange expectations of what they wanted to hear. If you came from East L.A., you were expected to represent. What about these other bands, like from Hollywood? Did they have to represent their cultures too? No. It was always like this double standard."

Not wanting to bow to management's manipulation or be the pawn of a major label, the band leaned into their politically charged themes, addressing the experiences of Mexican Americans in the U.S. and the injustices waged against Indigenous people and women. In "The Wolf," Teresa howls:

THE BRAT

STRAIGHT OUTTA EAST L.A.

Classic '80s Pop Thrash
East LA's Punk-Rock Pioneers

Cover of *Straight Outta East L.A.*, the Brat's retrospective CD released in 2017. From the collection of Jen B. Larson.

The star-spangled wolf comes side to side
This land was made for all
So hard to grasp the logic, coming
    from its rabid paw
You say it's democracy, beliefs in our
    equality, you lied
The wolf and the lamb, the wolf
    and the lamb
We are the lamb

And in the (recorded 1985, but not released until 2017) song "Slaughter of an Ancient Tribe," she sings:

Sturdy sailing soldiers only conquest
    on their mind
Slay them, betray them, rob them,
    harm them, shoot them, pollute them

The band has expressed their feeling that working with a manager began their eroding—that their genuineness and creativity were soured, that management wanted to change who they were. In the mid-'80s, the Brat lost focus, broke up, and didn't release a full-length album until decades later. Still, their story is largely hidden in most accounts of L.A. punk history. ●

45 GRAVE

Los Angeles, California   »   Formed in 1979

M E M B E R S

Original Lineup:
Dinah Cancer { VOCALS
Paul Cutler { GUITAR
Rob "Graves" Ritter { BASS
Don Bolles { DRUMS
(*a handful of additional members*)

>> With an ethereal demeanor—her dark eyeshadow and lips, ever-changing hair color, and all-black leather jumpsuits or dresses decorated with crucifixes and peekaboo lace—Dinah Cancer, singer of 45 Grave, founded a lifestyle thronged with nightmare themes, religious paraphernalia, and human skulls. The sexy but brutal vibe didn't belong to a specific subculture at the time and opened the doors to several: death rock, horror punk, and even goth.

Far before it became a fashion, Dinah's cemetery vamp expression was original. "Back in the day, I didn't have Bauhaus. I didn't have Sisters of Mercy. I didn't have any of those bands," she explains, naming artists she and her bandmates likely influenced. "I basically had Judas Priest, Ozzy Osbourne, Alice Cooper."

45 Grave hosted a long list of L.A. punks in their members: Rob Ritter of the Bags and Gun Club; Paul Cutler, who went on to play in Dream Syndicate; Don Bolles and Pat Smear of the Germs. Three members of 45 Grave also played in Nervous Gender at one point, and the band practically shared a lineup with Vox Pop in their early years. They recorded a few singles in their first few years together and then put out their first full-length album—and their only single with the original lineup—*Sleep in Safety* in 1983. The band name came from a thrift store pin. The pin, which said "We Dig 45 Grave," made so little sense it was the perfect band name.

45 Grave's music conjures hauntings—with topics ranging from violence, demons, phantoms, cannibals, and even the vicious murder of a child—and musically, it's a pyre lighting up the sky. The album *Sleep in Safety* opens with "Insurance from God" as the voice of a life insurance businessman leads into a funeral organ. After the first minute, the song morphs into spooky sludge metal for another minute, bursting into a fast punk tune, and transitions back to a sludge jam with soloing heavily effected guitar, and thrashes back to the punk song. 45 Grave's start-and-stop motifs and tempo switches with sprinklings of psychedelia set them apart from the straightforward rock of the time.

Dinah Cancer, who went by Mary Bat-Thing and Mary Graves at the time, was also a member of Castration Squad and one of their offshoots, Cambridge Apostles. She was in Nervous Gender, Penis Flytrap, and later Dinah Cancer and the 45 Grave Robbers.

Like many in the L.A. punk scene, she was forever altered by the experience of seeing the Ramones and Runaways at the Whisky a Go Go. "That was 1978. I was hooked and found music that I related to," she told Alice Bag in an interview. "And from then on, I decided singing was my calling. It made me want to go out and put together a project and that was when I found Castration Squad."

45 Grave opened for the Damned and worked on the soundtrack for the cult classic movie *Return of the Living Dead*. She remembers, "At the time, we were just having fun going to shows and making music. We had no grand plan to be this influential band. We were just having fun. We were just surviving the times."

When asked in conversation with Alice Bag about the challenges women in punk faced, she had this to say: "Women have been underrated for years," and "the punk scene has been and still is an all-boys scene."

Explaining her perspective of the scene's evolution, Dinah says:

45 Grave

Cover of *Sleep in Safety*, 45 Grave's 1983 12-inch. From the collection of Jen Lemasters.

"In the early days, you had bands that were female-fronted or had a female member. Like the Bags, the Avengers, the Alley Cats, X, and the Go-Go's (they were a punk band way back when). Then, there was a period or gap of bands that had lacked female energy. In my era, I played on mostly bills that were all male. Beki Bondage (Vice Squad), Kira Roessler (Black Flag), and Exene Cervenka (X) were a few that had notoriety. We girls fought hard for our spots. I was part of the 1980–1984 wave and it was tough. Either there were a lot around or none at all."

45 Grave began to unravel in the late '80s with the breakdown of relationships and members' priorities shifting; by 1990, the death of Rob Graves put a definitive end to 45 Grave. Dinah took a short break from music to raise her daughters. She worked as a preschool teacher and ran the Ragnarök occult bookstore. She has since put 45 Grave back together with a whole new lineup. ●

TEX & THE HORSEHEADS

Los Angeles, California » Formed in 1980

MEMBERS

Texacala Jones { VOCALS
Mike Martt { GUITAR, VOCALS
Gregory "Smog Vomit" Boaz { BASS
David "Rock Vodka" Thum { DRUMS

» In a 1983 interview with Ruben MacBlue of *Skratch* Magazine, the tameless Texacala Jones' first vocalization is a loud off-camera cackle. Taken aback, the interviewer nervously stumbles over his own name, and the view pans out to reveal Tex sitting next to him in a chair, a jet-black nest of hair piled on her head, swigging from a bottle of brandy. The two giggle and she pours brandy into a mug of coffee and, slurring her words, offers him some. "A little," he accepts the gift gleefully.

He asks her how long Tex & the Horseheads have been together, and she's caught stirring her coffee with her index finger. She flicks the liquid into the air, flips the whirl of teased black hair from her face, and asks if she smeared her eye makeup—a solid black stripe across her eyes, a narrow domino mask—then winks at the camera. She responds, "Since February."

When asked if Tex is her real name, she garbles, "Yep, it's my real name… at the moment." She sings part of a Hank Williams song upon request, role-plays her waitressing abilities (using the opportunity to pour more drinks for her and the interviewer), then she plays a cover of "Big Boss Man" on acoustic guitar in front of the fire.

At her bar shows, she was equally tameless—crucifixes and long necklaces swinging back and forth as she paces the stage, drinking straight from a bottle and throwing one arm up in the air as she attacked the mic. The feral nest of hair flies through the air, singing with hair covering her face while a few burly dudes keep the crowd under control.

"I didn't even know I was cowpunk," says Texacala Jones. Telling the story of when she first heard the term, she explains: "In New Orleans, I was at this bar… and the bartender says to me 'so you're cowpunk,' and I thought he was saying I was cow shit and I got mad and I picked my stool up and crashed it against the bar and broke glasses…I turned the tables and broke the door and ran for my life."

As a child, Texacala Jones wanted to be a bal-let-dancing nun and to join the school choir. "When I was in kindergarten or first grade, I wanted to join the chorus, so my teacher shoved me in there and the chorus teacher said, 'OK, give me a few notes,' and so I started singing and everyone started laughing and the teacher said, 'OK, you better go back to class now.' That always stuck in my head, but you know, later on, Jeffrey Lee said 'I like it, your voice is crazy, let's go with it!'"

In high school, she joined a few bands, playing bass. "Everybody wanted me to be in their band because I had this crazy, uncontrolled hair," she remembers. "At first I played bass and guitar; they had to show me note for note what to play—I had no dexterity or navigation on the instrument." Later, she learned how to play covers and developed as a songwriter. In a process as chaotic as her hair, she initiated some songs with vocals or lyrics and others with guitar. She remembers her adolescence: "No boys no proms cuz I was too weird I wore black and listened to John Coltrane alone by myself in the rain and I loved it."

So how did Tex & the Horseheads form? Well, in 1980, Tex played guitar in the Gun Club for one show. She says she played so badly that Jeffrey Lee Pierce had to fire her, but as a consolation, he helped her start her own band. Before she had a group

Texacala Jones performing live. Photo by Lyn Owen.

together, Gun Club even backed her up on an East Coast tour. She remembers playing with other bands in the scene: "After a few 12-packs, any band we played with was our kindred spirits."

Tex's aesthetic is bred from the confluence of death rock, burlesque, and cowboy fashion, wearing bandanas, knotted scarves, tattered tulle, frayed fishnets, and religious paraphernalia. In L.A. punk circles, friends called her Tex. She spoke with a Southern accent, and once Pleasant Gehman gave her a jigger glass with the word "Tex" and the name stuck. Wanting the name to be more elegant, she added the "acala."

She put out two records with the Horseheads. She sang of heartbreak, drug dependency, and grief over a fusion of blues, honky-tonk, and punk. In "Clean the Dirty," she croons:

Sitting here drinking, trying to wallow in my troubles

You come around my drinks they turn to doubles
You say you love me at least 50 times a day
But if you really loved me there's nothing to say...
If you really loved me you'd just go away

After the band broke up, Texacala formed Tex-orcist and participated as a storyteller and backup singer in an all-women performance troupe of L.A. scene-makers, the Ringling Sisters, whose members all fronted Los Angeles-based bands. Tex also acted in low-budget, independent films (including *Border Radio*, *Du-Beat-e-o*, and *Dr. Caligari*).

The band has reunited to play shows since, and Tex continues to play as a way to connect with nature. She says, "I just crawl through the swamp with my Vox mini amp and guitar strapped to my back, just a-croonin' for the frogs and gators." ●

SIN 34

Santa Monica, California   »   Formed in 1981

MEMBERS

Julie Lanfeld { VOCALS
Phil Newman | BASS
Mike "Geek" Glass { GUITAR
Dave Markey | DRUMS

》 Before kicking off a set, the band tunes their instruments, and SIN 34 singer Julie Lanfeld addresses the audience. "What tight security, they wouldn't even let me in…thanks a lot. I've only been waiting for 15 minutes! Thanks for waiting!" Showgoers meander around, beefy dudes extend their arms protectively, and the band launches into a song at rapid speed. Julie screams hoarsely. The audience is on the same level ground as the band and their mosh pit intersects with the performance.

Upon a quick Google search of SIN 34, the first result is the trig function. The second thing that comes up is the American hardcore band that formed in Southern California in 1981. SIN 34 is a name drummer Dave Markey had had in his head since he was 15; he even made a crucifix-centered logo that he drew on his backpack. When vocalist Julie Lanfeld noticed it, they both agreed it was a great band name. He said, "It sounded real cryptic, but in actuality, it was just [a reference to] Spanish International Network channel 34." While this is the explanation the band gave, punklorists can't shake information from the rumor mill: SIN 34, if displayed in a mirror, reads PE NIS.

Dave recalls meeting Julie: "I thought she had a very magnetic presence. Just by our shared interest in the music, we were drawn together. I had daydreams of forming a band, and I believe the first thing Julie ever said to me was 'Do you play an instrument?'" He met Julie at a Middle Class show at the Starwood in 1981, and, according to him, she promised she would steal a drum kit from a neighbor's garage. The kit she stole had a kick drum and high tom, and, according to Dave, probably hadn't been used since the '60s. Dave used a metal lampshade as a cymbal and would kick the kick drum with this foot.

The two high schoolers bonded over Devo and Black Flag. And with only a few punks at their respective high schools, decided to be friends, formed a band, and recruited bassist Phil Newman. They played without a guitarist for a while. They tried out many before finding permanent guitarist Mike Glass. Turned on to the intensity of Minor Threat, the group evolved into a hardcore band and played shows with Dead Kennedys, T.S.O.L., Social Distortion, Fear, and Circle Jerks.

Skating since she was nine years old and placing in amateur contests, Julie was a featured skater in *Thrasher* in 1983. When asked in an interview if she really skates ("Like that picture in *Thrasher*, was that real or did you pose for Dave?"), she replies, "That was the lamest picture. I have a trophy at my house if you want to see it." The interviewer also implied her boobs might get in the way while performing. She responded, "When I wear black, I wear a black bra…" and "I wear underwire."

Dave discusses her status as a rare female front person of a hardcore band—one of the first. "Julie was really the only girl fronting a band in the hardcore scene at the time," he says. "Julie set us apart from our peers. She was different, besides the fact she was female. She just had her own vibe. It worked within the context of the band. It was mostly a lot of fun, and Julie was a lot of fun to be around…Julie actually drew hardcore guys right into the thick of what we were doing."

Curiously omitted from certain versions of hardcore history, SIN 34 was listed in *American Hardcore*,

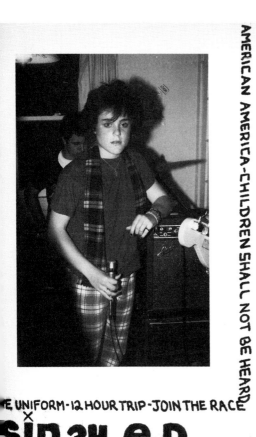

AMERICAN AMERICA-CHILDREN SHALL NOT BE HEARD

SIN 34 AT THE WHISKEY JUNE 30 9:00

E UNIFORM-12 HOUR TRIP-JOIN THE RACE

sin34 e.p. out soon

Julie performing live on a poster for a SIN 34 show. Poster by Dave Markey.

the book, but none of the members are interviewed in the film. The documentary leaves about five minutes for women to speak, almost an hour and a half in; Julie Lanfeld isn't one of them. But SIN 34 were prolific, recording upwards of 50 songs in three years and putting out exceptional albums, *Die Laughing* and *Do You Feel Safe?*

Some of their exploits are documented in *The Slog Movie* made by Dave Markey. (Among other work, Dave also directed *Desperate Teenage Lovedolls, 1991: The Year Punk Broke,* and a long list of essential music videos from the '80s until today.) SIN 34 got back together in 2008 and played local shows for a few years. Sadly, Phil died in a boating accident in 2015 and Julie passed away in 2018. ●

THE PANDORAS

Los Angeles, California   »   Formed in 1982

MEMBERS

Original lineup

Paula Pierce { GUITAR, VOCALS

Gwynne Kahn { KEYBOARDS, RHYTHM GUITAR

Casey Gomez { DRUMS

Deborah Mendoza, Bambi Conway { BASS

Later lineups

Paula Pierce { GUITAR, VOCALS

Melanie Vammen { KEYBOARDS

Karen Blankfeld, Sheri Kaplan, Kelly Dillard { DRUMS

Kim Shattuck, Julie Patchouli, Gayle Morency { BASS

Rita D'Albert, Billy Jo Hash, Lissa Beltri { RHYTHM GUITAR

» The Pandoras emerged from the L.A. mod and garage-rock revival movement, the Paisley Underground. Farfisa organ, jangle and fuzz guitar riffs, haunting hooks, Day-Glo fishnets, and vocals that go from sweet and sultry to mean and screeching in seconds, they pulled their look and sound from the psychedelia of '60s garage, and insulated with baroque pop riffs. After their first two albums (*It's About Time* and *Stop Pretending*), the group transformed to a heavy metal look and sound with extended guitar solos, emphatic chords and beats, thick eyeliner, and big hair.

In the mid- to late '70s, Paula, a teenager from Chino, California, traded her accordion for an electric guitar and played in a handful of bands, including the Rage and Action Now. In the local scene, she met and befriended Gwynne Kahn, who was dating her friend. When Paula decided to form her own band based on her fixation on '60s garage rock, she contacted Gwynne to play keys. Putting together a group through mutual friends and respondents to a newspaper ad, the girls considered a few names, including the Keyholes and Hole, but landed on the name the Pandoras. (Interestingly, Courtney Love was a fan!)

Over the years, the ever-evolving all-female garage punk group had a lot of members come and go, but singer-songwriter Paula Pierce remained the band's leader until her untimely death of a brain aneurysm in August of 1991 at the age of 31.

On the cover of 1984's *It's About Time*, the almost-original four-piece, consisting of guitarist and singer Paula, organ player Gwynne, drummer Casey, and bassist Bambi (who replaced Deborah Mendoza, the band's co-founder), plays in a hot pink room. With teased hair and beaded necklaces, they wear vintage minidresses, and with their positioning appear to be jamming. Paula's high ponytail is draped over the neck of her teardrop sunburst Vox guitar, Gwynne's left arm floats above the keys mid-dance-move, and Casey's hovering drumstick comes down on her high tom. Their band name and album title swoop across the top in a purple, green, and yellow bubbly retro font. The back of the album displays each band member's photo with a short third-person bio, reminiscent of boy-band regalia and fanzines featuring male garage bands of the '60s.

The Pandoras' beguiling band name was a coveted treasure[1]. After their first LP *It's About Time*, the Pandoras split into two factions. Gwynne, Bambi, and Casey decided to continue working together, leaving Paula Pierce on her own. Paula got a new lineup, but both parties laid claim to the name.

In 1984, Gwynne, Casey, and Bambi played shows with the name before Paula replaced them

---

1 An all-female garage group called the Pandoras played in New England throughout the mid-'60s.

It's About Time
The PANDORAS

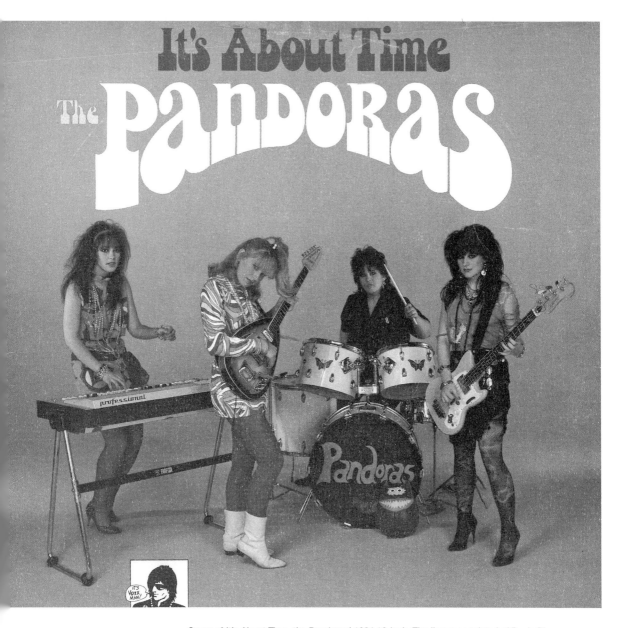

Cover of *It's About Time*, the Pandoras' 1984 12-inch. The lineup consisted of Paula Pierce, Bambi Conway, Gwynne Kahn, and Casey Gomez. From the collection of Jen B. Larson.

in a new lineup. The three ex-members also tried to use the name for a release with Enigma Records, but the label would not allow them to use it. Paula had legal rights to the name and her new group kept the name. Listening to the release, seeing the album, and hearing the interviews with the band at the time, however, it's hard to imagine that their relationships were so fraught.

During that time, the group appeared on KROQ with Rodney Bingenheimer, giggling, discussing their instruments and influences, and promoting their new music video shoot. Gwynne shouts out the Bangles and the Go-Go's. Casey says the Screamin' Sirens

(whom she later played with) are great. Paula says she's never seen them, but coolly says, "How about the Pleasure Seekers? That's an all-girl band that's good that I like." They also discuss the Runaways, and advertise an upcoming music video shoot—"like a shindig," calling for attendees to wear authentic '60s clothing: boys with Beatle boots and girls with white go-go boots and bangs and miniskirts.

Replacing the band a handful of times, Paula ended up with a few new Pandoras lineups, including the mid- to late-'80s roster of future Muffs Kim Shattuck on bass and Melanie Vammen on keys, and Karen Blankfeld on drums. They recorded *Stop Pretending* in their original

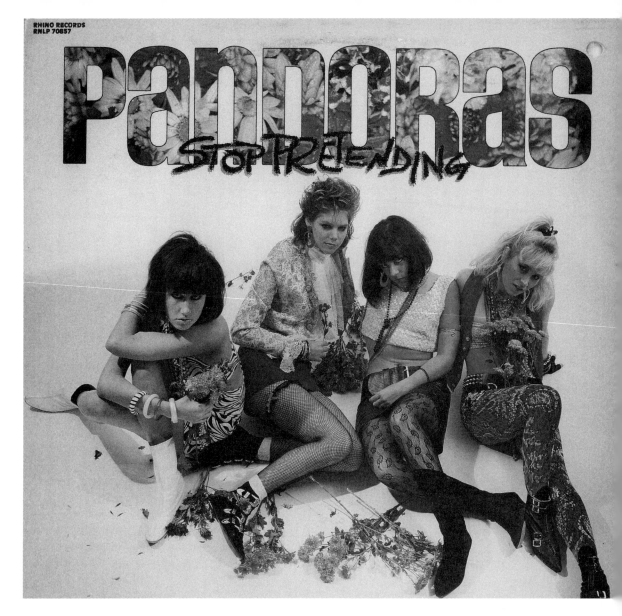

RHINO RECORDS
RNLP 70857

PANDORAS
STOP PRETENDING

Cover of *Stop Pretending*, the Pandoras' 1986 12-inch. The lineup consisted of Paula Pierce, Kim Shattuck, Melanie Vammen, and Karen Blankfeld. From the collection of Jen B. Larson.

style, but by the late '80s, Paula switched out her tear-drop Vox for a Strat and a black Les Paul. Their hard rock style didn't change the quality of their songs, and they still maintained a certain pop appeal, as the songs instrumentally contained keys and tambourine.

Based on interviews and recordings online, the group had a lot of fun and acted with total, untamed sexual ferocity. When promoting 1989's album *Live Nymphomania* on a KFJC-FM radio show, the girls ask Pandoras trivia questions on air to give away autographed band merch. One question was: "Which Pandora has the largest breasts, and which one has the smallest?" Paula's wild abandon coupled with the seriousness of her songwriting

was the energy of pure rock 'n' roll. The careful craft was demonstrated in the other question they asked fans on air: "What two songs have the Pandoras recorded twice?" A male caller taunted them, and they taunted him right back. They made lewd remarks about another DJ and finally, when asked about sexism in the business, Paula responded, "We basically don't really care. We just do what we want to do."

One member answered, "If people are going to be sexist toward us, we just don't deal with them." And Paula chimed in again, "People think we're the ones who are sexist…it's reverse sexism….Use 'em and lose 'em, that's what I say." ●

SCREAMIN' SIRENS

Los Angeles, California   »   Formed in 1983

MEMBERS

Pleasant Gehman { VOCALS
Diane "Boom Boom" Dixon,
Casey Gomez, Brie Howard { DRUMS
Annette Zilinskas, Fur Dixon,
Miiko Watanabe, Laura Bandit,
Arlo Zoos Keri { BASS, VOCALS
Rosie Flores, Genny Schorr,
Kathryn Grimm { GUITAR
Shayn Taylor-Shubert { BASS, GUITAR, VOCALS
Marsky Reins { FIDDLE, GUITAR

Pleasant Gehman in 1987 on the set of *The Runnin' Kind*. Photographer unknown. Courtesy of Pleasant Gehman archives.

In high school, Pleasant Gehman and her friend Randy Kaye would cut school and head to Hollywood Boulevard, where they would stay out nights at the Whisky, the Roxy, gay juice bars, and the Sugar Shack—a teenage disco where attendees would be carded to prove they were under 21. (The only people over 21 allowed in were rock 'n' rollers like Rodney and Kim Fowley.)

The kids on the L.A. scene had to talk face-to-face to know what shows were happening. Pleasant explains, "To this day, I try to figure out how I found out about shows. You had to go out. Most of the time you would hear about something, especially in those early days, and someone would tell you. It was seriously word of mouth." She continues: "Michelle Myers used to call the way that people found out about things, 'jungle drunks'—it was like 'smoke signals' or 'osmosis.'"

In 1978, she and Randy started the fanzine *Lobotomy*, a handmade Xeroxed gazette held together with Scotch tape and safety pins. Covering local gossip, informing people of upcoming shows, and taking on a humorous *Mad* Magazine-esque tone, they put out about 20 issues in three years. Pleasant and Randy wrote under pseudonyms to create original content,

and friend Theresa Kereakes became the main photographer. The reasons they published it included letting people know what was going on, and getting free records and free tickets to shows out of it. They began booking shows at the Whisky and raising funds to keep the paper in print.

In the first issue, Pleasant wrote a disparaging rant about Kim Fowley. She recalls, "I just said he was an idiot. I wrote that he was pretentious and always got dressed up." Calling her at home and screaming at her over the phone, he threatened to sue her and take her typewriter. Instead of printing a retraction, Pleasant found a more creative solution. She recalls, "I didn't have the money to reprint it… so instead I wound up hitchhiking and taking the bus to all the different record stores. I went there with scissors and cut out the offending paragraph [from all the copies of the magazine]!"

The *L.A. Weekly* got wind of her work and hired her to write a gossip column ("L.A. Dee Da") about the local music scene. Pleasant, a self-proclaimed unskilled typist, recalls the newspaper in retrospect:

Flyer by Pleasant Gehman. Courtesy of Pleasant Gehman archives.

"I'd go out every night, often to three or more places, scrawling a few notes in eyebrow pencil on a flyer. At the end of the week, I'd pop off a stream-of-consciousness column in my trademark one-fingered hunt 'n' peck."

As a writer, Pleasant wanted to convey the truth about the music scene, understanding the sound and influence of bands. "*Creem* was amazing but writers in many of the mainstream magazines were clueless," she says. "Stuff repeated from review to review, and I had suspicions people were just lifting information from press releases."

As someone in the center of the action, she could bring an important perspective. "They didn't understand the difference between punk and rockabilly in the slightest," she says. "A lot of young people turned to rockabilly because it had the same energy of punk but also because toward '79 or '80, the people who had been throwing garbage from the street suddenly decided punk was cool. That was when the punk scene changed and became dangerous for women, especially around the mosh pits."

In the early scene, the shows had been rowdy, but they were safe. She explains, "If someone fell over, someone else would pick them up. It was exceedingly different. It was a safe and cohesive scene. There were no gender boundaries, there were people who were queer and of all ethnicities."

Pleasant had always wanted to be in a band, but when she finally decided to form one, she wanted a band that was a little bit rockabilly, a little bit rock 'n' roll, and Andrews Sisters' vocal harmonies. She explains, "It came out punk speed because we were really excited."

In 1983, when power pop and new wave rocked the airwaves, Pleasant formed a rowdy punkabilly crew. She describes the Sirens: "We were like a band of female pirates." In an interview, she told *Flipside*: "I just wanted to have a really wild all-girl band that was like a gang or something." The group dressed in western attire, wearing cowgirl hats, boots, and western skirts. And they put on campy stage shows. With many members coming in and out over their four-year run, they resembled the swinging doors of a Wild West saloon. They even had members of Jimmy and the Mustangs play with them in drag.

The first person she called to get on board was her archenemy, Boom Boom Laffoon. She recalls, "The best drummer I could think of was Boom Boom. But we detested each other—we fucking hated each other. So, I got her number from someone, and I called her and was like, 'Hi, Boom Boom, this is Pleasant.' There was a big, long pause, and I said, 'what are you doing?' and she said, 'folding laundry,' and I went, 'oh, well do you want to start a band with me?'"

They met in person and discussed it. Turns out, they were exactly on the same page; they started sharing songs with one another and figured out that the reason they hated each other was that they were exactly alike. "She'd be getting thrown out of a club, struggling, and I would think, 'that girl's such a fucking mess' and she had seen me in the same situation. We ended up as best friends for ages."

Not explicitly country, the Sirens covered Tammy Wynette and sang songs with country-informed lyrics, including old gunfighter ballads like "Jim," and electric guitar-twang heavy jams like "I am the Queen of Kingdom Come." They also recorded hilarious tunes like "Mr. T Luv Boogie" and experimented with tracking lunatic laughing fits on "Maniac." Fittingly, they played with artists from Nicolette Larson to the Ramones.

While performing, Pleasant bit the buttons off a man's shirt, rolled them around in her mouth, and spit them at the audience like a machine gun. "That happened all the time," she laughs. Another night, she invited a heckler on stage and handcuffed him to a pole, feeding him drinks and cigarette puffs as the show went on. She recalls, "The guy was being so obnoxious that I called him on stage and cuffed him to a pole with a set of Smith & Wesson handcuffs a cop left me as a tip at a bar I worked at." After that show, people would approach the band and ask to be handcuffed on stage, and it became a regular stage antic.

In the studio for 1984's *¡Fiesta!*, the group laid down basic tracks live and then fixed them later. Working with Brian Ahern, she says he was "horrified" that the girls wanted to track breaking glass in the parking lot or add subliminal tracks (like whispering "buy our record!" under the guitar solo) in "Love Slave."

The group's lineup ran deep. Members came from other Hollywood bands, and several went on to join or form other groups. Genny Schorr of Backstage Pass was in the original lineup; Casey Gomez from the Pandoras joined later; and Brie Howard played with the band after shooting the film *The Runnin' Kind*, which Pleasant co-wrote.

Screamin' Sirens only put out two albums (*¡Fiesta!* and 1987's *Voo Doo*), but their music endures on a few movie soundtracks and the band even appeared in some films. In the movie *Vendetta*, the song "Love Slave" was changed to "Wild Thing." The band also portrayed the She-Devils in *The Runnin' Kind*.

On the power of women, Pleasant said: "Women did everything in the L.A. scene. Women had apartments that people crashed at, women made fanzines. Women were artists, writers, and storeowners. Women had equal power—the same as men, and no one questioned it."

Later, she formed the Ringling Sisters, wrote a handful of books, and became a world-traveling belly dancer. She had wanted to be a dancer her entire life. As a child, she was discouraged from pursuing the craft, told she was flat-footed. Still, she kept a photo of a belly dancer from a *National Geographic* article (her father wrote for the magazine) in her wallet for more than a decade. "People were like, 'what?' but my dance career came directly out of punk rock."

On her prolificness, Pleasant declares: "I wasn't a prodigy, I worked my fucking ass off!" ●

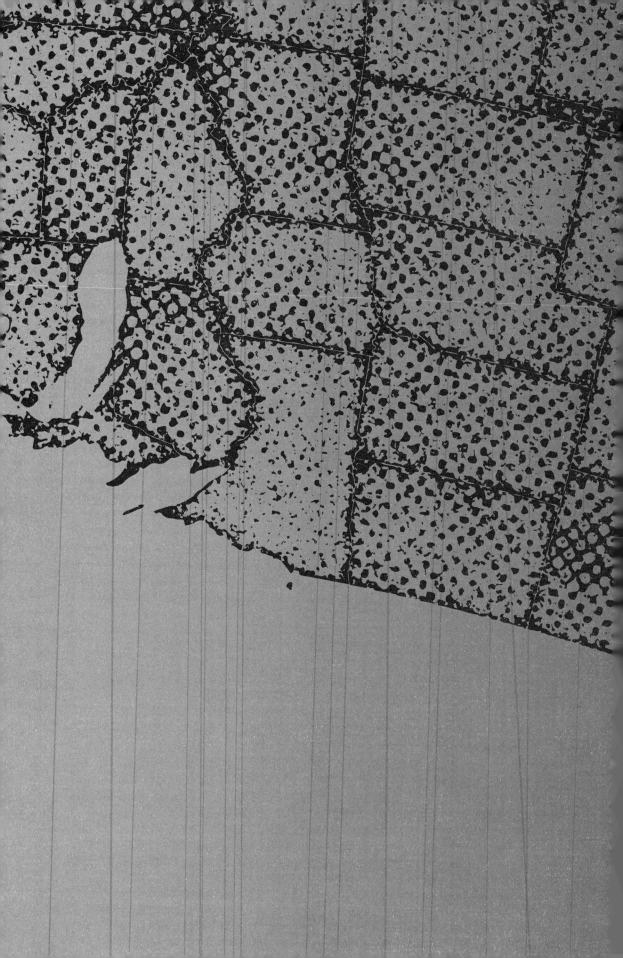

WEST COAST (NORTH)

Shake the Hands of Time

MARY MONDAY

San Francisco, California » Formed in 1976

MEMBERS

Mary Monday { VOCALS

The Revue
Vermillion Sands { VOCALS
Haiti
Lisa

The Street Punks
Don Lamb { BASS
Kenny Cimino { DRUMS
Rick Clare { GUITAR
Tony Laurenco { GUITAR

The Bitches
Maniff George, Tom Evoniuk,
George Falbo, Thomas Geiser { GUITAR
Steve Swan, Neil Peron { BASS
Bob Boginski, Don Peck { DRUMS

>> Donning short, brightly colored two-toned hair, thigh-high boots, a leather bustier ornamented with a cloud of feather boas, and red opera gloves, singer Mary Monday strutted the streets of San Francisco confidently. On and off stage, her production was one part punk, two parts cabaret; out of the spotlight, Mary was an enigmatic figure whose own family and close friends have struggled to piece together the story of her life.

What is known: She lived in St. Louis and Montreal before heading west. Mary began tap dancing at the age of five and taught herself how to sew. Later, she put together shows in downtown Montreal bars. She moved to Vancouver, where she performed burlesque, and in the early '70s Mary Monday migrated to San Francisco. In 1976, already in her late twenties, she dreamed up a punk band. Forming an all-female punk burlesque revue, she secured space at the Mabuhay Gardens to host shows. The revue played two shows and the group spun off into Mary Monday and Her Bitches (later, the Bitches, with a rotating cast of bands, including the Street Punks).

Few articles about Mary or the band exist, and few from the San Francisco scene discuss her, but rumors on internet message boards, mentions in *Punk Globe*, and a few short snips in *Search & Destroy* #1 give us a picture. On a KBD Records comments section, Edwin Craven (who identifies as a small-time promoter of punk bands in the San Francisco Bay Area and publisher of *New Wave Mag* in the mid-'70s) wrote, "She had an incredible gift for promoting herself on a shoestring budget…and was the first person I, or anyone else in San Francisco had ever seen with multicolored hair" and

Front cover of "I Gave My Punk Jacket to Rickie" / "Popgun," Mary Monday's 1977 7-inch. From the collection of Jen B. Larson.

Mary Monday at the Mabuhay Gardens in 1977. Photo by Jim Jocoy.

"most don't realize it…and she has never gotten the credit for it…but Mary brought the Punk scene to San Francisco…"

Commentor Karl Kotas echoes: "I concur with Edwin that Mary Monday was one of the first, if not THE first person to bring punk rock to [San Francisco]."

A feature article documenting the Mabuhay Gardens in *Search & Destroy* #1 from 1977 substantiates the claim, beginning: "In November 1976 a green-haired cabaret-glitter queen from Montreal named Mary Monday 'rented' a quiet Filipino supper club on Monday night to showcase her tap dancing, her songs, and theatrics. Because she attracted small but outrageous crowds, Ness Aquino, the owner (25-year lease) felt 'something was happening' and decided to

book more and more [acts]." Kathy Peck of the Contractions, at the time married to Don Peck, drummer in Mary Monday's band, also acknowledges that Mary started shows at the Mabuhay in a 2012 interview on Music Life Radio. *Punk Globe* creator and editor Ginger Coyote recalls her:

"She was an innovator, a very go-getter type. She was the one who approached Ness about doing shows at the Mabuhay. It was way before the Nuns or the Avengers or any of those bands played there…Mary was pretty haphazard. I did a Gong Show with her. Sometimes you couldn't even find her until the last minute…to find out what we were going to do. She made chaos. There are performers who know how to work with chaos and know how to make everything funny. She was fast-talking. And funny. She had a distinct look… small in stature and she had orange-colored hair with purple on the sides. She was a character. You remembered her."

As a performer, Mary Monday's show was energetic, engaging, and she gave crowds exactly what they wanted: rowdy, impromptu, out-of-control performances: "They rolled on the floor, pushed, shoved, ripped clothes. Microphones falling everywhere," (*Search & Destroy* #1). In a photo from the Mabuhay, balancing in ballet slippers, ripped shorts, polka-dot bra, choker, finger-wave hair, her black gloves grip a microphone which she devours on stage; alongside her, Vermillion Sands performs alongside her wearing black leather pants and an open jacket, otherwise topless underneath.

Search & Destroy documents the brief performances of Mary Monday's Revue:

"Mary Monday's revue played but two gigs—but what two gigs! For the first, Mary, Lisa and the black leather-jacketed furries, Vermillion and Haiti broke bottles microphones tables props, and costumes in a dangerous spontaneously incited girl gang war—the stage manager fought for the last surviving microphone—the bug-eyed audience could not believe their real-life trashing slugging and ripping of flesh. BY WOMEN! People were standing on tables and chairs! Their second gig was dramatic with a difference: no Haiti and Lisa but Bowie Iggy plus Blondie and Television members in the audience."

Categorized as a reaction band, the girls seemed to unleash cathartic violence with one another. An interviewer asks Vermillion, editor for *Search & Destroy*, and later singer for UK band Dick Envy, "Do you like working with Mary Monday?" Vermillion, whose brazen sarcasm through the interview only builds, responds, "She's a stupid cunt, but she's the only girl I hang out with. We like to yell at each other across the

room and barge stages and have bottle-smashing contests. Sometimes I have to keep her in line. She gets too sharp with her tongue."

"What's the future of your group?" the interviewer queries. "Today, New York. Tomorrow, the world," Vermillion snaps.

Mary's shows at the Mabuhay packed the room, and some sold out entirely. On occasion, she would include the teenage Lady La Rue's daughters, the Infant Terribles in her show. Ginger Coyote writes in *Punk Globe*, "After meeting the wild Mary Monday at The Palms they became Mary Mondays Bitches for a few performances at The Mabuhay Gardens…"

Next, the Street Punks—a local group founded by Don Lamb in 1974—became her backing band. Their first record, a split between Mary Monday and the Street Punks, "Out of the Alley," featured four songs including the original version of "Popgun." On the original "I Gave My Punk Jacket to Rickie" 7-inch, a Killed by Death Records blogger writes: "This was one of John Peel's (may he rest in peace) favorite records. The back of the sleeve is held together with two small safety pins. How punk rock!"

At the time and sometimes in retrospect, because of her age and theatrics, some accuse her of glomming onto the punk style. But by many accounts, it was Mary's determination that created space for the punk scene. Mary talked the owner of the Mab into letting her rehearse her punk cabaret there during the day when it was closed. She had talked up many artistic people in the area and a handful of them started showing up for the rehearsals to hang out. There were so many people, the owner decided to open up the bar to sell beer to the crowd. A scene began. On Sunday nights, the owner turned the bar into a punk club. Garage bands started to show up and the crowd gained more traction. No one had anywhere else to go and the owner was selling a lot of Budweiser. Slowly the restaurant turned into a punk club Sunday, Monday, and Tuesday, then it was seven nights a week. The restaurant closed and so began the Fab Mab—a popular Bay Area punk club whose regulars included the Avengers, Dead Kennedys, the Nuns, and more—all thanks to Mary's initial punk cabaret rehearsals.

Her true legacy exists in the energy she infused in the San Francisco scene. As it is aptly put in *Search & Destroy*: "Lest we forget there would be no punk rock New Wave scene in San Francisco without the Mabuhay Gardens." ●

THE NUNS

San Francisco, California » Formed in 1976

MEMBERS

Jennifer Miro { VOCALS, KEYBOARDS
Richie Detrick { VOCALS
Jeff Olener { VOCALS
Alejandro Escovedo { GUITAR
Pat Ryan { BASS
Jeffrey Raphael { DRUMS
(*a handful of additional members*)

"What is the perfect platinum blonde from the fifties doing with a New York street gang?"
(*Search & Destroy* #1)

》 Jennifer Miro was a sultry, icy icon whose who kept much to herself. Much of her story is unknown. But in a 1977 interview with *Search & Destroy* #1, she reveals a lot. In print, the interviewer's ridiculous, irrelevant questions ("Do you ever talk to kangaroos?" and "Do you believe in flying saucers?" and "Have you ever had an itch there?") make the interaction seem made-up, but Jennifer's responses are real. She tells about her childhood (raised in San Francisco, her mother had a degree in computer technology and her father was associated with the funk art movement), shares her feelings on punk, fashion, and experience as a homebody.

Jennifer insisted on taking piano lessons at five years old and was the only member of the Nuns who played an instrument before the band started. She wanted to be a jazz pianist until she heard Bowie's *Aladdin Sane*; after that, glitter rock was it. She told *Search & Destroy*, "Simultaneously I got into Jagger and theater although I've always been in theater…I'm always acting, you know." During high school, she dressed in all black, wore black eyeliner and pale white makeup. "They never accepted me.

Jennifer Miro playing live with the Nuns. Photo by Rikki Ercoli.

I could never get a tan!" She says her only friend resembled Patti Smith, and she recalls listening to records in her room, never going out and being depressed. As for the outdoors, she quips, "I like nature and looking at sunsets, but I hate the whole image that goes along with it…"

Her solitary nature turned out to be lifelong. While in the Nuns, she would stay home for weeks at a time until she had a gig. At home, she would lounge around without makeup and dance: "I have a huge room where I turn off the lights and dance for hours. It's my sports." She took a few lessons but learned from watching other

Cover of the Nuns' self-titled 1980 12-inch. From the collection of Jen B. Larson.

people. She speaks of her admiration of movie stars like Fred Astaire and Gene Kelly. "I've always been into movie stars. The first one I ever liked was Shirley Temple when I was four years old. I used to copy her dance and songs." Then, it was Julie Andrews. Though many make the comparison, she says she was not directly influenced by Marlene Dietrich, but Greta Garbo.

Members of the Nuns got together to create a joke band in 1975. Before Jennifer entered the picture, film students Alejandro Escovedo (Sheila E.'s uncle, who later went on to be a legendary country-punk pioneer) and Jeff Olener embarked on making a low-budget film about the strung-out rock singer of a band so terrible they could not play their instruments. The two art students play in the band, which they called the Trashcans, and then…they started to enjoy it, wanting to form a legitimate outfit.

Rehearsing in a warehouse in Terra Linda, Marin County, they met Jennifer Miro, an aloof, glamorous keyboardist, who had been playing for a band that covered the Doobie Brothers in a practice space nearby. She wasn't passionate about the cover band and when the guys invited Jennifer to join them, she did so enthusiastically, wanting to take part in the burgeoning punk movement. With another singer—Richie Detrick—recruited and with three lead singers in total, the Nuns began gigging around the San Francisco area in early 1976.

Jennifer told *Search & Destroy*: "I'm glad punk rock is happening. It has a new energy. The lyrics have to cut through, have an impact but very simple." Guitarist Alejandro described the band's set as a "block party."

A provocative, aggressive musical attack, the Nuns music mixed punk and goth with a disturbing sense of humor: socially aware without being political and radical without being sensitive. They intentionally pushed buttons with song titles such as "Mental Masturbation," "Cock in My Pocket," and "Decadent Jew" (apparently written for shock by a Jewish member); the latter song cost them a manager because they refused to drop it from the set.

Though it was difficult for the band to find regular venues to play, punk venues finally came into existence. The Nuns got popular quickly, even playing sold-out shows on consecutive weekends at the Mabuhay Gardens by the end of their first year as a band. And in January of 1978, they famously opened for the Sex Pistols' final concert at San Francisco's Winterland with the Avengers.

Jennifer's precisely applied makeup and retro glamour coupled with her deadpan delivery is sexy and acerbic. She sings:

I know you think you're the best
But baby you're just like all the rest…
You think you're chic
But I think you're passé

She won over audiences, and many musicians from the time cite her as an inspiration. The closing track for the Nuns' 1980 self-titled album features Jennifer's bewitching piano playing and stony lyrics. An ode to Peggy Lee and a reflection of her private life, "Lazy" could be considered her tour de force. The lyrics are:

I'm lazy, so lazy. I'm too lazy to fall in love.
It's such a bother, I'd rather stay home
    and watch TV
Such a bother, such a bore.
The same old lines you've heard
    a million times before.
I'm lazy, so lazy. I'm too lazy to fall in love.
It's such a bother. I'd much rather
    stay home and watch TV
Some say it's thrilling and can't
    live without it.
But (darling) I do very well without it.
I'm lazy, so lazy. I'm too lazy to fall in love.
It's such a bother. I'd much
    rather stay home and watch TV
Just stay home and watch TV

The band had a few opportunities that could have led to fame which didn't pan out. When the original lineup fizzled out in 1980, Jennifer and bassist Pat formed a short-lived side project in Los Angeles called the VIPs with Pat on guitar. After that, Jennifer returned to the Nuns, who had a totally different lineup. They dabbled in various genres, but nothing really worked the way the initial band did. Jennifer became a fetish model and wrote pilots for TV shows about vampires. Later she said,

"To me, the Nuns were really a cool band. We never sold out, we never made it big, we never became a big commercial thing. But so what? A lot of people don't make it in showbiz. I've been basically in and around showbiz people since then, and none of them make it either, so it's not just us. Showbiz is very, very cutthroat, very competitive. The weird thing is, I keep thinking it's going to end. But I'm still doing The Nuns. I'm still doing it."

Jennifer relocated to New York and renamed herself Mistress Jennifer. An intensely private person, she cut ties with close friends and family before dying of cancer at home early in 2012. ●

AVENGERS

San Francisco, California   »   Formed in 1977

M E M B E R S

Penelope Houston { VOCALS
Greg Ingraham, Brad Kent { GUITAR
Jimmy Wilsey, Jonathan Postal,
Joel Reader { BASS
Danny Furious (O'Brien),
Danny Panic (Sullivan), Luis Illades { DRUMS

>> With enormous all-knowing eyes, a brooding mouth, naturally platinum hair, Jezebel-inspired eyeshadow, and boyish fashion, singer Penelope Houston's look changed and challenged the parameters of normalcy in the regular world yet made her an icon in the art world. About dying her hair blue, she said, "People just turned around and their mouths would drop open, and their eyes would bug out. They didn't even pretend to be cool about it, they stared!" (*Search & Destroy* #2).

A few years before moving to San Francisco, Penelope had seen videos of Patti Smith at underground parties in Seattle. "She was so right…I agreed with everything she said…you don't have to compromise your intelligence to be attractive, punky, or sexual on stage," she explained.

Penelope's mother worked as a professional musician, and during Penelope's childhood, they bounced between the coasts. She was born in Los Angeles, lived in Long Island and upstate New York, Palo Alto, and then in Seattle. Attracted to art and the unconventional early on, she enrolled at Fairhaven College in Bellingham, Washington at the age of 16. She said, "It was kinda this write-your-own-classes type of school."

She acted in short films (*Nightcap*, *Honeymoon*, and *Virgil's Vigils*) and befriended artists. She met gay art collective the Whiz Kids in Seattle. (They later moved to Los Angeles and became the Screamers.)

While there were many avant-garde personalities in Seattle that influenced her, it wasn't until she moved to San Francisco in 1977 to attend the Art Institute that she met people involved in the punk scene.

That year, Penelope and a friend organized an art happening in San Francisco, and they titled the event "The Art Avengers." The name went on to inspire the name of future punk band. Penelope recalls that the group used the name "The Avengers" specifically because it sounded like a cliché rock band. The group was influenced by the resurrection of rock 'n' roll instigated by the Ramones, Sex Pistols, and the Damned. They played for a few months, tried out different bassists, and once they secured the lineup of drummer Danny Furious, guitarist Greg Ingraham, and bassist Jimmy Wilsey, with Penelope authoring lyrics and singing vocals, they composed prominent, powerful, and political punk anthems like "The American in Me." In it, Penelope sings,

It's the American in me that makes me
   watch the blood
running out of the bullet hole in his head
It's the American in me that makes me
   watch TV
see on the news, listen what the man said

and

Ask not what you can do for your country
what's your country been doing to you?

In "Fuck You," she sings,

Maybe the world's a mess
But baby I like your dress
Been seeing you around
You're the best in town
I want to fuck you

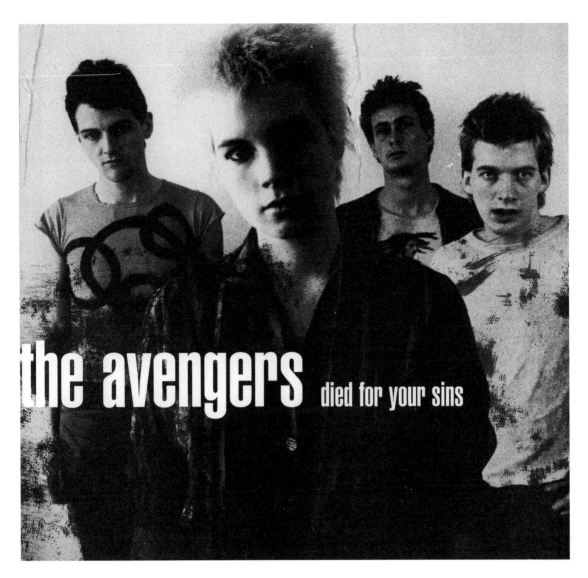

Cover of *Died For Your Sins*, the Avengers' compilation (recordings from 1977–1978 and songs by the Scavengers from 1998). From the collection of Jen B. Larson.

Musically, the Avengers were a torrent of crude, distorted guitar, root-note basslines, and standard 4-beat drums with transitions made by quick machine-gun snare rolls. Their simplistic punk sound leans on an easel like a blank canvas for Penelope to sling half-sung, half-shouted vocal lines. With in-your-face quips honed with a hopeful message, the band promised to set a better world in motion. In "We are the One," Penelope declares,

**We will build a better tomorrow
The youth of today will be our tool**

and

**I am the one who brings you the future
I am the one who buries the past**

Appearing as briefly as a supernova in the night sky, the Avengers lit a spark in San Francisco, preaching the spirit of unity without adhering to dogma. She sings,

**We are not Jesus Christ
We are not fascist pigs
We are not capitalist industrialists
We are not communists
We are the one**

Penelope and the band were regularly interviewed in *Search & Destroy*. In conversations, Penelope espoused her beliefs. She said, "People are brainwashed so easily. I don't want to be a typical punk," and "You don't have to be into violence or placidity." In a conversation about teenagers being interested in punk, she reacted:

> "If punk doesn't reach people and make things happen; if America turns punk into fashion, then fuck the fashion part of it just keep the part that's going to EXPLAIN something to people not the part that's going to divert them into spending their fucking money on shirts from seditionaries."

The Avengers headlined shows with legendary early first-wave punk bands, including the Nuns, X, the Germs, the Go-Go's, the Dils, and Dead Kennedys. Along with the Nuns, the band was also handpicked to play direct support for the Sex Pistols' legendary final show at the Winterland Ballroom. At the event, they met Pistols' guitarist Steve Jones, and he later produced and released their songs on a four-song 12" EP on White Noise Records. The original lineup played together for two years, performing a little more than 100 shows—an average of once a week—and still managed to leave an enduring mark on the Bay Area, where punk music would flourish long after their demise.

After putting out a handful of anthemic punk songs, the group parted ways, and Houston embarked on her own musical path, toward a career as an acoustic-oriented singer-songwriter. She is also a painter whose series "Muzzlers" renders originally black-and-white photographs of early-20th-century mugshots in color. Penelope's work skillfully inhabits political, personal, and academic spheres. In addition to her work as a singer-songwriter and painter, Houston also runs the San Francisco Punk Archive, where she salvages punk artifacts from San Francisco's rich punk history—a movement she helped set in motion.

In-Person interview with Penelope Houston, April 2019

Q: How did the Avengers get started? What drew you to make punk?

Penelope: Well, I moved here [San Francisco] on New Year's Eve 1976, going into '77. I was going to the Art Institute. I was 19 years old. And when I got there, I met Danny Furious, the drummer. He had been going to school there and dropped out. But he was still hanging out on campus. I guess we kinda started seeing each other. He had asked his friend Greg to move from Orange County, where they both grew up. They'd been in a band together down there called Head Over Heels. I guess he saw the Ramones—one of the first shows in the city was the Ramones in August of '76. I think they played three or four nights at the Savoy Tivoli. And Danny went there, saw the Ramones and was like "Oh yeah, I wanna do rock 'n' roll again."

So, he invited Greg Ingraham, who I still play with, from Orange County, to move up here and play guitar with him. Then Danny met me. At that point, they were living out in Dog Patch in a warehouse, or at least Danny was. He had amps and a PA set up so they could have rehearsals and stuff. He asked me to be the singer, and I was like "Eh, I dunno." Then one day, they were gone, and I put on some records—Patti Smith and Lou Reed and stuff. I started singing along with the records through the PA and I fell in love with the power of amplification. When they came back from wherever they were, I was like "Yes! I'm your singer!"

Then we found this bass player, who was a photographer named Jonathan. He was going to the Art Institute. We had him for about four or five shows—but he had totally different ideas. He wanted to do kind of a Blondie-type thing, and we were much more into the Sex Pistols and the Damned, the Ramones. So, we replaced him with Jimmy Wilsey, who just died this past Christmas. Jimmy was great. The four of us wrote all the songs and made the general Avengers.

Q: You mentioned some of the bands you listened to at the time. What did you grow up listening to?

AVENGERS

SIDE ONE
WE ARE THE ONE (10·23·77)
CAR CRASH (10·23·77)
I BELIEVE IN ME (10·23·77)
OPEN YOUR EYES (3·28·78)
NO MARTYR (2·9·78)
DESPERATION (2·9·78)
THIN WHITE LINE (3·28·78)

SIDE TWO
PAINT IT BLACK (3·28·78)
THE AMERICAN IN ME (10·12·78)
WHITE NIGGER (10·12·78)
UH-OH (10·12·78)
SECOND TO NONE (10·12·78)
CORPUS CHRISTI (5·13·79)
FUCK YOU/LIVE (10·18·77)

GUITAR/VOCALS · GREG INGRAHAM

VOCALS · PENELOPE HOUSTON

BASS/VOCALS · JAMES WILSEY

DRUMS/VOCALS · DANNY FURIOUS

IN SAN FRANCISCO, 1977-78, BEFORE THE PROLIFERATION OF TEN THOUSAND GARAGE BANDS ("HARDCORE" AND OTHERWISE), THE AVENGERS INVENTED AND PLAYED A FEW CLASSIC TEENAGE REBEL SONGS. THEIR MOTIVES WERE UN-SELFCONSCIOUS AND DIRECT—LIFE HAD TO BE CHANGED. PUNK ROCK WAS NOTHING BUT A SPONTANEOUS REVOLT BY YOUNG PEOPLE—WHO ELSE?—AGAINST A SOCIETY WHICH THOUGHT IT HAD PERFECTED THE MASS MARKETING OF A BILLION-DOLLAR-A-YEAR "YOUTH CULTURE."
CREATED AMIDST A GENUINE UNDERGROUND AS IT WAS ORIGINATING, THESE SONGS REFLECT A BREAKTHROUGH—HOWEVER BRIEF—INTO A VISION OF LIFE EXPRESSING FIRSTHAND PASSION AND REVOLT...BEFORE THAT REVOLT BECAME MERE STYLE...OR A VIOLENT SIMULATION...
WHAT THE AVENGERS PUT ON THIS RECORD ARE MUSIC AND LYRICS STRIPPED DOWN TO BASICS: SURVIVAL WITHOUT LIES, REBELLION WITHOUT GUILE. WHAT YOU HOLD IS A DOCUMENT REFLECTING A SPONTANEOUS BLACK-HUMOR RESPONSE TO A WORLD OF TOTAL CORRUPTION; AND, ALSO, WHAT YOU HOLD IS THE ONLY AVENGERS ALBUM EVER LIKELY TO BE: AN ALBUM CELEBRATING A WORLD WITH A GRIM HISTORY AND A GRIM FUTURE. BEFORE THE FINAL COLLAPSE, LAUGH IN THE RUINS OF TOMORROW, TODAY...
—VALE

Back cover of the Avengers' self-titled 12-inch ("the Pink Album"), released in 1983. From the collection of Jen B. Larson.

Penelope: I grew up in a household where I played violin, my sister played cello. It was classical music. We didn't grow up with very much rock 'n' roll or anything. I remember having, like, a Beatles album. We had like four albums. A Beatles album, a Joni Mitchell album, a Cat Stevens album, and what else was there? Hardly anything. So then when I was a teenager, in my early teens, I started to listen to my friends' older siblings' records like Bonzo Dog Band, the Incredible String Band—kinda out-there stuff. That's kinda what I got into. I was never like a real big rock 'n' roll fan, until punk.

Q: Does the name "Avengers" have a specific meaning to you? Has that meaning changed over time?

Penelope: When we were looking for band names, we had a huge list of ridiculous names. A friend of mine, who was an artist and lived in Portland, and I, we were gonna do some kind of art happening on July 7 of 1977—7/7/77—and it was gonna be called "The Art Avengers." When the Avengers got together—it was about May '77 or even April—we were trying to come up with a name, and I was thinking about the Art Avengers. Jonathan (the guy who was no longer in the band) said "Oh, there were always bands called the Avengers when I was growing up in Long Island."

It was like a generic rock band name, and we were just like "Oh, let's do the Avengers" [laughs].

Q: I know that you've had a long music career outside of punk, but that punk is what you are most known for. Do you think that punk opened doors for you in the other musical realm?

Penelope: I think there was a certain curiosity of people, like, "what's she doing now?" I started doing acoustic music in '84, and a little after that, I think, other punk bands were doing similar. X was doing the Knitters, and there was Billy Bragg. I think one of the things that made me go in the direction of acoustic music was the Violent Femmes and Tom Waits. That idea that you could have really dark themes, but the music didn't have to be super fast or super loud. After punk turned into hardcore in the early '80s, I was really not interested. I got more interested in sort of art-punk. But when I figured out that you could just get all these weird instruments and start making music that way, that's when I got into the more acoustic stuff.

But to answer your question, yes, I think having been in the Avengers helped people be interested in coming to see me, so it was helpful.

Q: Do you think as an artist, punk helped you express yourself clearly? Or in what ways did it impact your self-expression?

Penelope: Well, interestingly I started writing much more of the music once I started doing my acoustic thing. In the Avengers, the band members would bring in a riff or whatever and we'd work on it, and I would generally write the vocal melody and the lyrics, but with my later work I would write everything.

Q: With songs like "I Believe in Me," "We are the One," "The American in Me," and others, politics were a big theme of your early work, but later in your career, it feels to me your lyrics seem more personal. Do you feel that way? How did your approach change?

Penelope: Actually, I would say there are plenty of political songs in my later work, they just aren't anthemic. They are a different kind of political song. My last record was called On Market Street, written about this neighborhood [near the Civic Center]—the title track is quite political with social criticism.

Q: Overall, politics are a really important theme of your writing. What has been your goal with that? Where does it come from?

Penelope: I grew up in a pretty liberal household. Single mother, basically, well, divorced mother I guess you would say. And I just always felt strong in that I could do whatever I wanted. That I could be creative. There was no question about my expectations of life. So, when I got into this band and started writing lyrics, the idea that you would criticize the establishment or the administration or whatever, or the way things were going down, just seemed natural to me. I never really questioned it. "The American in Me" for instance was a song that someone, probably Greg, brought the music in to a rehearsal, and that was one of the songs that just poured out. It was all there. It was just all done. Somehow it just was inside my brain and it came right away. And "I Believe in Me," that's how I was brought up—to believe in me. We were not a religious family—I didn't have to get over any of that—it just came from a very self-confident place even though I was a 19-year-old girl.

Q: Who or what inspired you to be political?

Penelope: Just the world, how fucked up it was [laughs]. The more fucked up the world is [laughing], the more I want to write political things.

Q: Do you feel like that energy has changed at all?

Penelope: Well, interestingly, when punk first started happening in San Francisco, it was influenced by New York punk and English punk. I think when Jimmy Carter was president, in some ways there was less to complain about. Obviously, the young Brits had more to complain about. Like, I think more of the British punks were working-class, and more of the American punks were middle-class—educated white kids—but then when Reagan got in, ya know, like the Dead Kennedys wrote a lot of songs about Reagan and a lot of people wrote songs about Reagan. And that was easy [laughs]. It was an easy thing to react against. But over the years, there's always some fucked-up thing in society that people could and should rail against.

Q: *I wanted to go back to something you said earlier about the emergence of hardcore. What was that was like for you?*

Penelope: I was not interested in it at all [laughs]. It seemed like lyrics just kinda faded away. The music was super loud and fast. And I didn't like the way people sang. It was non-melodic. There was this horrible vocal style that was kinda like 'HUHRUHRUHRUHA' [makes a mouth noise]. It was just kind of a roaring lyric that's just…repulsive. That I'm just not interested in listening to. In fact, when that started, I was living in L.A. I moved to L.A. in the middle of '79, and I was there for a couple of years, so I kinda experienced the whole hardcore thing starting.

But, at the same time, there was a lot of art punk—the BPeople, Human Hands, and Minimal Man—bands with a lot more women in them or gay people in them, or whatever, and at the same time hardcore was really blistering its way around and it was just like… so straight white guy. I was just… not interested.

Q: *Was there anything about the way the crowds interacted that bothered you?*

Penelope: Oh, well, so I just basically didn't go to it. I wasn't one of those women that felt like I need to avoid these macho dudes who were moshing, because I…didn't go to hardcore shows. I just wasn't there.

Q: *Do you feel you or other women had obstacles in punk to overcome that men didn't have to deal with?*

Penelope: I feel like women who were in all-female bands definitely did. But as being just a vocalist, I didn't play an instrument, no one was ever questioning my prowess as a vocalist or lyric writing. But I would say for a woman instrumentalist there probably was a lot to overcome. Just, ya know, people's attitude that women can't play guitars or drums or bass, well sometimes bass, but not guitars or not drums, which it's like *fuck that*. But I personally didn't experience it because I was singing.

Later on, when I started writing my own music, performing my own stuff, I feel like there was definitely like—I feel like women in music are just taken less seriously than men.

Q: *Are you still painting and doing printmaking?*

Penelope: I went back to school after working at the library for a thousand years. I decided that my hands were not going to be able to shelve books forever and I needed to move up in the realm of things at the library, and so I went back to school maybe eight years ago. The thing I had the most credits in, the thing that would get me a bachelor's the fastest, was art, so I got back into painting and printmaking, and got my bachelor's in printmaking and studio art, with a focus on printmaking. I have gotten back into it lately. I mostly do portraits. That's my jam.

Q: *Any other passions outside of music and art?*

Penelope: Outside of music and art? Food! [laughs] Food has gotten to be very popular. I'm vegetarian. I've been a vegetarian for over 25 years, and I like cooking. I like baking bread, my own sourdough bread. When I'm traveling, I like to see what they can come up with. Sometimes it's hard, like there were times in Europe it was hard to be vegetarian.

Q: *You keep mentioning living in different places. Where did you grow up? Where have you lived?*

Penelope: I was born in L.A. a million years ago. Then I think we moved to the East Coast, to Long Island for a couple of years. Then we moved to upstate New York for a couple years, and that's where I experienced both hot and cold. Then we came back to the West Coast, and we lived in Palo Alto and then up to Seattle. And Seattle's kinda where I think I grew up.

The people who influenced me in Seattle were the Whiz Kids, which was this gay theater group—a couple of them became the Tupperwares, and then they became the Screamers, who are this fantastic L.A. synth-centered punk band. I had a bunch of friends in Seattle who were these out-there, crazy people that influenced me a lot too. And from Seattle I came to San Francisco at 19—well, I started going to college at 16. I went to Bellingham to go to Fairhaven, which was kinda this write-your-own-classes type of school. Then moved back to Seattle, and then moved back down here at the beginning of 1977 to go to the Art Institute, and that's where I started meeting a lot of the people in the punk scene and getting things started.

I lived in a couple of places in San Francisco, then I moved to L.A., and for a couple of years I moved to England, then I came back to the Bay Area, and I've been in either Oakland or San Francisco since I started doing acoustic music—so for the last 34 years, this is my home.

I was super lucky that when I started doing my solo stuff, it got popular in Europe. I got signed to a major label in Germany, and 20 years ago, and with that money, smartly—it didn't go up my nose—I put that money down on an old, old house in Oakland, and now it's all mine.

Q: Can you tell me more about the punk archive in San Francisco? How did it get started? What's your goal for it?

Penelope: I've been working at the library a super long time. I kinda worked my way up from a page to a library tech. When I actually got my BA, I decided I wasn't gonna go back to school and get a master's in library science—because I was like, it's too late, I was like 'I'm almost done, I'm not gonna go back to school.' But five years ago—I'd been a tech for about eight years in the information desk, where everyone comes up to you and says where can I find this or that—then this opening in the San Francisco History Center in the book arts and special collections department came, and so I jumped up there.

And once I got up there, I saw that they had all these collections on hippies. Boxes of stuff on hippies. People would come from the schools, the colleges, like 20 people would come and say, "we have to write something about the '60s"—and I was like "they need a punk collection; they need to know there is something after hippies!" And also, I've got all my stuff, and all my photos, and all my flyers and lyrics, and I was like "what am I gonna do with all this stuff?"

Being surrounded by archives, I was like, I am gonna talk to my boss, the city archivist, and see if she wants to start a punk archive, and she said, "yes, definitely." So, over the last four years or so, I've been talking to different people in the community. I've gotten a number of big collections, like I was telling you earlier—most from women—and I expect we'll get more. It's still getting processed. We're still waiting for an archivist to get assigned. But it's kinda great to know this is a growing thing and it will be archived and kept in good shape forever. So that when those college kids come and say, "my teacher wants me to write about punk rock," we'll be like "here's the stuff."

Q: Is there anything else you want to say about what we've been talking about? Or about punk or women in punk?

Penelope: I think it's really interesting that you are so focused on this early period. Because in my experience, that was a more open period. People didn't have an idea what punk was. You just went to the thrift shop and just got whatever kinda wacky clothes. Different people had different ideas. And there was quite a broad range of music styles and visual styles happening. And I think that openness also made it possible not just for women, but anybody to say, "I can't play guitar, but I can play guitar in this band because it's permitted," and then they would make some crazy sound that some untrained person would make that no one else would make. I think it was a real blossoming period. I'm glad so many women were involved.

And aside from women musicians, which is what you are focused on, there's many women photographers, women zine creators, women running clubs, women booking clubs. It just seemed like an inclusive time—the golden era [laughs]. After that, it kinda went through a couple other periods. And I think one of them would be hardcore, which I already dished on. Then after that, it was that pop-punk—popularity and punk becoming like mainstream. And that was its own thing and that's how a lot of people got introduced to it, and there's a lot of people into that and that's great. But for me, this period you are focusing on was a really important movement.

Q: What about riot grrrl?

Penelope: I feel like riot grrrl was in some ways a reaction to hardcore and the exclusivity to hardcore, and I can understand why people would react against that. But for me, I just went more towards more the art part and more wacky acoustic stuff. For women that wanted to do that and be in rock bands or punk bands, riot grrrl was also a great flowering of talents. But I always feel like if you have something that's very specific, then there's always people saying, "this is punk, this is not punk," "this is new wave, this is not new wave," or "this is riot grrrl, this is not riot grrrl" and breaking things up into a million classifications and that's kind of a pain in the neck. Ya know? [laughs]. So, I'm glad that riot grrrl happened—it's not something I have a huge collection of, but I like the fact that people just decided they were gonna do their own thing and have their own circle and make their own zines. And create their own scene. I think that's really important. So, I salute them. ●

THE BLOWDRYERS

San Francisco, California » Formed in 1977

M E M B E R S

Jennifer Blowdryer { VOCALS
Suzie { GUITAR
Judy Parks { BASS
Timmy Spence { KEYBOARD
Rotating drummers

>> In the mid-'70s, singer Jennifer Blowdryer's mom escaped the tyranny of her father's abuse and relocated the family near the Bay. She bought Jennifer a keyboard and paid for a piano teacher with divorce settlement money. Jennifer remembers reading her sister's *Creem* magazines and learning about punk. While in high school, Jennifer was subjected to a violent environment and graduated high school a year early.

Then in 1977, she started a band with a group of friends who called themselves the Blowdryers, because they were sick of bands with serious-sounding names. Jennifer remembers telling her bandmates, "We should just name it after something everyday like a blow dryer." The group practiced in bassist Judy's warehouse, and they covered songs such as "Liar Liar" by the Castaways, and "Bend Me Shape Me" by the American Breed.

Jennifer recalls that she didn't feel comfortable jamming on keyboard and was much more suited to be behind the microphone, but that she had never thought she would be a singer or ever thought about being famous. "It was a really primal thing," she says.

In an interview with Joe Biel in his book *Beyond the Music*, she expressed, "I loved punk because it was the funnest and I was the angriest girl on the planet."

"Punk rock was the right place for me to be," she says. But she also admits she was not in her best form and that she was often aggressive and bad-mannered toward other people in the scene. "I would just

Jennifer Blowdryer singing live. Photo by James Stark.

scream at people; I was really rude. I was foul. I was just an asshole with no training."

That brusqueness translated on stage as being raw rock 'n' roll. With a hoarse voice, she would curse on stage and say things on stage like, "If you don't like me, take some acid, squint and pretend I'm Blondie," and "let's go to the beach and freak out!" She wrote a song called "I Want to Take This Herpes and Give Them Back to You." She told interviewers things like "I'm not a woman in punk rock, I'm just me."

In San Francisco, she hung around strippers, sex workers, older people in leather jackets, people who

The Blowdryers playing live. Photo by James Stark.

THE BLOWDRYERS continued

were AWOL from the military. "People yelled 'freak!' at us on the street," she said. "San Francisco had an imprint on me." She recalls the difference between rock 'n' roll crowds and the art students. "The art kids were more put together—you know, now, they might own a house abroad and speak a few languages."

In addition to doing music, Jennifer always excelled at writing. According to Jennifer, she was horrible at getting jobs but was able to acquire student loans, so she enrolled at SF State and later UC Berkeley. She wrote for *Maximum Rocknroll*, and in 1981 collaborated on four issues of *Ego* Magazine.

In the early '80s, she started a party band called the White Trash Debutantes with Ginger Coyote, then moved to New York City at the end of 1984 when she got a fellowship to Columbia's graduate writing program. She's continued writing and authored several books including *White Trash Debutante*, *The Laziest Secretary*, *Good Advice for Young Trendy People of All Ages*, and *Kicked Out*, a collection of stories from an outsider's perspective.

Only one tape of the Blowdryers exists anywhere and it's a live gig from the Deaf Club. ●

THE URGE

San Francisco, California   »   Formed in 1978

M E M B E R S

Mary Lawler { GUITAR, VOCALS
Julie Lawler { GUITAR, VOCALS
Christeen Alicino { BASS
Kat Zumbach, Jean Caffeine { DRUMS

》》 When San Francisco's four-piece all-girl band the Urge played the Hong Kong Café in Los Angeles' Chinatown, the bar's owner told them that they were "the worst band [she's] ever heard"—so bad, she informed them, that Bill Murray had just walked out of the venue. Then the booking manager canceled their second night.

Jean Caffeine, the band's drummer at the time, who often makes light of others' judgments, later memorialized the moment in her song "All Girl Band" on a solo album, *Sadie Saturday Night*:

> **Hands greasy from Chinese food**
> **I played a sloppy set**
> **'You're the worst band we've ever heard'**
> **Bill Murray just left**

Whether the comments made by the bar owner were a product of sexism, internalized misogyny, or a general

The Urge on a boat. Photo by Ruby Ray.

The Urge goofing around. Photo by Ruby Ray.

THE URGE continued

misunderstanding of the band (or maybe they merely had a bad show?), they certainly reflect the reality that all-female bands weren't common, well understood, or respected at the time. Think about how poorly all-male bands can perform and still walk away with the recognition that they are "artists" or "counterculture."

Mary Lawler, her sister Julie, and Christeen Alicino formed the Urge with Mike Vacant on drums in 1978. Replacing Mike, their longtime friend Jean Caffeine joined them behind the kit, and they officially became an all-girl band. Later, Jean was replaced by Kat Zumbach, whose drumming appears on their only recording.

While very unheard, the Urge's only single "Bit by Bit" stands the test of time as far as underground pop music is concerned. The archival evidence of their work substantiates their songwriting strength. The songs feature a melodic garage style, perhaps best described as early lo-fi indie rock, disparate from what one would normally classify as mid-'70s punk. The B-side, "Baby Talk," demonstrates girl-group influences emerging with a surfy three-chord assault and progressing into a beachy, arpeggiated chorus with "wah wah" gang vocals.

Caffeine says, "We were our own thing. We had the punk attitude and punk primitivism, but we played several oldies covers. The Supremes' 'Love Child,' Santo and Johnny's 'Sleepwalk,' and the Shangri-Las' 'Sophisticated Boom Boom,' so I feel like we were more like a '60s girl-group hybrid with the punk primitivism and attitude."

The Urge seemed to be a band on the periphery of genres; they existed adjacent to the punk movement, and not necessarily part of it or because of it. Songwriter and lead singer Mary Lawler is a prolific and profound songwriter, whose work has gone largely unnoticed. The band also opened doors for its one-time drummer Jean Caffeine's long music career. Caffeine went on to play in legendary New York art punk group Pulsallama and form Clambake (with Holly George Warren and The Foams' Cathy Crane). She then moved to Austin to carry on with a solo career.

The Urge girls had been dear friends before joining musical forces, attending concerts such as the Who, Peter Frampton, and the Faces together. Their closeness and love of the medium solidified their friendships, but as bands and friendships go, it also contributed to heated conflicts that pulled them apart. ●

VS

San Francisco, California   »   Formed in 1978

MEMBERS

Olga De Volga { BASS, VOCALS
Anny Unger, Indian Wells { GUITAR
Carola B. Anderson { SAXOPHONE, VOCALS
Jane Weems, Alex MacNicols { DRUMS

>> At the crossroads of female-led bands in late-'70s San Francisco, VS was ground zero for artists from earlier outfits (such as the Offs and the Maggots) and the launching point for artists from later groups (such as the Gun Club and the Lewd). The original lineup consisted of only women but later admitted a few guys to their ranks.

On the cover of their *Girls in Leather 1978 Demo* (the only recording of them as an all-girl gang), four dude lookalikes wear leather and shades and pose in front of a Harley-Davidson sign. On the back, the girls sneer at the camera. They could have been, and easily were, mistaken for a gang. "Folk would cross the street to avoid us!" drummer Jane Weems recalls.

Their fearless leader, Olga De Volga, the Texas-born fetish leather fashion pioneer, was a real-life biker who had a side hustle leading funeral processions. Jane Weems, later of the Maggots ("Let's Get Let's Get Tammy Wynette"), was 17 and fresh out of high school when she was asked to drum for VS. She said:

"I answered an ad in a local paper for female musicians and got accepted immediately into

VS at an airport. Photo courtesy of Jane Weems.

the band (The Melting Pot) which was supposed to be a Motown/oldies revue, but I was still working with my own band the Maggots at that time. I was there when Anny Unger showed up to audition, and she noticed my Sex Pistols shirt. After practice, she said 'I know Olga from the Offs and she wants to start an all-girl punk group. Do you want to meet her?' Of course, I said yes. I was 17 at the time. They came to my parents' house to play with me and said I was in, just like that. I quit the oldies band right then."

She recalls in *Punk Globe*, "I was really thrilled to be playing such great shows with bands I really loved, like the Dils, the Avengers, the Zeros, Crime, & the Nuns… just a few months before, I had seen some of these bands open for the Sex Pistols, and now, I was opening for them!"

Olga's leather-wearing began when she got knocked out cold by a man at a Ramones show who was angry that she was dancing and blocking his view from a seated position. She wound up in the hospital. In a coma for days, her father came up from Texas and she told him she wanted leather chaps. Leather became an enormous part of her identity and her vision for the future. In one of the few VS songs ever recorded, "Leather Complex," she sings:

> Only salvation for a new race
> one way out of this place
> dressed in leather, ready for space

According to Jane, "[Olga] used to carry two little mini cans of spray paint in her bass case, one black, and one red, the colors of anarchy! We would spray paint everywhere! Olga never missed an opportunity to spray the band's name somewhere, or spray over Offs graffiti!"

The *Girls in Leather* demo (recorded in 1978, released in 2015) features four songs, all tool-chest-falling-down-a haunted-stairwell jams, all dynamic and well-written tunes with cool guitar riffs and socio-political lyrics. In "Magnetic Heart" (later a Lewd song), they sing melodically,

> Heavy metal
> Nothing can stop the power
> Nothing can stop the force

Anny Unger's song "Rigor Mortis" curses politicians to live and die as insects:

> Lies! Lies!
> The capital race is stuck like flies
> to useless ideals that absorb them
> they'd look so peaceful in rigor mortis

Their collaborative effort "Present from America" invokes military power plays:

> Nowhere to run when they drop their bomb
> Present from America, neutron hysteria
> Nowhere to run, shoot 'em with a gun
> They like to kill, they like to kill
> They love to kill, they make me ill!

After recording the early 1978 demo, VS disintegrated, breaking off into other bands.

Email interview with Jane Weems, Winter 2022

Q: What got you into punk music? What did you listen to growing up?

Jane: I first got into punk music from hearing about the Sex Pistols in magazines and on TV with their boat stunt during the Queen's Jubilee. My little foster brother Mike Muñoz was into KISS, and I had taken him to see them in 1977. When we found out that the Pistols were coming to San Francisco, my parents reluctantly let me take him with me. On the morning of the show, they regretted their decision and tried to buy our tickets off of us so we wouldn't go, first offering us $10 per ticket (the tickets were $5.50 each) and we said no, then my dad offered us $20 each but we still said no, so off we went.

We got there really early, at like 10 a.m. and were surprised to see two girls already in line. One was Devorah Ostrov (a.k.a. Betty Fremont), who would later become a dear friend; the other was her friend. We were sitting there, just the four of us, when Sid Vicious walked up and said "Hey! you guys are gunna be first in line, eh?" We were thrilled! Sid was too. He was stoked to see my little brother there and asked him if he had any sweets in his pockets but was bummed when he said no. The other two girls got him to sign their record covers and we had nothing for him to sign, but he stayed and talked with us. Later on, when he spotted us in the audience, he tried to pull us up on stage but security was throwing kids really hard off the stage and we didn't want to lose our spots up front so

VS all in leather. Photo courtesy of Jane Weems.

we said no. He was smiling and when they sang "Problems," he was pointing at us and was happy we knew the songs and were singing along. Most of the people there were only there to check out the freaks and to slam people around—kind of a bummer—but it was a life-changing event for me. After that show, I started looking around for bands to play with. That is how I found Anny, who introduced me to Olga.

I was raised listening to Top 40, Motown, Stax/Volt, the Beatles (of course) and everything Mersey Beat-related. My parents were into country and western. My father was a talented western musician who used to play his fiddle and guitar for us kids growing up. So I had a very broad spectrum of music growing up always.

Q: Can you tell me about meeting Olga and the other girls? What were your first impressions?

Jane: I was VERY IMPRESSED by Olga and Anny when I first met them. I met Anny through the ad that was running every week in the free San Francisco newspaper the *Advertiser*, looking for female musicians. I was already established in that band, but the other women who answered were all much older and seemed to come from more of a rock or blues scene, no punks, as punk was rare at that time in early '78. If you did see girls dressed as punks, they were mostly fans of the music and not musicians themselves.

When Anny came to one of these open auditions, we noticed each other right away. I noticed the safety pins in her shoes and she noticed my Sex Pistols T-shirt. We were the only ones dressed like that. After practice, she drove me home and asked if I wanted to join an all-girl punk band she was starting with Olga, and I jumped at the chance!

I loved the idea and the chance to play new music, as the other band was a golden oldies band, with the end goal of playing in Vegas wearing matching suits, horn section with onstage dancing…not my bag.

So, yeah, I jumped at the chance. I quit that band the next day, and the leader lady named Rosemary was very upset. She was crying, begging me not to quit, but I really wanted to be a part of something new and more my taste in music. When I met Olga I had NEVER seen anything like her before: tall, blonde and dressed in head-to-toe black, with a spiked dog collar, chains, handcuffs. My mom bought me a leather jacket for the group, so I would fit in and be accepted. But I had no problems there…there were no other female drummers in the San Francisco area, besides Tony Hotel, the drummer/guitarist for the band On the Rag (who became Noh Mercy), who had played their first show at the Mab in late 1977, just a couple of weeks before the Sex Pistols played Winterland. They were a two-piece "art punk duo," who had their own thing going and were not interested in joining any other bands, so I was the only working drummer who had played for years in my basement with my own kit and was available, loved the burgeoning new punk scene and was eager to be a part of it.

Q: *What was women's role and particular power in the SF punk scene?*

Jane: The role of women in the early scene was mostly of supportive girlfriend, driver, roadie, fan. The only people we saw were out front as "the pretty and powerful singer" types, like Penelope Houston, even Jennifer Miro was the minimalist keyboard player in the Nuns who only did three songs during their whole set. She was really pretty and they put her right up front, helping to bring guys up to the front of the stage. Also, those girls had boyfriends in their respective bands, not that there's anything wrong with that, but it made it hard for other girls who wanted to be taken seriously and weren't there to look for a boyfriend, I thought.

I remember seeing the Alley Cats when they first played and their bassist was great, but again, I think she was married to someone in the band. The whole thing with VS was we didn't want guys in our band, we wanted to be taken seriously on our own. Both Olga and Anny had boyfriends, but they helped drive us to shows, carry our equipment…

For a long time it seemed if there was a woman in any local band she was the pretty singer up front. That was not what we were into at all. While we loved those bands and their music, it wasn't our thing. We wanted to be respected as a whole band who didn't dress up to bring dudes up front to the stage to gawk at us, you know?

Q: *In what ways did the San Francisco punk scene change between 1977–2004?*

Jane: The punk scene changed in the ensuing years by our local San Francisco bands trying to copy the Los Angeles bands' success by speeding up their existing music until it was so fast it seemed all of the juice was squeezed out of it. Case in point: the Dead Kennedys. Their first album with Bruce Schlesinger on drums and 6025 (a.k.a. Carlos Cadona) on guitar was great. Biafra's lyrics were important and meaningful, worth hearing. After D.H. (Peligro) joined as drummer (and I was in a band with him and considered him a good friend), their songs were sped up so blisteringly fast that

it just sounded like sped-up mush. Biafra's lyrics weren't legible anymore, just fast screaming and wild gesturing, stage-diving and slam dancing…not something most girls wanted to get caught up in.

When I was drumming for the Cosmetics (from 1979–1980), we actually opened for Black Flag with Keith Morris singing. It was great fun. We had good friends and family in L.A. that came up with them and everyone was cool with us. Even showing us how to do the Huntington Beach shuffle, etc…it was great fun.

The next time they came up in 1980, Henry Rollins was the singer and was dressed just like a Charles Manson clone (even having Manson Family tattoos on his body like "Creepy Crawly"). Yawn. They had a bunch of "roadies" with them, who were bashing the fuck out of all the local San Francisco kids and really hurting people. They specifically came to San Francisco to put a hurt on the local kids who paid for that privilege, which was really fucked up. Years later, I watched the movie *American Hardcore* and actually watched an interview with Henry all these years later where he was laughing and bragging about "fucking up the San Francisco kids and beating them up" at the show. That hurt my feelings and made me mad, because a band I was in (The Conservatives) opened for them and our singer Donna got yanked into the pit and her foot got stomped on. Three of her toes were broken so we spent the night with her in the E.R. I went home and broke every Black Flag record I had.

Q: *What does "punk" mean to you?*

Jane: To me, "punk" means a sort of do-it-yourself type thing, like the Little Rascals "Hey gang! Let's put on a show!" type of idea, meeting like-minded people, especially in the beginning, when there weren't very many of us, so it meant finding members of our own "tribe" and actually writing songs and playing live shows. It was so much fun! I loved meeting kids my own age who were interested in playing music, making flyers and records and doing something worthwhile and real.

I was really disappointed when it became so commercialized and accepted later. Big huge crowds of people stage-diving, hurting other kids and in the background of TV commercials. People who had no real idea what "punk" meant, and like old Henry Rollins, only there to "fuck people up in the crowd" that paid to see them, which attracted more and more ex-jocks like him, who had no respect for any of the other people there. That was awful. Bands that came to shows or formed to specifically copy that sort of ultra-violent behavior against their own kind ruined the scene for me, and I quit going out much to shows unless I was playing. ●

VKTMS

San Francisco, California » Formed in 1978

M E M B E R S

Nyna Crawford { VOCALS, HARMONICA
Jay Davis { GUITAR
Jon Binkov { GUITAR, KEYBOARDS
Steve Ricablanca, George Ritter { BASS
Lou Gwerder { DRUMS

VKTMS playing live. Photo by Greg Gaar, courtesy OpenSFHistory.org.

>> The VKTMS LP features a pointillist illustration of a girl wearing headphones and smoking a joint; the girl holds another VKTMS record with the same girl facing the camera, holding another record. Like a set of Russian dolls, each cover is a variation on the same image. The subject of the image, singer Nyna Crawford, fronted the shock-rock San Francisco posse VKTMS.

Nyna Crawford answered a bulletin board advertisement the band put out in search of a singer. When she auditioned, she impressed them with her intensity and lyrical skills. She was the perfect singer for the band, and the meeting was kismet.

On stage, she burst with energy, once cracking solid concrete with her feet. She wore heels, smoked cigarettes, and drank cocktails on stage, somehow managing mid-range jumps and low kicks while singing. Guitarist John Binkov remembers, "No one crossed her. Toughest woman on the scene. No punches pulled."

Nyna's birth name was Nina Helen Crawford. "Nina," a Czech name, was pronounced with a long 'i.' She changed the spelling just to make sure everyone knew how to say it.

Nyna grew up in Long Beach. As a child, she had theater training and sang in a Los Angeles children's chorus. She was also a regular on *Romper Room*. She shared a passion for classic vintage movies with her father. Lines from those movies wound up in lyrics or inspired songs. For example, "Close But No Cigar" was an Annie Oakley reference; and "No Long Good-Byes" contains several lines from an assortment of noir films.

In other songs, the provocateur broached unspeakable topics with a brazen attitude. In some songs, her lewdness was about personal struggle. In "Teenage Alcoholic," which she calls a true story, she sings about addiction:

I'm a teenage alcoholic
Sex and drugs and rock 'n' roll
Don't mean shit to me

In "100% White Girl," she sings about not fitting in:

I'm a blue-eyed, blonde-haired white girl
and there is nowhere left for me
I feel like an alien in my own society

Cover of VKTMS self-titled 12-inch.
Recorded in 1982, but released in 1994.

In some songs, her songs were directed outside herself. In "Too Bad," she makes fun of sexually repressed synth players:

He said he couldn't do it
I knew that he could
I said come on and try
He said I'm not in the mood
What an ego-smasher
What a big disaster

And they take on the wealthy in "God Damn the Rich":

The motherfuckers, they always want more

In the ill-named "Midget," she sings about a lover in a way some might find offensive:

He's so short, he's so fine,
all 3 foot 3 of him is mine, mine mine

The politically incorrect and vulgar VKTMS were the original edgelords—stunning audiences with taboo topics, shocking speech, and a heavy onslaught of blistering tunes. The band members who were visual artists lived in a house together and worked closely together. They put out three 7-inches but their LP, produced and engineered in 1982, collected dust on a shelf until 1994, when the group reunited as a whole until Nyna died in 2000. The group got together once again in 2012 with new members and carries on today. ●

A FABLE
by Nyna Crawford

We rode up here on the FREELOVE EXPRESS, wearin' bells & beads; we were a tie-dyed mess. I thought that I was such a bitchin' chick I wore my hair just like Grace Slick. We were all just drop-outs who couldn't really do anything that society demanded. But, we could play rock and roll and I could sing and was a poet. We convinced each other that if we made it to Frisco we could become big rock stars in no time. Hell, we had our VW micro bus, our instruments, our talent and enthusiasm.

When we finally made it to Frisco we rapidly came to the realization that Psycho - delic music was no longer the big wazoo we had thought it was. PUNK ROCK WAS THE THANG! Well shucks that was no problem, we were versatile, accomplished rock musicians, punk rock was really easy to play. Heck, all you had to know is three or four chords and play the way you did when you were just learning in your daddy's garage. It was garage rock.

We soon found a house where we all could live. The best part about this house was that it had a fallout shelter under the garage that was soundproof and we could play anytime we wanted without becoming the neighborhood menace. We had since shed our hippie adornments and taken on the appearance of the COOOOL people. We got a big trash can and filled it with water and Rit dye (black, of course) and put all of our clothing including socks, underwear and even bed sheets into the trash can. You can never go wrong wearing black.

And, we did it. We started playing and recording and we played lotsa shows around the Bay Area. We even sold a few records and got the ever-bitchin' thrill of hearing our songs being played on the radio. It was a real blast.

—Nyna

U.X.A.

San Francisco, California » Formed in 1978

MEMBERS

Original Lineup

Denise Semiroux a.k.a. De De Troit { VOCALS
Michael Kowalsky, Billy Piscioneri,
Billy Southard, Dan "Bosco" Danford { GUITAR
Lynwood Land, Patrick O'Sullivan, Lisa Pifer,
Larry Go, Rick Dasher { BASS
Richie O'Connell { DRUMS

❯❯ In front of San Francisco City Hall, a woman with a brutal blonde mullet, wearing dark lipstick and a crisp, preppy collar, sneers, brandishing a spoof newspaper with the headline "World Governments Resign as Banks Fail." In Ruby Ray's famous low-angle 1978 photo, the subject, singer of U.X.A., De De Troit, looms over the audience.

U.X.A. transpired as the creation of De De Troit and her then-boyfriend Michael Kowalsky, who tragically died at the age of 26 in 1978. Michael was a thinker and writer, obsessed with parapsychology experiments and government mind control, and initially drafted many of the band's lyrics. De De Troit said of the band, "Ideas had to be fun, original, a bit insane…We exist with the spirit of a dead realistic, paranoiac genius."

In *Search & Destroy* #7 De De said, "When [Michael] came up with the phrase 'Paranoia is Freedom' I could only smile, wishing more people realized that fear is what secludes and binds you and that paranoia is knowing so much that it makes you pretty damn angry." The acronym U.X.A. stands for "United Experiments of America." De De explained the X stood for "the unknown, subtle factor pervading the American condition of controlled media and society." In interviews, both Michael and De De describe their outlook ("I laugh and shudder at the pain of authority") and process ("sparks thrive on shock and horror but that's reality") as if they were an ideology.

On their 1980 album *Illusions of Grandeur*, the lyrics—many written by Michael—reflect a disturbed suspicion of social organization and secret government plots; the music is both gothic and poppy, a proto-grunge drone carries De De's husky, all-knowing voice. Closing out the album, she shouts,

**No Savior with style!
Death From Above!
Death From Above!**

and

**Nobody's gonna save you
You gotta save yourself!**

Doomy guitars and swirling zombie backing vocals create a wall of sound, flaying religious dogma in favor of gloomy, macabre chaos. De De's devilish pose is layered in front of a spider web on the album's original cover.

Thirty-seven years later, the smiling band leader told Jet Wilson of Blast TV,

> "My story is that I was born and raised in Detroit, Michigan, and I was born again in south central Los Angeles."

She joined a church choir after a friend mentioned the idea to her; part of the reason she did so was because she wanted to sing R&B. She continues:

> "I was not even thinking about getting saved, but one Sunday morning, I took up with the altar call…"

Because she's relocated a lot, it's hard to tether De De to one region, but in the late '70s and early '80s, U.X.A. was a major player in the San Francisco

U.X.A. performing live. Photo by Ruby Ray.

U.X.A. continued

punk scene and considered one of the pinnacle punk bands on Posh Boy Records. Their 1980 album *Illusions of Grandeur* is classic old school: a few chords, chunky guitars, vicious solos, machine-gun drums and haunting Herculean vocals. The album boasts track titles like "Paranoia is Freedom" and the famous "Death From Above."

In "Immunity," De De introduces the song with the obligatory spoken-word intro in a faux British accent:

**My mommy died a social drinker
and my daddy still collects guns**

While she's distanced herself from her past, friends speak fondly of De De. A YouTuber writes, "De De has been like the fairy Godmother of wayward punks for over 40 years." On the blog Art for

Change, Slash Magazine artist Mark Vallan writes, "U.X.A. was ubiquitous in San Francisco and Los Angeles during the late 1970s. The full-throated atonal wailing, darkly poetic lyrics, and anti-fashion panache of lead singer De De Troit, made her a lightning rod for the underground scene."

After *Illusions of Grandeur*, U.X.A. disbanded. De De formed the De De Troit Band, which was shortened to De De Troit, and then she played with the Cotton Ponys before reforming U.X.A. in the '90s with Dasher of the Dickies and drummer Suzi Homewrecker, at some point moving to New York.

De De recalls she "came into relationship with Christ in the year 2000." UXA has played with many members over the last 40 years and played as recently as 2016. De De wants Christian members and while the two phrases tend to attract polar opposite politics, she changed the title of her song "Anarchy is Justice for All" to "Jesus Christ is Justice for All." ●

IXNA

San Francisco, California » Formed in 1978

M E M B E R S

Marina La Palma { VOCALS, LYRICS
Jay Cloidt { INSTRUMENTS

Cover of *Knotpop*, IXNA's 12-inch. Recorded in 1981, but released in 2019. From the collection of Jen B. Larson.

》On the cover of IXNA's "Mi Ne Parolas"/"Ixna Portal Exo," two hands face off holding collapsible push-button puppets—the creature is hard to make out, true to the group's minimalist, experimental nature. The lyrics on the album are sung in Esperanto, an auxiliary tongue meant to bridge language barriers between people who do not share a primary language. The first song translates, roughly, to "I Do Not Speak."

On Marina La Palma's website, she has a reading list, an astonishingly long one, logging the books she's devoured each year for the last four decades, most of which are quite obscure. The voracious reader is also a generous creator across media, as evidenced by the sections of her website: visual art, poetry, publications, and music.

She describes herself: "I am a human being, dedicated to learning as much as possible in this lifetime." Based on her personal appendix and creative output, the statement appears to be true. "I read a lot. Fiction, history, sociology, anthropology, developments in science and technology, global politics, the natural world and our impact on it, social justice," she writes on social media.

Born in Milan, Italy, she moved to the States early in life. With degrees in poetry and recording media, visual arts, and comparative literature, she also took graduate courses in film studies and romance philology. She met Jay Cloidt at Mills College, where she studied poetry and recording media in undergrad. Mills' music program was celebrated for its work in experimental sound study

and composition, and Jay was a graduate student at the school. The two formed IXNA and began experimenting with rhythm, lyrics, and sound, deconstructing both pop songs and the avant-garde. Notable composers like Luciano Berio taught there, and celebrated pop culture musicians like Laurie Anderson, Joanna Newsom, and Dave Brubeck all attended the program.

IXNA only put out one 7-inch in 1982, but recorded other songs, a collection of which were mastered from their original reels and released in 2018 on an album entitled *Knotpop*. The title describes the work's relationship to its perceived genres—a deviant new wave that builds on the wisdom of the avant-garde while radicalizing its dismissal of the status quo by embracing and distorting radio-friendly music, inverted or sideways, mutant in its embodiment of what's cool.

SIDE A

FUN FUN FUN

RIDI RIDI

BLACK SHIRTS

FLASHLIGHT

I CAN'T REMEMBER

SIDE B

GALILEO

SOMEBODY SAID

IN THE CITY

IXNA PORTAL EXO

MI NE PAROLAS

IXNA is Jay Cloidt and Marina La Palma

Back cover of *Knotpop*. From the collection of Jen B. Larson.

IXNA continued

The songs were recorded at the Center For Contemporary Music at Mills College in 1981 and feature Jay's studio mastery, subtly sampling perfect specimen pop riffs from songs like "I Want Candy" and "Johnny B. Goode." Combined with his precise musicianship on piano and bass, Marina's silver-tongued multilingual vocals (she sings in English, Italian and Esperanto) mutate between songs, layering both nonsense and sophistication.

Since the IXNA project, Marina La Palma has dedicated her life to the arts—founding a press, working as a performance artist and art critic, sitting on the board for a nonprofit dedicated to literacy-building in young children, and participating in every part of the publication process. Having lived in various cities, traveled all over the world, and practiced many disciplines, she's continued the quest for knowledge. ●

LOS MICROWAVES

San Jose, California   »   Formed in 1978

MEMBERS

Meg Brazill { VOCALS, BASS, SYNTHESIZER
David Javelosa { VOCALS, SYNTHESIZER
Todd "Rosa" Rosencrans { DRUMS,
ELECTRONIC PERCUSSION, BASS

Additional members
Caroline Canning { PERCUSSION
Pilar Limosner { KEYBOARDS

Los Microwaves as a four-piece. Photographer unknown. Courtesy of David Javelosa.

》 The synth-dominant trio performs in an underground vault with psychedelic lighting effects, swirling milk cartons, a tunnel, and flashes of silver party streamers in the Kim Dempster-directed music video for the song "Life After Breakfast."

Their bizarre sense of humor makes the video feel like a comedy sketch. The three-piece ham it up on synth, bass, and a snare and hi-hat in the video (clearly there are other drums on the recording). The members undergo cheesy transitions and costume changes. Musically, Los Microwaves' minimal electro-sound is danceable, kept together by bass and sturdy beat. The question is posed: "Is there life after breakfast?" Meg Brazill, who plays guitar in the short video, comes forth from behind a silver curtain wearing onesie pajamas. She affirms, "It takes more than Wonder Bread" as she squeezes two soft, starchy slices of white bread against her face, and then rolls them into snakes. "It takes more than Wheaties," she declares as bran flakes explode from under a shiny blanket. The trio's humor culminates at the end, where they chant in unison:

**Let them eat cake but give me
butter and toast**

Los Microwaves bassist Meg and synth player David met through work in 1978. They were both employed as nonprofit arts administrators in San Francisco. David recalls meeting his lifelong friend: "Originally I was going for the same job as her. There was a party fundraiser. And a postcard with Meg dressed as a musician with dark sunglasses. Each person on the card represented a different art form; music, dance, painting."

Meg told David she was an actress and he saw her perform in a theater collaboration called *Reckless Dialogue*. He began talking to her about music and she told him that she could play the banjo. He convinced her that the bass was similar (having four strings), and the two started writing songs, recording, and gigging together. Once they met drummer Todd through Meg's roommate, the three pillars of the band were set.

Early Microwaves recordings like "I Don't Wanna Hold You" and "Forever" have a different, psychedelic, baroque pop feel with rolling basslines and walls of organ. But the work they are most known for is primitive and melodic electronic drums, scheming bass, and hooky, spasmodic vocals. A single and a song off their only LP, *Life After Breakfast*, "Radio Heart" is

Los Microwaves as a three-piece. Photographer unknown. Courtesy of David Javelosa.

defined by its herky-jerky rhythms and cheeky chants. Los Microwaves' catchy tune "What's That Got to Do (With Loving You?)" is memorable and danceable, and it should be considered an electro-punk classic.

There were a few other synth bands in San Francisco that clubs would tend to book Los Microwaves with, but the group was also compatible with guitar-dominant bands. David said, "Our music was more power pop and beat-oriented, so we did well with most guitar bands. Our influences included Kraftwerk and Human League, but also Television and XTC, who we actually got to open for!"

During a cross-country tour in 1980, Los Microwaves met with Mark Kamins from Antilles/Island records (Kamins produced Madonna's first single "Everybody" in 1982). Kamins urged the band to add a fourth member to fill out their sound.

David Javelosa said, "When we got back to San Francisco, rather than getting a guitarist or another keyboard player like I'm sure Mark had envisioned, I wanted to get a percussionist to add to our drummer and rhythm machine. I had always wanted a salsa-sounding rhythm section. Also, we wanted to keep the band's co-ed image, so we were looking for another female. We found our female percussionist in Caroline Canning, a friend of friends of the band and it really worked."

Canning recorded the *Life After Breakfast* LP with the group and toured the West Coast. In early 1981, the group moved to New York City but Caroline stayed in San Francisco to attend law school.

San Francisco friends began relocating to New York. David said, "This included Pilar Limosner, who had performed with Baby Buddha[1] as a dancer. Meg and Pilar were good friends and Pilar could also play keyboards. So starting in mid-'82, Pilar started playing with the band and doing a fire dance with live torches for the finale!" Pilar left the band just before their last show at Danceteria in March of 1983 and didn't return for reunion shows, while Caroline did.

The band name—Los Microwaves—was a statement on Silicon Valley. The Spanish article ("Los") in their band name wasn't in vain either. The band was bilingual, singing in Spanish, and Javelosa grew up in a Spanish-speaking part of San Jose where his father was a Spanish teacher. He said, "Meg actually spoke better Spanish than I did!"

In 1982, Meg released music from a solo project called Maria De Janeiro. Recordings featured guest artists, including Margot Olavarria, the original bass player from the Go-Go's, and Caroline Canning on percussion and ankle bells. Sadly, Meg Brazill passed away suddenly and unexpectedly in December of 2021. ●

---

1 Baby Buddha is a side project of David Javelosa and Charles Hornaday. There were many members from San Francisco bands, including Meg Brazill and Kathy Peck.

ROMEO VOID

San Francisco, California » Formed in 1979

MEMBERS

Debora Iyall { VOCALS, LYRICS
Frank Zincavage { BASS
Peter Woods { GUITAR
Benjamin Bossi { SAXOPHONE
Jay Derrah, John "Stench" Hanes,
Larry Carter, Aaron Smith { DRUMS

» A snare hits milliseconds before a saxophone hook cuts through an eerie wave of percussion and keys. The camera pulls out to reveal a utility pole in front of a screen with one dark brown eye, half of an entire face. There is the face of a real person, speaking into a silver phone. A painter, all in white, strokes the screen-turned-canvas, emulating brush strokes—under and over the face's eyes and on the lips—as if applying makeup. The song is "A Girl in Trouble (Is a Temporary Thing)." Debora Iyall, the face on the screen, begins singing sensually and evenly, embracing the viewer:

> She's got a face that shows that
> she knows she's heard every line
> Tenderly she talks on the phone

The shot cuts to a man getting slapped across the face with the red-coated paintbrush. Debora cocks an eyebrow and sings,

> There's a way to walk that says 'stay away'
> And a time to go around the long way

The painter walks the telephone line like a tightrope with purple shoes and pink socks; she falls…into the rest of the video. A man, sleeping on an atmospheric beach, grabs her ankle.

The video is a near-literal interpretation of the opening lyrics and a rebuttal to "Billie Jean." Singer and lyricist Iyall explains, "the sentiment was a reaction to 'the kid is not my son'…I just thought…'that's so low, that's just so mean.'" The song is also about a real friend of Debora, a troublemaker. The saxophone expresses pain that cannot be conveyed in words while she sings,

> There's a time when every girl learns
>   to use her head
> Tears will be saved 'til they're better spent
> There's no time for her to be afraid
>   so instead
> She takes care of her business
>   and keeps a cool head

Romeo Void flyer created by Debora Iyall.
Oil crayon and mixed media.

Iyall grew up belting Lesley Gore's "You Don't Own Me," Dionne Warwick's "Don't Make Me Over" and recalls, "I really loved all the girl group sounds and Motown." Growing up in Fresno, she saw Janis Joplin at the Rainbow Ballroom, Jimi Hendrix, and the Doors, and once she ate KFC with Santana's family. She also sought out Patti Smith shows when she did poetry readings at a record store, an acoustic set with John Cale in Berkeley.

A Cowlitz Native American, Debora was born in Washington and raised in Fresno. She dropped out of high school and worked as a medical assistant in Eureka, Washington (a very small rural town). One day, Debora received a sign from the universe that there was something else out there for her. She opened a fortune cookie, and its message ("Art is your fate, don't debate") convinced her to move to San Francisco to enroll at the San Francisco Art Institute. At SFAI, she met joined a mixed-gender cover band called the Mummers and Poppers. (The group was Charlie from the Mutants' side project.) They played fun, danceable music, including versions of "300 Pounds of Heavenly Joy" and "Boy from New York City."

Debora remembers: "The first time I remember thinking 'I could do this… I could have my own band' was when I saw Penelope of the Avengers. I remember thinking 'I have something to say… like she did.' She was a role model of mine." But starting a punk band did not mean she was going to dress in a uniform or dye her hair green. "One thing I could not do was completely conform," she says.

Debora met bassist Frank when she worked for the video lab at school. He worked in a nearby gallery and began bringing a bass to work. Their first song was bass, drum machine, and vocals; then they added Peter on rhythm guitar to achieve a modern, danceable sound (à la Roxy Music) without long drawn-out guitar solos.

"[The saxophone] was the most beautiful accident," she says gleefully. "Benjamin came out of jazz tradition where there was a lot of improvisation… it was more like a lead instrument. [He] was just a listener. He would just listen to the band and take what was happening and elevate it and make it more intense and react to it, and I feel like, emotionally he was freer to say what I was saying than I was vocally saying it…as far as the intensity of emotion that could be behind the song."

Debora's lyrics were created in the spaces within the song. "I would hear a way in on top of what was going on. I never knew what the hell I was doing. If you ever asked me what's the difference between a verse and a chorus, I couldn't tell you…I was just winging it."

Debora says, "When I quit high school at age 16, I started sitting in on poetry classes at Fresno State. There were poets there out of the beat poetry tradition. It was always the image…not only the image but the specific image…the attention to the atmosphere is revealing the meaning, it's in the mood placements and transitions."

When choosing a band name, Debora made a list of words she liked. "We didn't want to be a 'the.' We were listening to bands like Joy Division. The 'the' era was over for us," she discloses. After reading an article in a local magazine titled "Why single women can't get laid in San Francisco," Debora connected the words 'Romeo' and 'Void.' She said, "Romeo and Void jumped together and said 'we want to be together and we want to be the name of your band because you write about relationships and sex and love.'"

Debora's lyrics detail the movement and emotion of a scene. Collecting images from real life and pairing them with words of advice, she writes in a cadence that meanders between the rhythms of the song, while her delivery and expressions on the saxophone underscore the intensity. In "Shake the Hands of Time," the lyrics:

He left a hole in the wall
You ask, did he call?

escalate to

You gotta shake the hands of time
Get that jerk off your mind

and

There's no money in boyfriends
Look ahead, don't look back
You gotta shake him off your back

In "Flashflood," a deluge symbolizes the end of a relationship in the lines:

The puddle in the apartment
The puddle in the market

Early 1980s Romeo Void promotional photo by Michele Clement.

and also in

Your green-tooled carpet
The weight of your footsteps
You gave out your number
Someone drowns in your flashflood

You used to smile when I walked
    out the door
Not anymore

The band's best-known song "Never Say Never" is often most remembered for its chorus, "I might like you better if we slept together," but panning out, the song is like an Impressionist painting, a collection of obscure details. Snippets strung together under the movement of the sun evince the mood of a dark world: girls being careful how they operate, a homeless man sleeping downtown, an ugly old couple in love. Debora stresses, "Women have to be careful, man. Sunsuit girls must be discreet. You have no idea what goes on in the mind of the misogynists or predators around you… sometimes the predators are people that we know… I can say that because I've seen it. Sunsuit girls should be discreet. We are not safe."

The song was featured in the film *The Wolf of Wall Street*. Debora says,

"When it came out, I was very excited and thought, 'Scorsese has a good person working on the music (Robbie Robertson). They know the song…and I was so hopeful…I'm thinking, it's gotta be they are using '[Slumped by the courthouse / With windburn skin / That man could give a fuck / About the grin on your face / As you walk by, randy as a goat / He's sleeping on papers / But he'd be warm in your coat]' — that could totally go in a movie about wolves of Wall Street…he'd be warm in your coat, you rich-ass fucker. Instead, it's like in a party scene with that one character who always annoys me so much jerking off with that woman he cheats on his wife with. All they really play in the whole thing is the chorus. Here I think it's going to be this moment of artistic understanding…[that] they get what the power struggle in the song is about."

She sighs and chuckles, "How privileged of a person am I that I have such a strong chorus that I am actually disappointed that that's what everyone remembers?"

As for misogyny in the music world, Debora affirms it is society-pervasive, and that with her mother's influence, she chose her way against the grain and has always lived by the motto "make a way for yourself in the world."

She explains, "I grew up as a girl who was not going to be a sex object, and I knew that and taught my role at a young age, like 'oh, you're not one of the attractive cute people but you're still female so what good are you?' I had the confidence to create my own way to be a person. I guess in a way if I couldn't be accepted as a female, I decided to be accepted as a person and I kept myself to some high standards."

The band's distinct sound was fused at the hands of a tight backline—guitar, bass, drums. The saxophone holds rhythm or solos alongside the vocals. And according to the band members, Debora's passion was truly the driving force behind them. Bassist Frank Zincavage said, "Debora was really positive. It was contagious to have that energy and that enthusiasm that she had, it was great."

The band's fan base grew and grew, and just as they were positioned for mainstream success, record executives at Columbia Records decided to drop the band while on a nationwide tour in support of "A Girl in Trouble," supposedly because Debora's look didn't fit the bill. The record executives didn't realize how much the public needs and relates to diverse identities, body types, and looks. Punk is about rebelling against the white middle-class status quo and that's exactly what Debora's presence represents.

Debora told *Rocker Zine* in 2012, "The [label's] marketing department wasn't sure about us. Had they had a little bit of vision they would have realized that I already had a lot of fans in the gay world and that a lot of disaffected youth were relating to me. I had a lot of girls of color, and bigger girls who were embracing me just as I am. That's why people loved Romeo Void because I wasn't a cookie-cutter girl singer. I don't have that in my being to ever be that, and that is a strength people love."

After focusing on a solo career and releasing an album, *Strange Language*, in 1986, Debora focused on printmaking, and poetry, and began teaching high school art. Debora returned to music in 2010 with the record *Stay Strong* and *Singing until Sunrise* in 2012. ●

THE CONTRACTIONS

San Francisco, California » Formed in 1979

MEMBERS

Mary Kelley { GUITAR, VOCALS
Debbie Hopkins { DRUMS, PERCUSSION, VOCALS
Kathy Peck { BASS, VOCALS

For a short time
Kim Morris { KEYBOARDS, VOCALS

Cover of *Something Broke*, the Contractions' 1984 12-inch. From the collection of Jen B. Larson.

》》A haunted guitar riff emerges, a bass line punctuates its root notes, and the shriek of a power drill looms behind it all in empty space. The thumping heartbeat of a kick drum and a skintight snare ground the fray. The song progresses, and wobbly footage from all angles of the stage—zooming in and panning out—reveals a power trio in action. Guitarist Mary Kelley in a jumpsuit wails on vocals, drummer Deb Hopkins keeps rhythm, and Kathy Peck bounces around on stage with a bass. Besides a multipurpose tool, the song "Tribute to Industry" showcases gang vocals, allusions to *West Side Story*, classical Japanese musical arrangements, and an Arabian snake-charmer riff.

Mary, Kathy, and Deb take turns on vocals. Kathy sings a simpler, punchy tune called "Magazine Phobia," and Mary takes lead again on "Water Beast." Opening with feedback, the guitarist croons soulfully while simultaneously and impressively riffing. With the same intensity at a different speed, the tune feels like a rock opera, equipped with ripping guitar and infused with drama; the prog-rock influence is palpable. From behind the kit, Deb takes vocals on "Rank and Vile," a critique of capitalism. She sings,

Checking their watches
They clock in at 9
going out to lunch
they drink white wine

The show was a 1981 performance at S.I.R., a studio instrument rental space, where arena-rock bands like Journey would rehearse before large events. The Contractions rented out the room and invited their friends for the shoot while a local porn company filmed it. A few weeks later, the group got together with the engineer in a studio built inside an old step van. Deb recalls,

"The board was in the truck. He and our sound crew set up all the mics and cables and ran them to his board. Then a few weeks later he drove the truck to our road manager's place in Sonoma County, out in the woods. We all stayed there for a weekend. There was a hot tub so we were partying and hot tubbing and then would run into the step van as needed for mixes."

Deb added auxiliary percussion, using gravel, shovels, and a chainsaw. She says,

"It's a musical reference to what happened between Japan and America after the war and how much industry developed as a result of World War II and where that had taken us…The first time we were going to perform it was at the Deaf Club, our first gig at a club. Mary had a chainsaw with the chain removed, I had a big piece of steel, a hammer, and a drill. We used these in the intro, but the club and all clubs thereafter would not allow the chain saw even with no chain."

In the studio, the band sounds very different from their live show. Two consistencies are the omnipresent time changes and inimitable musicianship. Their single "Rules and Regulations" demonstrates their penchant for pop, while on their full-length record *Something Broke* their sound on many songs is even more disparate—adding new-wave flair like saxophones, additional percussion, and piano.

Mary possessed important carpentry skills, and the group built their recording studio by hand. To accommodate a complaining neighbor, they even constructed a room within a room for added soundproofing. Deb recalls the process as a strange time for the band. They recorded their parts separately and even had the photos on the cover taken separately and edited together (if you look closely, Mary and Deb are even wearing the same jacket). "It's a mish-mosh," Debbie says.

In terms of the band's sound, bassist Kathy Peck disclosed that punk wasn't the goal. "[Mary] was a pretty great guitarist; she would not play the same thing twice," she says, and "we'd end up jamming, which wasn't punk rock at all…We'd end up going to some weird place…it was kinda experimental."

Live, the trio captivated the audience with mostly original tunes, and showgoers remember their performances as magical. The group all brought important aspects to their collaboration. They were professional and hardworking, rehearsing three times a week. Kathy socialized within the scene and guided their aesthetic, suggesting clothing and styles to the group. From behind the kit, Deb often directed the practices and remembers Kathy and Mary's influences and songwriting complementing one another: "Kathy's songs were more palatable and in a groove, while Mary's songs were intellectual; her lyrics were poetic and political."

Esoteric and sometimes macabre, all the songwriters' lyrics often reference lost loves, psychic energy, and death. In "Vampyre's Song," they sing:

Now I want for nothing on this
    physical plane
And so till my death will probably remain
I've seen governments and movements
    All Rise and Fall
No one has ever known my secrets at all
Now as the days turn to years
and my nights in my eyes sometimes
    turn to tears
and as my life operates away
Someone could swear somewhere they
    heard this melody being played

They also had songs with simple and precise lyrics, their vocals creating a wall of sound anchored by manic drum expressions and accompanied by an interpretive saxophone. They sang,

**Fuck you, fuck you
fuck you, fuck you**

As a child, Kathy's first instrument was piano. She says, "I would just get on the piano and space out." As a teenager, she found a bass stored under her brother's bed, and she took it. Mary was classically trained, starting with classical French horn, then shifting to guitar. Debbie was a serious, meticulous drummer with jazz consciousness, who started playing as a young kid, joining bands in sixth grade and in her high school band. She remembers:

"I used to get teased a lot in high school. I was first chair and that didn't go over well with the six other drummers who were all boys. They'd sit behind me and lift my dress up with sticks. I got called 'little drummer boy' all the time."

In the late '70s, Mary met both Deb and Kathy through friends and they formed the Contractions. Their band name is based on an inside joke. Kathy would inattentively leave her hollow-body Hofner bass on, leaning up against an amp. It would give feedback and the girls would chastise her: "Kathy, don't!" Then they began saying "Kathy Don't," "Debbie Doesn't," "Mary Won't." When a musician at their practice space asked their name, it was then decided: "The Contractions."

Before the Contractions, Deb played in Leila and the Snakes and a disco band. Kathy worked in a music studio in Los Angeles. The group found an opportunity in the punk scene but also floated between scenes, including the women's music scene. They wanted to be viewed as musicians and not lumped into any category. Kathy said, "In women's music, there wasn't any rock 'n' roll going on really,

Cover of "Rules and Regulations" / "You Touched Me," the Contractions' 1980 7-inch. From the collection of Jen B. Larson.

it was kind of soft rock, folk…" They were even negatively reviewed by an attendee of the Michigan Women's Fest as "that terrible male-energy band."

Deb, who identifies as gay, said, "I felt [the gay scene] was very confining. It wasn't acceptable to be a gay woman in 1976 and wearing makeup or dressing feminine."

Kathy said, "Being a woman didn't need to be a thing, but for many women in the scene, it was." Deb remembers bookers putting the Contractions on some shows just because there were other women in the bands, and hearing things like "you're good at drums for a girl," or telling someone she was in a band and them responding by asking "Are you the singer?"

The Contractions played with the Go-Go's plenty before the L.A. quintet got signed. Their last show with them was at the Go-Go's signing party in New York City. Before that, Deb recalls, "Everyone was telling us only one girl band is gonna get signed."

In addition to misogyny, homophobia was prevalent, too. Deb shares a horrifying story:

"I got my jaw dislocated at the Mab one time because I was watching my girlfriend play and standing at the front of the stage. Some guy made a nasty homophobic remark because I was looking at her, and I told him to fuck off. He took me and used my head as a battering ram into the cigarette machine. He really fucked me up."

A friend of the band, Kim Morris, from the Nervous (a Phoenix, Arizona band), joined them on keys for about a year. It drastically changed the feeling of the band and they mutually parted ways, going back to their power-trio roots. After the Contractions broke up for good, Deb played with Yvette and K.D. from Wilma in Impulse F. Kathy played in Baby Buddha and also founded H.E.A.R., a nonprofit volunteer organization dedicated to preventing hearing loss and raising awareness of the dangers of repeated exposure to excessive noise levels. Mary recorded solo work that showcases the depth of her talents. "I didn't recognize Mary's brilliance as much as I should have at the time," Deb says. ●

INFLATABLE BOY CLAMS

San Francisco, California   »   Formed in 1980

MEMBERS

Carol Detweiler { BASS, DRUMS, ORGAN, VOCALS
JoJo Planteen { BASS, VOCALS
Judy Gittelsohn { ORGAN, SLIDE GUITAR,
BASS, VOCALS
Genevieve Boutet de Monvel { SAXOPHONE

A large white space surrounds a black-and-white image. In it, there are four bodies from mid-torso to mid-ankle. Three are in long skirts—one A-line and two paneled—and one is in slacks. The middle figures hold hands, and a fatherly arm grips the farthest on the left. The Puritan, all-solid-colored cast could be attending a church social or pushing paper at an office. Who would think they were an art punk group, playing bizarre, inharmonic punk in the trenches of the San Francisco scene?

The quartet created one five-song EP. It included the childlike circus ditty "Skeletons" (a voice quivers "I am a skeleton dancing on the wall" and later "two little skeletons dancing on the wall" like a schoolyard chant) and "Snoteleks," the former song written and recorded backward. Another song, set to an ominous organ and background chanting, "I'm Sorry" consists of confessions of cruelty (stealing a boyfriend, smashing a car, destroying a tape collection) between two friends. Delivered apathetically, like a teenager forced to make amends with a sibling, all the admissions conclude with a canned, insincere apology:

> "You know your blue dress? Your favorite one with all the lace and the full skirt? Well, I wore it out the other night and I thought I would surprise you at that party we went to last Friday? So, it was real nice to wear and stuff. But I came home, and I had started my period. And it was all over the back of it, this big stain. And so, I tried to bleach it out because I knew that you liked the dress so much. But I bleached out the dress and it ate away all the fabric in the back, plus all the petticoats. So, there's this big hole all around the skirt. I'm sorry."

Inflatable Boy Clams formed in 1980. Judy and Carol, who met at the Art Institute of San Francisco, were embedded in the punk scene, also playing with Stephen Wymore and Matt Heckert in the new wave art-rock outfit Pink Section, a colorful co-ed group who took a more standard approach to writing and playing. Later, they also played in the neo-beat poetry Longshoremen with David Swan in the mid-'80s.

The Inflatable Boy Clams gave the girls space and autonomy to create on their own terms. "I'm young enough to not be intimidated by men, but I'm old enough to know that men kind of like ran the rock scene," Judy tells Please Kill Me. "It didn't bother me. But Boy Clams was the ultimate expressive woman thing, or girl-female thing. Where rehearsal for the Boy Clams was the four of us, or three of us, drooling on the floor, hollering. It was so intensely creative."

They'd conceptualize a song and then create it. They'd pare down the bass and drums and cherish their accidents. Genevieve would improvise on saxophone. They'd rotate instruments and plan their outfits for their performance. According to Judy, they wore layers of clothing—"bathing suits with a school-girl outfit on top of them, with a party dress on top of them, with business suits on top of them"—and take off a layer after each song.

Carol shares, "It just felt a lot more natural and there wasn't so much tension or expectation. As an all-girl band, it was like anything goes." ●

INFLATABLE BOY CLAMS

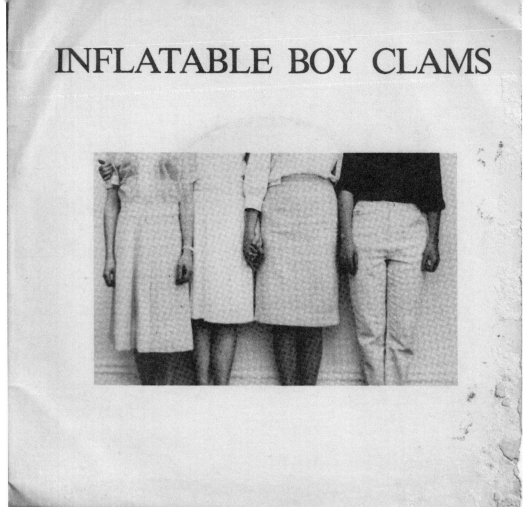

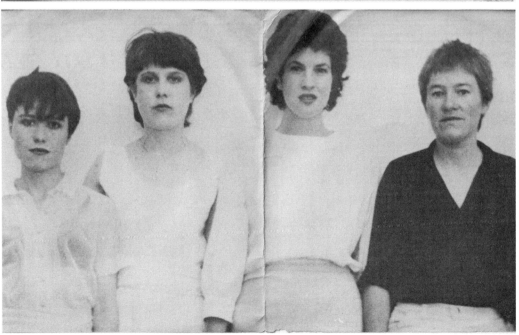

Top: Cover of Inflatable Boy Clams' 1981 self-titled 7-inch. Bottom: Insert for Inflatable Boy Clams' 1981 self-titled 7-inch. Both from the collection of Jen Lemasters.

WILMA

San Francisco, California » Formed in 1981

M E M B E R S

K.D. Davis { BASS, VOCALS,
KEYBOARDS, PERCUSSION
Louise Diedrich { SYNTHESIZERS,
VIOLIN, VOCALS
Yvette Kay { GUITAR, VOCALS, BASS
Kris Panebianco { DRUMS

» One chord strikes, and behind it, the hi-hat counts time. The chord doubles and rapidly a high-tuned snare rolls in a beat at breakneck speed. Yelping feverishly, the singer wastes no time condemning the Reagans:

He's a fast fascist, got a Christian smile
Got a funny haircut, got your name on file
He's a fast fascist, got a secret plan
To turn America into McDonald's land
Ronnie never does it 'cept to procreate
but late at night when the mood is right
Ronnie kneels down and opens up
and lets Christ come inside

The whole band joins the chorus "he's a fast fascist/he's a fast fascist," then the drummer plays breaks halfway through verse two:

Nancy is a Stepford wife
She's the latest gadget
She's a nuclear microwave
Womb unit, put an egg in her
She'll hatch it

Punchy and political, this is the opening song on Wilma's 45 "Pornography Lies," the only record they put out before breaking up (their full-length album came out posthumously). Side two features the title track, a down-tempo tune made with a drum machine, singular guitar plucks, and violin high in the mix. The lyrics critique the objectification of the female body:

Video simulation
The violence between her thighs
Disposable pleasure
In the feminine form
Girl fuck kill come
The patriarchal norm

Gigging as a group of out lesbians in the early '80s wasn't easy, not even in San Francisco, where people were experiencing a radical sexual revolution; not even in the punk scene where people were otherwise challenging the status quo. For the members, it was apparent they were outside the margins, both as punks and gay women. The women's movement wasn't for them or about them. The punk scene didn't know what to do with them. Gay culture wasn't really aligned with what they were doing. Bassist K.D. Davis says,

"The lesbian presence in punk music was completely invisible at that point—completely. As lesbian feminists, we didn't have a place for ourselves. It was not cool to be us. There was no riot grrrl, no guys thinking 'isn't it cool to have angry women on stage?'"

At shows, guys threw full beer cans at them and called them dykes. "It was constant conflict," lyricist and violinist Louise Diedrich remembers. "We had to develop thick skin."

"We had a reputation for being lesbian separatists," guitarist and songwriter Yvette Kay points out. "I wasn't a lesbian separatist personally," she muses. "It's possible we were…for like five minutes," she laughs. "Maybe we deserved the moniker, maybe we

Wilma as a three-piece. L–R: K.D., Yvette, Louise. Photo courtesy of the band Translator.

didn't. I don't know, but we did get a lot of shit."

People graffitied their band space and they beefed publicly with Jello Biafra. (According to various stories, he accused them on the radio and in zines of putting a hex on him, firebombing his house "or," according to K.D., "some weird shit.")

Louise responds, "I was moving in and out of separatism, but made no claims to the kind of purity of those ideals—at that time....It was *my* trajectory...but I don't think [the others were]. Lesbian separatism is almost impossible to realize in some kind of pure way, I mean just from an economic standpoint," Louise adds.

So, perhaps the term was mentioned, but it is unclear how the label stuck, other than the people using the term derogatorily or simply not understanding its meaning. Aside from the fact that lesbian separatists tend to live away from cities— buying land and settling away from men and heterosexual women—the group had a male drummer on their 7-inch, a male manager, a male-run record label, and played shows in San Francisco, which required them to interact with men and heterosexual women regularly. To an outsider, "separatist" seems like an illogical descriptor overall.

In general, neither feminism nor lesbianism were topics people were comfortable discussing in any real way in many art scenes, punk included. Interviewers regularly asked them why they hated men. The way the band responded was with absurdity: bringing in bizarre children's records to play on radio interviews, putting Barbie dolls on stage, collaging Wilma Flintstone's head onto the body of Patty Hearst holding a machine gun for show posters.

"It was upsetting to the conformists," Louise said. She also concludes, "Whether or not we were gay…We would have been called dykes anyway because that's what you'd call four women who hang out together."

While the members drew different conclusions about lesbian feminist politics, they seem to agree that they wanted to play rock music but not in the women's music scene, which was the main avenue for lesbian musicians to gig at the time. K.D. recalls,

"Back in the day, if you wanted a gig [at a lesbian bar], you had to play beautiful little sweet harmonies. You had to play at being utopian lesbians out in the country with no electric music and no anger. We were rejected flatly and resoundingly by the very community that inspired us to want to become a band and play for women. Ultimately, to keep playing, we had to play mixed clubs. We had a hell of a time attracting any women whatsoever to our gigs…Straight women in punk would never be caught dead at one of our gigs because we were the dyke band."

So, for Wilma, "challenging the patriarchy" ruffled some feathers. While women were far more accepted in punk than other rock genres, being out lesbians came with extra challenges. Without access to relationships with men in the same way straight women have, lesbians have to impress audiences and work twice as hard for opportunities. Homophobia from both men and women created obstacles.

"I think the hardest thing for lesbian bands is the lack of connections," Yvette says. "If you're a straight girl and you are in a band, you've probably got a boyfriend or some men in your life who are more willing to help you get places."

Additionally, straight women might snub you. The group idolized the UK all-girl band the Slits. And when they were booked to open for them, it was a dream come true until, a few days before the show, they were booted from the bill in favor of an all-guy reggae band.

"We had postered everywhere. It had been announced. People showed up to the show, thinking we were going to be playing," Yvette laments. "So, when I read Viv Albertine's book—which was very good, by the way—she talked about how hard it was for women musicians and how they were really into promoting other women and being very girl power. But I don't think that's very 'girl power' to bump us for a male reggae band. And if I ever talk to her, I am going to tell her."

It's unclear if the band made the decision to bump Wilma, or if it was their management or the venue itself, but the gig would have had a really big impact on their career. It would have been major exposure and validated them to the critics in their own city.

"[The punk scene] seems to remember itself as being much more open-minded than it actually was," Yvette laments. "It really wasn't open-minded about lesbians…"

Wilma as a four-piece. L–R: Kris Panebianco, Yvette, K.D., Louise. Photo courtesy of Translator/Julie Roxx.

While K.D. and Yvette agree there was a lot of homophobia, Louise chalks the discrimination up to misogyny in general. Even in retrospect. While their recordings tell a different story, most of the locatable reviews called them "pissed off" or "seething" lesbian separatists who lambasted the patriarchy. What's missing from the descriptors is that Wilma is also very funny and avant-garde while being pop-oriented. Influences like Laurie Anderson and Talking Heads are palpable. Their brand of art punk is absurd but accessible.

As a trio, Louise, K.D., and Yvette started out playing somewhat electronically with a drum machine while Louise ran a violin through a synthesizer she built herself (K.D. described her setup as a mad scientist lab where she made "all these Brian Eno boops and bops"). K.D., who had been educated in an experimental music school as a child, played a cherry-red bass she bought from a cult of Sun Myung Moon yard sale, and Yvette brought the rock element on guitar. For their 7-inch, "Pornography Lies," they recruited a drummer.

Later, a Juilliard-trained drummer named Kris joined them and played on their self-titled posthumous album. The album contains an unhinged rock version of "Georgy Girl" as well as some darker, intense songs like "Love Vaccine" and the melodic "Life Without Adjectives." The band broke up in 1982 before they put out their second album. Yvette and K.D. formed Impulse F with Deb Hopkins, drummer of the Contractions. Louise focused on visual arts; K.D. worked on film; Yvette recorded solo work and then began working in sound engineering. ●

FRIGHTWIG

San Francisco, California   »   Formed in 1982

M E M B E R S

Original Lineup
Deanna Mitchell { VOCALS, BASS
Mia d'Bruzzi, Susan Miller,
Rebecca Tucker { VOCALS, GUITAR
Paula Frazer { BASS
Rachel Thoele, Cecilia Kuhn { VOCALS, DRUMS
(*numerous additional members*)

》 On the back cover of their second album *Faster, Frightwig, Kill, Kill!* a verse is placed subtly like sun rays outside a block of text:

Wild Women
Never Die
Alter to
Survive.

Over their near-decade run as a band, the group hosted various lineups and never succumbed to their detractors.

In the early '80s, supporting their first album *Cat Farm Faboo* at their show at the Metroplex, a hardcore venue in Atlanta, Georgia, Frightwig's scuzzy mid-tempo stompers stir human bodies into a whirlpool. The girls, whose one- and two-chord wall of sound and multicolored hair electrify the audience, graciously accept the offer to play an encore on one condition: their audience be mindful of one another in the pit.

Exiting the venue, they narrowly escape a swarm of skinheads repeatedly jeering at them: "Are you dykes?"

As resilient women writing about sex and its effects, they responded to the bullying—in person and artistically—sometimes aggressively. They weren't afraid of their harassers; instead, they wanted their harassers to be afraid of them. At shows, the girls intended to look scary, wearing menacingly long eyelashes and freaky makeup. They would personally respond to catcallers and shoot back with offensive obscenities of their own. They called upon men to strip on stage during "A Man's Gotta Do What a Man's Gotta Do."

They cover songs by cultural icons like Muddy Waters, Lou Reed, and the Beatles, and they play raw, rage-filled originals. In "My Crotch Does Not Say Go," they crow,

There are times when I resent being alone
Yes, there are times when I just
     want to be owned
Yes, I base my worth on who I
     get to fuck me
Yes, I'll rut tonight, but you won't
     be so lucky
I don't know why it's true, I don't know
     why it's so
Why the hell should I fuck you when
     my crotch does not say go?

In "Vagabondage," they muse on the emptiness in meaningless, rough sex. They sing,

We're together with handcuffs
And we're playing with chains
Like a fish on a hook
Or sex with the insane

In "I'll Talk to You and Smile," they cast a critical eye on a suspicious character:

I know who you are, I know what you did
I'm watching you all the while

VOCALS ■ GUITAR

VOCALS ■ GUITAR

VOCALS ■ BASS

VOCALS ■ DRUM

Susan

Rebecca

Deanna

Cecilia

A
BEVERLY
CRAZY WORLD
BIG BANG
■PUNK ROCK JAIL BAIT
MANIFEST DESTINY

B
THE PRIZE
AMERICAN XPRESS
I AM HERE ALONE
FREEDOM

THIS ALBUM WAS RECORDED IN STUDIO D IN THE DEAD OF THE NIGHT ON JULY 24TH AND 25TH, 1986 AT HYDE STREET STUDIOS, S.F. CA. PRODUCED BY GARY CREIMAN, ERIC DREW FELDMAN AND FRIGHTWIG ENGINEERED BY GARY CREIMAN 2ND ENGINEER BY DAVID BLOCK PHOTOGRAPHY BY ROBERT CASTRO DESIGN BY MICHAEL MUNNA

WILD WOMEN NEVER DIE
ALTER TO SURVIVE

PSYCHO SAX ON *BEVERLY* BY FLATULA/KEYBOARDS ON *CRAZY WORLD*, *AMERICAN XPRESS*, AND *FREEDOM* BY ERIC DREW FELDMAN/SLIDE GUITAR ON *BIG BANG* BY SUSAN/EXTRA GUITAR DEMENTIA ON *MANIFEST DESTINY* BY REBECCA/INTRO TO *AMERICAN XPRESS* BY DEANNA/ 6 STRING BASS ON *I AM HERE ALONE* BY SUSAN/BACK UP VOCALS ON *FREEDOM* BY JENNIFER, CATHERINE, FLATULA, FRIGHTWIG/INSPIRATION BY RUBY ZEBRA, PATTI RAMELLI AND TIM FERRIS ■ CECILIA PLAYS GUITAR/ SUSAN PLAYS DRUMS.

EXTRA SPECIAL THANKS TO KEVO EDMISTON, ROBERT CASTRO, GARY CREIMAN, ERIC DREW FELDMAN, AND THE PARENTS AND FAMILIES OF FRIGHTWIG FOR THEIR CONTINUOUS FAITH AND SUPPORT . . . ALSO JIM RILEY FOR MAKING THIS RECORDING POSSIBLE. THANK YOU MIA LEVIN D'BRUZZI FOR YEARS OF LOVING SERVICE. BEVERLY IS DEDICATED TO BAMBI AND JOE MAMMA. GINGER, WE DID NOT FORGET.

Back cover of *Faster, Frightwig, Kill! Kill!*, Frightwig's 1986 12-inch. From the collection of Jen B. Larson.

The cover of *Cat Farm Faboo* is equally maniacal: a warm-toned painting of a woman smoking a cigarette and spilling dark blue liquid from a wine glass onto a small doll's head. With a limited budget and after playing together for two years, the band recorded the album quickly. It was reviewed in major publications and garnered attention for the band—which they ignored.

While Deanna and Mia originally formed the band and wrote most of the early material, Frightwig had no official front person—they were all the singers, and they all wrote songs. They played with bands like Flipper, D.O.A., Lydia Lunch, and Sonic Youth. They were recognized in the *Village Voice*, *Playboy*, *Spin*, and more. Kurt Cobain famously wore a Frightwig T-shirt on *MTV Unplugged*.

The band has continued to perform, adding members over the years. Their most recent single "War on Women" contains what they're best at, brazen lyrics and a threat:

> Vaginal ultrasound, legitimate rape
> You congressmen have sealed your fate
> If you get pregnant it's not a rape
> Just meant to be, give me a break
> Entitled men we're through with you
> We're going to vote you out of office too

Email interview with Mia and Deanna, Summer 2021

Q: When did you become conscious of your desire to make music? Were you in bands before Frightwig?

Deanna: It took me a while as I thought I wasn't thin enough or pretty enough or wild enough. I did love to go out and see punk bands, but I was a fan. I remember one night at the Mab watching some band and it hit me I could do this; I want to do this.

I played for a short time with a band called the Ghouls. I was a backup singer; the front person Jeff wrote the best deeply twisted lyrics, and he did a lot of hard drugs. This was a fun project for a little while before the drug use killed that project.

Mia: I grew up in a household full of music blasting nonstop, so I've always felt like I was part of whatever was playing at the time. I always felt like the music was me and I was the music. I loved Joan Baez and Janis Joplin, Buffy Ste. Marie, Joni Mitchell. I remember hearing Big Brother and the Holding Company and feeling that the guitar solos were the most intense and beautiful thing I had ever heard.

I "sang" in an early all-female art-damage band in 1981 called GOD. The name was an acronym for "Girls on Drugs," and that's pretty much all you need to know to imagine what we sounded like. My dad taught me how to write a limerick when I was about eight, and I've been writing and rhyming ever since. I think back to GOD and don't remember much about the music—we did play at the Mab, and I think there was a song which went "you're in jail, you're in jail, you're in jail and I don't care. Oh Honey!" Unfortunately, we had a band member tragically OD at a house party and the band never really got back together after that.

Q: Growing up, what did you think about or see in the differences between men and women in the music industry? What about outside the music industry?

Deanna: The music industry was and still is mostly controlled by men, it mirrors society. The sexism was and is loud. Early on we were asked to play a lot of shows not because we were such good musicians but because we were women. We were literally a novelty act.

Q: How did you get involved in the San Francisco punk scene?

Deanna: After being a fan for a few years and making friends in the scene I became part of it. I had a job working at a movie theatre where a lot of punks worked, they all played in bands or went to art school and I met Mia there, we became fast friends.

Mia: I moved to SF in 1980 after getting kicked out of, first, my father's house, and then three other living situations. I couldn't complete my sophomore year of high school because of all the disruption, and I took the California proficiency exam and moved to San Francisco in the spring of 1980. I looked for a job and finally was hired to sell popcorn at some movie theatres in downtown San Francisco. It turned out that just about all the cool, interesting artists and musicians in SF worked at these theatres and I ended up working with and meeting the San Francisco community of punk artists and musicians. It was a really integrated scene in those days, with all artistic disciplines cross-pollinating with each other, and everyone going out to the same shows, creating mob scenes of parties afterwards. It was a fantastic time to be a young punk in San Francisco!

Q: How did Frightwig form? What was your vision for the band?

Deanna: Mia and I formed Frightwig in the cold winter of 1981. We practiced by ourselves and wrote a few songs with like two chords. We were loud and yelled a lot and we thought we were so cool.

We wanted to play out, record and tour. We did all of those things. We were like the punk version of Laverne and Shirley, "give us any chance we'll take it, give us any move we'll make it, we're going to make our dreams come true."

Mia: Deanna and I worked together at the theaters, and I loved her from the moment I met her. Once I saw her sing with The Ghouls, she became the coolest chick I knew. I was doing my thing with GOD at the time, and there was always drama at the practices, and Deanna and I were bitching about our respective bands one day, and we stopped and looked at each other and just kind of went "hang on—we can just

Frightwig as a three-piece. Photo by Bobby Castro.

do it ourselves!" Shortly after that, we were both laid off and we went onto unemployment. It was the first time either of us had not had to work all the time to pay our rent. I had been paid for a drug deal with a semi-hollow-body Harmony Stratotone guitar (yes, I did a lot of drugs in those days, and sold them to support my habits—different times…). Deanna said she would play bass because there were fewer strings so it must be easier (hilarious! The hardest-working person on stage is the bass player). Also, Deanna already played violin, so the four-string thing must have been more familiar. We had no vision for the band. We spent the winter of 1981 drinking whisky and playing two-note dirges, AT VOLUME, in my unheated warehouse. A friend had taught me basic chords, and another friend had gifted me a huge

Roland distortion pedal which made my guitar feed back like hell, everything you played sounded like SATAN. I was truly in HEAVEN.

Q: What was your creative process like? How did you write songs?

Deanna: As we evolved and found other members, each member would come up with a song idea, have the lyrics, maybe a melody or beat and we would all jump in and pound it out. Once in a while, one of us would come in to practice with the song totally figured out and share what they wanted. In Frightwig we all wrote and sang songs, there was no front person, we all were the star. That made for less ego-stroking and more shared stardom.

Mia: Deanna and I wrote most of the early songs together. It was effortless because we had no agenda or investment in the outcome. These songs were gestated in suffering and pain and rage and inspired by all the respective shit we had witnessed and gone through in our young lives. They were super simple musically because we didn't know how to play. There was never a thought of making them polished—they emerged as if the result of a psychic emetic, and there was joy in performing them. Each time we would play, it felt like vindication. When Cecilia joined the band, we got a bit more sophisticated musically. She was an accomplished musician and would bring in complete songs which we would figure out and deliver the best we could. Songwriting was always a really communal and holistic process, with everyone adding what they thought should be in there.

Q: Your lyrics are still relevant today. What's your take on that/feeling about them?

Deanna: I honestly cannot write a happy song. I did write a song about this, "I Want to Sing a Happy Song" but the war goes on, the war goes on…My lyrics mostly come from despair and for me it's cathartic, a real release of the pain. I do stop and realize that in the big picture it hasn't been long since these songs were written and if goodness prevails, we will see change.

Mia: We always only write what we feel. There's no artifice or calculation behind what we do. I personally can't seem to write a catchy singalong chorus to save my life. We comment on the shit we see in the world; sometimes what we have to say is really funny commentary on a super-fucked situation. I think the Frightwig sense of humor is our best trait!

Q: How did you view gender in the early '80s San Francisco punk scene?

Deanna: My experience started in the late '70s in San Francisco, it was all in the mix together. In high school, most of my friends were gay, we would sneak off to San Francisco, to the gay bars starting when I was 14. I could get into the Stud at 14, dressed in '50s dresses, rhinestones, and lots of makeup. I was well developed at 14, when I was all done up, I really could pass for 21. In San Francisco, I met many transgender humans, drag queens and I loved them

and their scene. It was so colorful, creative and fun. This scene led me to the punk scene where one could dress as they wish, act as they wish, be loud, angry and/or fabulous. The punk scene in the early '80s was inclusive in style, music, and ethnicity.

Mia: From what I can remember, gender was a very fluid concept in the early '80s San Francisco punk scene. Keep in mind, it was (just barely) pre-AIDS epidemic, and the sexual revolution had happened not so long before, and San Francisco had been ground zero for that. I think it was a much freer time sexually; the punk scene certainly overlapped the gay scene and the drag scene. Bisexuality was not a big deal, and labels didn't seem very important. People had adventures with people and defined gender labels weren't such a thing in my circle, anyway. Sex was free and fun…Different times.…

Q: I read about men on tour harassing the group. Did men in San Francisco harass you?

Deanna: Yes, of course they did. We endured the sexist crap in San Francisco and everywhere else. "Show us your tits," et cetera. But in the end, we turned it around with Mia's song "A Man's Gotta Do What A Man's Gotta Do." When we were being treated in a sexist fashion, we'd shout out "Who wants to strip for us?" It was so much fun to watch men get up on stage and dance around trying to take off their tight black jeans, with big motorcycle boots on, tripping over themselves.

Mia: Of course we were harassed. It was common-place then, and it's commonplace now. I was not scared of harassment by men. My big thing with Frightwig was to look hot as hell from the back, and then turn around and stare them down with the scar-iest face I could possibly create. We would glue long fake eyelashes on our bottom lashes (à la Clockwork Orange), and just do crazy scary makeup—white pancake foundation and black eyeliner, red, red red lipstick—just be as shocking as possible. I wanted to scare them! Sometimes, in those days, if someone catcalled me, I would get all up close and personal with them and call their bluff: "You want me? Yeah, OK, let's go!" No one ever took me up on it. They would become uncomfortable and squirm away.

Q: What was touring in Europe like for you?

Deanna: The first time we played Europe was opening for D.O.A. First show was in Amsterdam and the last show of the tour was in Amsterdam. Word had gotten out about Frightwig. We had a huge, packed audience for our last show in Amsterdam, photographers lining the stage. The reception was overwhelmingly positive. We were invited back in the spring, but as is true of Frightwig herstory we had another member leave the band and that stalled our career again.

Mia: It's a long stupid story, but I didn't go on the first European tour with Frightwig. This is a regret I will take to my grave.

Q: What are some other all-female bands you remember seeing/performing with/hearing about in SF? Outside of SF?

Deanna: There weren't many. In San Francisco early on I remember the Contractions, Wilma. In L.A. early on, of course the Go-Go's, the Screamin' Sirens. In New York City I remember the Lunachicks.

Mia: The Contractions are the only all-female band I remember seeing in San Francisco in the early '80s. There were other bands who had fabulous female singers—Pearl Harbor, and Sally Webster and Sue White from the Mutants were all so inspirational to me because they were fearless and fun. I guess the Go-Go's, but I never went to see them because my taste ran rather rawer, and they were more "New Wave" than "Punk" in my eyes.

Q: How did you get hooked up with Caroline Records? How did the label impact your opportunities and experiences?

Deanna: In New York City we had a super fan in Jim Riley, and he worked at Caroline and secured our deal. Caroline was the most visible and well-funded label that we worked with. They were great to us, we received funds up front to buy a van, we were able to have the artwork we wanted, and we had the freedom to record what we wanted.

Mia: Deanna orchestrated the connection with Caroline Records. I was living in Honolulu with an infant daughter and wasn't playing with Frightwig then. I think the second album is extremely excellent!!!

Q: You all said in an interview you recorded Cat Farm Faboo *really fast just to get it done. What did you think of the reception of the album (by fans/non-fans/by the press, etc.)?*

Deanna: We had $2,000 to pay for recording the album, that's why we just got it done. We had a great reception for our first album from other band people and fans. Really, either you loved us or hated us and that reflected in the press.

Mia: I don't think we paid any attention at all to the reception of the first album—at least I didn't. We recorded the album, then drove to New York City to play with the Butthole Surfers. We were hustling our tits off. I don't think I ever read a review or knew what anyone thought of the album. It never occurred to me. I liked it but wished I had tuned my guitar more often during the recording.

Q: You are considered the harbingers of Riot Grrrl by many. What do you think of that?

Deanna: I think we were an inspiration and that brings me joy. I think we made it okay to play in a band without being traditionally beautiful or musically acceptable. Our lyrics resonated with a lot of young women and some men.

Mia: I think that we were an oddity at the time, in that we really didn't care what people thought about what we were doing. We did not present as "girls," we did not "play nice" in any aspect of the term, and we were on a mission to say it and play it loud. Perhaps that gave other women permission to do the same? I don't know, but if we have inspired anyone at all to say their piece to the world, I'm grateful to have helped that to happen.

Q: Do you think the music business has changed for women since the early '80s? How? Why/why not?

Deanna: In some ways yes, at the top of the "mainstream" field many women are number one on the charts, are making money and have more control. Things that haven't changed for women bands starting out is it's harder today.

Mia: One can only hope…I think it's still a boys' club, but I really wouldn't know. I think that there are more women working in the music industry than ever before. I know there are some excellent professional female audio engineers and front of house live sound people, and in the '80s there were none at all that I worked with. Progress has been made, and I believe that equality will prevail eventually. It's nice to see female artists at the top of many charts in all genres. ●

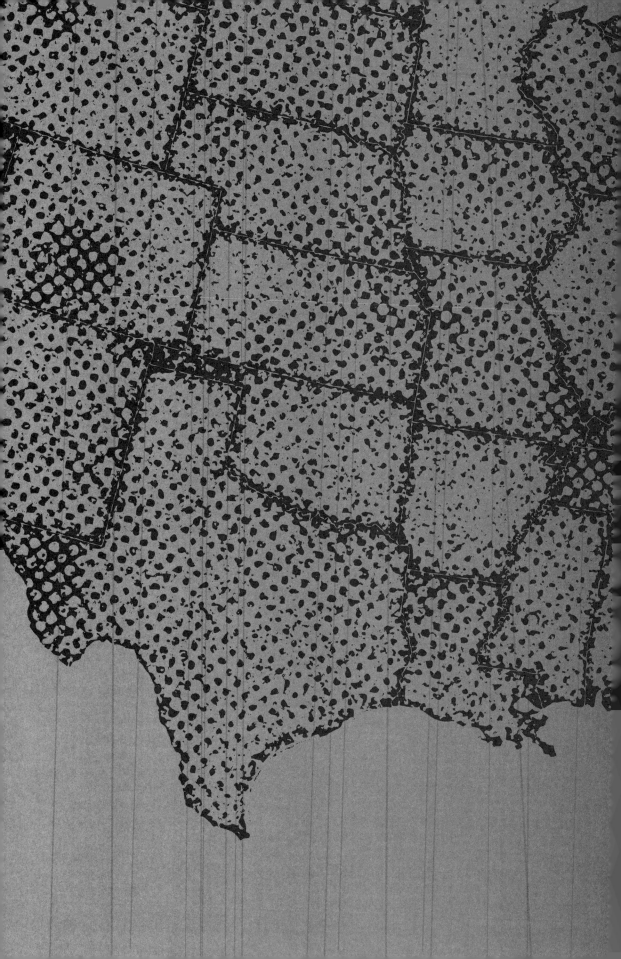

EAST COAST

Subversive Pleasure

JAYNE COUNTY

New York, New York   »   Formed in 1972

MEMBERS

The Backstreet Boys (formed 1974)
Jayne County { VOCALS
Eliot Michael { BASS
Greg Van Cook { GUITAR
Jett Harris { DRUMS

The Electric Chairs (formed 1977)
Jayne County { VOCALS
Greg Van Cook { GUITAR
Val Haller { BASS
Chris Dust, John Johnson { DRUMS
Eliot Michael { GUITARIST
Henry Padovani { GUITAR

》》 Lipstick and eyeshadow smeared across her face, sashaying across the stage in high-heeled shoes and a torn thrift-store dress held together with safety pins, Jayne County performs laying on her back, bicycle-kicking in the air as she belts the chorus to the original punk anthem "Fuck Off." The lyrics "If you don't want to fuck me, baby, baby fuck off!" evidence her X-rated aesthetic, one which would be replicated in punk and its many offshoots for decades to come.

Jayne's 1995 autobiography *Man Enough to Be a Woman* documents her experience growing up as a drag queen in rural Georgia and her move to New York City. In NYC, she transitioned, became a fixture at Max's Kansas City, and part of Andy Warhol's Factory, where she appeared in many productions including *Pork*. In the '70s, the rambunctious and theatrical performer fronted a handful of proto-punk and punk bands, influencing and working alongside illustrious artists like Bowie and Warhol. Jayne built her empire as a performer in the NYC punk scene, first with proto-punk group Queen Elizabeth in 1972, then with

her influential band the Backstreet Boys in 1974. In 1977, she moved to London and played with the Electric Chairs. Both a punk and queer icon, Jayne is one of the very few people in the '70s who both fronted a punk band and was present at the Stonewall Riots.

In a write-up about one of Jayne's performances in *Punk Diary 1970–1979*, George Gimarc notes that he saw her perform at a daytime show at Loeb College in 1972. Clad in a pink baby-doll nightdress, she sang a few songs that included a barrage of curse words and then squirted members of the audience with a water pistol shaped like a dildo. She underwent a costume change and emerged in ragged crepe long-john underpants and a revealing top. She was set to do another number that involved sitting on a toilet when the power was cut.

Over the years, Jayne's bands—Queen Elizabeth, the Backstreet Boys, the Electric Chairs, and her solo project as Jayne County with all the personnel changes—have kept the raw energy roiling, encountering some pushback along the way for controversial lyrics and performances.

The Electric Chairs attempted to move to the UK but were stopped at immigration, and then decided to change gears and move to Berlin instead, where the crowds were more interested in their music. Also, due to the nature of their pornographic content and performances, many record labels refused to put out their albums, and radio stations banned their songs, including their *Blatantly Offensive* EP. In 1978, the group recorded a squeaky-clean song for Safari Records called "Trying to Get on the Radio." On the back of the EP, they listed the radio stations that banned their previous songs.

The band put out another EP, *Things Your Mother Never Told You*, which was apparently packaged in the world's first washable album cover. Still, with radio airplay and legitimate record label releases, audiences continued to pelt the band with beer cans. One time, Jayne threw one back, hitting a concertgoer! Then, in 1979, the band broke up and Jayne moved back to NYC to

Cover of *Private Oyster*, Jayne County's 1986 12-inch. From the collection of Jen Lemasters.

make her first solo record (*Rock and Roll Resurrection*).

Jayne's look, attitude, and shocking behavior predated and outlived glam, GG Allin, and grunge's kinderwhore style. Mirrored by and possibly the inspiration for the fictional singer Hedwig from *Hedwig and the Angry Inch*, Jayne is widely considered the first transgender woman to front a punk band—but rarely acknowledged as one of the first people, in general, to ever front a punk band, which is also a title she holds.

Her career started in 1970; you can't enjoy punk, you can't love grunge, you can't revel in queercore without acknowledging the brilliance of Jayne County! Jayne has been highly influential across disciplines and genres, but she has hardly gotten due credit for being a hardworking artist, important influencer, and punk icon—not to mention a pioneer gay and transgender artist. And she's vocal about it. In 2003, Jayne told *Now* Magazine, "Record companies were so freaked out. You ask Bowie about me, and he pretends like he doesn't even know me now. Bowie wouldn't even have existed if it hadn't been for me and Cherry Vanilla and them. We made that asshole." She barely has to speak for you to know she's punk.

Her work in the '70s was not limited to foreshadowing future styles; she was also performing as an actress. In 1969, she performed in Jackie Curtis' play *Femme Fatale* alongside Patti Smith and wrote her own play *World – Birth of a Nation (The Castration of Man)*. Now back in Georgia, County has been focusing on her visual art. She creates colorful works of marker, acrylic, and glitter that feature fantastical and seductive original and Egyptian-adjacent creatures that expose a beautiful inner turmoil, an almost ritualistic, spiritual anger, directed externally at a world entirely unkind to outsiders. ●

MARS

New York, New York   »   Formed in 1975

MEMBERS

China Burg a.k.a. Lucy Hamilton { GUITAR, VOCALS
Nancy Arlen { DRUMS
Mark Cunningham { BASS, VOCALS
Sumner Crane { GUITAR, VOCALS
Rudolph Grey { GUITAR

In touch with a crazed extraterrestrial mental revolution, the mad and dissociative discord of Mars spurred an entire anti-rock movement into action. An inaugural no wave band, Mars found form in disorder and has been described as the "missing link between the Velvet Underground and Sonic Youth."

Mars played deconstructionist abstract art-noise. It was a cacophonous foundation for an anti-careerist, psychological uprising in the world of guitar-based bands and far more sonically radical than punk. The only things the band shared with punk music were the time period, the rebelliousness, and a few friends and influences.

The band formed when Nancy Arlen and Connie Burg called a meeting with their friends Mark Cunningham and Sumner Crane to discuss music. Nancy was an abstract cast-polyester resin sculptor, and Connie went by the name China.[1] The talk went well, and they decided to play together and continued to do so for three years.

Nancy and Connie hadn't played in bands before, but creating music came naturally to them. Connie rendered tunes on an acoustic guitar and Nancy percussed on paper bags. Sumner started out on piano and then moved to guitar. Before joining the others in Mars, Mark had tinkered with bass. While the group jammed briefly with a few other musicians, including the writer Rudolph Grey and future Contortions guitarist Judy Harris, they remained a four-piece for the remainder of their existence.

The group's carefully crafted chaos was far less ad hoc than it comes across. Most of Mars' songs were played live exactly how they recorded them. Practice was important to the group who perfected their sound for almost two years before ever performing in front of an audience when, in 1977, they booked their first gig as China. By their second show, they had renamed themselves Mars, when another, more commercial band laid claim to the name.

"It took us ages to decide on the name China and we were pissed. I still used China as my stage name in order not to relinquish it entirely," China Burg told *Vice* in 2015.

Bassist Mark Cunningham prophesied the new name. "Believe it or not, I did have a dream that we were playing at a theater and on the marquee, it said PATTI SMITH AND MARS…" he told *Vice*. "Later we were billed at [the short-lived] CBGBs Theater [on Second Avenue] with Patti." Patti Smith's record company had been interested in putting out one of their records, but according to the band, Patti never came around.

Innovative and bizarre, Mars challenged their audiences and sometimes elicited more than discourteous responses. Dead Boys singer and guitarist Stiv Bators' girlfriend once threw a chair at them. The audience also booed and cheered in equal measure when they opened for Patti Smith. While well-received by the right crowds during their short run as a live band, music crowds weren't ready for them. They were so strange and subversive, the punk scene mostly ignored them.

---

1 She also went by the name Lucy Hamilton when she played clarinet and piano on a collaboration with Lydia Lunch for Richard Kern's film *The Right Side of My Brain*.

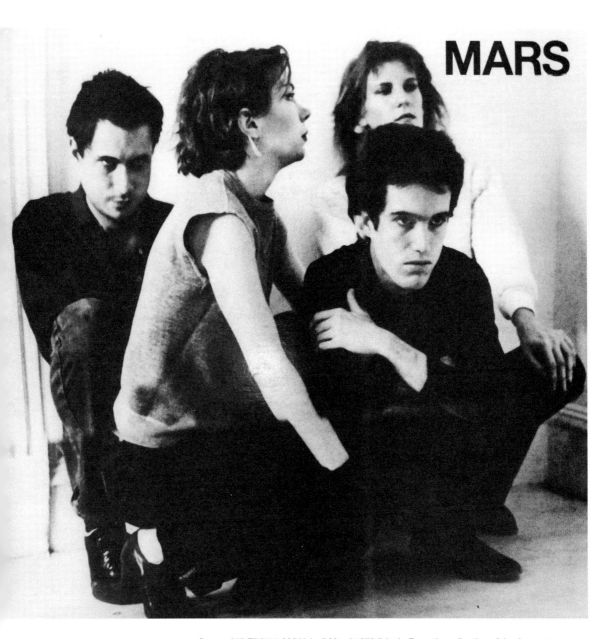

MARS

Cover of "3 E" / "11,000 Volts," Mars' 1978 7-inch. From the collection of Jen Lemasters.

Musically, Mars' primitive, angular compositions and freeform noise highlighted an abnormal, percussive bass with hypnotic vocals and indecipherable lyrics. Their vocals ranged from tempered murmuring to chaotic, ritualistic, high pitched bawling.

The group was made through synergy, and each member came up with their own parts. Their songwriting required a lot of time and focused attention; to achieve this, they played together nearly every day, allowing themselves to explore the depths of their psyches and musical connections. "Nancy always knew exactly how to keep things moving, and Connie was the loose cannon, always shaking things up," Mark remembers.

The energy and perils of living in New York City also possessed them, adding to the discordant tone in their songs. In *Vice*, China recalled a threatening encounter she once had on the city streets. "I wore men's clothing to be less of a target. Once, while walking in West Chelsea, a man approached me, asking if I was a TV. Stunned, I replied, 'A television set?' He took off after that."

Mars only performed live about 20 times before playing their final show in 1978. Mars' recordings include their debut 7-inch "3-E"/ "11,000 Volts," posthumous live recordings, and their inclusion on the famous *No New York* no wave compilation. ●

THE PHANTOMS

Boston, Massachusetts » Formed in 1976

M E M B E R S

Micky Metts { LEAD VOCALS, GUITAR
Angelo Aversa { DRUMS
Carolyn Casey, Tas Calo { BASS
Dash { KEYBOARDS
(*a handful of additional members*)

Above: The Phantoms as a trio. Opposite page: The Phantoms. Photos by Don Garner (a.k.a. Screeg Neegis).

>> When she was in her mid-twenties, Micky Metts had her bass guitar on her back on the subway in Boston when a stranger handed her a phone number she had gotten from an ad in a pizza parlor. The woman—a divine messenger—told her the ad was from a band looking for a bass player. The phone number Micky was given belonged to Angelo Aversa, her future Phantoms collaborator. This was sometime around 1976. Soon after, she, Angelo, and their friend Bob heard the Sex Pistols for the first time and jumped at the chance to start a punk band.

Micky wanted to be in on the action. As a nondrinker, Micky wanted to separate herself from the audience and that's one of the reasons she picked up the guitar. "And being short," she adds. "I could never see the band."

The band went through a few forms and names before landing on their name, the Phantoms. They were first called Carnelian, and also Little Frankie and the Boulevards. The group featured various players, but Micky and Angelo remained in the stable lineup: a rare '70s Boston punk band with a female-heavy lineup and a Black lead singer and guitar player. At one point, Angelo was the only male in the band.

Around 1978 Micky and Angelo made friends with coworkers at a car wash, where they worked day jobs. These colleagues quit the gig to run an ice cream truck, which they used to help Micky and Angelo haul gear to gigs, stacking instrument cases and amps on top

of freezers. "A few times we used those big old yellow checkered cabs to get to gigs with all our gear—two taxis with a drum kit and the three of us," she says.

They also lived in a punk house called Club 1 that could fit about 40 people. They would book about three bands a night and the space became an after-party hangout. Bar bands and DIY bands didn't typically overlap. Though they often played clubs themselves, the Phantoms booked shows at their house and gave space to other bands who weren't being booked at bars. She also notes that bar bands didn't often treat them with respect, recalling a "frat-boy vibe," and says, "We were laughed at by bands. They would roll their eyes if we were opening for them and not let us use their lighting. Even just the ones who were playing locally."

Labeled by fans as a "tongue-in-cheek act" and described by Lorry Doll's Boston fanzine-turned-NYC-tabloid and TV program *Neon* as "a band that was firmly punk in spirit and format and who embraced the absurdities of life in three-minute blasts of thought-provoking witticisms," their sound still veered into psychedelic territory. And even though they rarely played covers, the few

The Phantoms
Angelo + (Piggy) shelly (mickey)   1/29/78

they dared include the Yardbirds' "Shapes of Things," Fleetwood Mac's "Green Manalishi," and the Animals' "We Gotta Get Outta This Place."

Playing together a decade before morphing into hardcore bands the Organ Donors and then Diabolix, the Phantoms were fairly popular locally and released a 7-inch single, "Anyday" (Pressed for Time, 1982) and later, *Wagon Loopy*, a posthumous CD of live recordings from 1981. More comprehensive than any other recordings of the band, *Wagon Loopy* captures the essence of the group, as 11 tracks are from a live performance at Club 1, the basement venue run by Micky and Angelo. It even includes an audio portion of three songs from a TV appearance on Boston's Channel 5 from that same year (including station promos and disclaimer).

The Phantoms' dynamic and upbeat songs tend to also explore humor. The surfy, "ooh-ee-ooh"-infused "Blastphemy" contains the wordplay:

Blast for me and I will blast for you!

Other songs explored the macabre, "Bobby Franks," a sonically power-pop tune, is an ode to the 14-year-old victim of Leopold and Loeb, the creepy child murderers of Chicago.

Micky was also a foreign car mechanic. She created radically modified late-1960s VW Beetles and also worked as a welder, silversmith, and a formula racing pit crew member. Micky continues to work now for a worker-owned tech collective that advocates for privacy and freedom on the web. ●

HELEN WHEELS BAND

New York, New York » Formed in 1976

MEMBERS

Helen Wheels { VOCALS
Emanuel J. Caiati { BASS, SYNTHESIZER
Ed Steinberg, Albert Bouchard { DRUMS
Jack Rigg { GUITAR, SYNTHESIZER, PIANO
Joe Vasta { BASS
Tommy Morrongiello { GUITAR

A beloved, iconic, and way-out figure, Helen was an oddity even among the eccentric crowd at CBGBs. Helen was a keeper of snakes who obsessed over alien abductions and had a muscular build covered in tattoos. She stood just over five feet tall and struck up a friendship with the Hells Angels.

In 1976, she temporarily accumulated members of the Dictators as her backing band when they had broken up. Helen played with many musicians over the years from CBGBs but found it difficult to find stability in the scene or in-band relationships. She told *ROCKRGRL*, "It was a dangerous scene, there was so much heroin that punk became confused with the junkie scene." In 1981, Helen self-released an EP, *Post-Modern Living*, but it didn't boast major-label support, and it received little radio attention.

»» Helen Wheels' most lucrative hit was inspired by a horrific, psychotic encounter. During an unruly late-night party with early glitter-rock bands in the late '60s, Wheels' high and drunk tattoo artist friend was held at knifepoint by a crazed Eric Emerson (of Warhol Factory rank) and forced to tattoo Eric's name in capital letters across the buttcheek of the manic man's unconscious girlfriend. She purged the memory of this crude and abusive violation in the song "Tattoo Vampire," which became the B-side of Blue Öyster Cult's "Don't Fear the Reaper." Wheels told author Martin Popoff, "I wrote that song in the Café Figaro on MacDougal Street on a paper bag, and boy, it made me the most money of all my stuff."

Helen had linked up with Blue Öyster Cult as a student at Stony Brook. At the time, the band was known as Soft White Underbelly, and because of a bad review of a show, went by a few other names (including Oaxaca, Stalk-Forrest Group, and Santos Sisters). Helen, who had many years' experience writing her own songs, moved into a house with them and began designing their leather outfits and writing lyrics for their tunes. (Yet she is not even listed on the band's Wikipedia page!)

In the '80s, she turned to bodybuilding to curb her anxieties and wound up winning three Regional First Place Lightweight titles and a Women's Masters Championship. In the same *ROCKRGRL* interview, Wheels disclosed that her hobbies helped her manage her anger. She said that she no longer knocked over people's drinks or stuck knives in their tables at shows because exercise and writing about bodybuilding, UFOs, motorcycles, and magic helped her relax.

In the '90s, Wheels formed a band called Skeleton Crew, and in 1998 released a compilation of her recordings. The album, *Archetype*, was produced by Blue Öyster Cult's Albert Bouchard and rock writer Deborah Frost, and included cover art of her portrait by her fan and friend R. Crumb. In 1999, Helen began working on a book about the punk scene with photographer Mariah Aguiar, but both artists died before the book was completed. ●

Vinyl of "Destinations Unknown" / "Room To Rage," Helen Wheels' 1978 7-inch. From the collection of Jen B. Larson.

'B' GIRLS

New York, New York (by way of Toronto, Canada)   »   Formed in 1976

MEMBERS

Cynthia Ross ⎰ BASS
Xenia Holiday, Renee Schilhab,
Lucasta Ross ⎰ VOCALS, GUITAR
Marcy Saddy, Rhonda Ross ⎰ DRUMS

Promotional band photo by Rodney Bowes.

>> Four blonde girls with long hair and bangs wear relaxed sweaters with solid thick stripes, black pants, and calf-length boots. Each member has a different color: red, blue, pink, and purple. They play well-polished, upbeat pop tunes as they dance with their instruments.

At a Thin Lizzy hotel after-party in Toronto, 20-year-old 'B' Girls bassist Cynthia Ross and 19-year-old singer Lucasta Ross (not related) met while touching up their makeup in the ladies' room. Appreciating Lucasta's look, Cynthia asked if she'd ever thought about starting a band. The response was an enthusiastic "yes!" Neither played an instrument at the time, but they recruited Lucasta's friend Xenia and Cynthia's sister Rhonda. They got together, borrowed equipment from some friends, and learned "These Boots Are Made for Walkin'."

Cynthia shared great advice for any budding bassist with Amy Haben of Please Kill Me. She said, "I found the bass easy. I would just visualize the piano keyboard. The black notes and the white notes, the sharps and the flats. The dots are the white notes and the frets in between the white notes are the flats. So, I would just visualize that on bass."

The band name, short for "bar girl," came from a term used to describe women employed by bars and nightclubs to entertain or act as companions to male customers, persuading them to buy drinks. But it was tongue-in-cheek, as Cynthia recalls their motive was to be a good band and not just fluff.

She said, "We had a rule that you could never go home with a guy in the band that we were opening for. Then people could say that we only got the gig because we were sleeping with them." They also vowed not to wear short skirts, shorts, or cleavage-revealing shirts on stage. "We were going against the whole thing of being the sex object front person who didn't play an instrument. I think that was why we didn't get signed."

Playing a different cover every show or the same three songs twice, the girls were self-taught, wore matching outfits, and got their start playing regularly at a gay punk club in Toronto. Cynthia says, "We made mistakes and would just stop and start again. It was cute because the audience was rooting for us. People just wanted us to succeed."

Bomp! put out the "Fun at the Beach" 7-inch with the song "B-Side" as the B-side in 1977. Recorded shortly after they picked up their instruments, they played beachy, upbeat tunes using standard rock structures and surf riffs. They wrote about unserious song topics, including one about a gang of guys who wouldn't let them pass on the street, so the group ran after them. Another song, "Mystery," was a dark pop

'B' GIRLS continued

tune, with plaintive arpeggios, echoey vocals, and off-kilter chords.

Traveling to New York City once a month before moving there, 'B' Girls became regulars at CBGBs and Max's. They opened for the Ramones and Dead Boys, and Debbie Harry even did their sound. The film *Ladies and Gentlemen, the Fabulous Stains* is loosely based on the 'B' Girls' story. Cynthia even auditioned but the director went with experienced actress Diane Lane.

One night in 1978, the Clash arrived on the scene and despite their incredulous manager's advice, approached the 'B' Girls to ask if they would like to open for the European tour. Unfortunately, the tour was canceled when Topper Headon fell from the drum riser and broke a wrist. The 'B' Girls still got to open for them on a leg of their North American tour. Having fun (the impetus for being in a band in the first place), during the tour, the girls dangled a plaster fish over Joe Strummer's head during the Clash's political songs.

Brushing with stardom everywhere they went, another great feat is they sang backups on Blondie's *Autoamerican*.

Cynthia told *Gainsayer*: "Debbie gave me sage advice about the music business and also introduced me to her lawyer early on."

And shared with Please Kill Me,

Email interview with Cynthia Ross, September 2021

Promotional band photo by Rodney Bowes.

Q: 'B' Girls started in '77. Did you ever have any other band name ideas other than 'B' Girls?

Cynthia: The 'B' Girls formed on February 2, 1977, in Toronto, Canada. We were always the 'B' Girls and never considered other names. John Catto of the Diodes suggested the name and designed our logo. 'B' Girls referred to "bar girls" of the 1930s, '40s and '50s who made a living by getting guys (often soldiers) to buy them drinks. They were served soft drinks instead of champagne or alcohol and split the profits with the bartender. We loved the name immediately and wrote a song called "'B' Side" about being 'B' Girls… essentially a girl gang who were never intimidated or controlled by guys.

Q: From what I've seen/heard, I'm pretty impressed you hadn't played your instruments before starting the band. You had a very polished sound from early on! One approach you took to getting started was playing covers. How else did you learn chords and structures?

Cynthia: Yes. It's true that none of us played our instruments prior to forming the band. We learned to play together. Lucasta, the original singer, was a professional vocalist who sang jingles and I had taken piano lessons as a child so we both had a knowledge of music structure and theory. I would envision the piano keyboard when teaching myself to play bass. The black and white notes were the flats and sharps. We took playing seriously. We wanted to be good and practiced hard, often until our fingers bled.

Q: You wrote many of the songs. How did you approach songwriting? And how did the sound come together?

Cynthia: I always approached songwriting as storytelling. Mostly the words and the melody come together in my sleep. I used to keep a little cassette tape recorder beside my bed and would hum the melody, the hook and some of the lyrics into it, then expand later. Then I'd bring it to the band, and we'd learn it together and make changes.

"One thing she warned me about was to be very careful about who we signed with. 'These record company guys are gonna see you as their fantasy and try to mold you. Maybe tell you one has to lose weight, send you to choreography, maybe say this girl can't work on the record and use studio musicians. You're not that and that's what makes you different. You have to maintain creative control.' She said, 'it's a boys' club and very tough' and she was right."

In 2017, spearheaded by Suzy Shaw of Bomp!, they put out *Bad Not Evil,* a retrospective album of demos from 1977 to 1982.

Our sound was always clear to us from the beginning. We were melodic like the classic girl groups of the '50s and '60s (the Shangri-Las, the Ronettes, the Dixie Cups, Lesley Gore etc.) but we played our instruments. We were pop, rock 'n' roll, some blues and R&B influences and even had a rockabilly phase. We compared ourselves to the Rolling Stones and the Ramones. We existed as part of the punk scene but did not play punk music.

Q: How did you decide on the band's look?

Cynthia: I had dressed that way for years. It wasn't really a "look." It was heavily influenced by girl groups like the Shangri-Las and the Ronettes and guy bands we looked up to like the Rolling Stones, all the power pop bands and our friends like the Ramones. Our image suited our music. We knew we had to dress alike and have an identifiable image. We were the good girls next door who hung out with the bad boys down the street. We were 'B' Girls all the time, not just on stage. We hung out together. We were real friends. All of that was authentic.

Q: I love the song "Mystery." It feels very different from the rest of your songs, with plaintive arpeggios and echoey vocals. Can you tell me what inspired that song?

Cynthia: I love that song too. I wrote that about my dear friend John Genzale (a.k.a. Johnny Thunders RIP). We met in 1972 and stayed close friends until he left us. We were friends through girlfriends, boyfriends, wives, husbands, and children. All the ups and downs. He was a very sad and soulful guy, a great songwriter. He experienced a lot of hurt in his life and got tied up in addiction. Many of us did. That song was my questioning why he kept going back for more pain…before I truly understood. "Mystery" is the song most true to who I am, even the minor key. The other songs were lighter and happy.

Q: Of the songs you didn't write, how did you decide to play/record them?

Cynthia: Some songs like "Alibi" (Graham Stairs/ Roman Bish) were written for us by friends and totally fit our sound and image. Some songs like "I Need Your Love" (by the Boyfriends) and "Chi-

nese Rocks" (Dee Dee Ramone/Richard Hell) were written by bands we played with, and we decided to do our own versions. Same with "Hearts in His Eyes" by the Records. They taught it to us. We also covered songs by the Ronettes, Chuck Berry, etc. as a nod to our roots and influences. That was different though. We included one new cover like that every time we had to play a longer set because our sets were 20 minutes. We'd only ever play the cover once and only live.

Q: I know Debbie Harry was a very empowering figure for the 'B' Girls. Can you tell me more about that relationship and/or relationships with other women in the early punk/new wave scene?

Cynthia: Debbie was a key influence and advisor. Not only did she have us open for Blondie and produce us later on, but she also taught me a lot about the record business and what to watch out for, how to maintain creative control. In some ways, it prevented me from signing with a major label, but in the end, we stayed true to ourselves. No session musicians or Svengali-like managers or producers.

I often think about how Debbie helped us by sharing knowledge and experience, contacts and encouragement. I try to do the same now with younger bands and have helped a few get started with record deals, get gigs, and recently managed a band for a year. But in the end, I love playing.

There were other strong, independent women writers and photographers that were an integral part of the early punk/new wave scene. The Runaways were right before us, and we played gigs with them and my good friend Nikki Corvette from Nikki & the Corvettes (just after us and labelmates on Bomp). We had a lot in common and supported each other. Then there were other girl bands coming up at the same time as us like the Slits in the UK. We didn't know them personally, but reading Viv Albertine's book, their story pretty much paralleled ours. I'm friends with quite a few women from that time like Gaye Advert from the Adverts. What I found was that there was more camaraderie between all the bands at that time. We never thought about being women. The entire punk scene was DIY and we stuck together and supported each other. We were all outsiders, and it was us against the business, the man and the machine. ●

TEENAGE JESUS & THE JERKS

New York, New York   »   Formed in 1976

MEMBERS

Lydia Lunch { VOCALS, LYRICS, GUITAR
James Chance { SAXOPHONE
Kawashima Akiyoshi (Reck), Jim Scalvunos,
Gordon Stevenson{ BASS
Bradley Field { DRUMS

Lydia Lunch. Photo by Rikki Ercoli.

>> Lydia Lunch is a distinguished deviant and an underground oracle who flatly rejects "punk" as a label to describe her work. In the mid- to late '70s, the multi-disciplinary artist operated within the no wave sphere, a space parallel to punk. No wave was an anti-music movement that broke more boundaries than punk. Comparing the styles, she says,

"[No wave and punk] were the antithesis of each other… Punk rock is traditional rock'n'roll, sped up, with social consciousness and a fashion aesthetic. No wave, other than myself and James Chance, had no fashion aesthetic, it was about personal insanity. And none of it sounded the same, whereas punk rock pretty much has a sonic parameter, in the same way that country or opera does. No wave, in my view, was harking back to Dadaists and the surrealists because it was so absurdist and was only a movement outside of everything else."

When she landed in New York City, the 15-year-old runaway transformed her personal trauma into spoken word and prose. A master verbal assassin, Lydia's musical endeavors—including her first band Teenage Jesus & the Jerks—center her poetry. Layered in flesh-scraping screams over the brutal sounds

of abrasively strummed, untuned guitars, the raw inflection of her vocals rattle with rage, confessing her sins and desires. Disclosing personal stories of abuse and their relationship to collective traumas, Lydia's truth-telling has caused crowds to quiver for nearly half a century.

When performing, Lydia baits the audience with breathwork, builds momentum with cadence, changes the pitch of her voice to emphasize her pain. In her late-'80s poem "Daddy Dearest," she condemns her father's sexual abuse,

which began when she was six years old, decades before it became unobjectionable to do so. In "Conspiracy of Women," she bewilders audiences with her candor announcing her expertise with hostile events. She begins:

My language is not silence
My song is the scream

And then she lays the truth on so hard it hurts:

"So, ladies, I know you want to get into business, I know you want to improve your social status, your economic status, so I am going to appeal to you on a level you can all understand. Annie, get fucking your gun. Just get your fucking gun. Get your goddamn gun right now because there's a rumor going around. That the war has just begun, that the war is never over, that the war is never-ending, that the war is just an orgy of drunken hooligans, who in order to pop off that last fading trickle of their waning sexuality, they gotta pick up those bombs. They gotta pick up those bricks, they gotta pick up those bullets so they can better penetrate the flesh of my flesh, the flesh of my enemies, the breath of my breath, the breast of my breast. Hey fuck it anyway."

And advises:

"The only thing I fill myself up with is myself—and ladies I'm urging you to do the same: to fill up your hole not with another hole not with another vacancy not with another piece of shit, but with your own power, your own heat, your own energy, your own life."

Written prose and personal anecdotes in her books, *Paradoxia: A Predator's Diary*, *Will Work for Drugs*, and *So Real It Hurts*, reveal the darkest parts of her psyche and the foundation which caused it

to split. On her ability to speak the unspeakable, Jerry Stahl writes, "Lydia has emerged as a literary voice with an unparalleled genius for lending elegance to blunt-force trauma."

Having escaped the womb strangling her dead fraternal twin she believes to have murdered, Lydia's origin in Rochester, New York was the soil from which her life's work grew. Experiencing the race riots of 1964 out her front door gave her sight to the inhumanity of oppression up close. Later abandoned by her mother, and abused by her father and the men he brought around, she dropped out of high school, vanished out her bedroom window, boarded a bus to New York City, and never returned home.

As a teen, she developed an admiration for weirdos and a strong abhorrence for anything normal, reading the works of Hubert Shelby, Jr., Michel Foucault, Jean Genet, and Henry Miller. "How I found out about these authors in a family that never read a single book, I cannot recall," she writes in *So Real It Hurts*. In her small city, she experienced a feeling of exhilaration from the energy of rock concerts before ever setting foot in the East Village clubs. In the city, she was drawn to music and encountered artists who inspired her: the New York Dolls, Jayne County, Suicide, and Mars, to name a few.

For Lydia, passion is an art form. Writing is a burial ground for her pain, and her anger is a bullhorn warning for future societies. Her words shatter nicety, cut through pretense, and expose reality. With an exhaustive list of credits to her name, outside of music, Lydia's projects have ranged from starring in pornography and underground films to shooting photography and video and curating a cookbook and podcast (*The Lydian Spin*). No wave cohort Beth B documented Lydia's trajectory and her co-conspirators' experiences alongside her in a retrospective of her life's work in *The War is Never Over*.

There's little anyone can say or write that could eclipse all that Lydia's already put out into the world. We can merely accentuate the outlines to make them visible. ●

Opposite: Lydia Lunch. Photo by Rikki Ercoli.

CHEAP PERFUME

New York, New York » Formed in 1977

MEMBERS

Lynn Odell { VOCALS
Nancy Street { RHYTHM GUITAR
Alison Berger, Bunny LeDesma { LEAD GUITAR
Susan Palermo { BASS
Brenda Martinez { DRUMS

» For almost a year, two cocktail waitresses from CBGBs, Susan Palermo and Alison Berger, played guitar in secret for three hours every Saturday. Susan Palermo had started playing guitar at 13 and tried to start a band but hadn't formally formed a project until then. Lifting a line from a Rick Derringer song and using their boyfriends' gear and rehearsal space to their benefit, they gathered up a group of gals and formed a band they called Cheap Perfume.

With singer Lynn Odell, guitarist Nancy Street, and drummer Brenda Martinez in tow, the girls attracted large crowds and a dedicated following that bounced back and forth between Max's Kansas City, CBGBs, the Mudd Club, and all the clubs in lower Manhattan.

As punk was more welcoming to female musicians than were other genres, it put the girls both at an advantage and disadvantage. Guitarist Bunny LeDesma says, "That there were so few female musicians at the time proved to be helpful, but we felt we had more to prove to our audience—that we could play as well as the next band of male musicians—so in a way there was more pressure on the band to shine musically, as well as visually."

Palermo says, "You have to remember, there were few female musicians, and we really had no role models at that time."

The group recorded their high-energy earworm tunes but never put out an album. But their songs were so catchy fans still remember them decades later. There was the straightforward, loud and fast punk stomper "You Won't Stop Me"; in the lyrics, the girl defies a boy's expectations. Verging on metal, "Forever Damaged" is about a hard-living woman. They covered the Shirelles' "Boys."

Peter Crowley, manager of Max's Kansas City, says, "I remember they had lots of boy groupies, but also—because they played with as much energy and skill as any of their 'competition'—they attracted a much bigger following than they got from being pretty girls."

Of course, some of their fans' girlfriends didn't react in kind. A fan recalls, "I remember our girlfriends would get in a huff, '…oh, you wanna see Cheap Perfume because they're cute, right?'"

Though they toured up and down the coast, not recording an album and not having coherent guidance made it difficult for the group to gain recognition outside the city.

Bunny says, "We were a young band. We really did not have the management. We had no knowledge of which direction to go in a field that was not really open to female musicians until later."

The band regrouped for a few shows in the early 2000s, but without recordings from their early days, their legacy lolls in memory: New York punk lore, the recollection of their catchy chords by show-devotees, and the lingering taste of a cocktail named "Cheap Perfume" on Max's menu. ●

Undated promotional photo. Photographer unknown.

DNA

New York, New York » Formed in 1977

MEMBERS

Longstanding lineup
Arto Lindsay { GUITAR, VOCALS
Ikue Mori { DRUMS
Tim Wright { BASS

Original lineup
Arto Lindsay { GUITAR
Robin Crutchfield { KEYBOARDS
Gordon Stevenson
Mirielle Cervenka
(*Exene's younger sister*)

Cover of "You & You," DNA's 1978 7-inch. From the collection of Jen B. Larson.

Japanese drummer-turned-drum-programmer Ikue Mori joined New York no wave band DNA in 1977, just after she moved to the States from Tokyo on a whim. After original members Gordon Stevenson and Mirielle Cervenka (sister of X singer Exene Cervenka) dropped out, Arto Lindsay invited her to join. Before hearing artists from the punk scene in New York, Mori had not considered being a musician. She said,

> "I started listening to music in the late '60s—it was all rock music. Jimi Hendrix, the Doors. They didn't really influence me, I just listened to it. Then in '75, I'd listen to things happening in New York like Patti Smith, Television. I felt very close to that. There was a 'maybe you can do it too' kind of feeling to it. Then I got to actually see them when I got to New York in '77. When I saw them, I thought 'it's no big deal to do this.' When you're in Japan, it's like everything is more distant with the music, being far away. It really blew my mind though when I saw it."

In 1997, the band's founder Arto Lindsay said in an interview with Perfect Sound Forever, "She never played an instrument, but I liked her, and I invited her to play drums."

Mori describes her drumming in DNA: "It's a very primitive way of drumming like the way you play with big sticks: this is called 'taiko.' That was a big influence."

The band's sound, especially for the late 1970s, is singular. It didn't cater to the fashion of punk or its basic three-chord structure. It's the opposite of pop. Its insomniac whirrs drill into the caverns of the human mind and through all forms of matter. Its hypnotic chaos and sonic tantrums create a neurosis that escapes through a window, all while remaining worthy of dance. Arto Lindsay's atonal guitar screams into the wind and Ikue Mori's shipwreck drums respond to the waves in a storm at sea.

After the compilation came out, keyboardist Crutchfield left to form his own band and bassist Tom Wright of Pere Ubu stepped in. A musical minefield, the early recordings with Robin Crutchfield feature spiral-staircase keys, and later works with Tom Wright reveal a

Arto Lindsay

Robin Crutchfield

Ikue M

Cover- RL Crutchfield
Back Cover Photo- Diego Cortez

Produced by Bob Quine

YOU & YOU b/w LITTLE ANTS

©&℗ 1978 DNA. All rights reserved.
Released under license to Superior Viaduct PO Box 193563 San Francisco, CA 94119 USA

SV098

Back cover of "You & You." From the collection of Jen B. Larson.

DNA continued

labyrinthine bass, underscoring the primordial gallop of drums and the psychotic breaks in guitar. Unnerving as it was calming, as they evolved, the brevity and abstraction caused their songs to be compared to a haiku.

In 1982, the band dissolved. In 1997, Mori said, "We couldn't create new songs and then we all had different interests in musical things. Arto was already with the Lounge Lizards. We just naturally played out." They played three sold-out shows at CBGBs, recorded on the CD *Last Live at CBGB's*, released more than a decade later on John Zorn's Avant label. Not featured on the album was their final encore: a cover of Led Zeppelin's "Whole Lotta Love."

After the dissolution of DNA, Mori's work went in various directions. She also joined a handful of all-girl outfits. During a year when she lived in Japan in the mid-'80s and in 1985, she put together an all-girl art-rock band called Electrified Fukuko in Japan. She said, "It's like a mixture of DNA in a more rock way." Back in New York, she played in another all-girl crew called Sunset Chorus; they never recorded but played live in New York. She was also involved in a band called Toh Bandjan. She said, "[It] was mainly me with a bass player (Luli Shioi). We had the same kind of interest in music. She could sing and write lyrics. We started a unit together and different girls were involved as guest musicians."

She was also involved in electronic music, playing drum machines, sometimes modified to play samples, instead of her kit. Staying active in music over the last four decades, she has since been part of more than 20 bands with various sounds, as well as other projects. Throughout the '90s she continued to record solo music and collaborated with improvisers throughout the U.S., Europe, and Asia. In 1995, she began collaborating with Japanese noise-rock bassist Kato Hideki and experimental guitarist Fred Frith in the band Death Ambient. She's been active in music ever since. ●

NASTY FACTS

New York, New York   »   Formed in 1977

M E M B E R S

Kali/KB/Tuffnstuff /
Boyze/Boyce/Cherl { BASS, VOCALS
Brad Craig { GUITAR
Jeff "Range" Tischler { GUITAR, VOCALS
Genji Searizak { DRUMS, VOCALS

» The cloying sweetness of the three-track EP performed by an underage Brooklyn quartet can't be understated in its purity. Produced by Dizzy and the Romilars' Ramona Jan, and sitting at the vanguard of pop-punk, it entails three songs of infectious bops only the innocent could arrange.

Nasty Facts originally went by the name Pandemonium and played Kiss covers. They had at least 45 minutes' worth of original material, but when they secured studio time, they were only able to record three songs. Lead singer and bassist KB, who now identifies as two-spirit (using they/them pronouns), composed all three. "I wrote [them] in my room on a piece of crap guitar that only had three strings. I shit you not," they said in conversation with Osa Atoe in *Maximum Rocknroll*.

KB recalls starting the original incarnation of the band around 1975 at 12 years old. They told their mom they wanted to be in a band, and their mom took them down to the pawnshop to buy a guitar and amp. KB recalls they picked up the bass to impress a girl, started playing house parties and school dances, and by the time they were playing the NYC punk circuit—CBGBs and Max's—they were 15 and the oldest member of the band.

The title track of the EP *Drive My Car* crackles like an old film. Revving engines and screeching wheels make up the background, while blown-out, distorted guitars fill the horizon and a bassline flies

Back cover of "Drive My Car," Nasty Facts' 1981 7-inch (unofficial release in 2015). From the collection of Jen Lemasters.

like unbroken white lines shooting down the middle of the road. Sturdy drums and KB's glossy vocals confirm its status as proto pop-punk. They sing,

> I'm not as drunk as I look
> I'm not as stoned as I seem
> I'd rather dance than read a book
> I'd rather drive my car than a dream

"Get to You" and "Crazy About You" are upbeat, pining love songs where KB trades back-and-forth vocals with guitarist Jeff Range. Both songs boast tight drum rolls, saccharine vocals, and Cheap Trick solos.

As a punk, a queer, and a person of color, KB reveled when playing shows with ESG and Bad Brains. They recall,

> "[ESG] were people of color which was so rare to see back then in the scene! going to CBGBs & Max's was like swimming in a sea of

Cover of "Drive My Car." From the collection of Jen Lemasters.

NASTY FACTS continued

scruffy Caucasian bio-boys.…ESG was unique in so many ways. Like they were way laid back, and it came through in their music! Sexy grooves and off-kilter Beats!…And then came the Bad Brains. Opening for them gave me a whole new perception of what it meant to be a freak of color! Everyone respected the Bad Brains. Whites, blacks, everybody knew they were the shit. They made me feel so proud to be a POC punk. I mean a whole new sense of pride and power! It was not easy being a punk of color back then. And seriously there were no other out queers of color to be found and—I

was on my own there. But the Bad Brains doing what they did so well gave me a new perspective on life." (*Maximum Rocknroll*).

At the time, KB was still trying to find themself. "Trying to figure out what to do with myself as a queer. I was a baby butch and felt at odds with the lesbians I'd meet in clubs." Feeling strange among everyone, including lesbians, the punk scene was the most comfortable space. "Hell, 'queer' wasn't even an accepted term by gay folks back then, but I always felt queer—at odds with everyone."

They remarked, "Punk rock suited me just fine—and I felt more relaxed letting my freak flag fly."

Today, KB is a writer and performance artist in San Francisco. ●

UT

New York, New York   »   Formed in 1978

MEMBERS

Nina Canal { VOCALS, GUITAR, VIOLIN,
PIANO, BASS, PERCUSSION
Jacqui Ham { VOCALS, GUITAR, VIOLIN,
BASS, PERCUSSION
Sally Young { VOCALS, GUITAR, VIOLIN,
PIANO, BASS, PERCUSSION

》 Between songs at an Ut[1] set, the three members prepare for the next song, which means theatrically handing off instruments, adjusting straps and arranging percussion stands to their personal comfort. Each song the group constructs is led by a different member honoring a distinct vision, requiring diverse approaches musically. With no focal point for the band, no explicit leader, Jacqui, Sally, and Nina traded vocal, bass, violin, guitar, harmonica, and drum duties.

These exchanges broadened the sound, exploring new dimensions and making room for the songs to take on new characteristics. It was also more exciting for them to shake things up as artists. It was simultaneously anarchic and democratic and inclusive. In a *Warped Reality* interview, Jacqui explains, "We wanted to subvert the hierarchical thing, but we were mainly into the heightened perspective you get playing from every vantage point."

"I don't remember anyone at the time ever appreciating us changing instruments, and we got a lot of flak about how impractical it was," says Sally. "But we were very intent on making the kind of music we wanted to make…that involved us not being pinned down to just one instrument or role, so other people's disapproval didn't prove to be much of a deterrent."

Comparing band roles to community responsibility, Nina says, "We decided to change instruments as well as all other 'jobs' in the band—we had a kind-of saying that we each got to be both the 'controller and the dustbin collector' at different times!"

The freedom of expression led to unsteady and untamable friction, both an atmosphere and a plot. Scratching guitars and creaking violins, primitive rhythms, a threatening swell. Frightening, yet philosophical soundscapes. Author Andrea Feldman observes, "with Ut the journey was more important than the destination. You never knew where a song might veer next—they weren't built linearly but ran scattershot, pell-mell," and "the music is full of epiphanies."

In "Big Wing," over foreboding guitar and primordial percussion, Sally warbles,

> **There's a pedestal hidden
> in a bottomless ditch
> as this vision is wrenched
> from its lifeless niche
> like ghosts of our own theosophy
> kindred and riding roughshod
> to the sound of an army's boots**

In panning harmonies, Jacqui quavers,

> **turn over the earth you were crawling up
> you were crawling up**

Other songs like "Landscape" unleash a rumbling, otherworldly paranoia,

> **blue mountains
> where people are doing
> research, research**

---

1 "Ut" is the first tone or keynote of a scale set, superseded by "do."

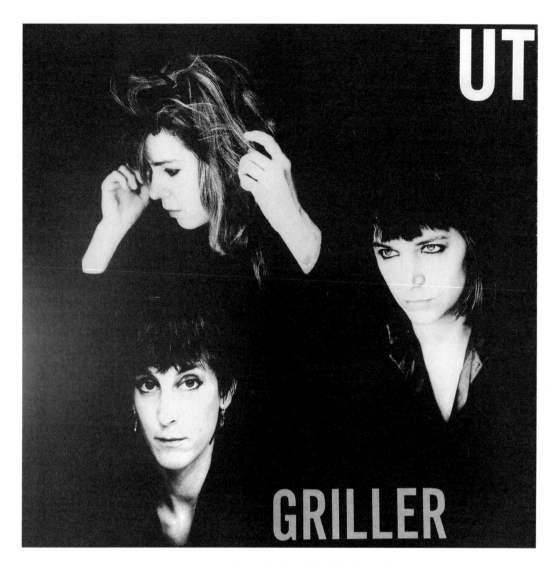

Cover of *Griller*, UT's 1989 12-inch. From the collection of Jen B. Larson.

UT continued

I know they're there
I see their smoke, I hear their noise
I know, I know they're there
I see their smoke, I hear their noise
noise noise noise
authorized personnel only
uniforms or is it know-how?
red red dust everywhere
red red red dust, it drives into my brain,
    into my brain
we are from another world, another world
remember that last last vista before
    we left our home

red red dust everywhere, it drives
    into my brain
life on Mars is like that sometimes
red red red dust it goes up up up
up my nose

In "Sham Shack," fervent tom rolls and clave-style bell accents underscore their poetics ("society see saw, inequity cribs"), which highlight their placement between the dirt and dissonance of no wave and the arty, intellectual indie rock (inspired by Mars and DNA while influencing Sonic Youth).

The trio signed to Blast First and relocated to England to record an album. Before dissolving, Ut put out three studio albums, a live album and tape, and two studio EPs. ●

ESG

New York, New York » Formed in 1978

M E M B E R S

Original Lineup:
Renee Scroggins { VOCALS
Valerie Scroggins { DRUMS
Deborah Scroggins { BASS
Marie Scroggins { CONGAS, VOCALS
Tito Libran { CONGAS, VOCALS

》 The moment ESG lays down a beat and plucks a single string, their cadence can convert a room of awkward crossed-arm concertgoers into a euphoric congregation of interconnected lightning rods. Through their incomparable blend of South Bronx funk, minimalist dance-punk, and no wave, ESG appeals to diverse crowds, influencing many artists over the last four decades. Their music is a staple at clubs featuring music across genres—funk, hip-hop, post-punk, house—but the only label the band likes to give itself is dance, which is exactly what the music will make you do.

ESG stands out, but not just because of their innovations, contributions to multiple music genres, and signature sound; they are also important because of their identity. Many post-punk bands in the late '70s chided rock 'n' roll groups for ripping off Black music while stealing from reggae, funk, and disco without acknowledgment. ESG's use of

Front cover of ESG's self-titled CD. From the collection of Jen B. Larson.

come away with ESG

Front cover of *Come Away with ESG* 12-inch. From the collection of Jen Lemasters.

ESG continued

funk basslines and polyrhythms came from authentic allusions to the music played in the neighborhoods they grew up in. They didn't mean to fit into the no wave post-punk scenes in New York at all; they were just trying to play the music they liked.

The visibility of Black women in punk has also helped future Black women envision themselves in similar roles. "Legendary, pioneering, and most importantly women-led, ESG at its core is a band of all black women," says Dina Bankole, a prominent Black feminist musician from Detroit. Bankole credits ESG for bringing representation to Black punk musicians and highlights how important that recognition has been to her own story. "As a Black woman myself, they are a band I particularly revere and look up to. Visibility is so important. A lot of people don't realize just how important it is to see people who look just like you do their thing in the spotlight, especially when you're female and brown. In the 'America' we currently find ourselves in, it's become even harder to just be if you're female and even more so if you're brown, let alone female and brown," Bankole told the Detroit *Metro Times* in 2017.

The sisters began playing music as a means to stay busy. As teenagers, the sisters were given musical instruments by their mother to keep them out of trouble. Sisters Renee, Valerie, Deborah, and Marie, along with their friend Tito Libran, made up the original lineup. ESG is short for Emerald, Sapphire, and Gold—Emerald and Sapphire are Valerie's and Renee's respective birthstones, and Gold is the record certification they aspired to, but have yet to achieve. Of course, though, other people riding their coattails have achieved successes by taking a big bite out of their work.

When they started, the band wasn't trying to make history, they were just trying to have fun and make their mom happy. "We started out playing cover songs—my favorite was (the Rolling Stones') 'Satisfaction,' and Rufus' 'Once You Get Started'—and we were horrible," Renee Scroggins told the *Chicago Tribune*, with a laugh. "I figured if I started writing my own songs, nobody could tell if we were messing up." Renee took it upon herself to learn the instruments her mom had saved up to buy, and once she learned, she taught her sisters. "It was like my mission, and I learned by doing," she says. "We were making a sound on instruments that we could afford. All the percussion we had, the claves, congas, cowbells, tambourines made it easy to incorporate a Latin feel into the funk because it wasn't expensive. I used to love when James Brown would 'take it to the bridge,' and he'd take away the horns and it would be just bass and drums. I thought, 'What if we made a whole song that sounded like that bridge?'"

Once they had built up a solid set list, the band began getting bookings at New York clubs. Their danceable, raw, and sparse sound unintentionally fit right in with the burgeoning post-punk and no wave scenes gaining traction in the New York City underground. They were signed to Factory Records and cut their first record. Their first session was recorded by Martin Hannett, who is famous for producing Joy Division among others, and turned out three songs that built the ESG legacy: "You're No Good," "Moody," and "UFO."

ESG's work proved to be so influential that throughout the '90s, a multitude of hip-hop producers sampled their work. The band's track "UFO" is one of the most sampled songs in history, having been used more than 450 times. Everyone wanted a piece of ESG's inimitable rhythms, from Wu-Tang, Kool Moe Dee, Big Daddy Kane to Gang Starr, TLC, and the list goes on. In 1992, ESG expressed their tongue-in-cheek opinion on this, releasing the EP called *Sample Credits Don't Pay Our Bills*. They've found ways to access some of their royalties, but they never did have positive experiences speaking with artists who sampled their work.

Though the members of the band are, in fact, humans tethered to the inconsistencies and unfairness of the world, their work transcends earthly life in more ways than one. As innovators who've inspired and birthed an entire universe of imitators, their work is essential to the canon of many genres. Funk, hip-hop, punk, and house music are greatly indebted to ESG. Another way their music feels all-powerful is in the blissful experience of their live shows. Their minimal instrumentation, sparse beats, and polyrhythms can move an entire room of people to dance. It's nearly impossible to stand or sit perfectly still with an ESG song playing, let alone while it's played live in front of you. Renee explains that her signature one-note guitar playing in the song "UFO" was inspired by extraterrestrial life. "I had to explain [to my mother] that I had just seen [Steven Spielberg's movie] *Close Encounters of the Third Kind*, and this was the sound of a spaceship landing."

In addition to funk music, science fiction movies, and Latin sounds, ESG was also heavily influenced by Motown. As children, the Scroggins sisters were enthralled specifically by the Jackson 5. Like the Jacksons, the band has maintained its connection as a family band and business. Their daughters have been part of their latest recordings and tours. Renee told the Detroit *Metro Times*, "It is very hard to work with your family because you will have disagreements and that can be hard to deal with if you are touring." But the positive side to working with family overrides any negatives that can come from it. If you argue with someone who doesn't love you like family, your relationship is bound to end. But, according to Renee, "Family to me means love, and someone that always has your back." ●

PLASMATICS

New York, New York   »   Formed in 1978

MEMBERS

Wendy O. Williams { LEAD VOCALS,
SAXOPHONE, CHAINSAW, SLEDGEHAMMER
Richie Stotts { LEAD GUITAR
Wes Beech { RHYTHM GUITAR, KEYBOARDS,
BACKING VOCALS
Chris Romanelli, Jean Beauvoir { BASS GUITAR,
KEYBOARDS
Stu Deutsch, T.C. Tolliver { DRUMS
Chosei Funahara { BASS GUITAR
(*a handful of additional members*)

»After simulating a blowjob and masturbation with a sledgehammer on stage in Milwaukee, Wendy O. Williams was arrested, kicked, beaten unconscious, pinned to the ground, groped, and tossed into a paddy wagon by the city's vice squad on a count of public indecency. Later arrested in other cities (once in Cleveland for wearing only pants and shaving cream), labeled anarchists, and banned in England, the Plasmatics were notorious for their dangerous and shocking performances. Their act was a rebuke of greed and materialism, representing the destruction of the American Dream. They blew apart full-size automobiles, fired shotguns, chainsawed guitars in half, toppled lighting trusses, exploded speaker cabinets, and sledgehammered television sets.

SoHo Weekly News writer Alan Platt declared "you will SHIT when you see the Plasmatics" and anointed Wendy the "Dominatrix of Decibels." The *Los Angeles Times* described Wendy's vocals as "so heavy, powerful and aggressive they made Pat Benatar and Ann Wilson sound like Judy Collins." Wendy wore leather chaps, skintight jumpsuits with cut-out breasts (nipples covered with pasties or pinched with clothespins, of course), high-heeled boots, chains around her neck,

and thongs. She sprang up and down across the stage, skulking like a feral animal, often in a spotlight. And she always had a new 'do: a thick black mohawk with blonde sides, a tall blonde signature 'hawk, or longer, colored or two-toned hair.

Wendy first found herself at odds with the law at 15 for sunbathing nude, and ran away from home as a teenager. When she was on her own, she worked odd jobs (as a macrobiotic cook, lifeguard, and dancer) everywhere from Colorado to London. Then, in 1976 in New York City, Wendy found an ad seeking a confrontational performer in a *Show Business Weekly* on the bus station floor and answered it. Anti-artist, neo-Dadaist, and Yale MFA alum Rod Swenson advertised his vision as an experimental show called "Captain Kink's Sex Fantasy Theater." The group was a shock-rock metal-punk fusion, which at the time was a sacrilege. They were determined to drop jaws and push the boundaries of conformity and consumerism. They were managed by Rod and began auditioning members in 1977. In 1978, Wendy and the Plasmatics erupted on the underground scene with their debut at CBGBs in New York.

In music videos and at live events, Wendy pulled off elevated stunts. Their culture-shattering shows, full of high-speed noise, were spectacles, almost like a monster truck rally. At shows, they spray-painted sedans with "Fuck the Status Quo" and exploded them on stage. She once drove a school bus through a wall of TVs. In 1980, at Pier 62, they managed to blow up an entire stage. At an outdoor event that attracted more than 25,000 people, Wendy drove a brakeless Cadillac loaded with explosives toward the stage. She jumped out moments before the vehicle hit the stage, detonating it and all the equipment on it. Another time, she hopped from a moving car to a rope ladder hanging from an airplane, without a safety harness.

Wendy's performances were also sexually aggressive. Their "Monkey Suit" video was filmed in

Cover of *Metal Priestess*, Plasmatics' 1981 12-inch. From the collection of Jen Lemasters.

The Plasmatics live at the Palms on January 18, 1981, Milwaukee. Image taken by Greg Kurczewski moments before Williams was assaulted by police and arrested on obscenity charges.

PLASMATICS continued

Sunshine Nudist Park. In the video, she sits in the driver's seat of a Cadillac half-submerged in a pool. Wearing cheetah-print spandex pants and a Day-Glo jacket, she pleasures herself and dry-humps the steering wheel. At Perkins Palace in 1981, the band plays amid smoke while Wendy teases the audience wearing a fetish schoolgirl uniform with the button-down top open, singing in sandpaper vocals, "You ain't got no nothin'." She spikes a bouquet of flowers mid-stage and hops into the crowd for the duration of the song. At another show, performing in front of a black pentacle engulfed in flames, Wendy croons huskily over screaming metal riffs in "Lunacy" to a whistling crowd:

Ancient forces from the tomb
Behold the power of the full moon
Dichotomy from outer space
Dominate the human race
Makes the casket overflow
Makes things die and makes things grow

Wendy contained multitudes, an on-stage and off-stage persona. On one hand, she was the first woman to appear on the cover of *Kerrang!*, the British heavy-metal music magazine. That same month she was featured on the cover of *Vegetarian Times*. "Those were both her," Swenson says.

Wendy said, "Ever since I was little, I've always liked to smash things. Basically, I hate conformity. I hate people telling me what to do. It makes me want to smash things. So-called normal behavior patterns make me so bored; I could throw up! The Plasmatics give me a chance to get this violence out of me and express it to other people. I don't like conformity. I don't like fashion. I don't like art. I do like smashing up expensive things."

The band worked with several labels including Stiff and Capitol. They put out five albums and four EPs in a decade and turned over more than a dozen members in its decade-long run; guitarist Wes Beach was the only other longstanding member.

After leaving music altogether, Wendy became a wildlife rehabilitator, and in 1998 chose to end her life. In her suicide note, she wrote:

"The act of taking my own life is not something I am doing without a lot of thought. I don't believe that people should take their own lives without deep and thoughtful reflection over a considerable period of time. I do believe strongly, however, that the right to do so is one of the most fundamental rights that anyone in a free society should have. For me, much of the world makes no sense, but my feelings about what I am doing ring loud and clear to an inner ear and a place where there is no self, only calm." •

TINY DESK UNIT

Washington, D.C.   »   Formed in 1979

MEMBERS

Susan Mumford { VOCALS
Michael Barron { GUITAR
Bob Boilen { SYNTHESIZER
Terry Baker { BASS
Lorenzo Jones { DRUMS

» As a waitress at d.c. space, Susan Mumford wore white rubber rain boots and a hacked-off asymmetrical pixie cut while absorbing the avant-garde jazz played regularly at the club. d.c. space owner and her boss, Bill Warrell, introduced her to guitarist Michael Barron and synth player Bob Boilen (later of NPR's *Tiny Desk Concerts*) and even suggested she sing in his new band. She had never sung in a band before, and her raw, untrained voice became an asset to the band's unique artistry.

Musically, the experimental jazz-inspired psychedelic dance music paired with Susan's beat poetry put them categorically in the description of "art rock." On stage, she wore black, emoted into the mic, smoked coolly, and grooved during instrumental jams. She sang in different pitches, churning out falsetto verses. She would stand perfectly still and then explode frantically with the mood of the music.

Witty, innovative, and sincere, she enjoyed using wordplay in her writing and honed a performance style that separated her from her low-key real-life persona. Michael describes Susan to the Washington *City Paper*: "She was magnetic. She had a real sense of time and space, and she got that thing—that the audience is full of energy, and they are totally willing to give it to you to do what you want with it," he says. "She would soak it up from the audience and shower it back on them. That was her greatest gift.

"She really loved the play of words, but she also really had this disdain for authorship," Michael continues. "You know, art in its purest form is anonymous, and that's what she strove for. She tried to use words almost as if they had no meaning, but they had a meaning anyway. Someone might say to her, 'I really loved your antiwar sentiment in this song,' and she would reply, 'What? I was just rhyming words that start with B.'"

And in "Sink Happy Ships," she sings:

Sink happy ship deep under the
    blue sea slip
Sink happy ship away beyond the
    sonar's blip
I was born dropped into the drink
Like the fly in my soup, I didn't sink
What's it all about I pondered to think
When a wave rolled me over the brink

And in "Another Way," she sang:

Stoke the coal fire
Burn my heart
Turn me into
Some purified art
Force the pressure
Feed the flame
Bleed my bones
Make me insane

Tiny Desk Unit playing live. L–R: Michael Barron, Terry Baker, Susan Mumford, Lorenzo 'Pee Wee' Jones, Bob Boilen.
Photo by Mark Gulezian.

TINY DESK UNIT continued

Tiny Desk Unit—the band name—came from the name Bill gave a wooden desk-drawer organizer that held paper clips, rubber bands, pencils, and glue sticks. The group played their first show at d.c. space in the fall of 1979. Their rehearsal space, in the vermin-infested basement of the Atlantic Building, would later become the original 9:30 Club.

At the 9:30 Club, the group was the first to play, and recorded their first self-titled LP live opening for Pere Ubu with their first lineup. Later, on their second album *Naples*, with bassist Terry Baker and drummer Lorenzo "Pee Wee" Jones holding together the rhythm, Susan, Michael, and Bob found more freedom in their playing.

The band reunited and put out a new album in 2007, and Susan Mumford sadly passed away in 2018. ●

DISTURBED FURNITURE

New York, New York   »   Formed in 1979

MEMBERS

Alexa Hunter { VOCALS, KEYBOARDS, PERCUSSION
Phillip Schofield { GUITAR
Stephanie/Ariel Hameon { GUITAR
Todd Crey { GUITAR
Jorge Arevalo Mateus { GUITAR
Mick Oakleaf a.k.a. Micki Crash { DRUMS
Tony Zebe { BASS
Steve Remote { BASS

Cover of "Information" / "Alors Allez," Disturbed Furniture's 1981 7-inch. From the collection of Jen Lemasters.

》 At the Peppermint Lounge in 1981, a co-ed coalition called Disturbed Furniture put on an unorthodox performance. The straightforward power-pop song "Breakdown" precedes a reggae-laced post-punk number where lead singer Alexa Hunter switches over to maracas. The stage goes dark, and the group emerges with a psychedelic dark-wave surf track; Alexa's vocals reveal their true power.

In between throbbing baselines and jagged guitar, she advises: "Be a hero to yourself." Singing in French and compared to a chanteuse, Alexa's elegant poise, old Hollywood style, and cabaret-quality vocal tone pair with her broad-minded lyrical themes. In "Alors Allez," the English translation comes out to "Don't stay in the same place…if you want to go with me, then go, but if you want to go with another, that's OK." Stage left, Stephanie (now Ariel) Hameon, an Asian American from Southern California, ensconced herself under a detective hat, strumming and noodling modestly.

While few of their songs are known to the public, their repertoire runs deep, and their aesthetic never stays in the same place, spanning from country & western to R&B and calypso, with a mood that is both paranoid Reagan-era warnings and an empowering 1940s Edith Piaf nostalgia. Guitarist Jorge

Arevalo Mateus says, "I always liked playing with Alexa. She was always willing to try a lot of things… she isn't stuck in one bag, so to speak."

When starting the band, Alexa's vision was to work together with other artists. She said, "Collaboration had to be part of it always. I was never going to be a dictator…" Working at both Danceteria and the Mudd Club, she was enmeshed in the Lower East Side art scene. She recalls the time as one of reciprocal expression, where people on the scene had many talents. She muses how "unbelievably rare it is to be part of that kind of community" and attributes the creative energy to the brilliant minds on the scene: "I was surrounded by very talented people."

In an article that appeared in the *East Village Eye* in 1980, Alexa explained the band name:

"We wanted a name that would not sound like a band and it doesn't, does it? It sounds like a line out of an Ionesco play. Disturbed Furniture! And I think that's what we look like. Throw five people in a room—five people who don't know each other very well—and put them in an intense working situation. It's a very disturbed situation… there's something unnatural about it. Also we're like furniture. We're moved around, manipulated. Not just us, but everyone. We start out thinking we've got a lot of power—like to change the world with all these ideals but the more involved we get, the more manipulated we are."

Members of the band came and went, and with them, various styles. When Jorge joined, he brought a funky soul vibe. Drummer Micki Crash describes past guitarist Stephanie's work: "Solid player, always had a good fat sound and put down solid rhythm tracks. She was a good songwriter." In fact, Stephanie wrote the beloved, depraved track "Bobby Beausoleil" (homage to the Kenneth Anger ex-lover and Manson Family murderer).

Alexa saw Patti Smith at 15 ("a transformative experience," she recalls), and she loved the Raincoats and the Slits.

She wanted to play with other women (and did with Stephanie on rhythm guitar) and was friends with women on the East Village scene, but also felt a tension in the air. "Even though we lived through the women's movement just in the '70s, so it was recently on the palette, women weren't always so nice to each other…I had definite vibes from women that were not in bands that we were in a competition. I didn't always feel embraced by other women in the community, as much as I would have hoped."

She notes "Men still had the dominance in bands musically… so it was still kind of a sexist music business, but not as bad." But it was a time when women were able to challenge sexist stereotypes. "There are a handful of women who did most of the writing and arranging…there were more women being taken more seriously. We did have people breaking the archetype of the cute, bubbly female in front or the sexpot."

Disturbed Furniture only put out one 45 ("Information"/"Alors Allez") during their initial run, but they made an impression on their scene, opening for the Go-Go's, the Psychedelic Furs, the Stranglers, Sector 27, the Waitresses, and Lydia Lunch.

The band's cult hit "No Information," written by original guitarist Phil Schofield, contains a hypnotizing formula, taking listeners on a paranoid journey into the future via scritching guitars, a punching bassline, deadpan vocals and ominous lyrics:

No information for me, no information for you
no information for free, no information it's true

Alexa discussed the song's lyrics with *Chaos Control*: "[It] is very much the voice of somebody being overwhelmed and disgruntled with the landscape of the Rupert Murdoch-ization of too much information coming at you. You're just back in the line of history, you're just a blob. It's the individual who has been overrun with too much, too much technology, too much information."

Drummer Micki Crash realized, "It just kept getting faster and faster and faster. I guess it was like we were in a rush, so we didn't have to pay for more studio time."

At a time when bands promoted shows by plastering up flyers on walls and spray-painting buildings, Alexa wasn't ready for the era of MTV, which she felt made external beauty the focal point of a band. She said, "I remember when MTV began, and I remember being horrified at the idea that the way you looked was going to be THAT important.…It just seemed tawdry… suddenly you have to wear costumes and make videos and tell stories on film."

Before that, the group made a music video. She says, "We tried making a video in 1979. I wrangled 15 people from the Mudd Club one night…" Thirty-five years later, in 2017, the video became part of a retrospective exhibit at the Museum of Modern Art (*Club 57: Film, Performance, and Art in the East Village, 1978–1983*), which spurred Alexa, Jorge, and Micki to reunite, reinventing old tunes and rearing new ones, including the punky "Hit or Miss" and the ballad "Halo of Pain." ●

BUSH TETRAS

New York, New York   »   Formed in 1979

MEMBERS

Cynthia Sley { VOCALS
Pat Place { GUITAR
Laura Kennedy, Julia Murphy,
Val Opielski { BASS
Dee Pop { DRUMS
(a handful of additional members)

» In 1980, Bush Tetras drummer Dee Pop and his mom (a photographer for *Downbeat* Magazine) went to see a show at Hunter College on the Upper West Side. During the event, someone pulled out a gun and began shooting. The crowd dispersed into the street. Squatting behind parked vehicles to evade bullets, they noticed Ed Bahlman and wife Gina Franklyn of 99 Records ducking nearby. Dee's mom shouted to Ed, "He's got a great new band! You should sign them!"

Emerging from the no wave and punk scenes, the Bush Tetras created danceable funk-forward post-punk with jagged rhythms and saw-toothed guitar. They settled into their sound by building songs from the ground up, often beginning with a drumbeat or bassline. Bassist Laura Kennedy and drummer Dee Pop played together incessantly, and guitarist Pat Place experimented on guitar, inventing chords and playing with the texture of sound (she previously played slide guitar in the Contortions); she played single, concise notes and sometimes just one chord per song ("Boom in the Night" and "Cowboys"). Among the first bands signed to 99 Records, they got together in 1979 and played for six months without a vocalist before adding Adele Bertei (of the Bloods, and other bands), parting ways with her, and then joining forces with Cynthia Sley.

Guitarist Pat Place had only been playing guitar for a few weeks before joining the Contortions. Pat told Perfect Sound Forever, "When the Beatles first played on Ed Sullivan, I said, 'I need a guitar,' and I went into the basement and drew pictures of the Beatles, constantly. I became obsessed because that was so cool, right? But they bought me an acoustic guitar. I think the action was probably an inch off the neck and I just said, 'Ugh…this is too hard.' And I didn't pick up a guitar again until I was probably, I don't know, like, 24."

When Pat came up with the name the Neon Tetras, and Dee suggested the Bush Babies, they combined the names, demonstrating their egalitarian process from the start. Connecting with audiences, the group was immediately popular in the Manhattan club scene and well-liked on college radio. They played shows with labelmates ESG and Liquid Liquid but also opened for the Clash and Gang of Four. On one occasion, they played with Gang of Four and Bad Brains but, Dee recalls, the Bad Brains were resistant to opening for women.

He says, "They were really pissed off that they had to open up for us." When asked by *Louder Than War* writer Audrey J. Golden if that happened a lot, Dee responds, "Uh, no…If we were on a bill with another band that had a frontwoman there'd sometimes be unease competitively, but that was more a band with a frontwoman and the rest of the band all male. Otherwise, we'd play with Delta 5 and the Au Pairs, and that was just like a big family party. It was all cool. There was never anything like, 'you're a bunch of girls.'"

Probably their most well-known song, "Too Many Creeps," responded to the crude leering from men experienced by young women in the city. In an interview published in issue #12 of *The Face* in April 1981, Cynthia stated: "You get bombarded all the time by so many different kinds of creeps…I

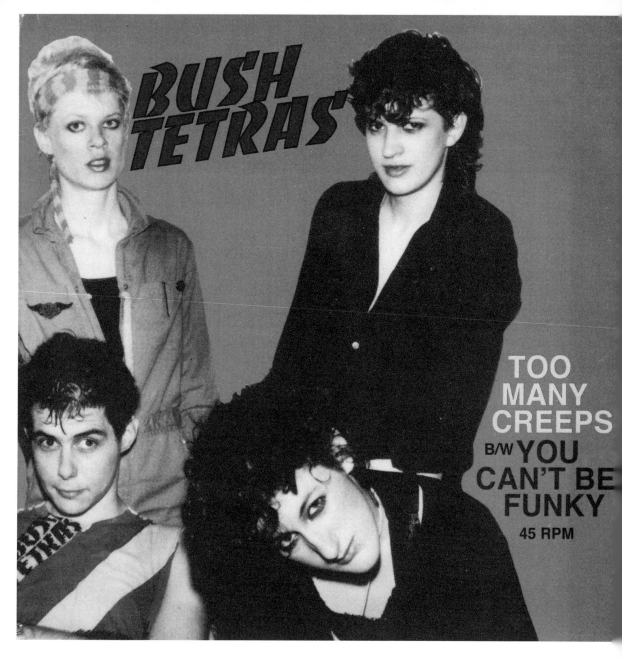

TOO
MANY
CREEPS
B/W YOU
CAN'T BE
FUNKY
45 RPM

Cover of "Too Many Creeps" / "You Can't Be Funky," Bush Tetras 2011 7-inch reissue. From the collection of Jen Lemasters.

BUSH TETRAS continued

suppose we get a lot of it 'cause we're girls and look the way we do." Later, in an interview in *Verbicide*, Pat recalls, "I was working at the Bleecker Street cinema and the people were getting on my nerves! Also, when we would walk around the streets, we would get hassled." Cynthia says, "Pat and Laura and I were always hassled on the street, so it felt right to lament about it…"

The Tetras worked with independent labels like Fetish, Stiff, and ROIR. Major labels sometimes looked their way but wanted to change them. The only way they can thrive and be happy with their work is to be themselves.

Pat told *Perfect Sound Forever*, "I used to be so insulted when people called us a punk band. We're not a punk band! I mean, we were some punk version of funk, and we were trying to write like funk or soul songs, and they came out… you know because we didn't know what we were doing. And they actually then got labeled as dance or whatever. Dance Funk or whatever. But I think we were trying to have some sort of funkiness, and I was trying to make up chords that sounded interesting and not, you know, the straightforward!"

Email interview with Cynthia Sley, August 2021

Q: When did you realize you would want to be in a band?

Cynthia: I was kind of coerced into joining Bush Tetras! I was mainly a visual artist who just loved music. In art school in Cleveland circa 1978 I started to be obsessed with Devo, Pere Ubu, and all the NYC and UK bands at that time. I remember thinking, when Pat and Laura asked me to join, "why not? What do I have to lose?" I had lots of poetry I was writing, and they had a sound. It just magically came together. It was pretty seamless. I was designing clothes at the time (I made all of Lydia Lunch's clothes for her ZE Records tour!) so made striped shirts for all of us for the first gig… Like a uniform!

Q: What other bands in the no wave/new wave/punk scene were you into?

Cynthia: I went to see the Contortions, DNA, Mars, and Teenage Jesus & the Jerks when I first moved to NYC in 1979. That helped cement my joining the Bush Tetras, also, because I could see that many of these were people like me who maybe had never picked up an instrument or had formal training to be a singer. It was the atmosphere of DIY…very freeing.

Q: When writing how do you/did you find your vocal melody? What about lyrics?

Cynthia: It was less of a melody than a phrasing thing. I was pretty monotone then! I wanted to find another thread to fit into the weave of the other instruments. The lyrics were sometimes pasted together from Dee, Laura, and my writing, done Burroughs-style, literally cut out and pasted like "Snakes Crawl" and "Cowboys in Africa"! Some were started by Pat like "Too Many Creeps" and then we added the second verse altogether. Some were mine, like "Boom in the Night" and "You Taste Like the Tropics." Dee wrote "Rituals."

Q: Dee mentioned a situation where the Bad Brains were unhappy to be opening for the Tetras. Do you recall this? Any other situations where you felt like artists or audiences, or men felt threatened by the band?

Cynthia: I don't recall that. I do remember seeing them perform there at Roseland for the first time and being both blown away and wanting to do a great show that night. The energy that night was amazing! Often the sound people or stage crew were condescending, especially to Laura and Pat. In the audience guy guitarists would stand right in front of Pat trying to figure out what she was playing! I had some bad experience in Boston once in the early '80s when a guy tried to take a swing at me as my mic stand broke and was tumbling into the audience, but others pulled him away. He was the same guy who had tried to pick me up before the show as I went to use the toilet. I turned him down and his retort was, "That's okay! You're the ugliest girl I've ever seen!" I answered that with, "Well! You just paid $25 to see the ugliest girl you've ever seen onstage, asshole!" He didn't like that. Guys could be intimidated by how androgynous we were….But at the same time intrigued.

Q: What was living in NYC and the city's nightlife like for you at the time?

Cynthia: It was a special time in the city. President Ford had just told NYC to Drop Dead and refused to bail it out. It was like a Wild West tumbleweed town full of danger and desolation. We owned it.

The clubs then were started by friends (TR3 and Miss Club) or had Hilly Kristal, the surrogate dad to us all running it (CBGB). It made for a very club-like feel and welcomed the freaks like us. The bands never paid for drinks at these places. We were always paid and treated with respect. That changed through the years and now after covid and even right before then, DIY joints in NYC are few and far between.

Q: What was the best part of being in Bush Tetras during that time period?

Cynthia: I got my chosen family. ●

Y PANTS

New York, New York   »   Formed in 1979

MEMBERS

Barbara Ess { BASS, UKULELE, VOCALS
Virginia "Verge" Piersol { DRUMS, VOCALS
Gail Vachon { KEYBOARDS, VOCALS

» When visual artists join together to make music, they don't always play weird music on toy instruments. But sometimes they do. In 1979, filmmaker Gail Vachon found a toy grand piano keyboard on the street and began building songs with photographer Barbara Ess on thumb drum, baritone ukulele, and electric bass. Their friend, a visual artist and novice percussionist, Virginia "Verge" Piersol, brought along her Mickey Mouse drumkit, whose skins were made of paper, combined with a standard tom (later, when it fell apart, she pieced together a simple trap kit).

The girls' spaced-out, overlapping melodies, diagonal rhythms, and affinity for acoustic toy instruments (and the melodica, Casio keyboard, other low-tech effects), won them admiration from audiences in the art gallery scene and at punk venues. They shared the stage with Bush Tetras, ESG, and Liquid Liquid. Part of the no wave movement, Glenn Branca (with whom Ess later worked in Theoretical Girls and the Static) recorded their debut EP for 99 Records, and two years later, they made their only EP, *Beat it Down*.

Their music is both a rebellion against post-punk's intellectualist posturing and a scholarly pursuit. They pay homage to Emily Dickinson (adapting her lyrics for "The Fly") and Bertolt Brecht's *Threepenny Opera* ("Barbara's Song"), and reimagine Lesley Gore's "That's the Way Boys Are" as a chilling hymn with a twist; a woman's bloodcurdling screams render it almost impossible to listen to all the way through without triggering panic.

Their sounds and lyrics are transcendental and unpredictable. The minimalist "Obvious," a collaboration between the band and its lyricist, novelist, and cultural critic Lynne Tillman, counsels artists' natural tendencies to be obscure ("Don't be afraid to be boring") while adhering to its freakishness. The meditative "Lulu" could be the soundtrack for a mindfulness session, evenly fading out and back in, while the off-kilter harmonies in "We Have Everything" hypnotize until its revelatory end.

After the group broke up, Barbara continued to play, not only with the Static, but also all-female no wave band Disband and Ultra Vulva; her photography work is in collections at the Museum of Contemporary Art in Los Angeles, the Whitney, and San Francisco Museum of Modern Art. ●

FAVORITE SWEATER
MAGNETIC ATTRACTION
BEAUTIFUL FOOD

OFF THE HOOK
LUEGO FUEGO
KUNG FU

45 RPM

Water Wing Records   WW17

Cover of Y Pants' self-titled 2017 12-inch. From the collection of Jen B. Larson.

EGOSLAVIA (A.K.A. R.E.M.)

Washington, D.C.   »   Formed in 1979

> ## MEMBERS
>
> Greg Strzempka { VOCALS, GUITAR, BASS
> Pam Lewis { ORGAN, MELODICA,
> SLIDE GUITAR, VOCALS
> Christopher Anderson { BASS
> Sally Ven-Yu Berg { DRUMS, VOCALS

» In Washington, D.C. between 1979 and 1982, a mixed-gender four-piece by the name of R.E.M. was gaining traction in the local music scene. With music in the vein of the Au Pairs, Wire, or Gang of Four, the band consisted of two guys—songwriter, guitarist, and singer Greg Strzempka and bassist Christopher Anderson—and the two aces up their sleeve, women: multi-instrumentalist Pam Lewis and drummer Sally Ven-Yu. The D.C. scene loved them.

When another band from Georgia with the same name—you may have heard of them—was booking shows around the D.C. area, this led to confusion selling tickets and promoting shows. Bassist (and future editor-in-chief of *Wired* magazine) Chris Anderson told *Ars Technica*, "We were releasing our first album and our manager came to us and he said, 'It's the weirdest thing, there's this other band called R.E.M. but don't worry, they're from Athens, Georgia, how good could they possibly be?'"

To resolve the issue, the two groups were invited to a friendly battle of the bands, in which the winner would get to keep the name. They flipped a coin to decide who would go first, which gave the local band the floor first. After playing a killer set, they assumed they'd won until the Michael Stipe-fronted outfit fired off with "Radio Free Europe."

The band who "lost" the battle was renamed Egoslavia with—for some reason—umlauts over the "a" and a slash through the "o." Who named them, no one is sure.

"R.E.M. to their credit didn't even stick around long enough to rename us except for the bass player, a guy named Mike Mills, is a sweet guy and he stuck around…I may be slightly misremembering the story, but it's too good to check. Basically, our overconfidence in assuming that we had won the battle of the bands spurred his suggestion that we name ourselves Egoslavia."

Rumors that he was intending to rename the band were dispelled on Twitter when R.E.M. bassist Mike Mills said, "We did not rename the other band. The 'playoff' story is otherwise essentially true, and as I recall it was a good-natured evening. Just a fun night of music by two good bands."

As Egoslavia, the group put out a seven-song LP. The cover of the LP is an altered illustration from an Italian fascist youth poster, which Sally and Greg collaborated on. Songs on the album range from poppy to experimental, but the overall sound fits neatly into the post-punk and new wave "categories." "Lost Song" kicks off with a steady dance rhythm, straightforward 4/4 drums, rattlesnake bass, call-and-response punctuated guitar, and ambulating arpeggios. Pam Lewis' auxiliary percussion—shaker and melodica—decorate. In "Girls Without Trying," Pam and Sally join Greg in chanting:

No this is no conversation
I got things to do

The contributions of the two women in the group, Pam Lewis and Sally Ven-Yu (Berg), set the group apart from other post-punk groups, bringing interesting flourishes to songs mostly written by Strzempka. Deeming the group's sound similar to

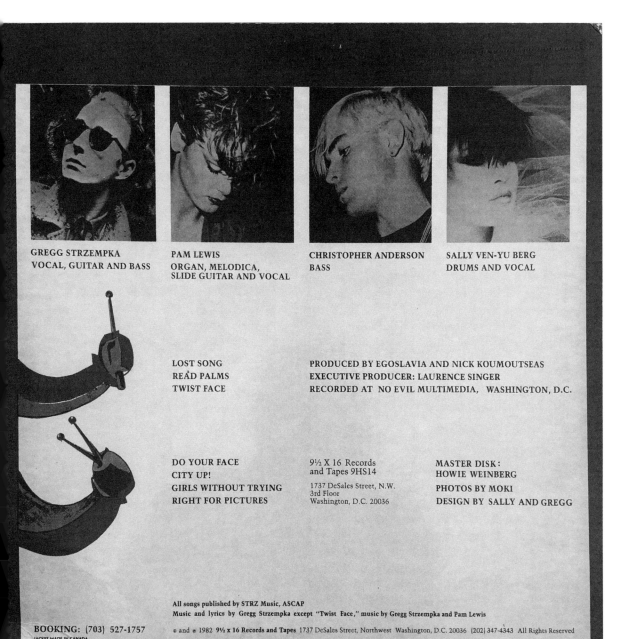

GREGG STRZEMPKA
VOCAL, GUITAR AND BASS

PAM LEWIS
ORGAN, MELODICA,
SLIDE GUITAR AND VOCAL

CHRISTOPHER ANDERSON
BASS

SALLY VEN-YU BERG
DRUMS AND VOCAL

LOST SONG
READ PALMS
TWIST FACE

PRODUCED BY EGOSLAVIA AND NICK KOUMOUTSEAS
EXECUTIVE PRODUCER: LAURENCE SINGER
RECORDED AT NO EVIL MULTIMEDIA, WASHINGTON, D.C.

DO YOUR FACE
CITY UP!
GIRLS WITHOUT TRYING
RIGHT FOR PICTURES

9½ X 16 Records
and Tapes 9HS14

1737 DeSales Street, N.W.
3rd Floor
Washington, D.C. 20036

MASTER DISK:
HOWIE WEINBERG

PHOTOS BY MOKI

DESIGN BY SALLY AND GREGG

All songs published by STRZ Music, ASCAP
Music and lyrics by Gregg Strzempka except "Twist Face," music by Gregg Strzempka and Pam Lewis

BOOKING: (703) 527-1757
JACKET MADE IN CANADA

℗ and © 1982 9½ x 16 Records and Tapes 1737 DeSales Street, Northwest Washington, D.C. 20036 (202) 347-4343 All Rights Reserved

Back cover of Egoslavia's self-titled 1982 12-inch. From the collection of Jen B. Larson.

other post-punk groups and contemporaries, *Trou-ser Press* wrote, "Pam Lewis's vocals and rubbery slide guitar, as well as some of the band's lyrics, showed Egoslavia's potential for transcending the sway of its influences."

In 1981, Sally Ven-Yu is credited with filling in on bass for all-girl riot grrrl precursor Chalk Circle's first show at d.c. space. Over the years, she later drummed for several bands, including Informa-tion Society and Death Comet Crew, and recorded drums and backing vocals on Indoor Life's "Search-ing"/"Hot and Cold." She also appeared in Richard Kern and Lydia Lunch's film *The Right Side of My Brain*. Ven-Yu died in 2015. ●

DIZZY AND THE ROMILARS

New York, New York » Formed in 1979

M E M B E R S

Ramona Jan Janquitto { GUITAR, VOCALS
Valerie Ghent { KEYBOARDS, VOCALS
Angelo Zarelli a.k.a. Angelo Romilar { BASS, VOCALS
Joe Klemmer a.k.a. Joe Romilar { DRUMS
Bob Riley a.k.a. Bob Romilar { GUITAR, VOCALS

» Named for the side effect of an addictive vintage cough syrup containing codeine, Dizzy and the Romilars began when Ramona Jan left the Comateens and joined forces with Valerie Ghent, Angelo Zip, and Joe Klemmer. In Dizzy and the Romilars, Jan wrote songs and collaborated with keyboardist Val, a 15-year-old who was a strong musician and demonstrated extreme confidence in the studio.

Dizzy and the Romilars centered around two potent women—Ramona, who was one of the first women sound engineers in New York City, and Val, who was to become an engineer herself. By the early '80s, though, she didn't buy into the idea of "rock star as omnipotent being"; Ramona worked with an impressive list of celebrity talent, including

Dizzy & the Romilars playing live. Photographer unknown. Courtesy of Ramona Jan.

ANGELO ROMILAR BASS & VOCALS BOB ROMILAR GUITAR, VOCALS
AND SYNTHESIZER ON ELIZABETH'S LOVER   JOE ROMILAR DRUMS
RAMONA LEE JAN GUITAR, VOCALS, SYNTHESIZER ON STAR TIME

JIMBOCO RECORDS
37 WEST 70TH STREET
NEW YORK CITY, 10023

Back cover of "Elizabeth's Lover," Dizzy and the Romilars' 1980 7-inch. From the collection of Jen B. Larson.

Brian Eno, Ramones, Talking Heads, and Frank Sinatra. She also worked with underground artists, producing the *Drive My Car* EP for the short-lived 1981 punk ensemble Nasty Facts (also included in this book).

Jan scored a job at Mediasound with the help of her then ex-boss' girlfriend and a few fabrications of the truth about her qualifications. Jan says she fibbed that her mother was an electrician, and her father was a piano tuner. (In reality, her father was a hairdresser, and her mother a housewife.)

To get the job, she was interviewed by the only other woman at the studio, Susan Planer, who cautioned her about what it meant to be a woman in the recording industry. In a blog post on her website, Jan writes, "During the interview,

[Susan] Planer forewarned me of the prejudice against aspiring women engineers in what was then a male-dominated industry." She got the job, and unsurprisingly, Planer's prophecy came true. Jan adds:

> "Engineering was fraught with sexism and even some bullying… since I had grown up with three brothers, I was able to circumvent some of the provocations during my twelve-hour shifts and six-day work weeks. At times though I'd just burst out in tears and when the crying was over, I'd soldier on. Media had become my college and I wasn't about to drop out."

The job at Mediasound meant not only fending for herself in a boys' club, but in a powerful one. The capital behind Mediasound came from two young men who were also the financiers of Woodstock. On top of that, Jon Bon Jovi's uncle Tony Bongiovi (formerly of Motown Records and Record Plant recording studio) was the head engineer and mastermind whose work attracted many of Mediasound's brilliant recording stars.

As a result of the power dynamic, women's presence in engineering wasn't common, but their visibility in it had profound effects on other women with an interest in the vocation. In 2016, Ghent told a West Beth website reporter:

> "The leader of Dizzy and the Romilars, Ramona Jan, was one of the only female engineers at the time… I could see how other engineers respected her because they knew she was also an engineer. So, it was important for me to know that was possible…besides Ramona, I rarely saw another woman engineer in the studio."

In addition to working together in Dizzy and the Romilars, the two women share other similarities: they both became musicians at young ages and have boasted impressive lifelong careers. While Jan plays in an alternative folk band with her husband Andre under the name JANTURAN, Ghent plays blues-rock and tours under her own name, Valerie Ghent.

In addition to being a musician and sound engineer, Ramona Jan began her creative life at a young age and has successfully pursued many creative ventures. The jewelry-maker, clothing-maker, and sculptor of vintage-baby-doll-head lamps, the indefatigable musician penned a poem at the age of three, picked up a guitar at 13, and began composing songs.

When she realized the creative life was her calling, she left the comfortable New Jersey suburb she grew up in for New York City at 19. Once in New York, Jan joined other musicians to form many bands, including new wave duo the Comateens; Dizzy and the Romilars, whose 1982 EP *Daily Dose* was recorded by Chris Butler of the Waitresses (another featured band); electronic duo Nursery School (Epic Records); and the all-girl folk-pop trio Venus Fly Trap.

Ramona has spent much time recently working with her husband in JANTURAN. In 2016, the duo recorded an album called *Legendary*, which honors the work of recording artists who recorded at Mediasound, reimagining songs critics never took to in an acoustic rock style. *Legendary* features songs by Millie Jackson, Laura Nyro, Frank Sinatra, Talking Heads, and more.

For the band's keyboardist, Valerie Ghent, "TVC-15" and *Daily Dose* were the first recordings of her career. She was 15 years old, still in high school, and rebelling against her parents. The child of a violinist and electronic-music pioneer, she began playing the piano at an early age and took up the synthesizer as a teenager. Ghent says, "My parents really didn't want me to become a musician. But I grew up with music. I was singing and making up songs as a very young child."

In Dizzy, Ghent played two monophonic synthesizers and sang. She later went on to tour with Debbie Harry, made a record with Maya Angelou, and played keyboards and sang backup with Ashford & Simpson. She also developed a therapeutic music program for 9/11 family members. ●

CHALK CIRCLE

Washington, D.C.   »   Formed in 1980

MEMBERS

Sharon Cheslow { GUITAR, VOCALS
Anne Bonafede { DRUMS
Mary Green { GUITAR, VOCALS
Jan Pumphrey, Tamera Lyndsay,
Chris Niblack { BASS

Front cover of *Reflection*, Chalk Circle's retrospective 12-inch (recordings from 1981–1983). From the collection of Jen B. Larson.

More than a decade after her first band broke up and amid the rise of riot grrrl, Sharon Cheslow scribed what could be construed as a necessary manifesto for anyone involved in punk music. A portion of the essay was published in *Interrobang?!* #2, a zine series she began compiling in 1989. The explication, as it lays essential groundwork for the topic at hand, can also be found in the preface.

The message of Cheslow's essay is urged throughout the text of this book. She writes,

"Respect is due. Women have been playing in punk bands since the beginning, yet only a handful have gotten recognition. Women have constantly been denied access to the male-dominated music world. I believe it has to do with society being threatened by women or girls up on a stage, displaying themselves in a manner that puts them in the public gaze, but in a way in which they have control" (Sharon Cheslow, 1994).

Guitarist and singer of the influential early-1980s outfit Chalk Circle, Cheslow cites the women of early punk as having opened doors for her and other women who came after them. "It's these women who first inspired me to play guitar in an all-girl band (back in 1981), and it's the era in punk history that preceded the more macho '80s hardcore."

Between 1976 and 1979, Cheslow identified as an avid underground radio station listener. She began tuning in to WGTB 90.1 FM in the ninth grade to hear the latest DIY playlist, curating punk, prog, new wave, and local music. When the station was shut down, she showed up to protest. She hung out at local record stores and even began volunteering at Limp Records her senior year of high school. There, she was introduced to influential post-punk bands, artists, and an entire circle of friends who became musical peers in the D.C. DIY community.

After meeting through local music heads and mutual friends, founding members of Chalk Circle, drummer Anne Bonafede and guitarist and vocalist Sharon Cheslow, began playing music in 1980. The group's original singer Cheryl Celso earned the lead vocal role over Henry Rollins but left the group relatively soon after (she had envisioned being in a more straightforward punk outfit, while the rest of the band imagined a more

SIDE 1

REFLECTION
UNEASY FRIEND
SCRAMBLED
PRIVATE LIE
TURNING UP THE COLLAR

SIDE 2

THE SLAP
RUN SO FAR
SIDE BY SIDE
EASY ESCAPES
HIGH STRESS
SUBVERSIVE PLEASURE

MARY GREEN - Vocals, Guitar
SHARON CHESLOW - Guitar, Vocals
ANNE BONAFEDE - Drums
TAMERA LYNDSAY - Bass (1981-1982)
CHRIS NIBLACK - Bass (1982-1983)

All songs by Chalk Circle 1981-1983
Audio compiled and edited by Sharon Cheslow
Mastered by Pete Lyman at Infrasonic Sound
Additional audio engineering by Timothy Stollenwerk
at Stereophonic Mastering

Tracks 1,2,10 from 1st demo recorded by Don Zientara
at Inner Ear Studios Feb. 1982, produced by Chalk Circle,
Howard Wuelfing — Tracks 1,2 mixed by Geoff Turner
at WGNS Studios May 1983

Tracks 3, 7, 12 from 2nd demo recorded by Don Zientara
at Inner Ear Studios Nov. 1982, produced by Chalk Circle

Tracks 6,8,11 from basement tapes recorded 1981-1982

Tracks 4,5,9 from live tapes recorded by Malcolm Riviera
and Chalk Circle Feb.-April 1982

Detailed information in booklet
Liner notes by Don Fleming
Designed by Sharon Cheslow
Front cover photograph by Devon Agaba
Back cover photographs by Mary Green, Devon Agaba

© 1981-1983, 2010 ℗ 2010
All rights reserved
Made in U.S.A.

Back cover of *Reflection*. From the collection of Jen B. Larson.

CHALK CIRCLE continued

inventive approach), creating the necessary space for Sharon and Mary to delicately craft unique interwoven vocal motifs.

Chosen by Sharon, the band's name is a reference to *The Caucasian Chalk Circle*, a Marxist masterpiece by the German modernist playwright Bertolt Brecht. The epic theater meta-play is a parable containing themes of justice, class warfare, and motherhood. Musically, Chalk Circle's songs capture a jubilant excitement for experimentation intent on disrupting standard rock structures. This can be viewed as another exposition of their critiques of class relations. Songs like "High Stress" and "Private Life" reference the "rat race" of American life. Lyrics in "The Slap" include:

> They gave me my first slap and told me
>   to be ready
> Now I'm quite prepared for the last slap

and

> It never stops

In their song "The Look," the band clanks a hammer as auxiliary percussion, which is perhaps as an allusion to the hammer and sickle.

In 1980, Chalk Circle played the Unheard Music Festival, a showcase intended to spotlight new D.C. hardcore bands. When they showed up, they discovered that even though there were a few in the scene, none of the other bands on the bill featured women. In March 1981, Chalk Circle rehearsed for the first time as an all-female quartet. Four months later, they opened for bands who did include women: record producer Don Flemming's band Velvet Monkeys, and Egoslavia (then called R.E.M.), with Sally Ven-Yu Berg, the drummer from Egoslavia, jumping in on bass for Chalk Circle's set.

They elaborated on their novel sound over time, drawing from '60s and '70s psychedelia, glam, go-go, and jazz. In D.C., go-go was a style of percussive funk that got crowds to boogie, and which artists like Chuck Brown made famous. Go-go's roots in R&B influenced both old-school hip-hop and post-punk.

In Chalk Circle, go-go's influence appears noticeably in the band's irregular rhythms and call-and-response vocals. Complementing the syncopated rhythms, Mary Green and Sharon Cheslow's angular guitar work laid a fertile foundation for Mary's existential lyrical arrangements to blossom. Green and Cheslow sometimes sang melodically, sometimes chanted. At times they did so in unison, and other times back and forth. Their influence on future hardcore bands is easily pinpointed, and their off-kilter, lo-fi cantillations inspired riot grrrl sounds.

D.C. later famously became an epicenter of riot grrrl—the feminist punk movement that would later sweep across the global underground—but Chalk Circle arrived too soon for it. Though the band predated the movement, Chalk Circle has often been referred to in the postscript of riot grrrl narratives. Just as the women before them did, Chalk Circle opened many doors for the women who came after them.

Prior to the days of hardcore and post-punk, D.C. experienced a 40-year drought of all-female performance groups. Since vocal girl groups of the '40s, Chalk Circle were the first all-female group to record and perform in the city. The golden era of D.C. hardcore was crowded by men, and so Chalk Circle not only had to break through stylistic barriers, but also gender barriers in order to be included in the scene.

Chalk Circle only played four shows, and three of them were booked at d.c. space, a popular and intimate artist-run performance space. They never played outside of the D.C. area, though. For bands who were not on major labels, touring was a near-impossible task.

Cheslow recounts, "It wasn't like today where it's easy to book shows in other cities. There was no infrastructure built up, no easy way to communicate other than by letter or phone (and remember this was before answering machines), no easy way to find out about places to play. And it was doubly hard for girls to tour. It was a big achievement for us to have played in the D.C. area, although I wish we'd been able to tour the U.S."

Their first studio demo was recorded at Inner Ear Studios in 1982 by Don Zientara (producer of Fugazi, Minor Threat and various other Dischord Records artists) and Howard Wuelfing (Slickee Boys, Nurses, Half Japanese). At the time, the collaboration was an auspicious sign that the album could be released on Dischord Records. But, disappointingly, label heads decided Chalk Circle did not belong on their roster. It wasn't until 1986 that Dischord Records opened the doors for bands fronted by women[1] (their first being Fire Party, whose singer fearlessly marched into the offices and ripped a sign off the wall that said "No Skirts Allowed").

Though the band never officially put out an album during their two-year lifespan, WGNS cassettes included Chalk Circle songs on compilations between 1982 and 1984. And in 2011, they released a retrospective album posthumously. Two demos, "The Slap" and "Subversive Pleasure" from their Inner Ear recording sessions, wound up on the Outside Records LP compilation *Mixed Nuts Don't Crack*. All of those tunes were eventually released on a vinyl LP called *Reflection* in 2011 via Mississippi Records.

Some members and collaborators of Chalk Circle continued playing music and participating in music scenes after the band called it quits in 1983. Bassist Tamera Lyndsay (and one-night-only bassist, drummer Sally Ven-Yu Berg) moved to New York, forming SHE with Claudia Summers and Bush Tetras' Laura Kennedy. Lyndsay also collaborated with Adele Bertei of the Contortions and Bloods as well as Lesley Woods of the Au Pairs and a few others. Sharon Cheslow joined Bloody Mannequin Orchestra, began publishing her zine *Interrobang?!*, co-published *Banned in DC: Photos and Anecdotes From the DC Punk Underground (79–85)*, and has since collaborated with various artists and musicians. ●

---

1 D.C. band Red C was featured on Dischord's *Flex Your Head* compilation. The group included Toni Young, an African-American woman, on bass.

THE EXCUSES

Philadelphia, Pennsylvania » Formed in 1980

MEMBERS

Lisa Mauro { VOCALS
Becky Wreck { DRUMS
Michael Dee { RHYTHM GUITAR
Beebe { LEAD GUITAR

》 As a high school student, Becky Wreck—the original drummer of Lunachicks—played in a band called Bondages. They were asked to play at a mental hospital as part of an experiment. She played a few shows with the band SicKidz, and then formed the Excuses with future Sadistic Exploits guitarist Pedrick and Michael Dee. When Pedrick left the group, they approached Lisa, a girl who worked at a local head shop, and asked her to be their singer.

"She had a great look, and she was so cool. We all wanted to be around her, and we all wanted to know her, so we asked her to be our singer."

Collectively, they had the look and attitude of old-school punk: wearing denim, leather, and studded jewelry, they played high-energy, loud three-chord-driven assaults like "Nazis Go to War" and "Slam."

On a 1982 appearance on *Music Menu*, where they performed live, an interviewer awkwardly asks the band, "Can someone tell me what hard-core punk is?" Becky quietly defers to Lisa, who, gripping a microphone with a wrist cuffed in a leather-studded bracelet, describes it as "loud, fast, high-energy music, noise, whatever you want to call it."

The interviewer asks how it's different from regular punk, and Lisa responds, "What do you mean by regular punk?" When the interviewer describes what she hears on the radio, such as Devo, as "regular punk," Lisa does a spit take. Coughing up a laugh, she pleads, "Someone else talk, please, quick."

The Excuses played locally but found it difficult to get gigs at venues playing original music. Many clubs preferred to showcase cover bands, which allowed them to make money on crowds. Their music attracted fewer audience members, as punk was still underground and less appealing to a mainstream audience.

"People aren't exposed to this type of music," Lisa explains, pressing the microphone up to her mouth. "So, they don't know what clubs to go to. Which is one in Philadelphia right now…"

The Excuses played locally, got airplay on college stations, and opened for the Bad Brains. The Philadelphia scene functioned like family. With strong women like Nancy Barile and Allison Schnackenberg writing the zine *Savage Pink*, a band like the Excuses gained exposure.

Becky was an out lesbian and explains that being gay didn't matter in the punk scene. She says, "What you were doing mattered. In high school I was bullied because it was pretty obvious I was a dyke.

"When I got into punk, the guys I played music with didn't care that I was gay. That was refreshing. I didn't have to hide anything or fight anybody. I felt safer there as a queer than anywhere else."

Lisa later became a body-builder, and Becky continued playing drums and famously made appearances as a "lesbian bachelorette," and later the girl-crush of a "straight" guest on the Howard Stern show. ●

RED C

Washington, D.C. » Formed in 1981

MEMBERS

Eric Lagdameo { VOCALS
Pete Murray { GUITAR
Toni Young { BASS
Tomas Squip { DRUMS

>> In 1981, Ian MacKaye played matchmaker for the short-lived hardcore group Red C. The band originally featured two women with androgynous names: Leo and Toni. Leo was replaced by Pete after a few shows, but Toni—a Black drummer—continued with the band until the end.

Tomas recalls meeting Toni when she was working at a pizza place. In an interview with DSI Records, he says, "We hit it off right away, it was brilliant" and that "playing with Toni was a real blessing."

He adds,

> "I call her my little angel. Toni was one of a kind. She was from the hood. So, she was authentically coming out of that scene where it was rebellious to be listening to rock music. She had a pretty broad perception of the world. She was a wonderful person."

One of the authors of *Banned in DC*, Cynthia Connolly, says in an interview with the *Washington Post*: "You could tell [Toni] was just a brilliant and outspoken performer. She was one of those people who didn't feel uncomfortable at any place that she was— she was totally herself." While retrospectives of D.C.'s punk scene recall the dominance of men, many women were involved. To give context for the scene in D.C., Connolly also explains: "There were so many women who were constructive and involved in the punk music scene."

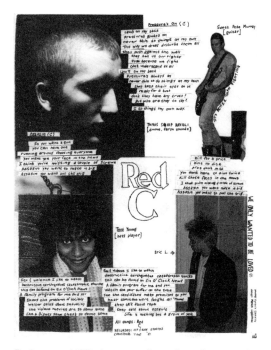

Back cover of 1981 demo recordings album. Courtesy of Dischord Records.

Tomas remembers that being involved in rock 'n' roll was fun for Toni, and that she used to go on tour with the Scorpions as a fan.

Red C laid down a demo tape at Hit & Run studios, and songs from that session appeared on Dischord's *Flex Your Head* comp, making Toni the only woman—and definitely the only Black woman—on the sampler, and the first woman to appear on the label's roster. Rumor is that there may have been another demo tape but that, if so, it disappeared after Toni's untimely death of pneumonia in the mid-'80s.

Groups in D.C. were mix-and-match; many lineups were different permutations of other bands. Before Red C, Toni played in a group called Peer Pressure, and after they broke up, she and Eric played in Dove. ●

THE BLOODS

New York, New York   »   Formed in 1979

M E M B E R S

Adele Bertei { VOCALS
Kathy Rey { GUITAR
Ann Phelan, Brenda Alderman { BASS
Anderson Toone { KEYBOARDS
Kathleen Campbell { DRUMS

In 1978, Kathy Rey worked as a makeup artist for the independent sci-fi film *Liquid Sky*. She picked up a guitar on set and started to play a few of her favorite songs, including "Ready for Love" by Bad Company and "All the Young Dudes" by Mott the Hoople. Out of nowhere, Adele Bertei, who happened to be on set for the film, started to sing the words.

Kathy recalls the connection: "It was immediate. Like meeting a kindred spirit. I was like 'I don't know who the fuck you are, but you have the most amazing voice, and you know all the music I love.' Music is such a powerful connector."

Soon after meeting, Adele went to Kathy's place and the two started playing Pretenders songs. Adele recalls, "We were in love with Chrissie Hynde and Patti Smith. Patti really gave so many women the strength to step out and start doing music. Because she was so androgynous and so creative and smart and made such intelligent references... She was like the Pied Piper and we were following in her footsteps."

Kathy had moved to New York to do music. Adele had come from Cleveland, where she and Peter Laughner played in the Wolves. The two had meant to move to New York together, but when Peter prematurely passed away, their plans were foiled, and Adele knew she was meant to be in New York City.

Once there, Adele played organ and guitar with James Chance and the Contortions for a short spell. She also worked in bookstores and film.

When Kathy and Adele met on the set of *Liquid Sky*, they clicked. By 1979, the girls decided they had to start a band. They put an ad in the *Village Voice* seeking musicians for an all-female band. Unaware of the L.A. gang at the time, they called themselves the Bloods. Adele writes, "We liked the name The Bloods because of being blood sisters... 'Bloods' as in 'only women bleed.'" She adds, "I do recall us pricking our fingers, doing that ritual."

During the band's short existence, the Bloods were thought to be the first rock 'n' roll band of publicly out-of-the-closet gay women.[1] (At least, as far as most people in New York were concerned.) Both in the city and abroad, they frequented lesbian clubs, played poker with switchblades out on the table, and partied with women on their laps. They had lesbian groupies. Outlaws by nature, they were doing all the things old-timey gangsters and the bad boys of rock 'n' roll were doing. They had a defiant bad-girl edge. In Amsterdam, they scrawled on the walls of clubs: "Lock up your daughters and one of your sons, the Bloods are in town." In Tompkins Square Park, they performed while tripping on MDMA, flinging copies of Valerie Solanas' *SCUM Manifesto* into the audience.

Musically, the Bloods' music was accessible but uncategorizable. Their sound was more funk than punk. Their songs were complex and harmonic. Adele sang in a three-octave range, Kathy played syncopated chords on high strings, and drummer Kathleen Campbell held steady disco dance grooves under Brenda Alderman's funk basslines. Unlike many of their punk and post-punk peers, they had a keyboard.

Kathy says, "We wanted to make rock 'n' roll. We were around a lot of bands of people who weren't

---

1 One member of the band no longer identifies as a woman.

The Bloods playing live at Tompkins Square Park. First row (L-R): Adele Bertei and Kathy Rey. Second row: Brenda Alderman. Photographer unknown. Courtesy of the Bloods.

musicians, who created a whole world of sound, a lot of visual artists, and such. We were proud of the fact that we knew what we were doing."

While they are often described as "no wave," Adele and Kathy challenge that descriptor. Adele says, "I wouldn't say we were no wave. No wave was more about busting music apart. Almost a brutalist version of music."

Despite their appeal, they had a hard time working within the commercial constraints of the music industry. Record labels didn't quite know what to do with the Bloods. They couldn't be boxed in, bought, or sold. The Bloods could never have been successful like the Go-Go's because they would have never conformed to what the industry wanted. Adele said, "Music is so much about commodification. They want to package you in a specific way, and if they don't know what to do with you, they can't. They certainly didn't know what to do with us—I mean, musically and image-wise we were these little hardcore dykes."

Kathy agreed: "We were the outliers, the outliers of the outliers. But ironically playing more accessible music than many."

While they acknowledge that most men in the scene treated them well, many other men took issue with their independence. Kathy said, "We were very tough women. Men do not like that ever. They don't like to be challenged. They think, 'Oh, some dyke is challenging me?' They just wouldn't take us seriously. And we would fight back. It was a lot of pressure for us to figure all of this out all on our own all the time."

At one time, Bleecker Bob intended to sign the group to his short-lived label. Adele recalls, "He took us into the studio and had us record a couple of things and had Mick Rock take our pictures. It was pretty fab. But he did that before he showed us the contract he wanted us to sign."

Then, he presented the band with a contract they considered tyrannical.

Adele said, "It was like, 'Your firstborn, every molecule in your body, belong to me forever more.' It was the most insane contract ever. We read it and we said there is no way we are going to sign this. And he freaked out. He called us every name in the book, and he was extremely hostile. Marching around, steam coming out of his ears. There was no negotiating with him. So, we didn't do that record. And people came to see us, but no one wanted to manage us or sign us until we met the Au Pairs."

In 1980, they were invited to play at an all-women festival called Venus Weltklang in Berlin, where they shared a bill with the Au Pairs, Malaria, and the Slits. After the fest, the Au Pairs brought the Bloods to Birmingham, England to record "Button Up," the band's only single, for Exit International Records.

The Bloods were featured on the genre-bending *New York Noise* compilation and also provided music for Lizzie Borden's feminist sci-fi fantasy *Born in Flames*. For the film, they wrote the song "Undercover Nation," about a women's army.

After touring Europe, the band broke up in 1981. Though short-lived, they had a lot of fun. Kathy said, "[Music] is a landscape of our lives. It's every memory. It's all that we went through. And we went through so much. It was not easy to do what we were trying to do." ●

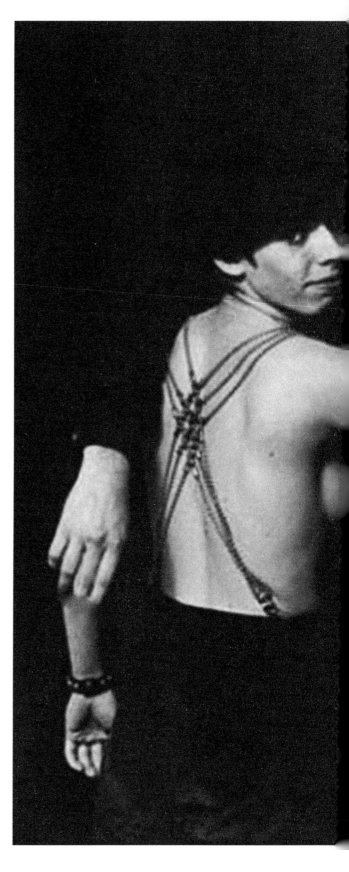

The Bloods. Photo by Pamela Camhe.

PULSALLAMA

New York, New York » Formed in 1981

MEMBERS

Ann Magnuson { VOCALS, PERCUSSION
Dany Johnson { VOCALS, STEEL DRUM,
SYNARE ELECTRONIC DRUM, PERCUSSION
Andé Whyland { VOCALS, BASS
Min Thometz-Sanchez { VOCALS, BONGOS
April Palmieri { VOCALS, MARACAS
Stacey Elkin { BASS, TIMBALES,
LINNDRUM SYNTHESIZER
Kimberly Davis { PERCUSSION, VOCALS
Lori Montana, Judy Streng { BASS
Jean Caffeine { DRUM KIT, VOCALS
Wendy Wild { GLOCKENSPIEL

» When Ann Magnuson and Dany Johnson saw the Bush Tetras live at Irving Plaza, they left the show inspired. The pair met at weekly meetings at Club 57 for Ladies Auxiliary of the Lower East Side, Ann Magnuson's "twisted version" of the 1950s-era Junior League. At their next meeting following the show, Dany shared an idea for an all-girl, all-percussion band with Ann, who scribbled the idea down in her notebook.

Recalling the invention of the band, Ann writes in the liner notes for *Rhythm and Paranoia: The Best of the Bush Tetras* in 2020:

"Watching the Bush Tetras that night brought the idea squarely into the spotlight. It was rare to see a band made up by three women with the guy as a drummer. We knew girls could rock but we had never seen evidence quite as compelling. We looked at each other and screamed, 'Let's do this too!'"

They came up with the moniker "Pulsallama" by fusing the name of a vintage blender, the Pulse-Matic,

with something that sounded funny—in this case, a camelid. The group, Pulsallama, was not supposed to be a serious band, but a performance art piece. Ann writes:

"Because Dany and I were part of the Club 57 crowd, our band was never going to be anything other than a laugh. You couldn't be serious about anything at Club 57. If you tried, you would be subjected to a hailstorm of ridicule."

Magnuson and Johnson envisioned a conceptual theater piece featuring a wild brigade of performers to create a frenzied racket on stage. They recruited members from the Ladies' Auxiliary of the Lower East Side. Ann writes:

"Our cacophony debuted several months later at a magic-mushroom-fueled 'Rites of Spring Bacchanal' at the club. A good time was had by all. Our percussive band was a novelty hit."

Pictures taken by Andé Whyland showed Pulsallama dressed in a secondhand mélange of draped fabrics and vinyl. "Rituals," "Isadoraesque dancers," "human sacrifices," and "pagan worship," with "BLOOD" scratched in by hand, appear in Magnuson's typed list for the first performance.

What was intended to be a one-off show was well received, and the group decided to continue performing. Vocalist and percussionist April Palmieri says she did not realize it was an ongoing commitment and missed the second show, an impromptu performance at Club 57. Additional shows throughout the summer of '81 generated buzz amongst the downtown cognoscenti. In a press release Magnuson wrote, the band was

Pulsallama circa 1981. Photo by Tseng Kwong Chi

described as "rabid girls harvesting crops of dementia in savage seasonal pageantry," and requests the audience dress "heathen."

Pulsallama explored the potentiality of what a performance-driven, pagan-ritual-inspired, all-girl percussion band could do. At the suggestion of the Bush Tetras' Laura Kennedy, they invited Jean Caffeine and her full drum kit to join the evolving group. The band also began rehearsing more, which made the performances tighter but came at the cost of Pulsallama's unique, brink-of-catastrophe energy that was the hallmark of early shows. Caffeine remembers, "The entire downtown NYC scene was pretty cool-conscious but also truly cool, full of unique, stylish and artistic/musical/theatrical individuals. Our band members had unique personalities, talents and strong individual styles."

Pulsallama gained press notice due to their over-the-top performances and promotional outreach to media fascinated by the downtown art scene. They were written up in the *New York Rocker*, the *Soho Weekly News*, *New York* Magazine, and *NME*. In 2012, in *Bedford and Bowery* online magazine, Magnuson described Pulsallama as "peddling in post-primal racket and a delirious expression of our blithe and extremely contrarian spirits. I always envisioned it as a conceptual theater piece."

Despite the sheer number of bodies on stage, none of the members played electric guitars. At the earliest conceptual stage, it was intended to create a rhythmic ritual-esque sound to summon primal urges. Instead of shredding on real axes, Wendy Wild created foam guitars purely for visual effect that were often destroyed during performances. With the primary focus on rhythm, Pulsallama sometimes featured two electric basses creating an even heavier propulsive sound.

The stacked percussion section had Caffeine playing a full kit, while Thometz handled the bongos, Johnson struck the steel drum and sometimes a Synare drum machine, and Wild rocked the glockenspiel. Stacey Elkin played some bass and kicked

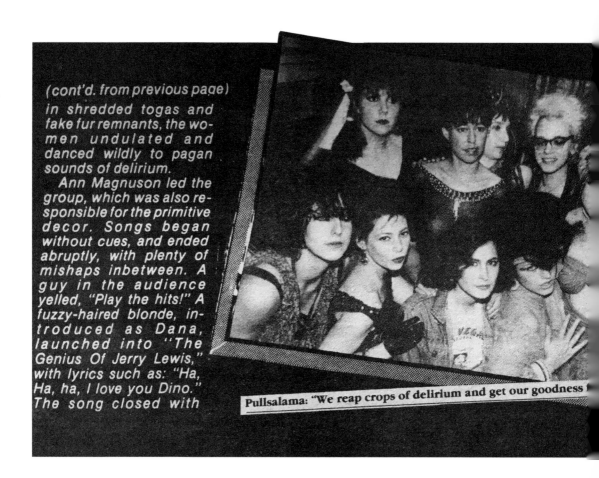

(cont'd. from previous page) in shredded togas and fake fur remnants, the women undulated and danced wildly to pagan sounds of delirium.

Ann Magnuson led the group, which was also responsible for the primitive decor. Songs began without cues, and ended abruptly, with plenty of mishaps inbetween. A guy in the audience yelled, "Play the hits!" A fuzzy-haired blonde, introduced as Dana, launched into "The Genius Of Jerry Lewis," with lyrics such as: "Ha, Ha, ha, I love you Dino." The song closed with

Pulsalama: "We reap crops of delirium and get our goodness

the beats up a notch with timbales and later, a Linn-Drum. The sound also included numerous smaller rhythm instruments, inspired by the hand instruments in elementary schools, such as go-go bells, cowbells, and tambourines.

The ten-piece crew developed themes and coordinated costumes for their performances, and with their wild and frenetic energy became a "must-see" event in the early '80s. With more shows and more rehearsals, the band morphed from spontaneous compositions based on a few lyrics or tempos to a band with defined songs. The band played shows in New York City as headliners and opening acts. The pinnacle was the opening slot on the East Coast leg of the Clash's 1982 tour. Wendy Wild, in an autobiography written just before her passing in 1996, remembers the Clash shows as a near-riot:

"Nothing could stop us, not even the hairbrushes or money or sneakers that were thrown onto the stage. Our finale was 'Rock-fest on the Meadowlands,' containing slurs of

all their icons including Bruce Springsteen, and ripping up the fake foam core guitars. This really infuriated them, but by the third night, we gained quite a sizable cheering section, including young girls in the front rows singing along to our songs."

During their short run, Pulsallama's rowdy stage antics, campy props and costumes, and jerky tempos turned heads in the New York underground. Their best-known single, "The Devil Lives in My Husband's Body," released on Y Records in 1982, turned out to be a minor college radio and cult hit.

Pulsallama was a force of pure female energy. Onstage, that collective power mesmerized and entertained. Offstage, it led to interpersonal conflicts. Ann Magnuson reveals the truth about the most infamous quote used to describe the band—13 girls fighting over a cowbell—which was mistakenly attributed to press: "There was fighting but never over a cowbell. Dee Pop said that in jest. Dany and I thought it was hilarious, so I always used that quote in the press releases. Not long before Dee died, he told me he loved the band."

The all-bass-and-percussion outfit had 13 members at its first performance but settled into a ten-piece outfit (the listed members above) during its most productive period. The band became a seven-piece band when founding members Ann and Dany, as well as Andé, left after the release of their first single, over creative differences and the ultimate intention and direction of the group.

Each member of Pulsallama had different reasons for leaving or staying with the band. Magnuson told *Bedford and Bowery* in 2012, "All bands are essentially dysfunctional families… and communism does not really work. For me, it was time to go." In a recent conversation, Magnuson and Johnson both remember that Pulsallama wasn't their sole creative project and that more opportunities to pursue work took precedence over the band.

The remaining seven members of Pulsallama carried on and rode the avant-garde soundwaves of the post-punk movement before calling it quits in July of 1983. ●

everyone in hysterics, clapping for more as she screamed, "Help my kids!"

Nothing was meant to be taken seriously, and it was truly the most refreshing fun a lot of us have had in a long time. To those who might have considered the fun to be a bit tacky, Wendy Wild, a punked-out cavewoman, who made Bo Derek look tame by comparison, dedicated the group's last song as follows: "This is Pulsallama, if you don't like it, then go f___ your momma!" My sentiments, exactly.

—K.B. Shoots

Excerpt of review and picture of the September 12, 1981 Pulsallama performance at the Cavern Club by K.B. Shoots (a.k.a. Karen Cohen). "The Aquarian," issue dated September 30–October 7, 1981. Courtesy of the Ann Magnuson Archive.

In Memorium

MAGGIE JOHNSON *of* ANEMIC BOYFRIENDS
passed away in May 2020.

ANGIE MIMA *of the* BRAPHSMEARS
passed away in October 2020.

BARBARA ESS *of* Y PANTS
passed away in March 2021.

DEE POP *of the* BUSH TETRAS
passed away in October 2021.

MEG BRAZILL *of* LOS MICROWAVES
passed away in December 2021.

KARLA MADDOG *of the* CONTROLLERS
passed away in October 2022.

Acknowledgments

I'M CORNY AS HELL and am brimming with gratitude. I am forever indebted to Jen Lemasters and Todd Novak whose knowledge and research fueled much of this project. Special thank you to CJ Del Mar whose mentoring, knowledge, and encouragement sparked the initial ideas for the project. Thank you to all of the artists and friends of artists who welcomed conversations, sent pictures, and graciously talked to me over video, on the phone, or through email. Thank you especially to the artists with whom I have developed friendships over the last few years. I am hugely grateful for the people who emailed me even one suggestion or shared excitement over these bands and artists. And I want to express my profound appreciation for Christina Ward and Jessica Parfrey of Feral House for taking a chance on my idea and my writing; it has opened up so many doors for myself and many women.

I will keep babbling…Thank you to my family. To my mom, who took me to see the Monkees reunion when I was 12. To my dad and my brother Matt who both passed away during the writing of the book. My dad read my first drafts and my brother was always cheering me on. To my sister Lisa who I stayed awake with for so many hours gabbing over '60s pop; though our obsessions have diverged over the years, we still share them with one another. To my stepmother Sandy who has always been on our side. To my sister Katie, who listened to my terrible high school album over and over in her room. To my oldest sister Amy who made me my first mixtapes. To Alex, who always keeps me laughing. To my aunts, uncles, and cousins who have always supported all of my endeavors.

To my perfect partner Erica for listening to all this music and getting into it with me. And going to shows and overall just being interested. Thank you to my friends who keep my spirits up and have helped me along this journey in so many ways: Nick Gamso, Erica Walker Adams, Oliv Roe, Asha Adisa, Kai Black, Clare Brighid, Jack Haynes, Frank Okay, Lucianne Walkowicz, and so many countless friends it would be impossible to name (I haven't forgotten you). Thank you to the girls of Swimsuit Addition, Sam Westerling, Becca Nisbet, Sarah Chmielski, and Susan Volbrecht, for allowing our relationships to grow even after the band dissolved. Without any of you, there is no possible way I'd be alive, or that this book would even exist…

Citations

Other than listening to bands' and artists' music, reading information on their records, watching all the live performances I could find on YouTube, I read the bands' and artists' websites, I gathered information from interviews, documentaries, books, magazines, newspaper archives, websites, radio, podcasts, and blogs. I read *Search & Destroy* magazines, *Maximum Rocknrolls*, the *Punk Diary* books, *Punk Globe*, and the *Punk Girl Diary* zines. I referenced *Punk Women: 40 Years of Musicians Who Built Punk Rock* by David Ensminger, *Rock and Roll Women: The Fiercest Female Rockers* (2018, Sterling) by Meredith Ochs, *Revenge of the She Punks: A Feminist Music History from Poly Styrene to Pussy Riot* (2019, University of Texas Press) by Vivien Golman, and *Typical Girls: Styles and Sounds of the Transatlantic Indie Revolution* (2017, Cicada Books) by Sam Knee. I read *She's a Rebel: The History of Women in Rock and Roll* by Gillian Gaar (2002, Seal Press). I tried to cross-check my information as much as I could. If there are any errors, which I am sure there are, I would be pleased to correct them.

OTHER WEBSITE SOURCES
Wikipedia, Discogs, Allmusic, Punkturns30, Punk77, Punkygibbon, Punk Girl Diaries

CHAPTER 1: MIDWEST

INTERVIEWS
Nikki Corvette
Susan Schmidt
Vivien "Vinyl" Rusche
Rockee Berlin
Members of the Welders
Lorrie Kountz
Audrey Stanzler
Stonie Rivera
Tracey Thomas
Kate Fagan

DOCUMENTARIES
If You're Not Dead, Play by Phil Hoffman (2005 PBS documentary)

OTHER
Geisha This by Destroy All Monsters (1995, Distributed Art Publishers)

"The True Story of Niagara, Destroy All Monsters, & the Desecration of Detroit" by Todd McGovern (2016, pleasekillme.com)

Niagara: Beyond the Pale by Various Authors (2005, 99mm Books)

"The Fabulous Nikki Corvette" by Ginger Coyote (*Punk Globe*)

"What's Shakin' with the Shivvers" by Bobby Tanzilo (2014, OnMilwaukee.com)

The Shivvers – Teen Line (2012, Cheap Rewards blog)

Tracy Wormworth interview by Joel McIver (2018, Music Radar)

We Were Living in Cincinnati liner notes by Peter Aaron (2019, HoZac Archival records)

Flirt (detroitpunkarchive.com)

"An oral history of long-lost St. Louis punks the Welders" by Mike Appelstein (2010, riverfronttimes.com)

(Sub)Basement Tapes by Steve Pick (2009, stlmag.com)

Ama-Dots by Jessie Lynn McMains (2014, rustbeltjessie.tumblr.com)

Ama-Dots: Ama-Dots (Rerun) by Mike Larson (2014, Shepherd Express)

Brick Through the Window: An Oral History of Punk Rock, New Wave, and Noise in Milwaukee, 1964–1984 by Various Authors (2017, Brickboys)

"The Return of DA!" by Chuck Nolan (2010, victimoftime.com)

In Memoriam: Lorna Donley of DA! by Kenneth Preski (2013, *New City Music*)

Preview of DA at the Abbey Pub Saturday by J.H. Palmer (2010, Gapers Block)

"An Artist's Work Lives On" by Jim DeRogatis (2007, *Chicago Sun Times*)

"Lydia Tomkiw: Like Royalty in Exile" by Bart Plantenga (2000, *Fringecore*)

"Please Respect her Decadence: Algebra Suicide: *Summer Virus Night*" by José Padua (*Brooklyn Rail*)

If You're Not Dead, Play by Phil Hoffman (2005 PBS documentary)

CHAPTER 2: SOUTH

INTERVIEWS
Vanessa Briscoe-Hay
Members of the Klitz
Neil Ruttenberg
Irene Hardwicke

DOCUMENTARIES
Athens, GA: Inside/Out by Tony Gayton (1987 documentary)

Invisible Bands by Greg McLaughlin (2011 documentary)

BOOKS, MAGAZINES, WEBSITES, RADIO, BLOGS
A Conversation with Vanessa Briscoe-Hay by *Life Elsewhere* radio show

Marcia Clifton Interview by Ryan Leach (2016, Terminal Boredom)

"Return of the Klitz" by Andria Lisle (2017, Memphis Flyer)

"After 40 Years, Memphis Punk Legends The Klitz Make Their Nashville Debut" by Edd Hurt (2019, nashvillescene.com)

The Delinquents – Alien Beach Party (2011, cheaprewards.blogspot.com)

"A World of Our Own: My Dolls and the Houston Punk Scene" (2016, wilddogzine.com)

Austin Surf Pop Punk: Alien Beach Party on Live Wire Records (wilddogzine.com)

"Teddy and the Frat Girls' Sheer Smegma" (2008, Detailed Twang)

Sheer Smegma – Audio Suicide 7" (2009, kbfarchive.blogspot.com)

Teddy and the Frat Girls (2010, ovarianfist.wordpress.com)

"Blast From the Past" by Abel Folgar (2010, *Miami New Times*)

Interview with Debbie DeNeese (2016, trashfever.com)

F-Systems – People (2012, cheaprewards.blogspot.com)

CHAPTER 3: NORTHWEST

INTERVIEWS
Cynthia Kraman (Genser)
Members of Art Object
Members of the Accident
Members of the Braphsmears
Scotty Buttocks
Louise Disease

DOCUMENTARIES
Northwest Passage: The Birth of Portland's DIY Culture by Mike Brainfollies

Madame Dishrags, a short documentary by Carmen Pollard

BOOKS, MAGAZINES, WEBSITES, RADIO, BLOGS
"Screams From the Vault: The Neo Boys" by Tage Savage (2004, psuvanguard.com)

"Neo Boys: Portland's Queens of Punk Recollect Their Roots" by Andrew Hamlin (2014, *Seattle Star*)

Interview with Louise Disease (2019, Evan "Funk" Davies Show, wfmu.org)

The Visible Targets by Dennis R. White (jivetimerecords.com)

Chinas Comidas by Dennis R. White (jivetimerecords.com)

"From the Vaults: Lost Cassettes, Digital Magic, and Sado-Nation" by Bryony (2011, *Maximum Rocknroll*)

"Tina Bell: a mulher negra que ajudou a fundar o grunge" by Tânia Seles (2017, Sopa Alternative)

"Bellingham Band Has New 'Constructive Anarchy' Sound" by Mark Higgins (1980, *The Herald*)

"New Disc A Work of Art Object" by Kevin Stauffer (1981, unknown newspaper clipping)

CHAPTER 4: WEST COAST (SOUTH)

INTERVIEWS
Pleasant Gehman
Members of Backstage Pass
Alice Bag
Joyce Rooks
Members of Frightwig
Dave Markey

BOOKS, MAGAZINES, WEBSITES, RADIO, BLOGS
"F! How About A to Z?" (2008, nathannothinsez.blogspot.com)

"Freda Rente': The Compassionate Outsider" (2015, *Random Lengths* News)

Violence Girl: East L.A. Rage to Hollywood Stage, A Chicana Punk Story by Alice Bag (2011, Feral House)

"On the Record: What Happened to Singer for Suburban Lawns?" by Bradford Brady and John Maron (2020, *Bristol Herald Courier*)

The Suburban Lawns Documentary Instagram

"Searching for Su Tissue" by Scott Beauchamp (2019, the Outline)

Suburban Lawns: Something Else! Interview by Steve Elliot (2015, Something Else Reviews)

"Looking Back on Suburban Lawns, the Great Forgotten LA New Wave Band" by Steve Eckhardt (2015, *Vice*)

Dinah Cancer interview (2014, eclecticartswa.blogspot.com)

"Catholicism and Death Rock Fashion" Part II by Sarah Schimek (lethalamounts.com)

"Texacala Jones: L.A.'s Cowpunk Pinup" by Sarah Schimek (lethalamounts.com)

"The Sin 34 Story" by Dave Markey (wegotpowerfilms.com)

March 1983 *Thrasher* Magazine

"The Pandoras: A Look Back, A Look Ahead" by Amanda Sheppard (2017, pleasekillme.com)

"The Dinettes" (*San Diego Reader*)

"The Dinettes Are Rocking Out Again After a 37-Year Hiatus" by George Varga (2017, *Chicago Tribune*)

Feature: "Black Punk History—Badass Drummer Karla Maddog" by Erin White (2016, afropunk.com)

"Flashback Interview: Pleasant Gehman" by Johnny Caps (2018, popgeeks.com)

"Pleasant Gehman Remembers the Wild, Wild Weekly of Yore" by Pleasant Gehman (2018, *LA Weekly*)

CHAPTER 5: WEST COAST (NORTH)

INTERVIEWS
Penelope Houston
Debora Iyall
Jean Caffeine
Texacala Jones
Members of Wilma
Members of the Contractions
David Javelosa

BOOKS, MAGAZINES, WEBSITES, RADIO, BLOGS
"Romeo Void: Another Unjustly Overlooked '80s Band" by Jeff Finkle (2018, culturesonar.com)

Debora Iyall of Romeo Void by Keith Valcourt (2012, Rockerzine.com)

Mary Monday (HoZac Records)

"Mary Monday – I Gave My Punk… 7″" by the Flakes (2006, kbdrecords.com)

"Songwriter/Musician Jean Caffeine Releases First Album in 6 Years Tomorrow" (2017, broadwayworld.com)

Hear This: Kathy Peck by Dan Sauter (2012, Music Life Radio)

Los Microwaves – *Life After Breakfast* LP DVD (Dark Entries)

"San Francisco Punk Prankers: Pink Section, Inflatable Boy Clams" by Richie Unterberger (2020, pleasekillme.com)

"The Bizarre Lost Art-Punk of Inflatable Boy Clams" by Ron Kretsch (2014, dangerousminds.net)

Countless newspaper and magazine clippings from 1977–1983 courtesy of the Punk Archives at the San Francisco Public Library

CHAPTER 6: EAST COAST

INTERVIEWS
Ramona Jan
Beth B
Lydia Lunch (for Please Kill Me article)
Jayne County (for Please Kill Me article)
Adele Bertei and Kathy Rey
Members of Pulsallama
Members of the Bush Tetras
Cynthia 'B' Girl
Members of Disturbed Furniture: Alexa Hunter, Jorge, Mick
Becky Wreck
Micky Metts

DOCUMENTARIES

Lydia Lunch — The War is Never Over by Beth B (2019)

Wendy O. Williams & the Plasmatics: 10 Years of Revolutionary Rock & Roll by Randy Shooter (2006)

BOOKS, MAGAZINES, WEBSITES, RADIO, BLOGS

Man Enough to Be a Woman by Rupert Smith and Jayne County (1996, Serpent's Tail)

"Life on Mars: The Surviving Members of the Earliest No Wave Band Talk Muggings, Warhol, and 1977" by Jordan N. Mamone (2015, *Vice*)

"How Mark Cunningham Blitzed the Bowery With No Wave Icons Mars" by Jordan Mamone (2017, *Observer*)

Paradoxia, a Predator's Diary by Lydia Lunch (1997, Akashic Books)

Will Work for Drugs by Lydia Lunch (2009, Akashic Books)

So Real it Hurts by Lydia Lunch (2019, Seven Stories Press)

"Dance to the Best of ESG" by Joe Tangari (2010, Pitchfork)

"It's Music That Makes You Dance" - ESG Interviewed by Melissa Rakshana Steiner (2015, The Quietus)

"ESG Turned Accident into Music History" by Greg Kot (2018, *Chicago Tribune*)

"The Devil Lives in My Husband's Body: Pulsallama, NYC All-Girl, All-Percussion New Wave Group" by Richard Metzger (2021, dangerousminds.net)

"Nightclubbing – Helen Wheels, 1979" by Emily Armstrong and Pat Ivers (2015, *Bedford and Bowery*)

"Helen Wheels, NYC Punk Bodybuilder, Blue Öyster Cult Songwriter and UFO Abductee" by Oliver Hall (2017, dangerousminds.net)

Chalk Circle "Reflection" review by Martin Douglas (2011, Pitchfork)

"Tiny Desk Unit: A Deeper History" by Michael Barron (bobboilen.info)

"Remembering Susan Mumford, Once the Voice of D.C.'s Punk Scene" by Alona Wartofsky (2018, *Washington City Paper*)

"Remembering the Time Wendy O. Williams Was Arrested in Milwaukee for Getting Freaky with a Sledgehammer" by Matt Wild (2017, *Milwaukee Record*)

"Plasmatics' Wendy O. Williams Commits Suicide" by Richard Skanse (1998, *Rolling Stone*)

An Interview with New York's Post Punk Icons Bush Tetras by Lola Pistola (2018, altcitizen.com)

"Bush Tetras at 40: An Interview With Drummer Dee Pop" by Audrey Golden (2020, louderthanwar.com)

Interview with Pat Place by Tim Broun (2011, furious.com, Perfect Sound Forever)

UT Interview by Andrea Feldman (2006, Warped Reality)

"The Collective Discordance of the No Wave Group Ut" by Marc Masters (2019, daily.bandcamp.com)

V-Day Throwback: Y-Pants (2011, Tom Tom Mag)

Disturbed Furniture by Richard Fantina (1980, *East Village Eye*)

Interview with Cynthia B. Ross of the 'B' Girls by Amy Haben (2017, pleasekillme.com)

"Underrated Classics: Nasty Facts" by Cory Clifford (2015, Heave Media)

Nasty Facts – Kali Boyce Interview by Osa Atoe (*Maximum Rocknroll*)

"Cherl Boyce – Nasty Facts" by Oihane Follones (2019, iamintheband.blogspot.com)

"Cheap Perfume – NYC's first all-female punk band…" by Bess Korey (2007, girlsinthegarage.wordpress.com)

Cheap Perfume by Chris Rocks On (*Punk Globe*)

Lorry Doll birthday Bash '78 (lorrydoll.com)

Ikue Mori Interview by Jason Gross (1977, furious.com, Perfect Sound Forever)

Index

A

Adams, Dale 72
  Gary 61
Akiyoshi, Kawashima (Reck) 253
Albertine, Viv 8, 232, 252
Alderman, Brenda 288
Aldridge, Lesa 96
Algebra Suicide 77-79
Alicino, Christeen 207–8
Alleman, Willie 100
Alley Cats, the 157, 168–69, 173, 179, 212
Ama-Dots 70–71, 298–99
Anderson, Carola B. 209
  Christopher 278
Andujar, Andres 107
Anemic Boyfriends, the 132–33
Arjavac, Chuck 134
Arlen, Nancy 244
Art Object 125, 138–41
Ash, Lorenda 107
Asheton, Ron 24, 26
Aston-Emerson, Lisa 173
Au Pairs, the 19, 273, 278, 285, 290
Austin, Gaye 164
Avengers, the 118, 125, 165, 179, 193–94, 197–202, 210, 222
Aversa, Angelo 246
Axley, Pam "Spam Ax" 109

B

B-52's, the 10, 54, 55, 87, 89, 92
Baby Buddha 220, 227
Backstage Pass 156–58, 189
Bad Brains 80, 260, 273, 275, 286
Bag, Alice 20, 156, 159–60, 166–67, 178

Bags, the 157, 159, 161, 165–66, 174, 178–79
Bain, Jill "Jade Blade"
Baker, Terry 269–70
Bam Bam 151–53
Bandit, Laura 187
Bangles, the 80, 95, 158, 185
Barron, Michael 269–70
Barton, Jerry 107
Bat-Thing, Mary 166, 178
Bauhaus 45, 178
Baum, Pat 128
Beauvoir, Jean 266
Beech, Wes 266
Bell, Tina 151–53
Bello, Elissa 166
Beltri, Lissa 184
Berger, Alison 256
Berlin, Rockee "Re Marx" 39, 80, 242, 290, 298
Bertei, Adele 11, 285, 288–89
Beth B 255
Bewley, Randall 86, 88, 92
Biafra, Jello 109, 173, 212, 231
Bickham, Becky 100
Bingenheimer, Rodney 157, 185
Binkov, Jon 213
Bitch 56–58
Black Flag 122, 134, 172, 179, 182, 212
Blackwell, Janna "Banana" 80
Blankfeld, Karen 184–86
Blondie 30, 36, 64, 149, 157, 164, 194, 205, 250, 252
Bloods, the 273, 285, 288–91
Blowdryer, Jennifer 205
Blowdryers, the 205–6
Boaz, Gregory "Smog Vomit" 180
Body, Genny 156, 158
Boginski, Bob 192

Boilen, Bob 269–70
Boisen, Myles 125, 138
Bojanic, Tony 61
Bolles, Don 178
Bonafede, Anne 283
Bondage, Mish (see: Miller, Michelle)
Bonebrake, D. J. 170
Bossi, Benjamin 221
Bouchard, Albert 248
Boutet de Monvel, Genevieve 228
Bradley, David 39
Braphsmears, the 134, 142–45, 147–48
Brat, the 175–77
Brazill, Meg 219–20
Brisco, Cindy 173
Briscoe Hay, Vanessa 86–87
Brown, David 170
Burg, China 244
Bush Tetras 11, 273–76, 285, 292, 294
Butler, Chris 53–55, 282
Butthole Surfers 102, 239
Buttocks, Scotty 151–53

C

Caffeine, Jean 207–8, 292, 294
Caffey, Charlotte 170
Caiati, Emanuel J. 248
Calo, Tas 246
Cambridge Apostles 166, 178
Cameron, Matt 151, 153
Campbell, Kathleen 288
Canal, Nina 261
Cancer, Dinah 166, 178
Canning, Caroline 219–20
Carter, Larry 92, 202, 221
Casey, Carolyn 246

Casmano, Steve 134

Castration Squad 166–67, 178

Cervenka, Mirielle 257

Chai, Dianne 168–69, 173

Chalk Circle 15, 283–85

Chanault, Mark 72

Chance, James 253, 288
   Meghan 124–25

Cheap Perfume 256

Cheslow, Sharon 15, 283, 285

Chilton, Alex 96–99

Chinas Comidas 119–20, 122–23

Chi-Pig 42–44

Church, Mickey 39

Cichlids 94–95, 104

Cicola, Tom 39

Cielen, Debbie 56

Cimino, Kenny 192

Clare, Rick 192

Clifton, Gail Elise and Marcia 96, 98–99

Cloidt, Jay 217

Cobain, Kurt 153, 235

Cold, the 106

Contortions, the 244, 273, 275, 285, 288

Contractions, the 225–27, 233, 239

Controllers, the 164–65

Conway, Bambi 184–85

Corboy, David 134, 145

Couch, Ric 134

County, Jayne 160, 162, 242–43, 255

Covarrubias, Teresa 175

Coyote, Ginger 193–94, 206, 298

Crafton, Kerry 107

Cram, Doug 124–25
   Lisa Nansen 124–25

Cramps, the 99

Crane, Cathy 111, 208
   Sumner 244

Crash, Micki 271–72

Crawford, Nyna 213–14

Creamcheese, Suzi 21, 142

Crey, Todd 271

Crowe, Curtis 86, 88

Crutchfield, Robin 257

Cubes, the 61, 63–65

Cunningham, Mark 244
   Sarah 111–12

Curley, Brian and Mindy 100

Currie, Cherrie 102, 127, 156

D

DA! 45–46, 70, 187, 299

Dadistics, the 59–60

Damned, the 157, 160, 178, 198, 200

Danford, Dan "Bosco" 215

Dash 246

Dasher, Rick 215–16

Davis, Jay 213
   K. D. 230
   Kimberly 292
   Michael 24, 26
   Nancy 56

Dead Boys, the 55, 65, 68, 134, 164, 244, 250

Dead Kennedys, the 182, 194, 200, 202, 212

Dean, Joanna "Spock" 156

Dee, Michael 286

Dee Pop 273, 275, 295

DeGeneres, Vance 106

Delguidice, Sue Ferguson 173

Delinquents, the 100–101

Del Rey, Marina 156, 158

Del Rio, Steve 80

Delta 5 273

Demme, Jonathan 172

Dempster, Kim 219

DeNeese, Debbie 94

Dents, the 72–73

Derrah, Jay 221

DeSavia, Tom 170

Destroy All Monsters 24–27, 41, 61

Detrick, Richie 195

Detweiler, Carol 228

Deutsch, Stu 266

Devo 41–44, 55, 142–43, 158, 171, 182, 275, 286

De Volga, Olga 209

Diedrich, Louise 230

Dietrich, Ed 59

Dillard, Kelly 184

Dillary, Hillary 164

Dils, the 165, 200, 210

Dinettes, the 173–74

Disease, Louise 132

Dishrags, the 116–18

Disturbed Furniture 271–72

Dixon, Diane "Boom Boom" 187
   Fur 187

Dizzy and the Romilars 259, 280–82

DNA 45, 257–58, 262, 275

Donahue, Patty 53, 55

Donley, Lorna 45

Donnas, the 15, 36, 139

Döring, Monika 80

Draper, Kelly "Rusty Welder" 28

Dummy Club 80–83

Dupont, Joesaphine 109

Dust, Chris 242

E

Eannelli, Jim 47

Eddinger, Gere 56

Egoslavia 278, 285

Elkin, Stacy 292, 295

Endsley, Fred 59

Escovedo, Alejandro 195–96

ESG 11, 259–60, 263–65, 273, 276

Ess, Barbara 276

Ethington, Jr., Bob 66

Evans, Mark 104

Evoniuk, Tom 192

Excuses, the 286

Eyes, the 165, 170

F

Fagan, Kate 74, 76

Falbo, George 192

Ficca, Billy 53–54

Field, Bradley 253

Firmin, John A. 132

Fisher, Dawn 45

Flirt 39, 41, 61

Flores, Rosie 187

Foams, the 111, 113

Fowley, Kim 58, 156, 158, 173, 187

Franklin, Randy 107

Fraser, Donna 56

Fremont, Tommy "Spud" 39

Fricke, Jim "Ed Media" 198, 200

Frightwig 139, 234–39

F-Systems 107

Fuertsch, Andy 100

Fujimoto, Caroline 28
   Jane 28

Fulcher, Sarah 96

Funahara, Chosei 266

Furem, Bob 45

G

Gangemi, Bud 104
Gang of Four 70, 72, 87, 108, 273, 278
Garcia, George 175
Gehman, Pleasant 156, 181, 187–88
Geiser, Thomas 192
George, Maniff 192
Germs, the 122, 128, 159, 165, 172–73, 178, 200
Ghent, Valerie 280, 282
Gittelsohn, Judy 228
Glass, Mike "Geek" 182
Gleur, John 171
Go, Larry 215
Goddard, Chris 132
Go-Go's, the 8, 15, 44, 97, 99, 122, 156–58, 166, 170, 174, 179, 185, 200, 220, 227, 239, 272, 285, 289
Golden, Pamela 149
Gomez, Casey 184–85, 187, 189
Goudreau, Gaylene 45–46
Graham, Terry 159, 252
Green, Mary 283, 285
Grimm, Kathryn 187
Gun Club, the 160, 178, 180–81, 209
Gwerder, Lou 213

H

Haller, Val 242
Hallet, Doug 72
Ham, Jacqui 261
Hameon, Stephanie/Ariel 271
Hamilton, Lucy (see: Berg, China)
    Rebecca 149
Hanes, John "Stench" 221
Hardwicke, Irene 111, 113
Harris, Jett 242, 244
Harry, Debbie 8, 10, 250, 252, 282
Hash, Billy Jo 184
Hayes, Mary "Boolah" 70
Heckert, Matt 228
Helen Wheels Band 248
Hell, Richard 134, 171, 252
Hendrickson, Tom 151
Hentges, Meg 128
Hernandez, Michael 59
Herrera, Trish 102

Hoffmann, Mike 50
Holt, Shawna 119
Hopkins, Debbie 225, 233
Houston, Penelope 139–40, 165, 198, 200, 212
Howard, Brie 187, 189
Hunter, Alexa 271
Hynde, Chrissie 10, 153, 288

I

Illades, Luis 198
Indian Wells 209
Inflatable Boy Clams 228–29
Ingraham, Greg 198, 200
Irving, Karen "Anna Klisis" 138–40
IXNA 217–18
Iyall, Debora 221–22

J

James, Pete 33, 37
Jan, Ramona 259, 280–82
Javelosa, David 219–20
Jendrisak, Mark 66
Jett, Joan 66, 108, 127, 156, 174
Johnson, Dany 11, 292, 294–95
    Ellen 132
    John 242
    Maggie 132
    Mike 66
Johnston, Kathy 102
Jones, Lorenzo "Pee Wee" 269–70
    Texacala 180–81

K

Kahn, Gwynne 184–85
Kaplan, Sheri 184
Kay, Yvette 230
Kaye, Leslie 56
KB (Boyze/Boyce/Cherl) 259–60
Keane, Laura 149
Kelley, Mary 225
    Mike 24, 26
    Jozann 111
    Trent 124
Kennedy, Laura 273, 285, 294
    Tiffany 166
Kent, Brad 198
Kincaid, Kim 128

King, Rob 24
Kirkendall, Donna 56
Klayman, Dan 53, 55
Kleinschmidt, Kim 138
Klemmer, Joe 280
Klitz, the 96–99
Kossoris, Jill 47–49, 51
Kountz, Lorrie 56, 58, 298
Kowalsky, Michael 215
Kraman (Genser), Cynthia 119, 123
Krueger, Scott 47
Kuhn, Cecilia 234

L

Lachowski, Michael 86–88
Lalonde, Chris "Dale Powers" 116
Lamb, Don 192, 194
Land, Lynnwood 215
Lander, Mark 107
Lanfeld, Julie 182–83
La Palma, Marina 217–18
Laurenco, Tony 192
Lawler, Julie 207–8
    Mary 207–8
Lawson, Paul "The Fly" 80
Lea, Tracy 166
Leach, Jimmy 170, 299
LeDesma, Bunny 256
Ledgerwood, Scott (see: Buttocks, Scotty)
Le Duc, Eve 80
Lee, Craig 159
Levin, Mia 234
Lewis, Pam 278
Liberatore-Dolan, Irene 173
Libran, Tito 263, 265
Limosner, Pilar 219–20
Lindsay, Arto 257
Lobiciano, Jennifer 128
Loren, Cary 24, 26
Los Microwaves 219–20
Loughran, Tim 100
Luckette, Chris 106
Lunch, Lydia 8, 11, 174, 235, 244, 253, 255, 272
Lyndsay, Tamera 283, 285

M

MacNicols, Alex 209
Maddog, Karla 164–65
Magnuson, Ann 9, 292, 294–95
Markey, Dave 182–83
Mars 244–45, 255, 275
Martin, Tommy 151–53
Martinez, Brenda 256
Martt, Mike 180
Marx, Skid 39
Mary Monday's Revue 194
Mateus, Jorge Arevalo 271
McBurney, John (see: Gleur, John)
McCarthy, John 168
Medina, Rudy 175
   Sidney 175
Mendoza, Deborah 184
Menendez, Barbara 106
Metts, Micky 246
Michael, Eliot 242
Michaud, Carmen "Scout" 116
Midtskog, Dag 119
Miller, Ben 24, 26
   Larry 24
   Michelle 134–35, 142, 144
   Susan 234
Mima, Angie 142
Miro, Jennifer 195, 212
Mitchell, Deanna 234
   Rod 156
Mold, Cookie 109
Monday, Mary 192–94
Montana, Lori 292
Morency, Gayle 184
Mori, Ikue 257–58
Morris, Kim 225, 227
Morrison, Patricia "Pat Bag" 159,
   166
Morrongiello, Tommy 248
Muhlfriedel, Marina (see: Del
   Rey, Marina)
Mulrooney, Robert "Bootsey X"
   33
Mumford, Susan 269–70, 301
Murphy, Julia 273
Murray, John 72, 207, 287
   Pete 72
Mydolls, the 102–3

N

Nanini, Joe 170
Nash, Lisa 94, 104
Nasty Facts 259, 281
Nation, Leesa 134, 136, 142–43,
   243, 290
Negrette Lair, Doriot 173
Neo Boys, the 21, 128–31, 142,
   147, 159
Newman, Phil 182
Niagara 24–27
Niblack, Chris 283
Nikki & the Corvettes 33, 36–38,
   61, 252
Nuns, the 19, 158, 193–97, 200,
   210, 212

O

Odell, Lynn 256
Olener, Jeff 195–96
Opielski, Val 273
O'Brien, "Danny Furious" 198,
   200
O'Connell, Richie 215
O'Sullivan, Colleen 28, 215
   Patrick 215

P

Padovani, Henry 242
Pagel, Andy 80
Palermo, Susan 256
Palmieri, April 292
Pandoras, the 184–86, 189
Panebianco, Kris 230, 233
Parks, Judy 205
Parsons, Sarah "Fish" 109
Patchouli, Julie 184
Paulson, Lynn 119
Peck, Don 192–93
   Kathy 193, 220, 225–26
Peron, Neil 192
Phantoms, the 246–47
Phelan, Ann 288
Phranc 166–67
Pierce, Paula 180, 184–86
Piersol, Virginia "Verge" 276
Pifer, Lisa 215
Piscioneri, Billy 215
Place, Pat 11, 273
Planteen, Jojo 228

Plasmatics, the 266–68
Pogue, Layna 100
Poot, Bruce 124
Portman, Allan 94
Post, Shellee Harper "Ami L.
   Nitrate" 142
Postal, Jonathan 198
Pozniak, Dan 134
Prendergast, Patti 56
Pretenders, the 43, 288
Propp, Dave 134
Pulsallama 208, 292–95
Pumphrey, Jan 283
Pyle, Mike 47
Pylon 86–89, 92–93
Pylon Reenactment Society 88, 93

Q

Quatro, Suzi 8, 30, 116

R

Radecker, Kevin 106
Ramirez, Joe 170
Ramones, the 28, 30, 33, 56–57,
   65, 73–74, 76, 92, 98, 113,
   116, 124, 128, 134, 144–45,
   157, 164, 178, 189, 198, 200,
   210, 250, 252
Ranson, William "Vex
   Billingsgate" 171
Raphael, Jeffrey 195
Ray, Dianna 102
Reader, Joel 198
Red C 285, 287
Reins, Marsky 187
Remote, Steve 271
Rey, Kathy 288–89
Reyes, George 102
Ricablanca, Steve 213
Richardson, Jim 47, 52
Riffle, Pete 72
Rigg, Jack 248
Riggins, Richard (Rich) 119, 122
Riley, "Bob Romilar") 280
Ritter, Rob "Graves" 159, 178
Rivera, Stonie 80
Roberts, Rich 42
Robins, Susan 94
Rodriguez, Charles "Chuck
   Roast" 171
Roessler, Kira 165

Rogers, Alison 111–12
Rollins, Henry 212, 283
Romanelli, Chris 266
Romeo Void 221, 223–24
Rooks, Joyce 173–74
Rosencrans, Todd "Rosa" 219
Ross, Cynthia 249, 251
    Lucasta 249
Ruiz, Corky "BamBam" 70
    Michael 156
Rummens, Michael 175
Runaways, the 8, 28, 30, 56, 58,
    66, 95, 156, 158, 173, 178, 185
Rusche, Vivian "Vinyl" 72–73,
    298
Russo, Joanne (see: Del Rey,
    Marina)
Ruttenberg, Neil 107
Ryan, Pat 195

S

Saddy, Marcy 249
Sado-Nation 134–35, 142, 148
Sanchez, Alan 61
Sands, Vermillion 192, 194
Scalvunos, Jim 253
Schilhab, Renee 249
Schmidt Horning, Susan 42
Schofield, Phillip 271–72
Schorr, Genny 187, 189
Schutt, David 59
Screaming Sneakers 104–5
Screamin' Sirens 158, 185, 187,
    189, 239
Scroggins, Renee 11, 263, 265
Searizak, Genji 259
Semiroux, Denise "De De Troit"
    215–16
Sex Pistols, the 65, 98, 143, 157,
    173, 197–98, 200, 210–11, 246
Shattuck, Kim 184–86
Shaw, Jim 24, 26
Shirley, John 134
Shivvers, the 47–52
Simmons, Ron 149
Siouxsie Sioux 10
Sley, Cynthia 11, 273, 275
Slick, Grace 10, 30, 52, 214
Slits, the 41, 63, 65, 232, 252,
    272, 290

Smith, Aaron 221
    Bert 106
    Deborah 42, 44
    Patti 8, 10, 15, 26, 32, 45, 61,
    63, 65, 73, 77, 92, 98, 145,
    195, 198, 200, 222, 243–44,
    257, 272, 288
Sonic Youth 11, 80, 235, 244, 262
Sortor, Steve 39
Soto, Luis 175
    Robert 175
Southard, Billy 215
Sparks 30, 55, 281
Spence, Timmy 205
Spike, Kidd 164–65
Squip, Tomas 287
Sreebny, Oren 138
Stace, Bill 70
Stanzler, Audrey 59
Starks, Amy Gassner 96
Stein, Michael (Mike) 124–25
Steinberg, Ed 248
Steinel, Carol 128
Stevenson, Gordon 253, 257
Stewart, Mark 175
Stingray, Johnny 164–65
Stodola, Randy 168
Stooges, the 26, 34, 37, 65
Stotts, Richie 266
Stranglers, the 45, 134, 144, 272
Strasburg, Gary 70
Street, Nancy 256, 286
Street Punks, the 194
Streng, Judy 292
Striho, Carolyn 61, 63–64
Strzempka, Greg 278
Suburban Lawns 171–72
Sullivan, "Danny Panic" 198
Sunshine, Gary 104
Swan, Steve 192
Swanson, Chuck 72

T

Talking Heads 8, 15, 55, 70, 92,
    171, 233
Teenage Jesus & the Jerks 253
Television 54, 107, 128, 194, 220,
    245, 257, 266
Tex & the Horseheads 180
Tiny Desk Unit 269–70, 301

U

UT 261–62, 301
UXA 216

V

Visible Targets the 149
VKTMS 213–14
VS 146, 209–12

W

Waitresses, the 44, 282
Whitney, Richard "Frankie
    Ennui" 171

Y

Y-Pants 301

Z

Zeros, the 165